KNOWLEDGE AND DEVELOPMENT

Volume 2
Piaget and Education

KNOWLEDGE AND DEVELOPMENT

A Continuation Order Plan is available for this series. A continuation order will bring delivery of each new volume immediately upon publication. Volumes are billed only upon actual shipment. For further information please contact the publisher.

KNOWLEDGE AND DEVELOPMENT

Volume 2
Piaget and Education

Edited by
Jeanette McCarthy Gallagher
Temple University
Philadelphia, Pennsylvania

and

J. A. Easley, Jr.
University of Illinois
Urbana, Illinois

PLENUM PRESS • NEW YORK AND LONDON

Library of Congress Cataloging in Publication Data

Main entry under title:

Knowledge and development.

Includes bibliographies and index.
CONTENTS: v. 1. Advances in research and theory. – v. 2. Piaget and education.
Vol. 2. edited by J. M. Gallagher and J. A. Easley, Jr.
1. Cognition. 2. Cognition in children. 3. Developmental psychology. 4. Piaget,
Jean, 1896-   5. Education – Philosophy. I. Overton, Willis F. II. Gallagher,
Jeanette McCarthy. III. Easley, J. A. [DNLM: 1. Cognition. 2. Child development.
WS105 K73]
BF 311.K6385   153.4   76-26163
ISBN 0-306-40089-8 (v. 2)

© 1978 Plenum Press, New York
A Division of Plenum Publishing Corporation
227 West 17th Street, New York, N.Y. 10011

Printed in the United States of America

Contributors

Paul Ammon, *School of Education, University of California, Berkeley, California*

Rheta DeVries, *College of Education, University of Illinois at Chicago Circle, Chicago, Illinois; University of Geneva, Geneva, Switzerland*

J. A. Easley, Jr., *Committee on Culture and Cognition, University of Illinois, Urbana, Illinois*

Jeanette McCarthy Gallagher, *Department of General Educational Psychology, Temple University, Philadelphia, Pennsylvania*

Doba Goodman, *Department of Psychology, York University, Downsview, Ontario, Canada*

Thomas Lickona, *Department of Education, State University of New York, Cortland, New York*

Kenneth Lovell, *School of Education, University of Leeds, Leeds, England*

Frank B. Murray, *Department of Educational Foundations, University of Delaware, Newark, Delaware*

Juan Pascual-Leone, *Department of Psychology, York University, Downsview, Ontario, Canada*

D. Kim Reid, *Department of Educational Psychology, New York University, New York, New York*

Michael Shayer, *Chelsea College, University of London, London, England*

Irene Subelman, *School of Education, University of California, Berkeley, California*

Acknowledgments

This second volume in the series devoted to issues concerning the development of knowledge represents efforts to link Piagetian theory to various curriculum areas.

A unique feature of the volume is the attempt by several of the authors to relate Piaget's new model of equilibration to various aspects of education.

The planning and execution by the editors of such a volume are significantly tied to the cooperation of many individuals. In the early stages, discussions with Constance Kamii, Hans Furth, Marianne Denis-Prinzhorn, and Bärbel Inhelder were most enlightening. Reviewers of first drafts included Richard Iano and Richard Mansfield, both of Temple University. Joseph Glick and Gilbert Voyat, members of the Publication Committee of the Jean Piaget Society, were a source of continuing support and encouragement. Toni D'Onofrio compiled the index.

Our students at Temple University and at the University of Illinois provided valuable insights on applications of Piagetian theory. Moreover, we appreciated the many scholarly exchanges with the other authors of chapters in this volume. Finally, the efficient editors at Plenum Press made the entire production phase an enjoyable experience.

JEANETTE MCCARTHY GALLAGHER

J. A. EASLEY, JR.

Contents

Chapter 2

Moral Development and Moral Education: Piaget, Kohlberg, and Beyond

Thomas Lickona

Chapter 3

Early Education and Piagetian Theory: Applications Versus Implications

Rheta DeVries

Chapter 4

The Impact of the Work of Piaget on Science Curriculum Development

Kenneth Lovell and Michael Shayer

Chapter 5

Four Decades of Conservation Research: What Do They Mean for Mathematics Education?

J. A. Easley, Jr.

Chapter 6

Two Models of Human Behavior and Reading Instruction

Frank B. Murray

Chapter 7

Genevan Theory and the Education of Exceptional Children

D. Kim Reid

Chapter 8

Piagetian Theory and Neo-Piagetian Analysis as Psychological Guides in Education

Juan Pascual-Leone, Doba Goodman, Paul Ammon, and Irene Subelman

Introduction

IRVING E. SIGEL

This volume of essays is a broad-gauged effort directed at reflections on the applicability of Piagetian theory to education. Identification and determination of the relevance of Piagetian theory to education is of course not new. The bibliographies in this volume do attest to that assertion. Then why the persistent interest and why still another volume? Rather than deal with the relevance of each article to these issues, let us deal with the basic question of why such continued interest in application of Piagetian theory to education, and further raise the problem of the feasibility of such a task.

Three questions come immediately to mind: Why the interest in applicability? What are some of the problems that arise in application? Is Piagetian theory applicable to education?

Why the continued interest in application of Piagetian theory in education? The answer to this question resides in the sociological and educational issues that arose twenty years ago and still persist in American education—namely, the need to upgrade the quality of education by providing a coherent conceptual system with a developmental emphasis. People gravitated to Piaget because it was the only major system sufficiently comprehensive, as well as substantive. While learning theories abound, they do not tie together general cognitive development with specific relevant content areas, e.g., development of such knowledge domains as number, time, space, geometry, etc. Thus, Piaget offers a development framework within which content areas are embedded. In this volume, Lovell and Shayer and Easley reflect this.

Not only did Piagetian theory fill a void in the educational arena, but it further provided a perspective that could be remedial, particularly with disadvantaged preschoolers. This group became a prime educational target population in the 1960s with the advent of Head Start and the move toward compensatory education. Thus, Hunt's (1961) discussion of the role of early experience and his concurrent rejection of the traditional IQ approach to assessment of intelligence provided impetus to the search for new models and conceptions of intellectual development. By concluding his discussion with an exposition of Piagetian theory, Hunt set the stage for Piagetian theory to enter the American scene in a new context evaluation of intellectual growth in a broader and more intensive way.

At the same time, more Piagetian writings became available to the English reading public, generating further interest. With the publication of Flavell's (1963) integration of Piagetian theory in a single volume, the professional public interested in cognitive development had a means to study and consider application of Piagetian theory to education. While many investigators were skeptical and critical of Piagetian theory and the accompanying results that Piaget reported, much research was undertaken either as efforts at confirmation (e.g., Elkind, 1961) or at disconfirmation (Kohnstamm, 1963; Sigel and Hooper, 1968). In the educational world, the biggest impetus was in the preschool field where Piagetian theory and research were seen as relevant to aiding the education of disadvantaged youngsters. Federal compensatory programs such as Head Start and others created a demand for innovative approaches to education. Piagetian theory offered a potential resource that would move the educational effort in new directions. In fact, for some it appeared that application of Piaget to the classroom had the earmark of a panacea. Various versions of preschool programming ensued, with the work of David Weikart and his colleagues being among the best known (Weikert, Rogers, Adcock, and McClelland, 1970). Thus, research and educational evaluation joined forces in making research within the Piagetian framework a highly popular and visible undertaking. Piaget was not idle during this period, producing more and more, so that the lag between what Piaget was saying and what his critics and friends were doing in the United States was virtually a constant. The net result was, as is frequently the case with comprehensive theories presented to many in secondary sources or in translations, a series of disputes about what Piaget really meant and what he originally wrote. In spite of all this controversy, Piagetian theory did offer a novel and significant perspective regenerating the quality and quantity of research in cognitive development, not only in the preschool field, but also in education as a whole.

What are some of the problems that arise in application? This burgeoning interest raised and continues to raise some critical problems. One of them was alluded to in terms of the lag beween Piagetian ideas and the awareness of them in the United States. Thus, critics are responding at times to points of view already discarded or not yet fully developed but in process. For example, Piaget's work on causality is a far cry from his early writings, similarly his concept of equilibration (Piaget, 1974, 1977). These are in part theoretical issues. The point of this volume is application to the field of education. Piaget is not an educator; he is not a psychologist; he is not a practitioner. His theories are not immediately applicable. Piaget is a genetic epistemologist, concerned with the processes involved in the acquisition of knowledge. He has developed, as the reader will discover if not already known, a system by which to examine this fundamental question.

Piaget is interested in the universal laws of development, thereby eschewing an orientation toward individual differences, as well as toward the intersect between the individual and the educational milieu. It is these latter two areas that educators and psychologists believe to be of critical concern for educational planning. Yet, these two objectives are almost antithetical because the study of universals does not provide a data base for individual differences. From a reading of Piaget's work, we note that he presents particular cases only as illustrative of general conclusions; he does not compare one case with another, for example. Yet, for the educator, there is a need to understand individual variability since teachers work with groups in which individual differences are critical.

Piaget has been criticized for his lack of attention to individual differences, which is patently undeserved since he intentionally has chosen different objectives. In fact, much of American psychology is also not oriented to individual differences. Criticizing Piaget in this regard is therefore not justified. However, this lack of emphasis places those interested in application of Piagetian theory to the classroom in a dilemma. Classrooms are organized on the basis of age. Yet, as will be noted in various places in this volume, age and stage are not closely related. If, on the other hand, stages of cognition are used as the criterion for grouping children, what are the implications in terms of other developmental criteria? Will the effect be an improvement over age? At first blush it might appear so, but on further consideration it may create the same set of problems, but from a different perspective.

Is Piagetian theory in fact a universalistic theory? Reading through this volume the reader will note that most of the papers describing Piagetian theory describe general features of development, e.g., Gallagher or Easley. How then does one translate these general principles to particulars in the classroom? This is one of the efforts attempted in this volume by Lovell and Shayer, Reid, Lickona, and DeVries among others.

Note, however, that these writers have to elaborate or interpret Piagetian theory to create the necessary operations for education. To derive the specifics necessary for education requires a thorough knowledge of Piagetian theory. Let us move on to this issue.

Knowledge of Piagetian theory is necessary for application. The chapter by Gallagher on reflexive abstraction provides an excellent example of why understanding of Piagetian theory is necessary prior to consideration of application. Her chapter deals with *but one* Piagetian construct. To understand that *one,* it is important to grasp the context and place of it in the theory. This is the way Gallagher develops her argument. Had she dealt with it in isolation, it would not have been very communicative. Other chapters in the book follow the same format.

Since Piagetian theory is comprehensive and holistic, focusing on any one part violates the theory and can produce a misapplication—if one is interested in applying *that* construct *per se.* Thus, a prerequisite to application is a knowledge of Piaget's basic assumptions and concepts. It could be argued that these are critical—more important relatively than just the results of his studies. In fact, it is because of this that virtually each author in this volume finds it necessary to describe relevant aspects of Piagetian theory. Thus, the reader should study these introductory sections with care.

Is Piagetian theory applicable to education? At this stage in the development of Piagetian theoretical development many hold that applicability is possible. Various efforts are being made to demonstrate where, how, and under what conditions. Is science education or is mathematics education the most appropriate? What about preschool? Or is Piagetian theory applicable not in a specific sense but in a more fundamental sense as basic to the educator's orientation toward all relevant phases of education?

At this stage then of the history of Piagetian theory, it is still a relatively new conceptual framework; questions as to how and under what conditions it is applicable are still to be answered.

The issues of applicability are joined in the essay by Pascual-Leone, Goodman, Ammon, and Subelman, as well as by Murray. For Pascual-Leone and his colleagues, the objective is to create a psychological theory out of Piaget's genetic epistemology. This is a formidable task. Yet, it is a necessary one for the reasons presented earlier in this discussion. In this regard, Pascual-Leone's theorizing is a *psychological* elaboration–extension of Piagetian theory. While less empirically oriented individuals might reject his theorizing, it should be kept in mind that Piaget, the scientist, does use empirical methods to study the phenomena of interest. In this connection, the issues raised by Murray vis-à-vis theoretical explanation are in the same genre.

This volume of essays is another admirable move toward enhancing the practical aspects of Piaget. These papers provide transitional perspectives to a developing conceptualization and application of a theory. But the reader must be warned, first, that the papers are pithy and require careful study and, second, that they will raise as many questions as they answer. Both these objectives signify a provocative volume that is a credit to the editors and their contributors.

References

Elkind, D. Children's discovery of the conservation of mass, weight, and volume: Piaget replication study II. *Journal of Genetic Psychology*, 1961, *98*, 219–227.

Flavell, J. *The developmental psychology of Jean Piaget*. Princeton, N.J.: Van Nostrand, 1963.

Hunt, J. McV. *Intelligence and experience*. New York: Ronald Press, 1961.

Kohnstamm, G. A. An evaluation of part of Piaget's theory. *Acta Psychologica*, 1963, *21*, 313–315. (Reprinted in: Sigel, I. E., and Hooper, F. H. *Logical thinking in children*. New York: Holt, Rinehart and Winston, 1968.)

Piaget, J. *Understanding causality*. New York: W. W. Norton, 1974.

Piaget, J. *The development of thought: Equilibration of cognitive structures*. New York: The Viking Press, 1977.

Sigel, I. E., and Hooper, F. H. *Logical thinking in children: Research based on Piaget's theory*. New York: Holt, Rinehart and Winston, 1968.

Weikart, D. P., Rogers, L., Adcock, C., and McClelland, J. *The cognitively oriented curriculum: A framework for preschool teachers*. Washington, D.C.: National Association for the Education of Young Children, 1970.

Reflexive Abstraction and Education

The Meaning of Activity in Piaget's Theory

JEANETTE McCARTHY GALLAGHER

1. The Meaning of Activity in Piaget's Cognitive Theory: An Introduction

It is no exaggeration to state that misinterpretations of the concept of activity in Piagetian theory have been the stumbling block to effective application of that theory to educational practice. The purpose of this chapter is to clarify the meaning of activity in relation to reflexive abstraction and to provide some new directions to interpretation and application.

The terms "to act on," "action," and "activity" occur repeatedly in Piagetian writings. The most common emphasis appears in the following quotation (Piaget, 1970, p. 704) and may be found in slightly different wording in each major work: "in order to know objects, the subject must act upon them, and therefore transform them: he must displace, connect, combine, take apart, and reassemble them."

JEANETTE McCARTHY GALLAGHER • Department of General Educational Psychology, Temple University, Philadelphia, Pennsylvania. This project was supported in part by funds and study leave from Temple University.

Here, the new Piagetian student, searching for applications to education, encounters a trap. Give children objects to manipulate or even sell a kit of "manipulators" and presto: instant Piaget! This commercialization of Piagetian theory is made even worse by the fact that the aim of the whole theory is to discourage an epistemological viewpoint in which understandings are gained through a "copy" approach from object to mind. In such a simplistic view of a copy epistemology, the longer and clearer the perceptions and manipulations, the clearer the understandings.

Other students get trapped not by kits but by arguments that appear very close to a definition of activity as "busyness." Silberman's concept (1970) of "I do and I understand," wherein he relates Piagetian theory to the open classroom movement, fails in that activity is not set within the context of the complexity of that theory.

Elkind (1976) describes an "active classroom" as the culmination of Piagetian psychology for classroom practice. Although this approach is important and well deserves our attention, another trap waits to be sprung. Elkind defines such an active classroom or school as "one in which there is a great deal of operative and connotative, as well as figurative, learning taking place" (p. 220). Elkind proceeds, however, to explain that the three types of learning are facilitated by materials that are brought into the classroom. Again, active and activity fall into an empiricist or copy form of epistemology. According to Elkind, interaction with materials such as workbooks (figurative), geoboards and attribute blocks (operative), and plants and flower arrangements (connotative) encourage learning. No one would argue against the importance of such materials in a classroom. What is missing is an explanation of the mechanisms of learning as related to the meaning of activity.

In sum, some interpretations of Piaget's meaning of activity for the educator may confuse more than assist. By placing the concept of activity within the broader Piagetian concepts of phenocopy and reflexive abstraction, a clarification may be reached.

2. Concept of Phenocopy

Piaget (1977a) describes himself as a psychological epistemologist who loves to return to his original biological interests. Therefore, when one attempts to probe a basic Piagetian term such as activity, it becomes necessary to return to the biological foundations of the theory.

In reading the early works of Piaget, one is struck by the statement of biological principles which today remain central to his unique discipline of developmental epistemology. Piaget wrote that at age 21, when he defended his thesis on the distribution and variability of land mollusks in the Valaisian Alps of Switzerland, he already had formulated his two central ideas:

> The first is that since every organism has a permanent structure, which can be modified under the influence of the environment but is never destroyed as a structured whole, all knowledge is always *assimilation* of a datum external to the subject's structure. . . . The second is that the normative factors of thought correspond biologically to a necessity of *equilibrium* by self-regulation: thus logic would, in the subject, correspond to a process of equilibrium. (Piaget, 1971b, p. 8)

Piaget's interest in merging biology and epistemology preceded his work on testing children's intelligence with Binet's co-worker, Dr. Théophile Simon. It was at this time, however, that Piaget realized such a merger was possible:

> At last I had found my field of research. . . . My aim of discovering a sort of embryology of intelligence fit in with my biological training; from the start of my theoretical thinking I was certain that the problem of the relation between the organism and environment extended also into the realm of knowledge, appearing here as the problem of the relation between the acting or thinking subject and the objects of his experience. Now I had the chance of studying this problem in terms of psychologenetic development. (Piaget, 1952, p. 245)

Reflection on these quotations leads to an understanding that Piaget's works (1967, 1971b, 1974c, 1975a,b, 1977a, in press-a) on the relations between biological regulations and cognitive processes are merely a continuation of a lifelong pursuit. When Piaget collects snails and herbs, therefore, we should not picture him as a frustrated biologist but as a scientist studying the development of knowledge. To emphasize this point, his two central ideas remain the meaning of assimilation in relation to the structured whole and the necessity of self-regulation as the individual grows in knowledge. To explore the meaning of these central ideas, one can turn to Piaget's interpretation of his work with snails (*Limnaea stagnalis*) that are common in the marshes and lakes of Switzerland and a juicy herb, *Sedum* (*Crassulaceae*), which he collected in many places that he has visited.

Piaget's work with snails and herbs laid the foundation for formulating the notion of phenocopy. Such a notion stands midway between the

theories of evolution or adaption to the environment proposed by the
neo-Darwinists and the Lamarckians. The neo-Darwinian view stressed
adaption controlled by internal, genetic mechanisms. Changes are due
to mutations controlled by chance factors. Emphasis here is on organismic or built-in mutational mechanisms.*

The genotype, the inherited makeup of the organism, is viewed by
neo-Darwinists as self-protected and isolated from the environment.
Changes caused by chance result not from the hereditary material working as a structured whole but from an "atomistic" or fractionated process. Recall that Piaget is searching for relations between biological processes and the development of thinking. Isolated or atomistic explanations do not fit the concept of a structured whole. "[N]eo-Darwinism
reasons as if the apple fallen by chance beside Newton was the source of
the theories of this great man on gravitation" (Piaget 1974c, p. 109).
Newton, however, assimilated this chance occurrence into a prepared or
comprehending mind. Thus, he was able actively to structure a new
idea.

Piaget (1971a) credits Lamarck with emphasizing the role of the
environment in development. Piaget's criticism, however, is that
Lamarck fails to explain how the organism reacts to the environment.
Piaget (1971a, pp. 106–7) elaborated that

> the organism is less passive than Lamarck supposed: it makes a positive
> reaction when it assimilates the environment to its structures instead of
> letting them give way in all directions through indeterminate accommoda-
> tions. It is true, of course, that the organism is capable of learning: but every
> time it registers some piece of information from the outside, this process is
> linked up with assimilation structures.

For Piaget, understanding development incorporated in his unique
discipline of genetic epistemology is a middle ground (*tertium quid*) position. This avoids the extremes: the environmental or empiricist position
of the Lamarckians and the hereditary or maturational position of neo-
Darwinians. In other words, Piaget's constructivist theory is intermediate between one emphasizing characteristics acquired by the pressure of the environment and one emphasizing characteristics acquired
by chance or by mutations.

The main biological evidence for Piaget's middle-ground position
on development (1971a, 1974c, 1975a, in press-a) is based on his lifetime
study of pond snails and, more recently, his studies of herbs. The pond

*It may be that the tendency to label Piaget incorrectly as a maturationist is due to confus-
ing *genetic* with *genes*. Genetic epistemology, of course, means developmental epistemology, with maturation as only one of the four factors of development (Gallagher, 1977).

snails have three separate habitats: (1) still, tranquil waters; (2) mildly disturbed waters agitated by waves; (3) severely disturbed waters agitated by strong winds and waves. The shape of the snail shell in each of the habitats is the important factor. In Habitat 1, the snail's shell is elongated and this shell is inherited by the offspring. In Habitat 2, however, the snail's shell is globular, wider and shorter than snails of the same species in tranquil water. The reason for this change in shape, according to Piaget, is adaption. As the snail attached itself to objects during agitation of the waves, the pull on the muscle gradually resulted in a shortening of the upper part of the shell. The offspring of the snails in Habitat 2 had globular shells. However, when Piaget moved these snails to an aquarium, the offspring were elongated, an indication that the changed shape was a temporary adaptation.

The snails in Habitat 3 are the puzzling group. Their shells are globular, of course, because of strong winds and waves. When these snails were moved to an aquarium, the shells of the offspring were globular—a change that continued for 16 years! Piaget claims this is evidence of a gradual reorganization of genetic material. This phenomenon of replacing external variation (the globular shell) by internal reorganization is called *phenocopy*. It is important that this reorganization did not occur simply because the organism reacted to external stress. The reorganization is a self-regulatory phenomenon, resulting in a new genotype imitating the previous phenotype. The change becomes, however, genetically fixed and nonreversible after adaption of the genes within a certain range of reaction (reaction norm).

What is important, then, and this will be more evident when an example of phenocopy is given from the psychological realm, is that the organism controlled the change because the reorganization was within the regulatory genes. Piaget found a similar phenomenon with field herbs (Sedum). When this herb grows at moderate altitudes, it is small but increases in size when transplanted to Geneva. However, when it is found at very high altitudes, the plant retains its small size when transplanted. This indicates that an internal control is manifesting itself by a "small-size" genotype, another example of phenocopy.

Why the stress on phenocopy? For Piaget, these phenomena from the biological world of snails and herbs are dynamic examples of the process of self-regulation or equilibration. Observe the behavior of children to see Piaget's parallels of cognitive (thinking) and biological processes. A simple experiment of Piaget and Inhelder (Piaget, 1975a) demonstrated this link between reconstructing or reordering on the biological level and the cognitive or thinking level.

Children were asked to place a marble into a container with their right hands and a blue marble into a partly concealed container with their left hands. They were asked two questions: (1) "As we put one in here and one in here, do we have the same amount?" (2) "If we were to continue for a very long time (large container, continue all day, etc.), would we still have the same amount?" The children, as young as four and five, had no difficulty with the first question. A typical response was, "Yes, both the same." However, the same children confronted with the second question, refused to predict the results of continuing the process; that is, they failed to understand that if $n = n$, than $n + 1 = n + 1$ (always). They relied heavily on what they perceived, the observables (empirical abstraction), and could not predict the future, the unseen.

An interesting variation of this experiment emphasized an even stronger difference between what is perceived and what is understood. The children were given a visible inequality: three marbles in the first jar and none in the second, before screening. Young children thought that equality eventually would be achieved ($n = n$) and somehow the initial inequality could be canceled by succeeding equal additions.

It was only when children reasoned on the coordination or relationship of equalities or inequalities to infinity (logico-mathematical abstraction) that they would overcome the observed (perceptual) features (empirical abstraction) of the situation. Thus, children, like snails in the process of phenocopy, reorder their structures. It is not so much what happens externally, but what happens during the reordering phase. This is the heart of Piaget's concept of equilibration: Children grow in knowledge by constructing their own understandings, which are not imposed from without but are reached by a reordering process.

In sum, the Piagetian position on cognitive development parallels that of biological development by arguing from a middle-ground, interacting position. This position avoids a view of development that permits the organism to be too easily affected by environmental stresses. On the other hand, it avoids the view that one waits for an unfolding process, that is, maturation. The environment is not ignored. As children learn something new, they register information from the outside. However, this information is always active and tied to assimilation structures: what has been learned before modifies what is learned in the future. The "reaction norm" (as in the snails), or the range of reaction, controls the learning experience. Remember that looking at the marbles did not lead to understanding. Progress in cognitive growth was tied to the construction of the rule that $n + 1 = n + 1$ holds for infinity. That is why Piaget repeats that growth in knowledge is not a simple registering of experience of perceptual givens that pass from eye to mind but a process of construction.

3. The Mechanism of Reflexive Abstraction

Our aim is to clarify what Piaget means when he repeats that knowledge is linked with activity. The idea is emphasized that children construct their own understandings. Reflexive abstraction is one of the mechanisms of cognitive development, that is, a means by which such construction takes place.* In addition, reflexive abstraction is one of the aspects of the key force in cognitive development: the process of equilibration. Recently, Piaget (1975b) reformulated his model of equilibration to incorporate infralogical aspects, especially the new research on causality, and to shift from a probability to a compensation explanation of conservation. It is not surprising, therefore, to note that the emphasis on relfexive abstraction is found threaded through recent volumes that expand on the meaning of equilibration (Piaget, 1974a,b,c, 1975b, 1977c).

This does not mean, however, that the mechanism of reflexive abstraction is new in Piagetian writings. In earlier works basic definitions may be found (Beth and Piaget, 1966; Piaget, 1969). What is new are volumes of experimental studies devoted directly or indirectly to expanding the meaning of reflexive abstraction as it relates to the broader issue of a constructivist epistemology. The following account of reflexive abstraction is drawn from several primary sources (Piaget, 1969, 1974a,b,c, 1975b, 1977c) and one secondary source (Brun, 1975) that had as one of its aims the clarification of the mechanism relative to education.

3.1. Basic Definitions

Piaget distinguishes between two types of abstraction: empirical and reflexive. A mathematician friend of Piaget's provided an example, cited in each major work, to clarify this distinction. When his friend was playing on the beach at the age of five, he reached the amazing conclusion that no matter in what order he arranged the pebbles he was counting; he always obtained the same number. Of course, the boy noticed that the pebbles were smooth and light and that they could be moved into any order. These learning experiences of smoothness, lightness and movability are labeled *empirical abstraction*. In this type of abstraction, information is drawn from objects through observation. In other words,

---

*The preferred translation of *réfléchissante* is *reflexive* (Sinclair, personal communication) rather than *reflecting* as in the translation of Piaget's (1975b) major work on equilibration. At the formal-thought level, the abstraction is labeled *reflected* (Piaget, 1976, p. 286).

information is drawn from an *exogenous* (extrinsic) or external source. Although this is a common form of learning, it can easily be over-stressed.

For further growth in knowledge, it is necessary to go beyond the observables or "beyond the information given" as in Bruner's terminology (1973). The boy on the beach reached the conclusion that no matter in what order the pebbles were arranged or whether he counted them clockwise or counterclockwise, he still obtained the same number. He constructed the rule: Sum is independent of order. (Unless he were quite precocious, however, we would not expect the child to express the rule in those terms!) The rule was constructed through the mechanism of reflexive abstraction. Whereas empirical abstraction is based on what is observed, reflexive abstraction is based on coordinating what is observed or a bringing into relationship (*mise en relation*).

It was noted that Piaget divided abstraction into empirical and reflexive. An important subdivision of reflexive abstraction is that of pseudoempirical abstraction, not to be relegated to a secondary status. In this type of abstraction the object is modified by the subject's actions and enriched by properties drawn from the coordinations. Thus, even though it may appear that a child is manipulating and observing an object, in some cases the manipulations may lead to higher levels of understanding. The child brings an enrichment to the object (Piaget, 1974c). A clear example of this type of abstraction is observed when the child seriates sticks and begins to grasp that, if there are seven sticks larger than A in a seriated array from A to H, then there would have to be seven sticks smaller than H. This understanding was not constructed by mere manipulation of the sticks but was drawn from the coordinations, that is, the grasped interrelationships among the seriated sticks. We will see that pseudoempirical abstraction is central to the understanding of activity relative to educational implications of Piagetian theory.

Reflexive abstraction is actually another term for logico-mathematical knowing which is of necessity *constructive* and *endogenous* (intrinsic). This endogenous aspect does not mean, however, that empirical abstraction ceases once reflexive abstraction is present. Piaget explains: "reflexive abstraction does not 'replace' empirical abstraction, but frames it from the start and then goes infinitely beyond it" (Piaget, 1974c, p. 88).

Thus, the "tools of assimilation" or the previously built-up structures are used when information is drawn from an object as in empirical abstraction. The tools of assimilation or the recording instruments make empirical abstraction possible. However, these tools or instruments are not taken from the object but

> are thus due to the activities of the subject, and as such, born of previous reflexive abstractions even if, let us repeat, the empirical abstractions they render possible draw their products only from the object. (Piaget, 1974c, p. 82)

The interplay between empirical and reflexive abstraction is crucial because it is at the center of what implications may be drawn from Piaget's theory to education. Consider the two fundamental characteristics of reflexive abstraction. First, reflexive abstraction is characterized by a *projection* in the physical sense. It is a transposing to a higher level of what is borrowed from a lower level. Such a characteristic may be found even at the sensorimotor stage when simple movements are coordinated and transposed to more complex movements to attain a goal (Piaget, 1977c).

Second, reflexive abstraction is characterized by a reflection in the sense of *mental reorganization,* that is, a need to reconstruct that which was abstracted from the lower level. This reconstruction is necessary since there must be an adjustment (accommodation) to the structure of the higher level.

Growth in knowledge at all levels is the constant spiral of projection and reorganization, then another projection and reorganization, and so forth. Before considering experimental evidence of the projection and reorganization processes, recall again Piaget's biological analogy.

3.2. Relationship to Phenocopy

Genetic epistemology is concerned with the parallels between the mechanisms on the biological level and those of the cognitive level. When the snails in the high winds and waves made an adaptation, it was a result of the replacement of an exogenous phenotype by an endogenous genotype of the same form. A parallel may be made with the cognitive level. Growth in structures on the cognitive level are due to the replacement of exogenous knowledge by endogenous reconstructions.

Piaget (1975a, p. 214) summarized:

> From the biological point of view, it seems clear that exogenous knowledge corresponds to phenotypical reactions, while endogenous knowledge is related either to a hereditary programming of structures or to the regu-

lations entailed in epigenesis, which are in part controlled by the genome and in part by adaptations to the milieu.

In both cases, biological and cognitive phenocopy, there are enriched reequilibrations because of internal reconstructions. Again, the middle ground must be stressed for in neither case is progress merely a result of pressures of the environment. Instead, one must stress the active organism or subject acting on the environment (Voyat, in press).

3.3. Experimental Evidence

Evidence for the distinction made between empirical and reflexive abstraction is given in two recent volumes in the series, *Etudes d'épistémologie génétique* (Piaget, 1977c, in press-b). Two experiments are summarized here which highlight some of the points made in previous sections, especially those of projection and reorganization.

3.3.1. The Study of Correlates

Piaget (with Montangero and Billeter, 1977d) presented children between the ages of 5 and 13 with arrangements of drawings that were to be paired. After the important step of identifying the drawings, the children were asked to put together the drawings that went well together. Next the children were asked to arrange the pictures into 2 × 2 matrices. If the child had difficulty in beginning to find such an analogy as "Dog is to hair as bird is to feathers," he was asked such questions as (in line with the Genevan method of critical exploration): "What allows the bird to stay warm in winter?" If the child still had difficulty, three of the cells were filled and the child was given a choice for the fourth cell among three cards. If he found the correlate or fourth term, he was given counterexamples. He was asked, for example: "Does a pump of a bike go as well as (fit into the matrix) the handle bars?" Such counterexamples were introduced to determine how strong the relations could be held by the child in spite of adult suggestions of another possible answer.

According to Piaget, the results lead to the designation of three distinct stages. The younger children, in Stage 1, ages 5 and 6, were more likely to arrange pairs but ignore the complete form of the analogy. They stated that the dog needs hair to keep warm and the bird needs feathers to fly. The relation between dog and hair (A is to B) was not compared to the relation bird and feathers (C is to D). For Piaget, this is an example of empirical abstraction, that is, attending to the observable content or objective characteristics which prevents true solution according to the analogical form of A:B as C:D.

Children in Stage 2, approximately ages 8 to 11, were able to complete the matrices; however, with the introduction of countersuggestions, the analogical form proved to be weak and the answers were changed. These children, according to Piaget, demonstrated reflexive abstraction, that is, a projection to a higher level of that which is drawn from a lower level. Such a process entails a coordination. In the case of analogy problems, the solution is based, as previously emphasized, on the coordination of the two separate relations (Piaget, 1977c,d).

In Stage 3, approximately ages 11 and over, the children were able to resist the countersuggestions. The form A:B as C:D is stabilized and it is possible for the subjects to reflect on their answers by consciously explaining the hierarchical relation obtained from the relations of both parts of the analogy. In addition, it is possible for children at this age to understand that the qualitative form used in the problems is based upon the mathematical or quantitative form which is the origin of the notion of an analogy as a double ratio. It would be possible, then, to understand that the same relation must exist between dog and bird as between hair and feathers (A:C as B:D) (Gallagher, 1978; Gallagher and Wright, 1977; Gallagher and Wright, in press).

As one studies the progress of the children in solving the correlates or analogies, the two characteristics of reflexive abstraction are apparent. A spiral process occurs: Every "reflecting" of content (the separate items in the cells) supposes the intervention of a form or reflection in the sense of a reorganization (A:B as C:D). The contents or observables transferred to a higher level require the construction of new forms, that is, the understanding of ratios. The construction of new forms are due to the reflection or reorganization at a higher level. "Thus, there is an uninterrupted alternation of   'reflecting'   'reflection'   'reflecting,'   and (or)   contents   forms   re-elaborated contents   new forms, etc. of always larger realms, without end or, especially, absolute beginning" (Piaget, 1977c [spaces in original]).

Reflexive abstraction, then, entails continual activity. It is akin to an operation for it deals with certain coordinations and ignores others. At first we may not be aware of these coordinations. Later, after we are aware, we may apply them in new ways to enrich our thinking.

In our research (Gallagher, 1978; Gallagher and Wright, 1977; Gallagher and Wright, in press) which extends the work of Piaget on analogies, we found clear instances of the reorganization process. The Piagetian format was adapted for group administration. One of the choices for each verbal analogy item was a countersuggestion, that is, a plausible but incorrect answer. At the seventh-grade level it became evident that children were able to reorganize answers from the traditional A:B as C:D form to A:C as B:D, a valid inversion which does not distort the relationship. For example, one of the items was:

Engine is to car as man is to: work   road   speed   *bicycle*

Responses of the younger children centered on the last half of the analogy ("A man rides a bike") or a linear ordering ("Engine makes car go and man makes bike go"). The older children were able to be flexible in reorganization of contents due to stability of form. Note the variety which still preserves form: "Because engine and man power the car and the bicyle;" "Because man is a bicycle's engine;" "The first words provide power to the second." The higher-order mapping of A to C (Sternberg, 1977) seems to be evidence of a higher projection and reorganization, the double aspect of reflexive abstraction.

3.3.2. The Study of Intersections

Reflexive abstraction is closely related to constructive generalization (Inhelder, 1977; Piaget, in press–b). The common meaning of generalization is psychology is that it is an extension of an already existing concept. However, when new combinations are introduced, Piaget uses the term constructive generalization. The following experiment highlights the links between reflexive abstraction and constructive generalization.

Bourquin (Piaget, in press–b) conducted an experiment on the discovery of the center of gravity with subjects from 12 to 15 years old. The subjects were asked to find the middle, that is, the point of balance or equilibrium of various shaped objects such as circles, rectangles, and disks of irregular shapes. After the subjects were permitted to use the edge of the table to discover the lines of equilibrium (for the intersection of these lines would be the center of gravity), they were asked to place the shapes on a cylindrical support 5 mm in diameter until each in turn balanced.

Note the answers of Cla, age 12 (incomplete protocol adapted from Bourquin):

Adult: [*Gives Cla a rectangular board*] You have to find the middle, the point of equilibrium.
Cla: [*She divides the large side in two and traces the two medians*] There where these two lines join in the center.
Adult: There are how many of these lines in all that are possible with the rectangle?

Cla: [*She places it along a diagonal on the edge of the table*] That makes four lines (possible).
Adult: Is that all?
Cla: Yes, I think so, you can't make any more lines.

Cla tries several disks of irregular shape and rectangles and comes to the conclusion that if a shape has equal sides and equal angles you can "do more things with it."

After manipulating the irregular disks, however, she decides that only one line of equilibrium can be drawn. Further manipulations lead her to change her mind with a summary statement about the disks and the rectangles: "That everywhere there are an infinite number of lines that cross the same point. . . . To find the equilibrium there must be [and that suffices] two lines, not necessarily in the middle [spatial] of the figure."

Contrast the conflicts and hesitancies of Cla with the quick, self-assured answers of Mil, age 15½:

Adult: [*Starts with the diagonals*] How many possible straight lines are there?
Mil: An infinity.
Adult: [*Shows rectangles which are thicker on one side and thus off-centered*] Where will the point of equilibrium be?
Mil: If there is more weight on one side, the center will not be at the intersection of the diagonals.

For adolescents who are at Mil's level of thinking, it seems very normal to state that the figures may be turned in all directions, and all the imaginable lines may be understood as passing through the center. However, by reflecting upon her activity of turning the irregular disk on the side of the table, Cla is able to generalize from regular shapes to irregular shapes and thus to move gradually to almost the same level of understanding as Mil's.

Just as the little boy on the beach advanced in knowledge by projecting to a new level and by reorganizing, so we see Cla constructing an understanding: "There is an infinity everywhere because you can always turn it."

Return to the notion of pseudoempirical abstraction. The manipulations alone did not lead to the projection and reorganization, that is, the realization of the infinity of intersecting lines. The enrichment was a result of the activity, the middle-ground position. Activity is not an ideal, abstract state "in the head" nor is it within the objects, to be discovered by more and more manipulations. The activity is the process of constructing between the enrichments brought to the object by the child and the object, including reactions of that object (Piaget, 1977b).

3.4. Theoretical Considerations and General Educational Implications

At the beginning of this chapter, several traps were noted in attempts to translate Piaget's concept of *activity* or *educational practice*. With a background of such concepts as phenocopy and reflexive abstraction, we are in a better position to avoid such traps and to move on to more meaningful applications of the theory.

A diagram of the Spiral of Knowing is a "constructive" starting point. Note in Figure 1 (adapted from Piaget, 1974c) that the diagram is of an inverted cone with a peripheral envelope that surrounds spiral A. The envelope surrounding the spiral represents interactions with the environment, and E and E' symbolizing empirical abstraction with the "reflexive" frames which operate as recording instruments (see Section 3.1.). Spiral A is the endogenous process of reflexive abstraction or logico-mathematical knowing. Vector a represents the successive and hierarchical levels of the cognitive structures. Vector b represents the changes x', y', and z' due to the environment and the disequilibriums x'', y'', z'' that result. Note that here the direction of vector b is horizontal, but

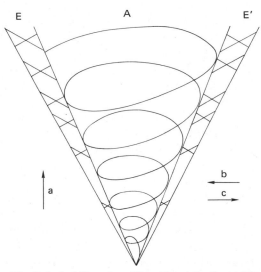

Figure 1.   The Spiral of Knowing: The epigenesis of cognitive functions.

it could be inclined slightly toward the base or toward the top. Thus, the environmental events may interact with the endogenous processes (spiral *A*) of the same level, or possibly at a slightly lower or higher level (those in the process of construction). Following the traditional Piagetian maxim that learning is subordinated to development, we would not expect these environmental events to destroy previous constructions nor that learning experiences would be functional well beyond a certain structural level.

Vector *c* represents explorations that may be of a trial-and-error nature leading to partial reorganization or to a complete endogenous synthesis; the latter is analogous to the snails in the high winds and waves—replacements of exogenous characteristics by an endogenous reconstruction.

Note that the spiral is open and ever-widening. This represents the more and more complex set of endogenous synthesis previously explained by the alternation of "reflecting" and "reflection" that are the two characteristics of projection and reorganization of reflexive abstraction. Piaget (1975b, p. 36) summarizes the meaning of the ever-widening spiral: "All knowledge consists of raising new problems in proportion as it resolves the preceding ones."

Let us consider three implications of the Spiral of Knowing for those who seek practical applications of Piagetian theory. First, when activity is translated too narrowly from Piagetian theory, one leaves the store with the exogenous or extrinsic "cone" of the spiral, failing to get at the real substance, the endogenous "cream." If Active School means *activity* in the narrow sense, that is, free movement to learning centers, or manipulation of objects, then to base such schools or curricula on Piagetian theory is a superficial application.

Second, if activity is taken in the broad sense of projection and reorganization to ever higher levels, then what children do in quiet times of reflection may be equally or more important than stress on "busyness" as the basis of learning.

Third, spiral *A* with the movement of vector *a* represents the "tools of assimilation," that is, all the cognitive structures: innate coordinations and reflexes, circular reactions, sensorimotor intelligence, the preoperatory forms of representation, the constituent functions, concrete operations and, finally, propositional operations. Concentration on the spiral may help to avoid an overstress on labeling curricula as appropriate for "concrete" or "formal" levels. A too rigid adherence to curriculum development in relation to the structure of stages instead of to the function of reflexive abstraction leads to narrow and arid applications of the theory. The Spiral of Knowing fits all stages. Thus, dynamics of the activity inherent in reflexive abstraction are central to all levels of learning.

4. Reflexive Abstraction and Contradiction

Emphasis upon a phenocopy thrust in the understanding of Piagetian theory and its implications for education leads to the sources of "agitation." In other words, why does the child search for another explanation when an old one ceases to be functional? What is the motivating factor in Piagetian theory? It is not enough to state glibly that equilibration is *the factor*. It was noted that reflexive abstraction was a mechanism of equilibration. The fourth factor of development, therefore, has levels of meaning far beyond a simple statement of "interaction."

An understanding of reflexive abstraction is not complete until one considers the meaning of conflict and contradiction in Piaget's theory (Inhelder, Sinclair and Bovet, 1974; Piaget, 1974a,b,c; 1975a,b; 1977a; Moessinger, 1977). It is in the area of contradiction that the most fruitful applications of Piagetian theory to education have their foundation. Here again is the heightened equilibration, the spiral of knowing model, which views cognitive development not in terms of static returns but of the opening to new possibilities. Moessinger (1977, p. 182) commented on the Piagetian view of contradiction: "The solution of every contradiction brings in a new contradiction, either because one discovers new contradictory facts, or because the new theory contradicts an older one."

4.1. Basic Notions of Contradiction

For Piaget (1974a,b; 1975b), contradictions are created by an incomplete or a lack of compensation between the positive and negative characteristics of reality. Turn to a familiar example. When one of two equal balls of clay is rolled into a sausage, the small child attends to the length (positive characteristic) and fails to notice the accompanying "thinning" (unnoticed negation). Thus, for the "conquest of conservation" (Piaget, 1975b), there must be a balance between the positive and negative characteristics. What part does contradiction play in this conquest? If the child becomes puzzled (facial or verbal expression) when lengthening is accompanied by thinning out, the thinning is a disturbance. Such a disturbance is a source of contradiction.

What must be made clear is that contradiction is not used as a term in logic, that is, a return to a state of noncontradiction. We are in the realm of natural thought. Contradiction, therefore, is not a return to a previous state of equilibrium but to a disequilibrium leading to a re-equilibration.

The motivating source for the successive forms of equilibrium, Piaget's (1975b) heightening equilibration (*équilibration majorante*), is to be found in the disturbance or disequilibrium. Such a disturbance "incites the subject to go beyond his present state in search of new solutions" (Inhelder, Sinclair, and Bovet, 1974). Such "goings beyond" (*dépassements*) have two characteristics. First, there is *compensation* (assimilation) in relation to the disturbance and second, there is *construction* (accommodation) in relation to reflexive abstraction.

The disturbance or disequilibration is the source of the reordering process emphasized in the earlier sections on phenocopy and reflexive abstraction. The "goings beyond" the contradiction is essentially an active and constructive process. As Piaget (1975b, p. 45) states in his comment* on the research of Inhelder, Sinclair, and Bovet:

> In their study of the relationship between learning and development, these authors have shown that the most fruitful factors in the acquisition [attainment of understanding] were established by the disturbances giving rise to situations of conflict... which, once they are measured out in a systematic fashion, bring about "goings beyond" [dépassements] and new constructions.

The specific experiments that Piaget referred to here are the conflict situations created when "paths" are to be compared which are made up of the same number of matches having different lengths. Numerical conservation conflicts with conservation of length (Inhelder, Sinclair, and Bovet, 1974, ch. 6).

4.2. The Meaning of Activity and Anticipation

The search for the meaning of activity has lead us to the sources of contradiction. A major source is the request for the child to anticipate the outcome of an event. There is no disturbance if the discrepancy is ignored. If there is an awareness of the contradiction between the prediction and the observation, however, such an awareness is the basis for

*Unfortunately, this important section is mistranslated in the English edition (1977, p. 39).

the projection to a new level of understanding and a reordering or re-equilibration (Brun, 1975; Piaget, 1974c, 1975b).

Activity in the Piagetian sense is essentially tied to an awareness of the coordinates or inferences between the subject and object. To repeat, activity is not manipulation of objects. Neither is it simply a mental reordering. These inferences or "goings beyond," as was noted, may be sparked by discrepancies between what was anticipated and the real events.

5. Conclusions and Future Directions in Applying Piagetian Theory to Education

The route from snails to reorderings sparked by contradictions is a complex one, far removed from the selling of Piagetian kits at the pre-school level or the division of "concrete" and "formal" thinkers into separate classes at the college level. What the route of reflexive abstraction means is that, in the search for implications drawn from Piaget's theory (see DeVries in this volume), we need to stress mechanisms and not stages (Gallagher and Reid, in press). No doubt the stress on stages and centration on the tasks of the Genevan School were, in the past, the stumbling blocks to creative uses of the theory in education.

A shift to mechanisms means renewed research on old questions. For example, what is the best procedure for training teachers to ask conflict-producing questions? What teaching strategies are most effective in fostering such representational thinking as anticipation? The groundwork for research on this question is provided by Sigel (Sigel, 1970; Sigel and Cocking, 1977) but more work is needed to highlight the importance of anticipation in levels beyond that of preschool.

To educate is to lead. There is no return to a static state in the search for the implications of Piagetian theory education. The ever-widening Spiral of Knowing forces us to seek for a better equilibrium: continual "goings beyond."

ACKNOWLEDGMENTS

The author wishes to give special thanks to Dr. Sarah Campbell for translation assistance and Professor Bärbel Inhelder and Mr. Nicole for library assistance at the Archives of Jean Piaget, University of Geneva.

References

Beth, E. W., and Piaget, J., 1966. *Mathematical epistemology and psychology.* Dordrecht-Holland: D. Reidel.

Bourquin, J. F. A case of constructive generalization typical of stage III. In J. Piaget (Ed.), *Constructive generalization,* in press.

Brun, J., 1975. *Education mathématique et développement intellectuel. Recherche à propos de l'enseignement rénové de la mathématique sur des enfants en fin de scolarité primaire.* Thèse pour le Doctorat de 3e cycle (Psychologie) présentée devant l'Université de Lyon II.

Bruner, J., 1973. In J. M. Anglin (Ed.), *Beyond the information given: Studies in the psychology of knowing.* New York: Norton.

Elkind, D., 1976. *Child development and education: A Piagetian perspective.* New York: Oxford University Press.

Gallagher, J. M., 1977. Piaget's equilibration theory: Biological, cybernetic, and logical roots. In M. Appel and L. Goldberg (Eds.), *Topics in cognitive development.* New York: Plenum.

Gallagher, J. M., 1978. The future of formal thought: The study of analogy and metaphor. In B. Presseisen, D. Goldstein, and M. Appel (Eds.), *Studies in language and thought.* New York: Plenum.

Gallagher, J. M., and Wright, R. J., 1977. *Children's solution of verbal analogies: Extension of Piaget's concept of reflexive abstraction.* Paper presented at the symposium "Thinking with the left hand: Children's understanding of analogy and metaphor." New Orleans: Society for Research in Child Development.

Gallagher, J. M., and Wright, R. J. Structure of analogy items: A Piagetian interpretation. In J. Magary (Ed.), *Piaget and the helping professions.* (Vol. 8). Los Angeles: University of Southern California, in press.

Gallagher, J. M., and Reid, D. K. *The learning theory of Piaget and Inhelder.* Monterey, Calif.: Brooks/Cole, in press.

Inhelder, B., 1977. Genetic epistemology and developmental psychology. In R. W. Rieber and K. Salzinger (Eds.), *The roots of American psychology.* Annals of the New York Academy of Sciences, p. 291.

Inhelder, B., Sinclair, H., and Bovet, M., 1974. *Learning and the development of cognition.* Cambridge: Harvard University Press.

Moessinger, P., 1977. Piaget on contradiction. *Human Development, 20,* 178–184.

Piaget, J., 1952. Autobiography. In E. G. Boring *et al.* (Eds.), *History of psychology in autobiography* (Vol. IV). Worcester, Mass.: Clark University Press, pp. 237–256.

Piaget, J., 1967. Intelligence et adaptation biologique. In F. Bresson (Eds.), *Les processus d'adaptation.* Paris: Presses Universitaires de France.

Piaget, J., 1969. *The mechanisms of perception.* New York: Basic Books.

Piaget, J., 1970. Piaget's theory. In P. H. Mussen (Ed.), *Carmichael's manual of child psychology* (Vol. 1). New York: Wiley.

Piaget, J., 1971a. *Biology and knowledge.* Chicago: University of Chicago Press.

Piaget, J., 1971b. *Insights and illusions of philosophy.* New York: World. (Original French edition, 1965.)

Piaget, J., 1974a. *Recherches sur la contradiction* (Vol. I). *Les différentes formes de la contradiction: Etudes d'épistémologie génétique* (Vol. XXXI). Paris: Presses Universitaires de France.

Piaget, J., 1974b. *Recherches sur la contradiction* (Vol. II). *Les relations entre affirmations et négations: Etudes d' épistémologie génétique* (Vol. XXXII). Paris: Presses Universitaires de France.

Piaget, J., 1974c. *Adaptation vitale et psychologie de l'intelligence: La notion de la phenocopie.* Genève: Droz.

Piaget, J., 1975a. From noise to order: The psychological development of knowledge and phenocopy in biology. *The Urban Review, 8.*

Piaget, J., 1975b. *L'équilibration des structures cognitives: Problème central du développement.* Paris: Presses Universitaires de France. (Trans. A. Rosin, 1977. *The development of thought.* New York: Viking.)

Piaget, J., 1976. The grasp of consciousness: Action and concept in the young child, Harvard University Press.

Piaget, J., 1977a. Chance and dialectic in biological epistemology: A critical analysis of Jacques Monod's theses. In W. F. Overton and J. M. Gallagher (Eds.), *Knowledge and development* (Vol. I): *Advances in Research and Theory.* New York: Plenum.

Piaget, J., 1977b. The role of action in the development of thinking. In W. Overton and J. Gallagher (Eds.), *Knowledge and development* (Vol. 1): Advances in research and theory. New York: Plenum.

Piaget, J., 1977c. *L'abstraction réfléchissante.* Paris: Presses Universitaires de France.

Piaget, J. (with J. Montangero and J. Billeter), 1977d. Les correlats. In *L'abstraction réfléchissante.* Paris: Presses Universitaires de France.

Piaget, J. *Behavior—motor of evolution.* New York: Pantheon Books, in press (a).

Piaget, J. *La généralisation constructive.* Paris: Presses Universitaires de France, in press (b).

Sigel, I. E., 1970. The distancing hypothesis: A causal hypothesis for the acquisition of representational thought. In M. R. Jones (Ed.), *The effects of early experience.* Miami: University of Miami Press.

Sigel, I. E., and Cocking, R. R., 1977. *Cognitive development from childhood to adolescence: A constructivist perspective.* New York: Holt, Rinehart and Winston.

Silberman, C. E., 1970. *Crisis in the classroom: The remaking of American education.* New York: Random House.

Sternberg, R., 1977. *Intelligence, information processing, and analogical reasoning.* New York: Wiley.

Voyat, G. Preface. In J. Piaget, *Behavior—motor of evolution.* New York: Pantheon Books, in press.

2

Moral Development and Moral Education

Piaget, Kohlberg, and Beyond

THOMAS LICKONA

1. The Case for Moral Education in the Schools

Convincing people that moral education deserves a high place on the public-school agenda was once an uphill battle, but now American advocates of moral education are surrounded by an embarrassment of supportive evidence. Fresh scandals break with such numbing regularity that the list grows almost too long to remember: Watergate, international sabotage by the CIA, domestic spying by the FBI, assorted corruption in Congress, routine bribery in big business, widespread fraud in Medicare, another rash of cheating at a military academy, reports of premed students destroying each other's lab work, and steady increases in almost every category of crime.

The public schools, faithful to their role as microcosms of society, reflect the moral malaise at large. For the last six years, the Gallup Poll of Attitudes toward Education has named discipline the number one problem in the schools. Such a verdict is not merely the complaint of teachers

THOMAS LICKONA • Department of Education, State University of New York, Cortland, New York. This chapter was prepared with the support of a sabbatical from the State University at New York at Cortland.

or parents who want their children to sit still and be quiet. An even higher percentage of high school juniors and seniors, tired of theft, classroom disruption, gang beatings, and shakedowns in the washrooms, ranked discipline as the most serious problem facing their schools. Testimony given to the U. S. Senate Subcommittee on Violence and Vandalism in the Schools (*Today's Child*, 1975) suggests the dimensions of the problem:

> The cost of vandalism, arson, and theft in America's public schools is now estimated at 500 million dollars each year, a sum comparable to the entire national annual expenditure for textbooks.
> There were 100 murders in American schools during a three-year period in the 1970s; approximately 70,000 teachers are attacked each year during the course of their work, and hundreds of thousands of students are assaulted every year.
> Students in some schools are operating flourishing narcotics, prostitution, and extortion rings.

How all of this affects day-to-day education is graphically conveyed by a teacher's letter to *Today's Education*, describing what was once an excellent high school in Detroit:

> Absenteeism on a typical day runs from 30 to 40 percent—or more. Hallways are congested with students after classes have supposedly begun. Students are free to enter classes any time they wish. . . . Increasing numbers of brazen students and nonstudents challenge staff members with threats and obscenities. Teachers' purses are snatched—even in the classroom. Fires, smoke bombs, knifings and shootings within the building have become common occurrences. In recent weeks two students have been shot and killed at two Detroit high schools, one of these killings at my wife's school. These worsening conditions have resulted in extremely low staff morale. (March–April, 1975, p. 26)

Not all schools have disintegrated into this kind of moral jungle. Many of them, critics charge, are still doing their job of socialization all too well, demanding and getting uncritical conformity to the dictates of authority. Two psychologists (Hainey and Zimbardo, 1975) recently drew parallels between high schools and prisons. Both institutions, they observed, subject their clientele to endless regimentation and regulation such as how long they may wear their hair and when they may go to the bathroom. In schools as in prisons, power is in the hands of the authorities. Students do not complain about unfair teachers because, as one student said, "No matter how bad it is, you're gonna end up worse than you started" (p. 30). Prison guards turn inmates against one another by discriminatory use of privileges and favors; schools do the same thing to students through competition, whereby one person's success comes at the expense of another's failure. To the extent that schools train students to toe the line and fit into the system, they share at least some of the responsibility for all those subjects in Milgram's experiments (1974) who gave what they believed to be intense electrical shocks to protesting victims, simply because the experimenter told them to do so.

In the face of this sorry state of the moral ship, it is not surprising that two thirds of Americans recently told the Gallup Poll that they believe people no longer "lead as honest and moral lives as they used to" (*The New York Times*, April 18, 1976). An even larger majority, 79% of all respondents and fully 84% of parents with school-age children, endorsed "instruction in the schools that would deal with morals and moral behavior."*

That seeming consensus, however, masks a potentially divisive question: What kind of moral instruction should the schools perform? What should be its goals and how should it be carried out? By what criteria can developmentally legitimate, ethically defensible aims of moral education be defined?

Piagetian developmental psychology stands ready to respond to this challenge. Indeed, it has already aggressively presented itself as a major contender for the allegiance of moral educators. Lawrence Kohlberg's Harvard-based Center for Moral Development and Moral Education, deeply immersed in theory development, research, and an expanding variety of intervention projects, is one of a growing number of examples of what cognitive-developmental psychology can contribute toward fostering moral maturity in children and adults. This chapter will present the theory and research undergirding the developmental approach to moral education, particularly Piaget's pioneer research in moral judgment development and Kohlberg's important extensions of Piaget's work. Concrete examples of developmental moral education at the secondary, elementary, and preschool levels will be described, and its uses in other settings will be indicated briefly. The chapter will also include criticisms of Piagetian and Kohlbergian theory and practice and will attempt to identify needs and new directions in this rapidly developing field.

*The current call for moral education in the schools is a return to a much older theme. Thomas Jefferson, well aware that the new American government rested on moral principles the people should understand, urged that moral education have an important place in the public schools (Peterson, 1970).

2. Piaget's Theory of Moral Development

One of the happy legacies of Piaget is that he has made it scientifically respectable to tell stories about one's children. In the spirit of that heritage, I would like to introduce Piaget's contribution to the psychology of moral development by relating three experiences with my son.

By the time he was 6 years old, Mark had developed an unwavering addiction to one particular comic book, *Richie Rich*. Young Richie, "the richest kid in the world," is portrayed as a model of courtesy and generosity who gives much of his weekly allowance of $100,000 to the poor and to other altruistic causes. My concern was that Mark was reading nothing else. I thought he should be getting a more balanced diet of children's literature. So one night, as he was tidying up his mounting stack of "Richies" behind the living room sofa, I said, throwing subtlety to the winds, "Mark, how about reading a regular book once in a while instead of just Richie Rich comics? I'm beginning to think that when you grow up to be a man, you'll still be reading Richie Rich and people will say, 'There goes Mr. Mark Lickona, reading a Richie Rich comic.'"

Whereupon Mark rose to his full four feet and said calmly but with a look of deep disgruntlement, "Dad, you shouldn't tell me what to read. I have my own human personality, and I should read what my human personality tells me to. If I read Richie Rich comics when I grow up to be a man, that's okay, because that's just the way I'll be. We each have our own human personality. You read what you want to read, and I'll read what I want to read."

In addition to being properly humbled by this moral reprimand, I was surprised by Mark's spontaneous articulation of two fundamental moral principles: personal liberty (he should be free to choose his own reading) and equality (I was just as free to choose mine).

A year and a half later, Mark was still defending his autonomy against the assaults of adult authority. The occasion this time was our preparation for the annual family trip to the 4th-of-July fireworks at Cornell University. Mark was bringing along his best friend David, and both of them, in keeping with their current obsession, had donned their respective "Superhero" outfits. Mark, beaming in his blue and red "Mighty Mark" suit that his mother had sewn for him the Halloween before, announced that he was ready to go. Noticing immediately that Mark was wearing no shoes, only red socks, my wife said, "Where are your shoes?"

"Mom," Mark patiently explained, "Superheroes never wear shoes.

Besides, I think these red socks look kind of neat with my Mighty Mark suit."

"Well," his mother replied, "we have to walk across a big field to get to the fireworks, and the grass will be wet coming back. Besides, Superheroes don't wear socks with their suits, they wear boots."

Now visibly frustrated, Mark protested, "But Mom, I don't have any boots like that!" He then left the room in great distress.

Moments later he reappeared, looking very pleased with himself and wearing matching red rubbers over his socks. "I know, Mom," he said, "I'll wear my rubbers! That way I won't get my feet wet and I won't have to wear shoes. Neither of us will get everything we want. But, you see, I'll get part of what I want, and you'll get part of what you want. Okay?" The dispute was thereby resolved.

To our knowledge, Mark had never heard us use the language of compromise that he brought to bear on this moral conflict, and it seems doubtful that he would have heard it in school. Like a good Piagetian, I duly recorded this event, noting that Mark was apparently developing a sense of justice, an ability to give all parties to a conflict their due.

One final fatherly tale before drawing the full Piagetian meaning from these incidents. This last anecdote began when Mark was 6½. I mentioned that I was on my way to giving a talk to the Cortland Rotary Club "about how children grow up to know the difference between what's right and what's wrong." "Well," he said, "I have something to say about that." "Okay," I said. "What do you think is right for children to do?"

Mark replied, "Children should be good to their parents, and parents should be good to their children. That's the way they get along."

"That's very interesting," I said. "Suppose one day Mom and I weren't very nice to you; you asked if you could have a new *Richie Rich* comic book, and we just said no without any good reason. Then, later in the day, because we were going to have company, we asked you to do us a favor like vacuuming the rug. Do you think you should do it for us?"

Mark said without hesitation, "Well, no—because you weren't nice to me. I'm sorry, Dad, but that's just the way it works, you see."

Six months later, I decided to do a little longitudinal research. I again raised the question of what Mark should do if we asked him to vacuum the rug after unreasonably refusing his request for a new comic. He paused, then said, "I think I should vacuum the rug. It would be a good way of earning the new comic book."

I clarified: "No, we wouldn't pay you any allowance, this is a favor we're asking."

After another pause, he said, "Well, I would still do it."

"Even though," I reminded him, "we weren't nice to you and wouldn't get you the comic when you asked?"

"I'd still do it," he said, "I just like doing favors for people."

"Why do you like doing favors for people?" I asked.

"Because then they don't have to do all the work themselves."

"Why is that important?"

"Well," Mark said, "if they can do only part of the job, how can they get it done if they don't have help?"

How do these observations by one child's father illuminate Piaget's contribution to our understanding of moral development? They bear witness, I believe, to the truth of at least two basic principles that Piaget helped establish in his seminal book, *The Moral Judgment of the Child* (1932). One of these principles, illustrated by the story of the vacuuming-the-rug dilemma, is that conscience or moral judgment does not suddenly appear full-blown at a given age; rather, it develops through a sequence of stages. Mark's first statement that he would refuse to do the rug was characterized by a strict reciprocity; no comic, no chore. A half a year later, his reasoning was qualitatively different, more flexible and forgiving, more focused on the ideal of helping people meet their needs, regardless of what was in it for him. Similarly, Mark's early focus on his own rights when I vainly sought to alter his reading habits later broadened to a consideration of two persons' perspectives, as in the case of the rubbers-on-the-feet compromise.

The second core Piagetian idea, exemplified by all three stories, is the notion of the child as moral philosopher. Just as Piaget's research on logical thinking has depicted the child as the chief architect of his own mental model of the world, so *The Moral Judgment of the Child* paints a picture of the child as someone who constructs his own moral world view, who forms ideas about right and wrong, and fair and unfair, that are not the direct product of adult teaching and that are often maintained in the face of adult wishes to the contrary. In all three of the above examples, his parents' influence notwithstanding, Mark presented an independent moral viewpoint on the situation at hand that gave testimony to a constructivist force at work in the child's moral growth. Certainly, for example, he was not subscribing to adult prescriptions when he explained that he could not be nice to us (and vacuum the rug) if we had not been nice to him. Parents, fairly or not, want their children to do what they are asked, regardless of prior parental shortcomings.

These two key concepts, that children can and do think for themselves in the moral sphere and that their thinking goes through progessively broader, more mature stages, have, as we shall see, profound implications for the enterprise of moral education. There are, however, other important findings and ideas in Piaget's work on moral judgment that bear at least brief sketching here.

Piaget (1932) studied the moral development of children by observing their games of marbles and by interviewing them for their judgments regarding hypothetical stories of clumsiness, lying, cheating, punishment, disobedience, and so on. On the basis of this research, Piaget postulated two broad, overlapping phases in the child's moral growth: a morality of constraint, typically dominant until middle childhood, and a morality of cooperation, on the rise after 7 to 8 years of age. In the first phase, Piaget observed, children regard rules as unquestionable, unchanging absolutes handed down by adult authority. In the second phase, they tend to see rules as a code of action freely agreed upon in order to make group activity possible. Children reflecting a morality of constraint equate justice (the distribution of rewards and punishments) with whatever adults say and do, and are firm believers in severe punishment as a way of atoning for an offense. By contrast, children who have developed cooperative morality believe that justice means treating everyone equally and that punishment, when administered, should be aimed at restoring normal social relations by making the transgressor realize how he has broken a social bond. Someone who lies, for example, should understand that lying is bad not because adults say so and punish it, but because it destroys mutual trust. The younger child, Piaget found, is also likely to ignore intentions in evaluating a person's responsibility for an action and focus instead on the external consequences of the deed. A boy who broke fifteen cups accidentally is thereby judged naughtier than a boy who broke one cup while stealing some jam. The older child reverses the criteria and gives primary consideration to intentions when evaluating another's behavior.

Though he did not give it a name, Piaget also described a third stage of moral functioning, during which the ethic of cooperation becomes more adaptable to social-moral complexities and at the same time more attuned to moral ideals. Rules can now be bent according to extenuating circumstances. In a spirit of equity, for example, children who once insisted on strict equality are now willing to share some of their portion of cake with a small girl who accidentally dropped and spoiled her first piece (Piaget, 1932). By this third moral level, reciprocity has also evolved from a concrete rule of action into *ideal reciprocity*—from "Do unto others as they do unto you" to "Do as you would be done by." One of Piaget's 10-year-old subjects, reflecting this golden-rule reciprocity, rejected the idea of striking back a boy who had hit with the explanation that "there is no end to revenge" (Piaget, 1932, p. 323).

What transforms the child's moral philosophy from a morality of constraint to one of cooperation? Piaget theorized (1932) that three interacting factors account for this fundamental shift. First, the child's pervasive intellectual egocentrism, of which moral immaturity is only one manifestation, diminishes with age and experience. Second, the child's conscience becomes less a prisoner of *adult constraint*. Piaget defined *constraint* as authority's tendencey to impose unilaterally on the child rules whose basis he does not understand, thereby retarding his progress toward understanding the mutuality of moral obligations. The child's increasing independence of adult constraint, Piaget believed, develops partly as a result of his emerging awareness that authority's rules are psychosocial expectations rather than external absolutes, partly as a consequence of observing that adults are neither perfect nor omniscient, and partly as a result of social experience with other children. This last factor is the one that Piaget pinpoints as the most important impetus for moral development: the child's increasing interchange with his social peers on a basis of mutual respect and equality.

For Piaget, social interaction on an equal-to-equal footing has three clear consequences for the child's moral development. (1) The first is disequilibrium, arising from the incompatibility between the new experience of social equality with peers and the child's previous tendency to submit his conscience to the mind of the adult. This incompatibility upsets the old cognitive equilibrium represented by a morality of obedience and motivates a gradual equilibration or reorganization of moral values on a more rational and more stable basis, namely, cooperation among equals. (2) Second, peer relations force the child out of his socially egocentric mentality by confronting him with several points of view to which he must adapt. As Kohlberg puts it: "In order to play a role in a group, the child must learn to *take* the role of others toward himself and toward others in the group" (1964, p. 395). Once the child can shift perspective and coordinate different social viewpoints, he can begin to·understand that reciprocity and agreement among equals, rather than authority, constitute the basis of rules and obligations. (3) Finally, equalitarian peer interaction helps the child to "discover the boundaries that separate his self from the other person [and] to learn to understand the other person and be understood by him" (Piaget, 1932, p. 95).

Piaget's *Moral Judgment* book has left an unmistakable stamp on the field. As Weinreich observes: "Throughout the last 40 years, research on moral judgment has not departed in any significant sense from the Piagetian framework" (1975, p. 201). Most of the progressions in judgment that Piaget described in Swiss children have stood up, after scores of studies, as universal trends in the development of moral thought. There is, moreover, additional research, much of it done by Kohlberg (1973a, 1976b) and his colleagues, that supports Piaget's identification of cognitive development, peer interaction, and freedom from coercive authority as factors contributing to advance in moral judgment. (For more comprehensive treatments of Piaget's theory and the research it stimulated, see Gibbs, 1975; Lickona, 1976c; and Scaplehorn, 1974).

Any evaluation of Piaget's contribution to moral development and moral education must ultimately include what this work has in large part inspired: the moral development theory and the research of Lawrence Kohlberg.

3. Kohlberg's Theory of Moral Development

3.1. Kohlberg and Piaget: How They Compare

As a doctoral student at the University of Chicago in 1955, Kohlberg (1958) began a still-continuing longitudinal study of the moral reasoning of 50 Chicago working-class and middle-class males. (Subsequent researchers, e.g., Belenky, in progress; Gilligan, Kohlberg, Lerner, and Belenky, 1971; Haan, Smith, and Block, 1968; Holstein, 1976; and Turiel, 1974, have found the same stages of moral reasoning in females.) On the basis of that research, and drawing from the moral theories of Dewey and Tufts (1932), Mead (1934), and Baldwin (1906) as well as from Piaget's work, Kohlberg has advanced a "cognitive-developmental" approach to understanding moral growth that has been judged as "perhaps the single most fruitful exploration" in the field (Stewart, 1975). The similarities and differences between Piaget and Kohlberg, described in detail elsewhere (e.g., Duska and Whelan, 1975; Gibbs, 1977; Krahn, 1971; and Weinreich, 1975), can here be summarized as follows:

1. Like Piaget (1970; 1971a,b), Kohlberg (1969b) adopts the basic developmental-structuralist assumptions that the life of the mind is organized into *holistic structures,* that these organized patterns of thought are *constructed* by the individual through interaction with the environment, and that such psychological structures develop in a natural *sequence of stages* which occur, like biological differentiation and integration, in human cultures everywhere. (For an elaboration of these shared assumptions, see Gibbs, 1977.)

2. Like Piaget, Kohlberg (1973b) postulates that each higher stage provides a more stable or equilibrated structure for assimilating and accommodating to new experiences.

3. Like Piaget, Kohlberg (1969b, 1976b) defines moral judgment according to how an individual reasons (structure) rather than according to what he thinks (content); unlike Piaget, Kohlberg has used open-ended "moral dilemmas" and in-depth questioning (as opposed to Piaget's story pairs and relatively brief interviews) to try to probe beneath the content of a person's judgment to the structure of his reasoning. (Kohlberg's dilemmas pose such problems as: Should a doctor mercy-kill a fatally ill woman who pleads to be put out of her pain? Why or why not? If the doctor gives her the drug and is later found guilty of murder by a jury, what sentence should the judge give him? Why?)*

4. Like Piaget, Kohlberg defines moral development in terms of maturity of moral reasoning rather than in terms of particular moral behaviors (which may reflect any number of different levels of reasoning).

5. Whereas Piaget studied children from age 5 to 13, Kohlberg began his longitudinal investigation with 10- to 16-year-olds and charted the course of their moral thinking over a 20-year period—a program of research that has yielded a profile of moral development in adolescence and early adulthood as well as in childhood. As a result of the greater scope of Kohlberg's work, he has been able to describe three additional moral stages beyond Piaget's three stages of childhood.

Kohlberg has continued to refine his six stages on the basis of his on-going research and theory construction. His most recent revision (1976b) of the stages and the three levels (preconventional, conventional, and postconventional) into which he groups them are presented in Table I. An individual's stage is always based on the kind of thinking he uses to justify his solution of a range of moral dilemmas. The interviewer typically asks a series of probe questions designed to elicit the subject's reasoning on several of 10 value issues that Kohlberg (1975) believes all people, regardless of class or culture, deal with in their social relations: punishment, law, property, roles and concerns of affection, roles and concerns of authority, the value of life, liberty, truth, sex, and justice.

The six stages are perhaps best illustrated by successive views of justice, the central issue in Kohlberg's concept of morality. He holds that a person's view of justice permeates his approach to solving all moral

*For an increasingly popular, short-answer approach to assessing the stage of moral reasoning, see Rest (1976).

Table I.   Kohlberg's Six Moral Stages[a]

Level and stage	Conception of the right
Level I: Preconventional Stage 1: Heteronomous morality	To avoid breaking rules backed by punishment, obedience for its own sake, and avoiding physical damage to persons and property.
Stage 2: Individualism, instrumental purpose, and exchange	Following rules only when it is to someone's immediate interest; acting to meet one's own interest and needs and letting others do the same. Right is also what's fair, what's an equal exchange, a deal, an agreement.
Level II: Conventional Stage 3: Mutual interpersonal expectations, relationships, and interpersonal conformity	Living up to what is expected by people close to you or what people generally expect of people in your role as son, brother, friend, etc. "Being good" is important and means having good motives, showing concern about others. It also means keeping mutual relationships, such as trust, loyalty, respect and gratitude; golden rule.
Stage 4: Social system and conscience	Fulfilling the actual duties to which you have agreed. In order to maintain the system, laws are to be upheld except in extreme cases where they conflict with other fixed social duties. Right is also contributing to society, the group, or institution.
Level III: Postconventional or principled Stage 5: Social contract or utility and individual rights	Acting so as to achieve the "greatest good for the greatest number." Being aware that people hold a variety of values and opinions, that most values and rules are relative to your group. These relative rules should usually be upheld, however, in the interest of impartiality and because they are the social contract. Some nonrelative values and rights like life and liberty, however, must be upheld in any society and regardless of majority opinion.
Stage 6: Universal ethical principles	Following self-chosen ethical principles. Particular laws or social agreements are usually valid because they rest on such principles. When laws violate these principles, one acts in accordance with the principle. Principles are universal principles of justice: the equality of human rights and respect for the dignity of human beings as individual persons.

[a] Adapted from Kohlberg, 1976b.

conflicts and defining human rights and obligations. The concern for justice, like thinking about other moral issues, is given a new and wider definition at each higher stage. At Stage 1, the conception of justice is a primitive "mechanical equivalence," an eye for an eye and a tooth for a tooth. At Stage 2, when the individual becomes conscious that he and others have different viewpoints and interests of which they are mutually aware, fairness takes on a positive dimension: you help me and I'll help you, let's make a deal. At Stage 3, justice becomes ideal reciprocity, being a nice guy, putting yourself in the other person's shoes regardless of what's in it for you.

At Stage 4, the relatively simple morality of interpersonal reciprocity is broadened: the person now thinks that getting along in a complex society and the just distribution of rights and duties require a social system of roles, authority, and law. At Stage 5 comes the recognition that the social-legal order does not dispense rights to individuals but exists by social contract between the governors and the governed to protect the inalienable equal rights of all and to settle conflict by democratic process (the heart of the morality of the American Constitution) (Kohlberg, 1975).

Ideal justice, at Stage 6, involves what Kohlberg describes as a "second-order conception of Golden Rule role-taking" (1973b, p. 643). Consider the well-known Heinz dilemma: He has to decide whether it is right to try to save his dying wife by stealing a drug that is priced beyond his means. At Stage 6, a highly formal-operational Heinz would imagine the greedy druggist putting himself in the shoes of Heinz's dying wife and conclude that the druggist, once back in his own shoes, could no longer maintain his "claim" of refusing to sell the drug at an affordable price. If, on the other hand, Heinz imagined his wife putting herself in the druggist's place, he would see that she could still maintain her claim to the life-saving drug. It would therefore be justified to steal it, a solution that anyone would choose as fair if he did not know in advance which role in the dilemma he would have to occupy.

Kohlberg has made the claim, vigorously debated among social scientists and philosophers (see Mischel, 1971, and Lickona, 1976b, for various views on this issue), that each of the successive moral judgment stages he has described is "objectively preferable to or more adequate than an earlier stage" according to both psychological and philosophical criteria (1971; 1973b, p. 630). From a psychological standpoint, he argues that the higher stages are better because they are more equilibrated, more capable of handling diverse moral conflicts within their problem-solving framework. From a philosophical standpoint, Kohlberg maintains that each higher stage does a better job of measuring up to the long-standing criteria of reversibility, consistency, and universalizability that Kant (1787), Rawls (1971), and other "formalist" philosophers have viewed as the essence of rational moral judgment. Kohlberg's defense of Stage 6 as the most just stage of all attempts to show how moral judgment that meets his philosophical criteria is simultaneously more equilibrated in Piagetian psychological sense:

> For developmental theory, meeting these philosophical conditions of moral judgment is parallel with the equilibration of fully logical thought in the realm of physical or logical facts. According to Piaget and others, the keystone of logic is reversibility. A logical train of thought is one in which one can move back and forth between premises and conclusions without distortion. Mathematical thinking is an example; A + B is the same as B + A. . . . Reversibility of moral judgment is what is ultimately meant by the criterion of the fairness of a moral decision. If we have a reversible solution, we have one that could be reached as right starting from anyone's perspective in the situation, given each person's intent to put himself in the shoes of the other. . . .
>
> It is [also] clear that universalizability is implied by reversibility. If something is fair or right to do from the conflicting points of view of all those involved in the situation, it is something we can wish all persons to do in all similar situations. (Kohlberg, 1973b, pp. 641–642)

Clearly, one cannot achieve a more stable moral equilibrium than a stage of principles that guide what all persons should do in all situations. As an example of how lower stages lack the fully equilibrated reversibility of Stage 6, Kohlberg cites how Stage 3 role taking would see-saw in the face of the capital punishment dilemma: "If we put ourselves in the shoes of the murderer, we are opposed to the death penalty; but if we put ourselves in the shoes of the victim whose muder would be deterred by the death penalty, we favor it" (Kohlberg and Elfenbein, 1975, pp. 634–635). Stage 3 tells you to consider the viewpoint and welfare of another, but it does not tell you whose viewpoint to take or how to resolve competing claims.

Logic and morality are similar, Kohlberg says, but they are also different. A new logical stage is only a necessary, not a sufficient, condition for a new moral stage (see Colby and Kohlberg, in press; Keasey, 1975; Kohlberg and Gilligan, 1971; and Tomlinson-Keasey and Keasey, 1974, for an elaboration of the conceptual and empirical relationship between Piaget's logical stages and Kohlberg's moral stages). Kohlberg (1973b) argues that moral judgment goes beyond logical judgment in two ways: (1) "Moral judgments involve role-taking, taking the point of view of others conceived as *subjects* and coordinating those points of view, whereas logic involves only coordinating points of view upon objects"; (2) "equilibrated moral judgments involve principles of justice or fairness," restoring equilibrium in a moral conflict by giving each party his due according to a standard that all would accept as impartial and fair (p. 633). An educational implication of Kohlberg's theory that morality is more demanding than logic has a clear message to schools: Making students smarter will not automatically make them more moral.

3.2. Research on Kohlberg's Theory

What does the research say about Kohlberg's sweeping claims? He supports his "higher-is-better" assertion with evidence that children reject lower-level reasoning as being inadequate (Kohlberg and Turiel, 1971) and that subjects tend to prefer reasoning above their own stage even though they cannot produce or accurately paraphrase such higher-stage thinking themselves (Rest, Turiel, and Kohlberg, 1969). Another study (Erdynast, 1973) showed that Stage 5 subjects asked to engage in Stage 6 ideal role-taking often subsequently change their judgments about a moral dilemma and feel that their new Stage 6 solution was more adequate.

Critical support for Kohlberg's theory of an invariant developmental sequence in his moral stages is provided by newly published data from his longitudinal research (Kohlberg and Elfenbein, 1975). Findings are reported for 30 subjects interviewed at 3-year intervals since the beginning of the study, when they were 10 to 16 years old. "At every 3-year interval, subjects had either remained at the same stage or had moved one stage ahead" (p. 622), with some subjects showing advance all the way from Stage 1 to Stage 5 over the course of the investigation.

An interesting short-term approach to validating Kohlberg's assertion of stage sequentiality assessed the moral reasoning of 50 kindergarten to second-grade children on two Kohlberg dilemmas, administered three times over a one-year period (Kuhn, 1976). Over the six months between the first and second assessment, 25 subjects showed an increase in stage level, 15 subjects no change, and 10 subjects a decline. Over the 12 months from first to third assessment, 32 subjects showed an increase, 13 no change, and only 5 a decline. Most of the observed change was an increase in the stage of reasoning that had been present earlier but not yet dominant. Kuhn interpreted her results to indicate that there is considerable short-term fluctuation in moral judgment level, but that over a longer interval of one year, there is significant progressive change in the direction Kohlberg predicts.

The cross-cultural case for the universality of Kohlberg's stages is weakened somewhat by the fact that only a fraction of the relevant data has been published. The major portion is promised in Kohlberg's long-awaited edited book, reportedly still in preparation. The findings that have been published show the predicted upward-stage trends in adolescent moral reasoning in countries as varied as the United States, Great Britain, Israel, Mexico, Turkey, and Taiwan (e.g., Kohlberg, 1969b). More recently, Kohlberg and Elfenbein (1975) report that "although no reasoning above Stage 3 or Stage 4 occurs in some of the primitive cultures studied, some Stage 5 thinking occurs in all complex societies with a literate urban component." (For an argument that Kohlberg's system is culturally biased, see Simpson, 1974.)

Kohlberg's longitudinal data have also yielded new support for his thesis that the moral stages are genuine "structures" of thought, producing a fair amount of consistency in stage of moral thinking across different dilemmas. In only 10% of the 105 interviews scored in Kohlberg and Elfenbein's longitudinal report (1975) did a subject's overall stage score (based on nine dilemmas) differ from his stage score on a particular dilemma concerning capital punishment. Broughton (1976) presents other recent evidence for "structural wholeness" in moral thought, such as Lieberman's reported statistical identification of a first-level factor accounting for 85% of the variance in moral judgment. (For another discussion of the "stage mix" issue, see Turiel, 1969.)

Kohlberg (1969a, 1976b) has been careful to point out that people do not always act according to their highest stage of reasoning, but he has nonetheless boldly asserted that "moral judgment . . . is the single most important or influential factor yet discovered in moral behavior" (1975, p. 672). Social learning theorists like the Mischels balk at such a statement, marshaling evidence that they feel shows moral reasoning to be a relatively undependable predictor of behavior, no better than "other individual difference variables" (1976, p. 101). Studies cited as buttressing Kohlberg's claim showed that Stage 6 subjects were much less likely than lower-stage subjects to continue shocking the victim in Milgram's experiment (Kohlberg, 1969b); that higher-stage subjects cheated less on a test than lower-stage subjects (Grim, Kohlberg, and White, 1968); that the higher a college student's moral stage, the greater the likelihood that he or she would resist authority to help someone in distress (McNamee, 1968); and that fulfilling a commitment to return a questionnaire, ostensibly needed for the experimenter to pass her research course, increased dramatically as a function of stage of moral reasoning (Krebs and Rosenwald, 1973). Kohlberg also reports that

criminal offenders are considerably lower in moral judgment development than nonoffenders from the same social background. Most adolescent delinquents, for example, have reached only Stage 1 or Stage 2,
whereas the majority of nonoffending adolescents and young adults
are at Stage 3 or 4 (Kohlberg, Kauffman, Scharf, and Hickey, 1975).

Some of the most interesting data on the moral behavior question
may come from a study in progress on the relationship between moral
judgment and life outcomes (Graham, Lieberman, and Candee, 1976).
Of 74 subjects interviewed, 23 of the 25 who had reached the highest
job status categories (on the Hollingshead scale of preferred occupa-
tions) also exhibited at least one of the two highest moral stages (Stages
4 and 5) found in the study. By contrast, persons who held lower-status
jobs were more likely to be at lower stages. The study's tentative interpretation: "The reason higher-stage subjects were found predominantly in high-status jobs seems to be that they possessed the social
skills and moral judgment needed to decide what an individual or organization ought to do in a complex situation" (Graham *et al.*, 1976, p.
6). Subjects' political activities and attitudes toward personal success,
marriage, and family are also among the life outcomes being examined
by the researchers.

The discussion turns now to the pragmatic issue at hand: Does the
theory work in a school? If so, how? Kohlberg's final claim, resting on all
the others, is that a cognitive-developmental approach to morality offers
the most ethically and developmentally sound solution to the problem of
moral education in the schools.

4. Developmental Moral Education: Putting Piaget and Kohlberg into the Classroom

4.1. Goals and Means of Developmental Moral Education

Kohlberg and Piaget are strikingly similar in how they see the moral
mission of the schools. In 1932 Piaget wrote that

> The essence of democracy is to replace the unilateral respect of authority by
> the mutual respect of autonomous wills. . . . The modern ideal is
> cooperation—dignity of the individual and respect for general opinion as
> elaborated in free discussion. How are we to bring children to this spirit of
> citizenship and humanity which is postulated by democratic societies? By
> the actual practice of cooperation, by democracy at school. . . . It is unbe-
> lievable that at a time when democratic ideas enter into every phase of life,

they should have been so little utilized as instruments of education. (1932, p. 366)

Over 40 years later, Kohlberg is sounding essentially the same call:

the school has a right and the mandate to develop an awareness of justice, of the rights of others, (an awareness) necessary for a citizen in a democracy if democracy is to be an effective process. . . . While our political institutions are in principle Stage 5 vehicles (for maintaining universal rights through the democratic process), our schools have traditionally been Stage 4 institutions of convention and authority. Today more than ever, democratic schools systematically engaged in civic education are required. (1975, pp. 674–676)

Just as the development of the individual (to higher stages) should be the end of education, Kohlberg says, so should democracy be the means of education.

Not surprisingly, Piaget and Kohlberg also advanced their views on authority in the school in remarkably parallel ways. Anyone weary of hearing that "Piaget himself has little or nothing to say about the application of his work to education" should be refreshed by the force and directness of his statements on educating for moral growth in the closing chapter of *The Moral Judgment of the Child* (1932). The results of his research on moral development, Piaget argued,

are as unfavorable to the method of authority as to purely individualistic methods. It is absurd to impose upon the child a fully worked out system of discipline when the social life of children amongst themselves is sufficiently developed to give rise to a discipline infinitely nearer adult morality. (p. 404)

The sense of a common law, which, as we have shown in connection with the rules of a game, is possessed by children of 9–12, shows clearly enough how capable is the child of discipline and democratic life when he is not, as at school, condemned to wage war against authority. (p. 364)

In the same spirit, Kohlberg writes, "If schools wish to foster morality, they will have to . . . provide an atmosphere in which interpersonal issues are settled on the basis of principle rather than power" (1972). Such an atmosphere can be created, Kohlberg points out, only if *"both students and teachers* are willing to modify their decisions and behavior as a result of democratic discussion" (1976a, p. 6). From a Piagetian or Kohlbergian perspective, then, "schools would be radically different places if they took seriously the teaching of real knowledge of the good" (Kohlberg, 1970, p. 83).

For both Piaget and Kohlberg, becoming morally mature means two kinds of growth: (a) *vertical development* to higher stages of moral reasoning, and (b) *horizontal development,* or the widening application of one's highest stage of reasoning powers to analyzing moral situations and choosing a moral course of action. From this viewpoint, moral education is not indoctrination but rather it is supplying the conditions that stimulate this natural development, or at the very least not interfering with it. Kohlberg and his colleagues (Kohlberg, Kauffman, Scharf, and Hickey, 1975) have spelled out six such conditions or experiences that they believe foster progress through the moral stages:

1. Being in a situation where seeing things from other points of view is encouraged—important because upward stage movement is a process of getting better at reconciling conflicting perspectives on a moral problem.
2. Engaging in logical thinking, such as reasoned argument and consideration of alternatives—important because one cannot attain a given stage of moral reasoning before attaining the supporting stage of logical reasoning.
3. Having the responsibility to make moral decisions and to influence one's moral world (e.g., through participation in group decision making)—necessary for learning to apply one's moral reasoning to life situations.
4. Exposure to moral controversy, to conflict in moral reasoning that challenges one's thinking and may lead to rethinking at the next stage up.
5. Exposure to the reasoning of individuals who are one stage higher than one's own—offering a new moral structure for resolving the disequilibrium caused by moral conflict.
6. Participating in a just social environment where day-to-day human relations are characterized by concern for mutual respect and fairness.

4.2. Applications of Kohlberg with Adolescents

Providing all of the above conditions for moral development is clearly a tall order. Early Kohlbergian efforts were much more modest, utilizing the moral dilemmas Kohlberg had used in his research and offering them for discussion in the classroom. The teacher's role was to "introduce the dilemma; encourage class members to take a stand on what ought to be done and explain why; encourage confrontation and mutual probing by the class members of each other's reasoning; encourage listening and paying attention to each discussant's points and evaluation of the adequacy of the argument; furnish occasional high-stage responses; interject a probe question here and there; reflect and summarize group deliberations; and facilitate good group discussion process" (Rest, 1974, p. 247).

Blatt (1969; Blatt and Kohlberg, 1975), a clinical psychologist and colleague of Kohlberg's, pioneered in the dilemma discussion approach. The very first project used a combination of Biblical and non-Biblical dilemmas (e.g., Was it right for Abraham to offer Isaac for sacrifice? Should a boy give up a scholarship to college in order to work to provide needed support for his family?) with a Reformed Jewish Sunday School class of 30 children, ages 11 to 12. The classes met for one hour each week for 12 weeks. By the end of the sessions, 63% of the children had moved up one stage in moral reasoning, 9% had moved up half a stage (a mixture of their pretest stage and the next higher), and 28% had remained the same. Control group subjects showed no change. On a follow-up test one year later, the experimental subjects retained their advantage. Significantly, Blatt also found a close relationship between how much interest a student expressed in the discussions (e.g., "I liked them because they really made you think hard") and how much stage change he experienced. This may be a lesson for teachers who wonder if they should let a moral debate get off track. If a tangent is where the students' interest is, then that is probably where the discussion should go.

Blatt and Kohlberg (1975) report a second study that performed several twists on the first. This time moral dilemma discussions were carried out in four public-school classrooms in Chicago, chosen to vary age (6th versus 10th grade) and socioeconomic status (lower-middle class versus lower class). For each age and status group, three subgroups were set up: Group I was led by a trained adult using developmental principles; Group II discussed the same moral dilemmas but without active leadership by an adult; and Group III was a control. Eighteen sessions, held twice a week for 45 minutes, dealt with moral issues such as law, conscience, parent-child relations, crime, punishment, love, and sex. Change in reasoning for the experimental subjects was on the average one third of a stage—only about half what it had been in the Jewish Sunday School study—but superiority to controls was still evident one year later. Social class and age did not relate in any systematic way to amount of stage gain. What did matter was whether the group was conducted by an adult: peer-run discussions produced significantly more stage change than that experienced by controls but only one-third as much change as experienced by students benefiting from an adult's guidance and questioning. Leadership made a difference.

An interesting sidelight was the study's finding that on three Hartshorne and May (1928) paper-and-pencil tests of cheating, experimental students actually cheated slightly more at the end of the program than they had at the beginning. Blatt and Kohlberg reasoned that the Hartshorne and May measures were a poor device for picking up the impact of judgmental advance on behavior. The study's behavioral results can also be taken as a caution against expecting better moral conduct as a result of merely talking about what it means to be moral.

Aside from being all talk, a steady stream of moral dilemmas, as Rest (1974) points out, can be a rather dull academic diet. Inspired by Kohlberg's theory, Ed Sullivan and Clive Beck, two Canadian educators (E. Sullivan, 1975), set out to broaden his educational methods, although still staying within a verbal-discussion format. Meeting twice a week with juniors and seniors in two Ontario high schools, they discussed a dozen or so general social-moral questions (e.g., What does it mean to be "good"? Why do people need each other? Why do moral codes vary from one society to another?). They also tackled such relevant issues as abortion, drugs, school rules, and relations with parents. Significant increases in Stage 5 reasoning—the main objective of the intervention—occurred in only one of the two schools, was quite slight (16%), and took two years to show up in the comparison with controls. Sullivan also reported that students frequently gave more lower-stage arguments (especially Stage 2) during discussion with their peers than they did on individual written assignments, and that supercharged issues like abortion and mercy killing generated much more emotional reaction than enlightened exchange of reasoning.

The Canadian studies—combined with a Minnesota project (Schaeffer, 1974) showing no stage change at all in high school students following a semester of dilemma debate—reinforced the impression that discussion alone will not always do the job. Growing from that insight is a new direction in developmental moral education that turns away from hypothetical moral dilemmas and concentrates instead on changing the social role of the person, coupled with guided reflection on the meaning of the new social experience. This is a balanced mix of practicum and seminar, which Mosher and Sprinthall (1971) report works better than either practicum or seminar alone.

Called Deliberate Psychological Education by its originators, this more applied approach has been used with adolescents in a number of ingenious ways. In one high school course (Mosher and Sprinthall, 1971), students learned counseling techniques and listening skills and used these skills with one another to discuss personally meaningful issues in their lives. Not only did they develop these observable interpersonal competencies, but they also showed average gains of about one third to one half a stage in measured moral reasoning—without any involvement in a formal curriculum for moral thinking. Initially surprised by this outcome, the course instructors reflected that counseling had after all involved the students in two processes that are at the heart of moral stage development: developing a more complex understanding of the principle of justice in resolving conflict in human relationships, and developing the capacity to empathize with or take the role of another.

Something like the same processes appear to have been at work in a half-semester course on The Psychology of Women (Erickson, 1975). This course trained its female students in listening and Piaget-style questioning in preparation for doing field interviews of girls and women across the life span. In their interviews they asked such questions as, "What is one thing in life that you really value?" and probed for reasons that would enable them to characterize the major motivational and value position of their female subjects. In seminar sessions, the students examined their interview data for complexity of thought and feeling and were able gradually to construct rough stages of female development throughout the life cycle. The seminar was also used to discuss current and historical literature about sexual stereotypes, inequality, and the rights and roles of women—frequently searching for parallels between the behavior or reasoning of a female figure in literature and the processes they had found in their field interviews of women. Finally, course participants began to make connections between the interviews and the reading and their own emerging life choices and patterns of personal growth.

By the end of the quarter, students involved in this imaginative curriculum had shifted one third of a moral stage, from Kohlberg's Stage 3 (other-directed conformity as a basis for moral judgment) toward Stage 4 (judgment based on general rules, rights, and duties). Moreover, they kept right on developing, showing an additional gain, equal to the experimental-phase advance, on a follow-up assessment one year later. Finally, they made significant gains in complexity of thinking about self and others as measured by the Loevinger Sentence Completion Test of ego development (Loevinger and Wessler, 1970).

Programs like the ones just described, in addition to treating moral reasoning development as only one objective embedded in a broader program for personal growth, demonstrate that the readily available high school course can be a powerful vehicle for developmental values education. Another notable venture along these same lines (P. Sullivan, 1975) stimulated a half-stage change in moral reasoning in Boston high school students and an advance of one full stage on Loevinger's ego development scale. The catalyst in this case was a course lasting an entire year, with four segments: (1) moral discussions, making heavy use of popular contemporary films (e.g., *The Godfather, Serpico, Judgment at Nuremburg, On the Waterfront*) that dramatize ethical dilemmas; (2) training in and application of counseling skills; (3) comparative moral philosophy and developmental psychology; and (4) a two-part moral practicum which involved students in leading moral-dilemma discussions among 6th graders and in setting up a high school board of appeals to handle their own discipline problems. The students' new social responsibilities and their sense of having an impact on their social-moral environment, Sullivan observed, stimulated the greatest interest during the course and may have been largely responsible for their substantial developmental change.

Since the early dilemma discussion efforts, Kohlberg's own thinking about what optimizes moral growth has taken some important turns. "Prior to 1974," he writes, "our moral education efforts viewed moral development as an attribute of an isolated individual. . . . This conception of individual stage change ignores the fact that 'real life' reasoning and action in school are largely a response to the moral reasoning and behavior of others" (1976a, p. 10). This fact of moral life, Kohlberg says, was brought home to him when he set up moral dilemma groups in prisons and found discussions competing with the sounds of guards beating up inmates and inmates beating up each other. The behavior of others, Kohlberg suggests, constitutes a "group level" and creates a "moral atmosphere" that may strongly influence the members of the group. Also contributing importantly to the moral atmosphere is the perceived "justice structure" of an institution. In the eyes of its members, how fair are the rules, the privileges, the responsibilities, the rewards and the punishments? If the moral atmosphere is "low"—either because group behavior is low-level or the institution is perceived as operating according to a low-stage ethic (as prisons, for example, are typically seen)—it may cause people in that environment to function at a moral level well beneath their own highest stage. In a significant and positive sense, Kohlberg's addition of the moral atmosphere construct represents the sociologizing of a developmental theory.

In educational practice, developing a positive moral climate has meant creating the kind of "democracy in the school" that Piaget urged so strongly in 1932 and that now constitutes for Kohlberg the vital core of effective moral education. In 1974, Kohlberg's Center received grants to begin fashioning such a participatory democracy within a large urban high school in Cambridge, Massachusetts. Set up as a school-within-a-school, the Cluster School at last account (Wasserman, 1976) involved 7 staff members and 72 students, about one third of the students coming from academic professional homes, one third from working-class homes, and another third who had been dropouts and troublemakers or petty delinquents. Aimed at "making moral education a living matter" (Kohlberg, 1975), the "just community school," as Kohlberg calls it, features five interweaving strands of effort:

1. A core curriculum in English and Social studies that frequently centers on moral discussions, role taking, communication, and experiences such as visiting and studying the functioning of real-life communities like churches, Alcoholics Anonymous, and prisons.
2. Weekly community meetings of all students and staff where everyone has one vote and the goal is to reach fair decisions on issues that matter to students (e.g., drugs, stealing, disruptions, grading).
3. Small-group meetings that clarify issues to be raised at the larger community meeting and provide an opportunity for greater personal involvement in moral discussions.
4. Weekly advisory or counseling groups, led by a staff member, in which the focus is on providing peer support regarding personal (rather than community) problems.
5. A discipline committee, comprised of rotating student representatives from each advisory group, that is charged with the responsibility of making decisions (which may be appealed at the community meeting) about how to deal with rule offenders.

Social-moral education on this scale is clearly a long way from the early days when the Kohlbergian moral curriculum was discussing the likes of Heinz and the avaricious druggist. Does the new, broad-gauged approach work? Forthcoming research evaluation of the just community school will compare its students' moral judgment development and perception of school moral atmosphere with those of a control group in another school (Kohlberg, 1976a). A descriptive report of results thus far is encouraging:

> The clearest signs of success in the Cluster School lie in an emerging sense of community and in high morale. Students have assumed increasing responsibility for their own behavior and for the behavior of others. Many students have become competent at participating in community meetings, and a smaller number have learned to lead community meetings skill-

fully.... Friendships have formed among students of widely different background who might never have had an opportunity to interact in a traditional, tracked high school. The staff has also observed some positive changes in the behavior of students with long histories of difficulty in school. These students say that the changes in their behavior came about mainly because the Cluster School treats them fairly and gives them a forum in which they can protest unfair treatment. (Wasserman, 1976, p. 207)

4.3. Developmental Moral Education with Elementary School Children

Early endeavors to put Kohlberg into the elementary classroom, like the maiden undertakings at the secondary level, consisted of talking about the right thing to do in fictitious situations. Working with fifth graders in Canadian schools, for example, Ed Sullivan (1975) stimulated some movement toward conventional-level reasoning by having students discuss hypothetical moral events—e.g., to decide in town-meeting style what to do about a principal who strapped seven pupils in violation of school policy against corporal punishment.

Another effort to improve on the verbal dilemma discussion approach took the form of sound-filmstrips, produced by Guidance Associates (1972) in collaboration with Kohlberg and Selman. Two filmstrip series, *First Things: Values* (1972) and *First Things: Social Reasoning* (1974), were respectively designed to develop moral reasoning and the social understanding of how people think and feel, the latter being an apparently necessary intermediate step between Piaget's logical stages and Kohlberg's moral judgment stages (Selman, 1976). Each filmstrip dramatizes a dilemma that children presumably can identify with. For example, should 10-year-old Holly respond to a small boy's plea to rescue his stranded kitten from a tree, or should she keep her just-made promise to her father not to climb any more trees? An evaluation of this approach (Selman and Lieberman, 1974) found that second-grade children advanced a half stage in considering others' intentions after they had participated in twice-weekly filmstrip discussions over a five-week period and small-group discussions of actual classroom problems for another five months. Controls showed no significant change. Selman speculated that it was the teachers' follow-up discussions of real classroom concerns, weaving moral thinking into the fabric of everyday life, that interacted with the filmstrip sessions to bring about developmental gains.

Enright (1975) took moral discussions a step further. He had sixth graders not only debate dilemmas themselves but also, working in pairs, lead discussions of the same dilemmas twice a week with first graders. He reports "dramatic changes" in these sixth-graders' stage of interpersonal reasoning (role-taking ability) but no superiority to the control group on a test of "means-end social problem solving and referential communication" (1975, p. 6). Enright also observed in some of his "teachers" a considerable gap between a high stage of interpersonal understanding and a low level of actual interpersonal behavior. One sixth-grade boy, for example, was a sophisticated reasoner but retaliated in a primitive eye-for-an-eye fashion whenever a younger child called him a name. Enright concluded that the integration of social reasoning and behavior would be more likely if children had an opportunity to play teaching or helping roles on a more regular basis in the classroom.

Using dilemma discussions to work directly on moral reasoning continues to be honed to a fine art. Recent books on the market (e.g., Galbraith and Jones, 1976; Lockwood, 1973; Mattox, 1975) and articles (e.g., Beyer, 1976) provide an abundance of dilemmas for use with both elementary and secondary students and spell out the steps the teacher should follow in order to initiate, sustain, and conclude a fruitful discussion. In our own work with elementary and preschool teachers in Project Change (Lickona, 1976a; 1977a and b), however, we have moved away from hypothetical moral dilemmas toward what we consider a more holistic approach, one that defines the moral curriculum as all the human interactions and relationships in the classroom. Moral discussions are still on the agenda, but they center on real problems arising from the children's own experience and are only a part of the larger task of creating a moral atmosphere of mutual respect and support that would pervade the human environment entirely. This is plainly parallel to the new direction that Kohlbergian moral education has taken in the secondary school.

In another basic sense, our approach is a return to the kind of naturalistic moral curriculum that Piaget called for in his *Moral Judgment* book in 1932. He never suggested that educators use his stories about broken cups or stolen apples to directly induce moral conflict, just as he never meant for teachers to use his logical research tasks as classroom curriculum. In the desire to create disequilibrium and cognitive advance, it is possible to overlook a fundamental principle of Piagetian epistemology: that knowledge is slowly constructed out of personally meaningful interaction with one's environment. In the moral as in the intellectual sphere, this principle for Piaget called for the "Activity School, in which the child works of his own free will" (1932, p. 364) and is able to follow "his interests and the special laws of his activity" (p. 366). At the same time Piaget rejected education that "lets children do exactly as they like" because such a Philosophy fails to realize that "for work and discipline to come into being, there must be *an organized social life*" (1932, p. 366) (italics added). His harshest words, however, he saved for traditional schools,

> whose ideal has gradually come to be the preparation of pupils for competitive examinations rather than for life. . . . They have found themselves obliged to shut the child up in work that is strictly individual. . . . This procedure, which helps more than all the family situations put together to reinforce the child's spontaneous egocentrism, seems contrary to the most obvious requirements of intellectual and moral development. (1932, p. 405)

"Only the Activity School," Piaget emphasized, "is able to realize cooperation and democracy in the classroom" (1932, p. 364). He urged schools to become places where children are allowed

> to follow their interests together, either in organized teams or simply according to their spontaneous groupings . . . where individual experimentation and reflection carried out in common come to each other's aid and balance one another. (1932, pp. 404–405)

Such cooperation, because it allows for coordination of actions and objective comparison of ideas, "suppresses both egocentrism and moral realism [constraint] and thus achieves an interiorization of rules" (1932, p. 404).

As an example of how to bring Piaget's prescription to life in an elementary classroom, let me share with you a semester-long project organized by a third-grade teacher (Hophan, 1977) in our graduate program at Cortland. Her strategy for fostering cooperative experimentation began with a deceptively simple question put to her children: How can you make different kinds of dried beans sprout, and what factors affect their growth?

Working in pairs, students tackled this task with great enthusiasm, the teacher reports, but showed "a surprising lack of familiarity with the requirements for growth: Beans were pierced, stomped, smashed, peeled, drowned, and parched. . . . Some teams chose to do as many as twelve experiments covering every possible combination of container, light, moisture, and bean variety, rather than pursuing a few experiments in a logical, coherent pattern" (Hophan, 1977, p. 9). The teacher decided to allow this scatter-gun approach and deal with their reasoning in whole-class meeting: "I devised a 'Class Bean Book' and, as teams reported on what they had learned, I continually asked, 'How do you know that?'" When children offered their results as proof, others in the group challenged with counterevidence from their experiments. Only agreed-upon claims could be entered as facts in the Bean Book. As a consequence of the discussions, "teams began communicating with other teams outside the whole-group sessions in an effort to make use of others' findings to substantiate or disprove their own theories" (p. 10).

Children showed a good ability to divide their labor, the teacher observed, and demonstrated respect for one another's competencies and preferences. Said one boy to his teammate: "You write down what we found, okay? You write neater than me. I'll empty the water 'cause I don't care if it smells."

Two weeks after the project began, the teacher introduced real planting, using soil, along with a new rule: Each team had to write down their prediction for each experiment they chose to do, to post this prediction on the wall, and to report on the progress of the experiment at the class meeting. The new rule was followed by "a great deal more order to the processes the children used." Intense interest in charting growth rates, however, led to an unexpected eruption of competition between teams: "Partners blamed each other for over or under watering. Teams taunted other teams when their plants grew faster or larger. There were even several cases of sabotage, as when the class discovered many containers virtually swamped in water and a book placed squarely on top of a lush crop of soybean plantings" (p. 11).

This whole-class meeting now served as a vehicle to talk about issues of competition, jealousy, and cooperation. About half the children said they wanted to work alone, caring for their own plant, rather than having to work with a team member. The teacher agreed to this change, but a week later almost all of the children, acting on their own initiative, were back together again. One boy explained that he needed his partner because "I can't hold this paper (on which he had been recording the plant's growth rate) and mark it, too." Another reunited team said that apart they forgot to water their plants, but together they could remember.

Strengthened by their survival of a crisis, the class went on to higher things: a visit to a greenhouse at Cornell University, and a decision to construct their own greenhouses and plant gardens of flowers for the whole school. This altruistic venture involved the children in "selecting the seeds, drawing plans to scale for our greenhouses, constructing the greenhouses, preparing the soil mix and seed trays, reading the planting instructions, sowing the seeds, measuring and selecting the garden sites, preparing the soil, and transplanting the plants"— activities undertaken in spontaneous groupings according to interest and ability. "The accepting of group goals and responsibilities," the teacher reported, "developed to a gratifying degree," along with a marked improvement in children's self-esteem and tendency to contribute to each other's feelings of competence by saying to classmates "You're really good at that" (p. 15).

A long-range, cumulative project like teacher Hophan's can have an especially profound impact on children, but smaller-scale ways to foster cooperation in the classroom are also effective. Ann Caren, a Project Change participant, has found a class newspaper to be an excellent way to develop cooperative effort and group cohesion among her second and third graders. In addition, she recommends stocking the environment with materials—blocks, lincoln logs, lego, animals, plants, clay, scrap materials, and plenty of paper and pencils—that naturally stimulate children to work together on activities that are meaningful to them. Another teacher (Kur, 1977) introduced regular small-group projects with her seven-year-olds—constructing a building, drawing a picture, making a circus mural, doing a terrarium—and found that with time children's groups became less dominated by one or two strong leader types and more respectful and solicitous of contributions from all members. General helping and communication in the classroom increased noticeably, while disruptive behavior, a problem before the group activities, seldom occurred.

In addition to active cooperation, Piaget (1932) recommended a second critical ingredient in a curriculum for moral growth: the opportunity for children to govern themselves. Rules imposed by external constraint, his research on children's games of marbles showed,

> remain external to the child's spirit and do not lead to as effective an obedience as the adult would wish. Rules due to mutual agreement and cooperation, on the contrary, take root inside the child's mind and result in an effective observance in the measure in which they are incorporated in an autonomous will. (1932, p. 362)

As a practical procedure for helping children regulate their own behavior, our program at Project Change encourages teachers to hold class meetings, an idea advanced by the humanist psychiatrist-educator, William Glasser (1969). Class meetings are conducted in a circle, usually last from 20 to 30 minutes, and are most effective when held every day. They can be used to share experiences, plan classroom events, and solve or prevent problems. From a moral standpoint, the most important kind of problem solving the class meeting provides for is the involvement of the children in defining, enforcing, and revising the rules that regulate the life of their classroom. In this sense, the class meeting makes contact with a universal concern of teachers: discipline.

No teachers have more trouble with discipline than those whose fate it is to substitute teach. Children, accustomed to external restraint, almost invariably test the limits of the substitute teacher and generally conspire to frustrate that harried pedagogue into wielding the club of Stage 1 authority. How to avoid this trap is demonstrated by Debbie Wilcox (1977), one of our graduate students, who used the class meeting to create the elementary classroom equivalent of Kohlberg's just community. When a group of third graders greeted her with the announcement "This is the bad class of the school," she decided that their first day (she was to have them for six weeks) would begin with a meeting to talk about rules.

"What rules do we need in this classroom?" she asked. Many children volunteered answers. The teacher noticed that most children stated rules negatively: "Don't push" or "Don't punch anyone."

"What does it mean when we push or punch someone?" she asked. "It means we don't care about the person," one child said. The teacher pursued this. "What can we do to help make this a better class?" The children's response: "Care for each other." This, the teacher says, became their primary rule, from which other more specific rules could be derived.

Meetings continued daily, and changes began to appear. "Children stopped running to me with every small problem and instead decided what was wrong and worked it out among themselves. Sharing increased, and schoolwork improved. Class meetings became more open as many children introduced topics that they believed were important for all to discuss. They made a real effort to listen quietly when someone else was speaking. Serious behavior problems virtually disappeared" (Wilcox, 1977, pp. 29–30). This and many other teachers' comparable experience bears testimony to the truth of Piaget's statement that the only true discipline is that which *"children themselves have willed and consented to"* (1932, p. 364).

Curiously, the conventional educational wisdom has more trouble assimilating that basic insight than it does the Piagetian notion that children must develop their own logical understandings. The same teachers and parents who in the logical realm grant that the child is the architect of his own mind, in the moral sphere treat him as a blank slate to be written upon. The understanding of the rules of social interaction, every bit as much as a grasp of the rules of logic, must be constructed by children as they wrest meaning from their encounters with the world. "In the moral as in the intellectual domain," to use Piaget's words, "we really possess only what we have conquered ourselves" (1932, p. 366).

The class meeting provides a context uniquely suited to children's collaborative construction of rules. It also provides an opportunity for a teacher to follow what many adults would regard as radical advice: to "place oneself on the child's own level, and give him a feeling of equality by . . . drawing attention to one's own needs, one's own difficulties, even one's own blunders, thus creating an atmosphere of mutual help and understanding" (Piaget, 1932, pp. 137–138). A teacher can use a class meeting to say, "Look, I'm having a problem here, things aren't working out as I planned, can you suggest some improvements?" or "This has been a tough day for me; I'm not in a very good mood, and I need your help." Setting that kind of example, Piaget points out, can have "an enormous positive influence" (1932, p. 319) on children's moral development by teaching them that morality is "not a system of commands requiring ritualistic and external obedience but a system of social relations such that everyone does his best to obey the same obligations, and does so out of mutual respect" (1932, p. 138).

To say that cooperative learning and self-regulation through democratic decision making are the crucial processes of moral education in the elementary school does not exclude using curriculum content as grist for the moral mill. The Tacoma City School District in Washington has launched an ethical reasoning project spanning grades 1 to 12 that will design strategies around moral issues present in the existing social studies, health, and language arts curricula (P. Sullivan, 1976). At the secondary level, Fenton (1975) has written persuasively about how to refocus the traditional social studies course on the social-moral functioning of "a variety of voluntary, blood-related, geographic, or economic communities to find out who joins, what benefits they receive, what obligations they have, and how the communities treat members who fail to meet their obligations" (p. 47). One goal of Fenton's formal curriculum is to enhance students' ability to run their own community meetings in the school. In this way, curriculum content and the process of education that students experience themselves become two sides of the same coin.

Some curriculum-oriented projects, however, may end up centering on content goals and losing sight of the deeper moral lessons the student learns from the way the curriculum is implemented. One individualized social studies program for ages 6 to 9 describes itself as Piaget-based because "the learner acts upon the content of the learning, must assimilate it to what he already knows, and must extend his new learning" by relating it representationally to life situations. Though the program affords children a more active role than they have in many traditional classrooms, students for the most part work alone on individual tasks, develop concepts based on two-dimensional materials rather than real personal experiences, and follow closely prescribed steps in a predetermined curriculum. This approach seems a far cry from the kind of experiential social studies curriculum that Piaget urged, in which children can follow their own interests in cooperative relationships. There is a real danger that the American movement to individualize instruction will partially assimilate Piaget while missing his more fundamental message: that developing "the independence of the person" and "respect for the rights and freedoms of others . . . demand a return by their very make-up to a *lived experience* and to *freedom of investigation*, outside of which any acquisition of human values is only an illusion" (Piaget, 1975, pp. 125–126) (italics added). A recent study (Bennett, 1975) adds empirical evidence to Piaget's exhortation: an individualized, programmed approach to fostering moral reasoning among college students proved inferior to an approach that emphasized social interactive discussion of moral issues.

Perhaps the best tool for dispelling any remaining fuzziness about the operational details of how to promote moral development in the classroom is an instrument developed by Lengel (1974). Titled "Classroom Process Objectives for Moral Development," this observational rating scale consists of 50 objectives pertaining to the everyday operation of the classroom. These objectives correspond to 12 dimensions of developmental moral education that Lengel has carefully derived from the writings of Kohlberg and Piaget: (1) general classroom interaction, (2) opportunities for role taking, (3) presentation of moral problems, (4) use of real-life problems in class, (5) peer discussion, (6) teacher's knowledge of and accommodation to children's developmental level, (7) teacher's focus on reasoning, (8) presentation of alternative solutions, (9) absence of a right-answer approach, (10) presence of stage mixture among the children, (11) opportunities for children to structure their own solutions to social problems, and (12) challenges to children's reasoning. For purposes of classroom observation, these 12 dimensions are grouped into four major areas: general classroom procedures, children's work activities, nature of class discussions, and teacher's actions. Sample items for each of these areas are presented in Table II. Lengel's scale offers an excellent device, much needed, for either outside assessment or teacher self-evaluation of a classroom as a total moral environment. By concentrating on readily observable process objectives, his instrument also responds to the vexing problem of how to evaluate a moral education program in terms other than students' stage change, which is typically small and very slow to appear. Lengel plans validation

Table II. Classroom Process Objectives for Moral Development[a]

	\multicolumn{5}{c}{Evidence}				
	None	Slight	Moderate	Extensive	Cannot make judgment
Part I: General procedures					
1. Children interact with each other in many different situations.	1	2	3	4	X
2. Rules and discipline are discussed freely by children and teacher.	1	2	3	4	X
3. Problems of the school and community are presented for class discussion.	1	2	3	4	X
Part II: Children's work activities					
1. Children are engaged in a cooperative venture with a group.	1	2	3	4	X
2. Children talk among themselves during class time.	1	2	3	4	X
3. Children use their own methods to solve problems in class.	1	2	3	4	X
Part III: Nature of class discussions					
1. Children share ideas with others.	1	2	3	4	X
2. The reasons behind answers and positions are stressed in discussions.	1	2	3	4	X
3. Conflict between alternative ideas is pointed out.	1	2	3	4	X
Part IV: Teacher's actions					
1. Teacher keeps notes and histories of each child's progress and development.	1	2	3	4	X
2. Teacher listens with respect to each child's thinking and reasoning.	1	2	3	4	X
3. Teacher helps children look at things from different viewpoints.	1	2	3	4	X

[a] Sample items from Lengel, 1974.

research to determine whether classrooms high on his scale do in fact eventually stimulate greater moral stage advance, as Kohlberg's theory would predict, than classrooms low on his scale.

4.4. Fostering Moral Development in Early Childhood

What form does developmental moral education take at the pre-school and kindergarten levels? How much can be done? Although young children are egocentric, efforts at early moral education can build on their budding social and moral capacities, which are impressive. One study (Mueller, 1972) of communication patterns among pairs of pre-schoolers found that fully 62% of children's statements received a verbal response from their playmate, while an additional 23% at least attracted the listener's attention. Damon, studying the development of positive justice in children as young as four, finds that "young children are able to make certain fine distinctions that are not revealed by the Kohlberg methodology . . . they can say very clearly that the neighborhood bully's commands are not 'right' or 'fair' in any sense, even though these commands carry with them the force of physical power" (1975, p. 27). Peterson (1976) describes an incident in which her 2½-year-old daughter forced her to do some role-taking in the interest of fairness. The daughter asked the mother if *she* liked getting spanked when she was a little girl, and when the mother said "No," the 2½-year-old said, "Well, I don't *either*!" Hoffman (1976) provides anecdotal accounts of astonishing feats of role-taking by children not yet two years of age. In the realm of behavior, Murphy's extensive naturalistic observations of pre-schoolers (1937) recorded many spontaneous demonstrations of compassion and kindness.

The major objective of early childhood moral education is the same as the goal for the elementary school: to lead children out of their egocentrism toward relations of cooperation and mutual respect with others. One means to this end is to try to develop the child's ability to empathize, to become sensitive to how another person experiences a situation (Kuhmerker, 1975; Wolfe, 1975). There are a number of commercial discussion programs (e.g., *Developing Understanding of Self and Others*, Dinkmeyer, 1970; *Magic Circle*, Bessell and Ball, 1972) designed to stimulate empathic awareness, but teachers can also use natural interactions to enhance interpersonal sensitivity. Everyday situations, for example, can be opportunities to foster awareness of intentions: "Do you think David stepped on your drawing on purpose?" or "Do you think Billy was trying to help or not when he knocked over your tower?"

It is also helpful to point out the positive effects of a child's behavior on another, e.g., "You gave Karen a push on the swing and that made her smile." Similarly, a teacher can ask children what *they* think are the effects of their actions, e.g., "How does Bob feel when you won't let him join in the game?" Better still, a teacher can help children learn to give each other direct social feedback so that they can reduce each other's egocentrism without the intervention of an adult. One preschool teacher I observed taught her youngsters how to say, "I don't like that!" whenever anyone hit, grabbed a toy, or otherwise infringed upon their rights.

A Headstart teacher (Peterson, 1977) in our program used class meetings to increase empathy among her 4- and 5-year-olds. In a series of discussions, the children expressed their negative feelings about one boy's aggressive behavior, learned from the boy that he was very worried about going into the hospital for an operation, talked about various fears each of them had experienced, and decided upon things to do, such as all writing letters, that would help the troubled boy's stay in the hospital to be a nicer time. The teacher reports that this event had a very positive effect on the social climate in the classroom as evidenced by children's heightened regard for each other. Her experience is noteworthy for two reasons: (1) It demonstrated the effectiveness of using an important real-life situation to engage the children's interest and expand their moral awareness; and (2) it followed the children's experience of increased empathy with a concrete opportunity to help the person in need. Staub's research (1975) has revealed this combination of awareness and action to be especially important in developing prosocial behavior. If young children cannot figure out for themselves how to go from empathy to action, they can be shown. One training program (Yarrow, Scott, and Waxler, 1973) explicitly modeled both empathic awareness and helping behavior for 3-, 4-, and 5-year-olds and thereby increased the children's subsequent altruistic behavior in response to another's need.

Another approach to emancipating young children from their social-moral egocentrism has been to ask them to construct alternative solutions to imaginary conflicts. Chittenden (1942) used this technique in preschool children to increase cooperative behavior among initially domineering 5-year-olds. Another preschool intervention (Rosenhan, 1969) used stories and puppets over a 10-week period to encourage different solutions to various interpersonal disputes, and found that, the longer the children participated in the program, the fewer the aggressive solutions they offered. Still another experiment (Doland and Adelberg, 1967) had an adult act out opposing solutions to a conflict using a set of dolls. In one episode, for example, two dolls fought over a wagon, the wagon broke, and both were unhappy. In the cooperative solution, they took turns, which satisfied them both. Children who observed and discussed these little dramas became less aggressive and more cooperative in their preschool play.

Early childhood environments can also structure opportunities for children to work or play in pairs or small groups, similar in spirit to the effort to foster cooperative learning in the elementary classroom. Shelton (1975), in an excellent discussion of ways to stimulate young children's social development, suggests providing equipment such as rocking boats or horizontal tire swings that either requires or allows cooperative use. She reviews a variety of evidence that "children tend to behave more cooperatively after participating in situations where they have shared a group reward, operated with a group ('we') orientation, or received reinforcement for cooperative behavior" (p. 51). Karrby (1974) describes a partnership program in which 6-year-olds, working in groups of 3 and 4, role-played conflicts with puppets and then considered how the conflicts and outcomes were like situations in their real-life relationships. Of 18 small groups, 10 showed a rise in spontaneous partnership (versus solitary) behavior following the role-playing exercises.

Group games are advocated by DeVries and Kamii (1975) as being uniquely suited to fostering social-moral growth in the preschool years. Quoting Piaget's statement "How much more useful is a well-regulated game than a lesson in morals" (1932, p. 307), they give the following reasons for considering games ideal moral education for young children: (1) They are fun; (2) game rules, since they are made up and enforced by children, are experienced as useful social regulations rather than as arbitrary demands; (3) children participate as equals; even adults must follow the rules of a game; (4) in deciding the rules—e.g., where the safety zones should be in a game of tag—participants have to confront each other's ideas and reach a consensus: (5) children get corrective feedback from each other if they break the rules; (6) games, unlike other forms of social interaction such as dramatic play, require the child to regulate his behavior according to some objective, agreed-upon norm. DeVries and Kamii go on to discuss different kinds of games—parallel (e.g., racing), collaborative (e.g., "Keep the ball in the air"), and complementary (e.g., hiding and finding)—that are useful in developing children's cooperation and their moral understanding of rules as mutually determined obligations rather than as unilateral impositions of authority.

Rules can also be the topic of class discussions in the preschool years. It may be necessary for the teacher to lay down some ground rules, especially at the outset, but even preschool youngsters can begin to share responsibility for formulating rules—those governing clean-up time, for example, or the use of materials, or the number of children who can participate in one activity at a time. Not surprisingly, teachers in our program report that the most effective, easily enforced solutions to everyday problems like these are the ones the children invent themselves.

A good program for moral development, like any good educational program, will also pay attention to the level and progress of individual children. Acting on this principle, Fulda and Jantz (1975) provide the teacher with a "Morality of Constraint versus Morality of Cooperation" checklist, comprised of 12 dimensions corresponding to Piaget's description of these stages. They suggest that by concentrating on the reasoning

Table III.   Dimensions for Documenting a Child's Moral Development

A.   What is the child's understanding of rules?
  1. Can he name classroom rules?
  2. How does he explain the reason for various rules?
  3. What does he think will happen if someone breaks a rule?
  4. Can he say why an existing rule is fair or unfair?
  5. Can he suggest a rule appropriate to a particular situation?
B.   Does the child follow rules?
  1. What rules does he follow? How consistently?
  2. What rules does he not follow? How consistently?
  3. When he breaks a rule, is he aware of it? What does he say when he is asked to describe what he is doing?
  4. Can he make a plan for improving his behavior and follow through on it?
C.   Does the child take others' point of view?
  1. In a conflict situation, can he describe what the other child thinks, feels, and wants?
  2. Can he describe the effects of his behavior, both positive and negative, on other people?
  3. Does he demonstrate concern when others are hurt and upset?
D.   Does the child understand how to be fair?
  1. Can he settle a conflict in a way that takes into account the needs of another as well as his own?
  2. Does he take turns?
  3. Does he share?
  4. Does he do his fair share in a group task (like clean-up)?
  5. Can he explain why a particular action or solution to a problem is fair or unfair?
E.   Does the child participate in positive social interactions?
  1. In group discussions?
  2. In individual conversations?
  3. In collaborative play?
  4. In work on a group task?
  5. In helping others?

and behavior of no more than three children a day, a teacher can gain a greater knowledge of each child's moral development. My own suggestion to preschool and elementary teachers wishing to document the moral progress of individual children has been to use the set of questions provided in Table III to construct a profile of each child at the beginning, middle, and end of the year.

5. Conclusion: Critique and New Directions

Both Piaget and Kohlberg have come under fire from many camps. Piaget has been criticized for being too maturationist and too behavioristic (see Lickona, 1969, for a review of misunderstandings), for causing educators to underestimate children's capacity for sound reasoning (Lipman, 1975), and for romanticizing the contribution of the peer group to poisitive morality (Hogan, 1973). Kohlberg has been taken to task for centering too much on Justice in defining the moral (Orr, 1974; Peters, 1971, 1975); for being culturally biased in his definition of morality (Simpson, 1974; E. Sullivan, 1977; Wilson, 1976); for going from a description of what moral development is to a prescription of what it ought to be (Alston, 1971); for devaluing conventional morality (Hamm, 1976; Peters, 1975); for overestimating the role of reasoning in moral functioning and underestimating the role of other factors such as affect, personality, habit, and expectations of consequences (Alston, 1971; Aronfreed, 1976; Mischel and Mischel, 1976; Simpson, 1976); for failing to take into account the impact of the particular nature of a moral dilemma on the stage of moral reasoning elicited (Levine, 1976); for lack of validity and reliability of his research methodology (Kurtines and Grief, 1974); for having insufficient evidence for his two highest moral stages (Gibbs, 1977); and for failing to respond to his critics (Peters, 1975; Sichel, 1976; E. Sullivan, 1977). Since dealing with all of these criticisms is impossible here, I would like to focus on one issue that is high on the list of both theoreticians and practitioners: the relationship between moral reasoning and moral behavior, and the mediating role of emotion.

If we reflect on our own moral lives and those of the people we know, two psychological facts are readily apparent. One is that we commonly do what we want to do, and then find reasons to justify our behavior. Moral reasoning in such cases is clearly the servant of self-interest. Another fact is that we very often do not in the first place even see a situation as involving a moral issue: We don't see somebody's rights getting trampled, somebody's legitimate interests being ignored, somebody's dignity being demeaned. Men who are on their way to being "liberated," for example, are often astonished at all the sexist things they used to do or condone without realizing how those behaviors violated the value of equality. Orr has argued plausibly that "the problem with children, as with anyone else, is usually one of value blindness, not immaturity of moral reasoning" (1974, p. 367). If that is the case, then the job of moral education may be less a matter of promoting vertical stage development than a matter of opening students' eyes to the moral dimensions of their lives, to the countless ways in which they act, consciously or not, either with respect or with disregard for the rights, needs, and worth of other people.

A study by Leming (1974) speaks to the importance of raising moral issues that penetrate the psychic space of students. He asked 8th and 12th graders to judge classical moral dilemmas like the Heinz story, but also to say what they would do in personally relevant situations, e.g., "A girl wonders if she should lie to her parents about where she is going in order to attend a party that her parents have forbidden. What would you do?" Leming found that low-level (Stage 2) reasoning was used much more in solving personally relevant dilemmas than in judging classical story situations. More surprising was his finding that on personal dilemmas there was *no significant difference* in the average stage of reasoning of 8th and 12th graders. Leming concludes that students' moral reasoning about personal-life issues may remain at a relatively low level, even if their reasoning about Kohlberg's classical dilemmas improves.

What are the educational implications of Leming's findings? He sees three: (1) teachers need to find out what's on student's minds, and this should be the stuff of moral discussions; (2) teachers need empathy and communication skills to get students to open up and disclose their thoughts and feelings, and (3) moral discussions should ask students to deliberate about what they would do in a moral conflict and why, rather than simply to judge what someone else has done. Without these features, Leming predicts, moral education efforts, like so many drug education programs, will not affect students' behavior because they will fail "to touch their life concerns—sex, love, joy, self-doubt, fear, pain, anxiety, loneliness, belonging" (1974, p. 22).

To touch the lives of students, Leming makes clear, is to touch their emotions as well as their minds. Howard Gardner, assessing Piaget's contribution to our understanding of the human mind, observes: "We learn much from his writings about children's conceptions of water, little about their fear of floods, their love of splashing, their desire to be minnows, mermaids, or mariners" (*The New York Times Book Review*, August 1, 1976, p. 2). In the realm of morality, Piaget and Kohlberg's focus on moral judgment may face a similar indictment. We have learned much from their work about how individuals analyze moral issues and justify hypothetical choices when asked to do so, but we have learned less about how they function as whole people, how they make personal moral decisions, or whether they reason morally at all under the stress of the real world, where morality may have a low priority. Was it underdeveloped moral reasoning that kept "the best and the brightest" from making different decisions about Vietnam, or was it, as Halberstam (1969) suggests, their ego-investment and inability to admit error, their capacity for self-deception, and their fear of appearing weak or unmanly if they raised moral questions about the war? Was it poor moral reasoning or was it the lust for power and the desire to be a good team player that led Watergate figures to play their parts in that moral debacle? Do stages of moral reasoning adequately explain Richard Nixon? Why is it that so few people publicly protest what they privately know and feel to be wrong? We must pay much more attention to such dynamics as the need to be liked and thought well of, the fear of losing face, the desire to control others, the sense of failure we feel when others succeed, our capacity for taking pleasure in other's misfortune, and the deeply rooted, lifelong tendency toward egocentrism and self-interest if we wish to understand how a principled moral concern for others can work its way past the obstacles of human nature into the mainstream of everyday consciousness. In short, we need to go beyond moral reasoning to a comprehension of moral personality.

To seek a broader understanding of moral personality is to want to know how knowledge of the right becomes commitment to doing the right. Piaget (1967) touched on this issue when he spoke of the developing "will" of the child as a regulator of moral feeling and action. How is it possible to develop people whose moral emotions do not lag far behind their highest stage of moral reasoning (Sichel, 1976)? How can we foster what Peters (1970) calls the "rational passions"—a genuine devotion to principles of fairness and freedom, an in-the-bones respect for the rights of others, and an intense concern when others suffer? One way, it seems to me, is to involve people, as peer teaching or counseling programs in schools and prisons have done, in active helping relationships so that they begin to identify on a personal and emotional level with the welfare of others. One learns to care by giving care. Another approach is to provide a supportive social-moral ecology, like the just community school, where students are asked to see the world through a moral lens and where they can practice making real-life moral decisions in an environment where reflection, strong emotions, and self-interest all have a chance to come into play.

Another emerging strategy of much promise is to treat moral reasoning as only one strand in a broad program for value development that includes helping students define lifestyles and life goals, develop an appreciative sensitivity to others' values, needs, and feelings, clarify their own needs, values, and emotions, and act upon their new moral awarenesses (Allen, 1975; Beck, 1976; Meyer, 1976; Superka, Ahrens, and Hedstrom, 1976). Selman's research (1975, 1976) underscores the need for children to understand themselves and others before they can make sound moral judgments. Colby (1975) has written lucidly of how values clarification (Raths, Harmin, and Simon, 1966), which focuses primarily on defining one's own values and acting on them consistently, can complement a Kohlbergian concern for the development of a sense of justice.* Finally, deliberate psychological education, incorporating goals of interpersonal and ego development, is a wise step toward anchoring moral development in the deeper substrate of personal identity.

The maturing of developmental education may also see a meeting of the minds with didactic approaches that most Piaget and Kohlberg disciples have heretofore been prone to regard as pernicious forms of adult constraint. The philosopher Cornel Hamm (1974), for one, has quarreled with Kohlberg for ignoring the positive role that didactic instruction can play in helping children develop a behavioral disposition to do the good. Hogan (1973) has made a similar case for a strong adult hand in moral upbringing by calling attention to Baumrind's finding (1971) that moral autonomy in young children was fostered not by parental permissiveness but by "authoritative" parents who clearly label certain actions right or wrong, explain their rules and encourage verbal give and take, and make their praise contingent upon the child's meeting specified standards of performance. As anyone who has faced the considerable challenge of rearing children knows, the role of Baumrind's moral manager is difficult to escape. It is reassuring to know that a dose of well-directed didacticism is good moral medicine after all. At the same time, Piaget's prescription for parents to deal with their children on a basis of mutual respect gains support from Baumrind's finding that "authoritarian" parents, who dominated their children to the exclusion of give and take, failed to foster moral maturity.

This review is only a sample of what is happening in developmental moral education. New directions are emerging all the time. John Whitely (1976), Dean at the University of California at Irvine, has taken Kohlberg to the college level by implementing a year-long program of moral/psychological education for 45 Irvine freshmen who live together in a

*For a review of Kohlbergian and values clarification programs and their effects on students, see Lockwood, 1977.

closely knit community of their own making. Moral reasoning development is an intended by-product of 10 educational modules that include developing empathy and communication, assertion training, conflict resolution, life planning, career decision making, sex-role concerns, and rendering service to the outside community. At the secondary educational level, new frontiers for Kohlberg's just community school include developing a cooperative process for defining and achieving learning objectives, identifying a curriculum that better integrates democratic moral education processes with academic content in social studies and English, and extending the just school concept down to grades 6 to 9 (Kohlberg, 1976c). A project to train high school counselors and teachers to integrate moral education into psychology and history courses is under way in Brookline, Massachusetts (Mosher and Sullivan, 1976). Adolescents have also been taught to take a moral reasoning approach to interpersonal sexual dilemmas (DiStefano, 1976). At the junior high level, Paolitto (1975) has conducted a successful program providing role-taking opportunities. In the middle school years (10 to 14), Selman (cited in Kohlberg, 1976a) is adding a democratic community component to his social reasoning curriculum for children having learning or behavior problems. At Project Change (Lickona, 1976d), we are documenting the impact of class meetings and cooperative learning on moral climate and children's behavior in elementary and early childhood classrooms. At the preschool level, Peterson and McNamee (1976) have done important research on the development of sharing in naturalistic settings that promises to have practical utility for early childhood teachers.

The moral education movement in the schools has also turned a spotlight on moral development in the home. Holstein (1972) found that parents who encourage their child to participate in family discussion of moral issues and to share in family decision making have children who are relatively advanced in moral judgment. Grimes (1974) brought sixth-grade students and their mothers together to write and discuss moral dilemmas. One of the spin-offs, mothers reported, was that at home they spent a lot more time talking with their children about moral issues, and the children made progress from Stage 2 toward Stage 3 moral reasoning. Still more ambitious was Stanley's (1976) 10-week workshop that taught parents and their adolescents how to communicate, resolve conflicts democratically, conduct a family meeting, and discuss value differences and moral dilemmas. By the end of the course, parents had become more equalitarian in their attitudes toward family decision-making, families were better at solving conflicts fairly, and adolescents had advanced in their moral reasoning.

Also at the cutting edge of developmental interventions are

Kohlberg's New England just community prison projects (Kohlberg *et al.*, 1975; Scharf and Hickey, 1976). Best known among these is the Connecticut Women's Correctional Center in Niantic, site of a cottage in which inmates and staff collaborate in a process of democratic self-government. Project evaluation shows that cottage inmates see their environment as much more fair than do inmates in traditional prisons, that the program stimulates progress in moral reasoning, and that the percentage of cottage participants who return to prison after release is only half what it is for similar offenders in the state of Connecticut (Scharf and Hickey, 1976).

What may be missing from these brief accounts is a sense of the struggle involved in putting developmental theory into practice. Impersonal, one-way, teacher-centered education, though it is now breaking down, is a good deal less work than the kind of education described in this chapter. I was recently reminded of this in a letter (Parham, 1976) I received from the principal of a California high school that, working with Scharf, Mosher, and Kohlberg, has taken seriously its responsibility to teach the good:

> When we began, I dreamed of a utopian school. When we sit by the campfires of creativity, we can build new worlds in a moment. I've learned that social experimentation requires patience. It takes more than a year or two years or even three to realize a workable modification of an established system. What we have created is a process whereby people can come together and grow ... an organization that allows for democratic participation. This participation is sometimes painful for all of us. It requires a level of commitment not ordinarily given in more traditional schools.

One of the most encouraging aspects of the moral education movement is that it has brought practitioners like this principal into a partnership with developmental theorists like Kohlberg and his colleagues. Schools have learned something about human development, and developmentalists have learned much about schools. It is this kind of "combined effort of practical workers and educational psychologists," Piaget said at the end of his *Moral Judgment* book, that is essential for finding out what works in the classroom.

5.1. Summing Up

As they test the waters of social-moral education, a growing number of teachers are turning to Kohlberg and Piaget for a way to chart their course. Their chances of success in the classroom will be better if they begin with a clear picture of both the strengths and the problems of the cognitive-developmental approach. Its strength, I believe, are these:

1. It offers a well-worked-out theory, grounded in psychology and philosophy, of what morality is and how it develops over time.

2. Though some of its research claims are debated (see, for example, Fraenkel, 1977), the cognitive-developmental approach rests on a broader base of longitudinal, cross-cultural, and experimental research than any other contemporary approach to moral values education.

3. Stages of moral reasoning offer a way of defining the process of maturing in at least one area of moral growth; they thereby provide a clear educational goal—namely, to help students progress toward higher stages of moral reasoning and to apply their highest available stage to the moral issues they encounter.

4. The Piagetian/Kohlbergian approach provides a theoretical framework capable of assimilating a variety of humanistic methodologies. In the graduate course I teach in moral development and moral education, for example, teachers come to see the class meetings of William Glasser (1969), the empathic communication techniques of Haim Ginott (1972), and the no-lose conflict resolution of Thomas Gordon (1975), all as means of creating a positive moral climate, developing students' ability to take the perspective of others, and ultimately helping them move to more mature stages of moral reasoning.

5. Both the democratic methods and developmental goals of Piaget and Kohlberg are strongly consistent with the social education objectives of a constitutional democracy. To become competent citizens in a democracy, students need to experience the democratic process and realize respect for persons in their education and, eventually, to develop principled understanding and valuing of the human rights that a democracy is meant to secure. From this point of view, education for high-stage moral reasoning is not only permissible in a democratic society, it is essential.

6. By advancing the notion of the just community as the ideal moral society, whatever the scale, Kohlberg has fused a concern for justice with a concern for human community. This union of two such powerful themes greatly deepens and broadens the cognitive-developmental concept of moral education. It also responds to critics (e.g., E. Sullivan, 1977) who have accused Kohlbergian structuralism of centering on the individual-in-isolation, contributing to the problem of social alienation. To be a member of a just community, at least ideally, is not only to strive to reason and act justly as an individual but also to identify with and fully participate in a community of persons who support each other and who celebrate the shared values, traditions, and reason for being that make them part of a larger whole.

What problems or weaknesses of the cognitive-developmental approach should the moral educator bear in mind?

1. The moral stages, though they provide a useful way of thinking about moral development, pose several hazards. For one, the stages can be used destructively by teachers as another way of stereotyping and labeling students (Bolt and Sullivan, 1977). Ed Sullivan reports an instance of a teacher who asked a student to leave class "because he was a wise guy and a Stage 2" (1975, p. 140). Graduates of workshops or short courses on Kohlberg have been heard in discussions to put down a peer with the statement, "That's a Stage 2 argument." Educators being exposed to the moral-stage approach should clearly recognize that morality means respect for the rights, needs, and worth of people and that to use the moral stages as put-downs is essentially immoral.

A second danger of the stages is that they may lead a teacher to underestimate seriously the moral capacities of young children. Preschool children, for example, though they may not yet have reached even Stage 1 on Kohlberg's hypothetical dilemmas, often reveal in their natural interactions with other children a capacity for empathy, altruism, and fairness. Damon's work (1975, 1977) with young children has done much to shed light on the development of their thinking about fairness issues in real-life situations.

A third problem is the persistent debate about whether the higher stages of reasoning are really objectively superior to the lower stages and therefore desirable as educational goals. Kohlberg's critics, especially philosophers, like to sharpen their axes on this grindstone. A straightforward way for any educator to deal with this issue is to argue that as students progress to higher stages, they get better at understanding and respecting the rights of others, something that will serve them well both in their personal relationships and in their role as members of a democratic society.

2. A second major problem is that despite Kohlberg's new emphasis on just community, many educators still identify his approach with the discussion of hypothetical dilemmas. Discussion of fictional dilemmas, by itself, is an extremely limited and superficial approach to moral education, as teachers will attest. I recently received a letter from the director of a Kohlbergian moral education project at the elemetary school level saying that his teachers were complaining that moral dilemma discussion had failed to produce a more positive moral climate in the classroom. A first-grade teacher recently described to me how her children enthusiastically discussed the filmstrip dilemma of "Cheetah the Cat Man"—whether he should keep his solemn oath to the Cat people never to reveal his superhero identity, or break the oath and tell

his son Marcus he is Cheetah in order to allay Marcus's fears that his father was involved in a bank robbery. Following the discussion the children proceeded to the playground for recess, where they promptly began fighting with each other. Similarly, a high school teacher lamented that he had to call a moral dilemma discussion of nuclear energy to a halt when the debate between two students in one of the small groups erupted into a slugging match.

What do these experiences tell us? First they tell us that moral dilemma discussions do not necessarily improve the moral atmosphere and human relations in a classroom; they may in fact even worsen them. Second, they tell us that students may need training in some basic human relations skills, such as good listening and expressing disagreement respectfully, before they will be ready to enter productively into moral dilemma discussions. Third, they suggest that moral behavior is more likely to be changed by class meetings discussing real-life problems of the classroom, such as rules and discipline, than by discussions of hypothetical dilemmas. Such meetings require students to act on the basis of their moral reasoning by implementing the class' agreed-upon solution to a problem and by having follow-up discussions to evaluate how well the solution is working and what people can do, if necessary, to make it work better. Teachers in our program (see J. Lickona, *Mini-Book*, 1977) report excellent results in using the class meeting to foster responsible moral conduct in the classroom.

Even if one wishes to deal with hypothetical moral dilemmas, which can be a valuable way of expanding students' moral horizons, the standard moral dilemma debate format (e.g., Galbraith and Jones, 1976) may not be the only or the best way to encourage thoughtful moral reasoning. As Hall and Davis (1975) point out, "philosophers do not normally recommend adopting moral positions first and defending them later" (p. 144). These authors favor the values analysis or cognitive decision-making approach which teaches students to go step by step through a process of considering alternative solutions to a problem, calculating the probable consequences of each, evaluating each solution from the point of view of each person affected by it, identifying the moral value or principle underlying the different solutions, and finally, on the basis of all these considerations, choosing the best solution. Training in such a procedure may prepare students to participate more effectively in the kind of moral dilemma debate traditionally associated with Kohlberg's approach.

3. Even if the moral educator understands that a Piaget or Kohlberg-based approach means having students live out the value of justice rather than simply talk about it, many questions remain. How

does one go about developing a strong sense of justice and community among students? Teachers need to go beyond Piaget and Kohlberg for an understanding of how to get students to know and like each other, to feel a bond of caring and mutual support, and to be able to solve difficult interpersonal conflicts when they arise.

What skills do students need to be able to talk civilly to one another, and how can they acquire these skills? Do students need to feel good about themselves before they will respond to the needs of others? Teachers I have talked to who are attempting to have democracy in the classroom or the school say that students do indeed need to develop respect for themselves before they begin to respect the rights and needs of others. Morality starts with self-esteem. How does one build this sense of worth in students and extend it into respect for others? Once again, teachers in our program at Project Change say that the class meeting, with its emphasis on good listening and the thoughtful exchange of perspectives, is an effective way of developing students' feelings of importance and mutual respect.

Similarly, many of the values clarification activities (e.g., Simon, Howe, and Kirschenbaum, 1972), stressing disclosure of personal thoughts, feelings, ambitions, and accomplishments, are a good way to foster self-esteem, as well as the feelings of community and good will without which attempts at conflict resolution may explode in the teacher's face. Values clarification, to date a target of criticism from cognitive-developmental partisans, may go a long way toward creating the community half of Kohlberg's just community. So may the prosocial learning approach of Staub (1975) and others, whose research points to ways of teaching children how to be helpful. The child who develops such social skills will experience many more positive social interactions and relationships of the kind that Piaget and Kohlberg see as essential for moral stage development.

4. Ralph Nader (1972) has written, "The fiber of a just society is a thinking, active citizenry. If we do not perform our civic duties, who will?" Moral educators who take Nader's charge seriously will have to go beyond Piaget and Kohlberg to find ways to help students extend their concern for justice past the boundaries of the school and into the community at large. What skills do students need for tackling problems like vandalism, pollution, and discrimination against the poor or minorities? What teaching strategies help students pursue such problems? For answers to questions like these, teachers can turn to the *Values Education Sourcebook* by Superka, Ahrens, and Hedstrom (1976) and to the excellent work of Fred Newmann (1975) and his colleagues. In the belief that students will not exercise civic responsibility as adults without

having had practice in doing so, Newmann and his co-workers have advocated "action learning" as a vital component of moral and civic education in a democracy. Moreover, the action-learning approach is far superior to mere discussion as a way of developing students' first-hand understanding of problems of social injustice and the complexity of efforts required to correct them.

No single methodology, then, will do the whole job. The cognitive-developmental approach provides neither the theory nor the practice adequate to the full challenge of social-moral education. This should not be surprising, since Piagetian/Kohlbergian structuralism does not give us a complete model of the person. There is much more to people than their stage of thinking—a fact now recognized by Kohlberg's concepts of moral atmosphere and just community. We need a moral psychology that speaks to feeling, motivation, personality, and behavior as powerfully as it speaks to moral reasoning. Until the complete theory comes along, however, teachers and schools would do well to begin with Piaget and Kohlberg and pursue an intelligent eclecticism that integrates the expanding array of ways to help students become good persons.

References

Allen, R., 1975. But the earth abideth forever: Values in environmental education. In J. Meyer, B. Burnam, and J. Cholvat (eds.), *Values education*. Waterloo, Ontario: Wilfrid Laurier University Press, pp. 1–24.

Alston, W. P., 1971. Comments on Kohlberg's "From is to ought." In T. Mischel (Ed.), *Cognitive development and epistemology*. New York: Academic Press, pp. 269–284.

Aronfreed, J., 1976. Moral development from the standpoint of a general psychological theory. In T. Lickona (Ed.), *Moral development and behavior: Theory, research, and social issues*. New York: Holt, pp. 54–69.

Baldwin, J. M., 1968. *Mental development in the child and the race: Methods and processes* (3rd ed., rev.). New York: Augustus M. Kelley (originally published 1906).

Baumrind, D., 1971. Current Patterns of parental authority. *Developmental psychology, 4,* 1–103.

Beck, C., 1976. The reflective, ultimate life goals approach to values education. In J. Meyer (Ed.), *Reflections on values education*. Waterloo, Ontario: Wilfrid Laurier University Press, pp. 149–161.

Belenky, M. *The moral reasoning of adult females*. Research study, Goddard College, in progress.

Bennett, A. C., 1975. *A cognitive-developmental orientation toward moral education: An experimental study in "developing moral judgment" through the comparable efforts of two teaching strategies*. Unpublished doctoral dissertation, The Pennsylvania State University.

Bessell, H., and Ball, G. 1972. *Magic circle guide for preschool and kindergarten*. La Mesa, Calif.: Human Development Training Institute.

Beyer, B. K., 1976. Conducting moral discussions in the classroom. *Social Education, 40,* 194–202.

Blatt, M., 1969. *Studies of the effects of classroom discussion upon children's moral development.* Unpublished doctoral dissertation, University of Chicago.

Blatt, M., and Kohlberg, L., 1975. The effects of classroom moral discussion upon children's level of moral judgment. *Journal of Moral Education, 4,* 169–172.

Bolt, D. J., and Sullivan, E., 1977. Kohlberg's cognitive-developmental theory in educational settings: Some possible abuses. *Journal of Moral Education, 6,* 198–205.

Broughton, J. M., 1976. *The cognitive-developmental approach to morality: A reply to Kurtines and Grief.* Unpublished paper, Wayne State University.

Chittenden, G. E., 1942. An experimental study in measuring and modifying assertive behavior in young children. *Monographs of the Society for Research in Child Development, 7,* (1, Serial No. 31).

Colby, A., 1975. *Values and teaching* and *Values clarification* (review). *Harvard Educational Review, 45,* 134–143.

Colby, A., and Kohlberg, L. The relationship between moral and cognitive development. In D. Bush and S. Feldman (Eds.), *Cognitive development and social development: Relationships and implications.* Hillsdale, New Jersey: Lawrence Erlbaum Associates, in press.

Damon, W., 1975. Studying early moral development: Some techniques for interviewing young children and for analyzing the results. In J. Meyer, B. Burnham, and J. Cholvat (Eds.), *Values education.* Waterloo, Ontario: Wilfrid Laurier University Press, pp. 25–40.

Damon, W., 1977. *The social world of the child.* San Francisco: Jossey-Bass.

DeVries, R., and Kamii, C., 1975. *Why group games? A Piagetian perspective.* Available from Educational Resources Information Center (ERIC), ED 110 159.

Dewey, J., and Tufts, J. H., 1932. *Ethics* (rev. ed.). New York: Henry Holt and Co.

Dinkmeyer, D., 1970. *Developing understanding of self and others.* Circle Pines, Minn.: American Guidance Services.

DiStefano, A., 1975. *Teaching moral reasoning about sexual interpersonal dilemmas.* Unpublished doctoral dissertation, Boston University School of Education.

Doland, D. L., and Adelberg, K., 1967. The learning of sharing behavior. *Child Development, 38,* 695–700.

Duska, R., and Whelan, M., 1975. *Moral development: A guide to Piaget and Kohlberg.* New York: Paulist Press.

Enright, R. D., 1975. *A social-cognitive developmental intervention with 6th and 1st graders.* Paper presented at the annual meeting of the American Psychological Association, September, 1975.

Erdynast, A., 1973. *Relations between moral stage and reversibility of moral judgment in an original position.* Unpublished doctoral dissertation, Harvard University.

Erickson, V. L., 1975. Deliberate psychological education for women: From Iphigenia to Antigone. *Counselor Education and Supervision, 14,* 297–309.

Fenton, E., 1975. A developmental approach to civic education. In J. Meyer, B. Burnham, and J. Cholvat (Eds.), *Values education.* Waterloo, Ontario: Wilfrid Laurier University Press, pp. 41–50.

First things: Social reasoning (sound filmstrips). New York: Guidance Associates, 1974.

First things: Values. (sound filmstrips). New York: Guidance Associates, 1972.

Fraenkel, J. R., 1977. A response to Edwin Fenton. *Social Education,* January, 57–61.

Fulda, T. A., and Jantz, R. K., 1975. Moral education through diagnostic-prescriptive teaching methods. *The Elementary School Journal, 8,* 513–518.

Galbraith, R. E., and Jones, T. M., 1976. *Moral reasoning: A teaching handbook for adapting Kohlberg to the classroom.* Anoka, Minn.: Greenhaven Press.

Gardner, H., 1976. The grasp of consciousness (review). *The New York Times Book Review*, August 1, pp. 1-2.

Gibbs, J. C., 1975. The Piagetian approach to moral development: An overview. In J. Meyer, B. Burnham, and J. Cholvat (Eds.), *Values Education*. Waterloo, Ontario: Wilfrid Laurier University Press, pp. 51-64.

Gibbs, J. C., 1977. Kohlberg's stages of moral judgment: A constructive critique. *Harvard Educational Review*, 47, 43-61.

Gilligan, C. V., Kohlberg, L., Lerner, J., and Belenky, M., 1971. *Moral reasoning about sexual dilemmas: The development of an interview and scoring system* (Technical report of the commission on obscenity and pornography, Vol. 1, No. 5256-0010). Washington, D.C.: Superintendent of Documents, U.S. Government Printing Office.

Ginott, Haim, 1972. *Teacher and child*. New York: MacMillan.

Glasser, W., 1969. *Schools without failure*. New York: Harper and Row.

Gordon, T., 1975. *Teacher effectiveness training*. New York: Peter H. Wyden.

Graham, R., Lieberman, M., and Candee, D., 1976. *Moral judgment and life outcomes*. Unpublished paper, Center for Moral Education, Harvard University.

Grim, P. F., Kohlberg, L., and White, S. H., 1968. Some relationships between conscience and attentional processes. *Journal of Personality and Social Psychology, 8*, 239-252.

Grimes, P., 1974. *Teaching moral reasoning to 11-year-olds and their mothers: A means of promoting moral development*. Unpublished doctoral dissertation, Boston University School of Education.

Haan, N., Smith, M. B., and Block, J., 1968. Moral reasoning of young adults: political-social behavior, family background, and personality correlates. *Journal of Personality and Social Psychology, 10*, 183-201.

Hainey, C., and Zimbardo, P. G., 1975. The blackboard penitentiary: It's tough to tell a high school from a prison. *Psychology Today*, June, 26-30.

Halberstam, D., 1969. *The best and the brightest*. New York: Random House.

Hall, R. T., and Davis, J. U., 1975. *Moral education in theory and practice*. Buffalo, New York: Prometheus Books.

Hamm, C. M., 1974. Can moral judgment be taught? *Journal of Educational Thought, 8*, 73-86.

Hamm, C. M., 1976. Dialog with Don B. Cochrane. *Moral Education Forum, 1*, 3-7.

Hartshorne, H., and May, M. A., 1928. *Studies in the nature of character*. New York: Macmillan.

Hoffman, M., 1976. Empathy, role-taking, guilt, and the development of altruistic motives. In T. Lickona (Ed.), *Moral development and behavior: Theory, research, and social issues*. New York: Holt.

Hogan, R., 1973. Moral conduct and moral character: A psychological perspective. *Psychological Bulletin, 79*, 217-232.

Holstein, C. B., 1972. The relation of children's moral judgment level to that of their parents and to communication patterns in the family. In R. C. Smart and M. S. Smart (Eds.), *Readings in child development and relationships*. New York: Macmillan, pp. 484-494.

Holstein, C. B., 1976. Irreversible, stepwise sequence in development of moral judgment: A longitudinal study of males and females. *Child development, 47*, 51-61.

Hophan, P., 1977. Beans, kids, and moral development. in J. Lickona (Ed.), *Mini-book on fostering moral development in the classroom*. Cortland, New York: Project Change, State University of New York.

Kant, I., 1787. The critique of pure reason. In *Great books of the western world* (Vol. 42). Chicago: Encyclopedia Britannica, 1952.

Karrby, G., 1974. *The socialization process in preschool.* Available from Educational Resources Information Center (ERIC), ED 104 562.

Keasey, C. B., 1975. Implicators of cognitive development for moral reasoning. In D. J. DePalma and J. M. Foley (Eds.), *Moral development: Current theory and research.* Hillsdale, New Jersey: Lawrence Erlbaum Associates, pp. 39–56.

Kohlberg, L., 1958. *The development of modes of moral thinking and choice in the years ten to sixteen.* Unpublished doctoral dissertation, University of Chicago.

Kohlberg, L., 1964. Development of moral character and moral ideology. In M. L. and L. W. Hoffman (Eds.), *Review of child development research* (Vol. I). New York: Russell Sage Foundation, pp. 383–432.

Kohlberg, L., 1969a. *The relations between moral judgment and moral actions: A developmental view.* Unpublished paper, Harvard University.

Kohlberg, L., 1969b. Stage and sequence: The cognitive-developmental approach to socialization. In D. A. Goslin (Ed.), *Handbook of socialization: Theory and research.* Chicago: Rand McNally, pp. 347–480.

Kohlberg, L., 1970. Education for justice: A modern statement of the Platonic view. In N. F. Sizer and T. R. Sizer (Eds.), *Moral education: Five lectures.* Cambridge, Mass.: Harvard University Press, pp. 57–83.

Kohlberg, L., 1971. From is to ought: How to commit the naturalistic fallacy and get away with it in the study of moral development. In T. Mischel (Ed.), *Cognitive development and epistemology.* New York: Academic, pp. 151–235.

Kohlberg, L., 1972. A cognitive-developmental approach to moral education. *The Humanist, 32,* 13–16.

Kohlberg, L., 1973a. *Collected papers on moral development and moral education.* Cambridge, Mass.: Center for Moral Education, Harvard University.

Kohlberg, L., 1973b. The claim to moral adequacy of a highest stage of moral judgment. *Journal of Philosophy, 70,* 630–646.

Kohlberg, L., 1975. The cognitive-developmental approach to moral education. *Phi Delta Kappan, 56,* 670–677.

Kohlberg, L., 1976a. *The effects of democratic governance on the development of high school moral climates and student moral judgment.* Unpublished proposal, Harvard University.

Kohlberg, L., 1976b. Moral stages and moralization: The cognitive-developmental approach. In T. Lickona (Ed.), *Moral development and behavior: Theory, research, and social issues.* New York: Holt, Rinehart and Winston, pp. 31–53.

Kohlberg, L., 1976c. *A three-year just community school intervention project.* Unpublished proposal, Harvard University.

Kohlberg, L. (Ed.), *Recent research in moral development,* in preparation.

Kohlberg, L., and Elfenbein, D., 1975. The development of moral judgments concerning capital punishment. *American Journal of Orthopsychiatry, 45,* 614–640.

Kohlberg, L., and Gilligan, C. F., 1971. The adolescent as philosopher: The discovery of the self in a postconventional world. *Daedalus, 100,* 1051–1086.

Kohlberg, L., and Turiel, E. Moral development and moral education. In G. S. Lesser (Ed.), *Psychology and educational practice.* Glenview, Ill.: Scott Foresman, pp. 410–465.

Kohlberg, L., Kauffman, K., Scharf, P., and Hickey, J., 1975. The just community approach to corrections: A theory. *Journal of Moral Education, 4,* 243–260.

Krahn, J. H., 1971. A comparison of Kohlberg's and Piaget's type I morality. *Religious Education, 66,* 373–375.

Krebs, D., and Rosenwald, A., 1973. *Moral reasoning and moral behavior in conventional adults.* Unpublished manuscript, Harvard University.

Kuhmerker, L., 1975. Learning to care—the development of empathy. *Journal of Moral Education, 5,* 25–34.

Kuhn, D., 1976. Short-term longitudinal evidence for sequentiality of Kohlberg's early stages of moral judgment. *Developmental psychology, 12,* 162–166.

Kur, J., 1977. Love is working together. In J. Lickona (Ed.), *Mini-book on fostering moral development in the classroom.* Cortland, New York: Project Change, State University of New York.

Kurtines, W., and Grief, E., 1974. The development of moral thought: Review and evaluation of Kohlberg's approach. *Psychological Bulletin, 81,* 453–470.

Leming, J. S., 1974. *An empirical examination of key assumptions underlying the Kohlberg rational for moral education.* Available from Educational Resources Information Center (ERIC), ED 093 749.

Lengel, J. G., 1974. *Explanations of developmental change applied to education: Atmospheres for moral development.* Available from Educational Resources Information Center (ERIC), ED 104 738.

Levine, C., 1976. Role-taking standpoint and adolescent usage of Kohlberg's conventional stages of moral reasoning. *Journal of Personality and Social Psychology, 34,* 41–46.

Lickona, J. (Ed.), 1977. *Mini-book on fostering moral development in the classroom.* Cortland, New York: Project Change, State University of New York.

Lickona, T., 1969. Piaget misunderstood: A critique of the criticisms of his theory of moral development. *Merrill-Palmer Quarterly of Behavior and Development, 16,* 337–350.

Lickona, T., 1976a. *The challenge of Watergate to American schools: Fostering the moral development of children.* Cortland, New York: Project Change, State University of New York.

Lickona, T. (Ed.), 1976b. Critical issues in the study of moral development and behavior. In T. Lickona (Ed.), *Moral development and behavior: Theory, research, and social issues.* New York: Holt, Rinehart and Winston, pp. 3–27.

Lickona, T., 1976c. Research on Piaget's theory of moral development. In T. Lickona (Ed.), *Moral development and behavior: Theory, research, and social issues.* New York: Holt, Rinehart and Winston, pp. 219–240.

Lickona, T., 1976d. *Teacher approaches to moral education: An interview and observation study.* Unpublished proposal, State University of New York at Cortland.

Lickona, T., 1977a. Moral education in the classroom. *Learning,* March, 36–43.

Lickona, T., 1977b. Creating the just community with children. *Theory into Practice,* Summer.

Lipman, M., 1975. Philosophy for children: Learning to be a moral individual. *Ethical Perspectives,* No. 6. New York: New York Society for Ethical Culture. (Monograph)

Lockwood, A., 1973. *Moral reasoning—the value of life.* Middletown, Conn.: Xerox Education Publications.

Lockwood, A., 1977. *The effects of values clarification and moral development curricula on school-age subjects: A critical review of recent research.* Unpublished paper, University of Wisconsin.

Loevinger, J., and Wessler, R., 1970. *Measuring ego development: Construction and use of a sentence completion test.* San Francisco: Jossey-Bass.

Mattox, B. A., 1975. *Getting it together: Dilemmas for the classroom.* San Diego, Calif.: Pennant Press.

McNamee, S., 1968. *Relation of moral reasoning to experimental helping behavior.* Unpublished manuscript, Case Western Reserve University.

Mead, G. H., 1934. *Mind, self, and society.* Chicago: University of Chicago Press.

Meyer, J., 1976. Where are we and where might we go in values education? In J. Meyer

(Ed.), *Reflections on values education*. Waterloo, Ontario: Wilfrid Laurier University Press, pp. 213–221.

Milgram, S., 1974. *Obedience to authority*. New York: Harper and Row.

Mischel, T. (Ed.), 1971. *Cognitive development and epistemology*. New York: Academic Press.

Mischel, W., and Mischel, H., 1976. A cognitive social-learning approach to morality and self-regulation. In T. Lickona (Ed.), *Moral development and behavior: Theory, research, and social issues*. New York: Holt, Rinehart and Winston, pp. 54–69.

Morals instruction favored in schools by 79% in survey. *The New York Times*, April 18, 1976.

Mosher, R., and Sprinthall, N. A., 1971. Psychological education: A means to promote personal development during adolescence. *The Counseling Psychologist, 2*, 3–83.

Mosher, R., and Sullivan, P. R., 1976. A curriculum in moral education for adolescents. *Journal of Moral Education, 5*, 159–172.

Mueller, E., 1972. The maintenance of verbal exchanges between young children. *Child Development, 43*, 930–938.

Murphy, L., 1937. *Social behavior and child personality*. New York: Columbia University Press.

Nader, R., 1972. *Public citizen report*, No. 2.

Newmann, F. M., 1975. *Education for citizen action: Challenge for secondary curriculum*. Berkeley, Calif.: McCutchan.

Orr, J. B., 1974. Cognitive-developmental approaches to moral education: A social-ethical analysis. *Educational Theory, 24*, 365–373.

Paolitto, D., 1975. *Role-taking opportunities for early adolescents: A program in moral education*. Unpublished doctoral dissertation, Boston University School of Education.

Parham, J., 1976. Personal communication.

Peters, R. S., 1970. Concrete principles and the rational passions. In N. F. Sizer and T. R. Sizer (Eds.), *Moral education: Five lectures*. Cambridge: Harvard University Press.

Peters, R. S., 1971. Moral development: A plea for pluralism. In T. Mischel (Ed.), *Cognitive development and epistemology*. New York: Academic Press.

Peters, R. S., 1975. Why doesn't Lawrence Kohlberg do his homework? *Phi Delta Kappan, 56*, 678.

Peterson, C., 1977. Developing empathy in preschoolers. In J. Lickona (Ed.), *Mini-book on fostering moral development in the classroom*. Cortland, New York: Project Change, State University of New York.

Peterson, J., 1976. Personal communication.

Peterson, J., and McNamee, S., 1976. *Role-taking and moral reasoning about distributive justice in preschool children*. Paper presented at a Conference on Moral Development in Young Children, Case Western Reserve University.

Peterson, M. D., 1970. *Thomas Jefferson and the new nation*. New York: Oxford University Press.

Piaget, J., 1932. *The moral judgment of the child*. New York: The Free Press, 1965. (Originally published, 1932.)

Piaget, J., 1967. *Six psychological studies*. New York: Random House.

Piaget, J., 1970. Piaget's theory. In P. H. Mussen (Ed.), *Carmichael's manual of child psychology* (3rd ed., Vol. 1). New York: Wiley and Sons.

Piaget, J., 1971a. *Biology and knowledge: An essay on the relations between organic regulations and cognitive processes*. Chicago: University of Chicago Press.

Piaget, J., 1971b. *Psychology and epistemology: Toward a theory of knowledge*. New York: Viking Press.

Piaget, J., 1975. *To understand is to invent*. New York: Grossman.

Raths, L., Harmin, M., and Simon, S. B., 1966. *Values and teaching: Working with values in the classroom*. Columbus, Ohio: Charles E. Merrill.

Rawls, J., 1971. *A theory of justice.* Cambridge: Harvard University Press.

Rest, J., 1974. Developmental psychology as a guide to value education: A review of "Kohlbergian" programs. *Review of Educational Research, 44,* 241–258.

Rest, J., 1976. New approaches in the assessment of moral judgment. In T. Lickona (Ed.), *Moral development and behavior: Theory, research, and social issues.* New York: Holt, Rinehart and Winston, pp. 198–218.

Rest, J. R., Turiel, E., and Kohlberg, L., 1969. Level of moral development as a determinant of preference and comprehension of moral judgments made by others. *Journal of Personality, 37,* 225–252.

Rosenhan, D., 1969. Some origins of concern for others. In P. Mussen, J. Langer, and M. Covington (Eds.), *Trends and issues in developmental psychology.* New York: Holt, Rinehart and Winston.

Scaplehorn, C., 1974. Piaget's cognitive-developmental approach to morality. In S. Modgil (Ed.), *Piagetian research: A handbook of recent studies.* NFER Publishing Co., Ltd., pp. 352–368.

Schaeffer, P., 1974. *Moral judgment: A cognitive-developmental project.* Unpublished doctoral dissertation, University of Minnesota.

Scharf, P., and Hickey, J., 1976. The prison and the inmate's conception of legal justice: An experiment in democratic education. *Criminal Justice and Behavior, 3,* 107–122.

School violence, vandalism a national crisis. *Today's Child,* June–September, 1975, *23,* 8.

Selman, R., 1975. A developmental approach to interpersonal and moral awareness in young children. In J. Meyer, B. Burnham, and J. Cholvat (Eds.), *Values education.* Waterloo, Ontario: Wilfrid Laurier University Press, pp. 127–140.

Selman, R., 1976. Social-cognitive understanding: A guide to educational and clinical practice. In T. Lickona (Ed.), *Moral development and behavior: Theory, research, and social issues.* New York: Holt, Rinehart and Winston, pp. 299–316.

Selman, R., and Lieberman, M., 1974. *The evaluation of a values curriculum for primary grade children based on a cognitive-developmental approach.* Paper presented to the American Educational Research Association, Chicago, April, 1974.

Shelton, W., 1975. *Social development in young children.* Available from Educational Resources Information Center (ERIC), ED 110 166.

Sichel, B. A., 1976. *Can Kohlberg respond to his critics?* Paper presented to the annual meeting of the Jean Piaget Society, Philadelphia (June).

Simon, S., Howe, L. W., and Kirschenbaum, 1972. *Values clarification.* New York: Hart.

Simpson, E. L., 1974. Moral development research: A case of scientific cultural bias. *Human Development, 17,* 81–106.

Simpson, E. L., 1976. A holistic approach to moral development and behavior. In T. Lickona (Ed.)., *Moral development and behavior: Theory, research, and social issues.* New York: Holt, Rinehart and Winston, pp. 159–170.

Stanley, S. F., 1976. *A curriculum to affect the moral atmosphere of the family and the moral development of adolescents.* Unpublished doctoral dissertation, Boston University School of Education.

Staub, E., 1975. To rear a prosocial child: Reasoning, learning by doing, and learning by teaching others. In D. J. DePalma and J. M. Foley (Eds.), *Moral development: Current theory and research.* New York: Lawrence Erlbaum.

Stewart, J. S. 1975. *The school as a just community: A transactional-developmental approach to moral education.* Unpublished paper; portions presented to the Philosophy of Education Society, Kansas City (March).

Sullivan, E., 1975. *Moral learning: Findings, issues, and question.* New York: Paulist Press.

Sullivan, E., 1977. *A study of Kohlberg's structural theory of moral development: A critique of liberal social science ideology.* Toronto: Ontario Institute for Studies in Education.

Sullivan, P., 1975. *A curriculum for stimulating moral reasoning and ego development in adoles-cence.* Unpublished doctoral dissertation, Boston University School of Education.

Sullivan, P., 1976. Personal communication.

Superka, D., and Johnson, P. L., with Ahrens, C., 1976. *Values education sourcebook.* Boulder, Colo.: Social Science Education Consortium.

Today's students are impossible (name withheld). *Today's Education,* March–April, 1975, p. 26.

Tomlinson-Keasey, C., and Keasey, C. B., 1974. The mediating role of cognitive development in moral judgment. *Child Development, 45,* 291–298.

Turiel, E., 1969. Developmental processes in the child's moral thinking. In P. Mussen, J. Langer, and M. Covington (Eds.), *Trends and issues in developmental psychology.* New York: Holt, Rinehart and Winston, pp. 92–133.

Turiel, E., 1974. *A comparative analysis of moral knowledge and moral judgment in males and females.* Unpublished paper, University of California at Santa Cruz.

Wasserman, E. R., 1976. Implementing Kohlberg's "just community concept" in an alternative high school. *Social Education, 40,* 203–207.

Weinreich, H., 1975. Kohlberg and Piaget: Aspects of their relationship in the field of moral development. *Journal of Moral Education, 4,* 201–214.

Whitely, J. M., 1976. *The Sierra Project.* Unpublished paper, University of California at Irvine.

Wilcox, D., 1977. "Miss Wilcox, this the bad class of the school." In J. Lickona (Ed.), *Mini-book on fostering moral development in the classroom.* Cortland, New York: Project Change, SUNY at Cortland (Spring).

Wilson, R. W., 1976. Some comments on stage theories of moral development. *Journal of Moral Education, 5,* 241–248.

Wolfe, L. C., 1975. Children's literature and the development of empathy in young children. *Journal of Moral Education, 5,* 45–50.

Yarrow, M. R., Scott, P. M., and Waxler, C. Z., 1973. Learning concern for others. *Developmental Psychology, 8,* 240–260.

3

Early Education and Piagetian Theory

Applications Versus Implications

RHETA DeVRIES

Preschool educators have struggled for a number of years with the question of the educational significance of Piaget's research and his theory of knowledge. This question is difficult for at least two reasons. First, the theory is not a theory of teaching, and its educational significance is thus not obvious. Second, the theory is a dynamic one, and the significance of any part must be understood in relation to its role in Piaget's continuing epistemological search for answers to the question of how knowledge develops. In preschool education, the first efforts to use Piaget's work have been direct applications of a few isolated parts taken out of their epistemological context. Unfortunately, these applications have had the effect, in practice, of reducing Piaget's theory to something less, and even to something different, than it is. Later efforts are only just beginning to shift the emphasis away from direct applications of isolated parts to broader implications of the theory as a whole. At this point in the history of early education, it seems useful to review the assimilations of Piaget's theory in preschool education. The purpose of this chapter is to consider the applications in light of the theory as a whole, to outline

RHETA DeVRIES • College of Education, University of Illinois at Chicago Circle, Chicago, Illinois. This chapter was written during a sabbatical leave at the University of Geneva, Geneva, Switzerland.

aspects crucial to education that are unrecognized in these applications, and to consider the direction of future efforts.

1. Applications of Isolated Parts of Piaget's Work

Most educational applications have centered on aspects of Piaget's work related to the stages of development. The following discussion deals with the ways in which the theory is reduced by applications centered on the stages generally, on the research tasks which revealed the structural differences giving rise to the notion of stages, on the areas of knowledge in which Piaget identified stages, and on superficial interpretations of the notion of action. Examples are given of the general theoretical contradictions in specific practices to which these applications have led practitioners.

1.1. Stages

The broad stages of development described by Piaget are so impressive and persuasive that they are sometimes mistaken for the theory itself. Preoccupation with the stages has led to the preschool objective of moving children from the preoperational level to the stage of concrete operations.

This direct application of the notion of stages has two basic shortcomings. The first shortcoming is that *the focus on stages reduces the theory to a theory of the development of scientific knowledge.* Piaget's research yielding the description of stages deals with a limited area of scientific knowledge. The stages, therefore, do not describe all areas of development and, by themselves, suggest educational applications which are limited to a very narrow range. They reflect not at all the aspects of Piaget's work bearing on socioemotional and moral development. Although these latter aspects have not been studied in the same depth as the scientific reasoning process, they constitute, together with the scientific aspects, an interrelated network in terms of the theory as a general theory of the development of knowledge.

The second shortcoming is that *the focus on stages reduces the theory to its structural aspects.* Here, it is important to recognize the role of the stages in the development of the theory. For Piaget, the stages simply signify the mental structures which enabled him to show that knowledge, especially logic, is not innate, but develops itself little by little. The

stages are merely a description of discontinuous organizations in operational structures during development and do not, in themselves, signify anything with regard to how one gets from one stage to the next. By
focusing on the stages which are the *result* of development, one misses
entirely the theme of Piaget's theory—constructivism—which deals with
the *process* of development. It is the constructive process in Piaget's
theory which deals with the way in which operations develop and which
thus accounts for continuity between stages. In describing the stages,
Piaget always pointed out dynamic processes, but it was only later that
this part of the theory began to be elaborated. As will become clear, a
focus on the stages is a focus on logico-mathematical structures apart
from their roots and connections in experience.

1.2. Tasks

One of the most common applications of Piaget's work has been to
try to teach the research tasks such as conservation and classification.
This application is a natural outgrowth of the preoccupation with stages
which led to the objective of moving children to the stage of concrete
operations. Once this objective was accepted, it was a short step to the
conclusion that the way to make children concrete operational is to make
them more logical on the tasks with which Piaget demonstrated operational structures. In addition to the general shortcomings of a focus on
stages, teaching the tasks further reduces the theory in at least three
ways.

First, *this application reduces the theory to the content of the tasks*. Actually, the tasks represent an extremely limited content that is not in itself
worth teaching. They were created by Piaget and his collaborators to
study certain epistemological questions about how knowledge develops.
The tasks are *not* the result of research showing that this specific knowledge is crucial to intelligent adaptation, but are simply the context in
which the structure of thought was studied. It is true that the tasks were
not chosen arbitrarily and that they *represent* important aspects of intellectual adaptation. Nevertheless, they only represent a limited content related to these aspects and cannot be assumed to be the same as
adaptation in life. Focusing on teaching the tasks has the effect of reducing Piaget's theory to one of his research methods.

A second shortcoming, related to the first, is that *this application
effectively reduces the theory to isolated operations*. Even when looking beyond the task content to the theory of operations, by teaching the tasks

educators remain bound by the limited content and end up trying to
foster the development of single operations in isolation. Piaget, however, has made it very clear that operations neither exist nor develop in
isolation (see, for example, Piaget, 1970a,b,* 1971). One *can* teach the
task content, but this does not necessarily reflect any change with regard
to the basic structure of thought.† It is even possible, as Inhelder,
Sinclair, and Bovet (1974) have shown in their research on learning, by
taking account of the constructive process, to teach the tasks so as to
accelerate operational development with regard to these situations.
However, this research led them to the conclusion that "training procedures in which one type of reasoning is artificially isolated and exercised . . . are not, in our opinion, very useful . . ." (Inhelder, Sinclair, and
Bovet, 1974, p. 265). If what one hopes is to foster the long-range development of operational thought, the tasks appear an extremely poor
way to go about it. In comparison with the child's task of constructing
his logic, learning a task is trivial. Sinclair (1971) has drawn an instruc-
tive analogy in this regard by pointing out that teaching the tasks is
like trying to enrich an entire field by fertilizing just a few soil
samples.

The third shortcoming of teaching the tasks is that *this application has
the effect of reducing the broad stages to the stages on the tasks*. That is, it is
assumed that the stages described for the tasks have the same characteristic of invariant sequentiality as the broad stages, and that a child
must thus go through all the stages on the tasks in order to get to the
next broad stage of development. This assumption reflects a confusion
of two kinds of stages which are not of the same order. While the broad
theoretical stages do represent the sequence of development in life, this
is not necessarily true of the empirical stages on the tasks. For example,
the child does not have to go through a stage in which he believes that
there are more girls than children in a class in order to become capable of
operational quantification.‡ The problem of comparing the number in a
class with its largest subclass is unlikely to occur to young children in life.
It is only in the psychologist's research situation that children have any
reason or motivation to think about such questions. To organize an
educational program on the basis of sequences found for the tasks is,
therefore, to reduce the sequence of development to sequences which
are research artifacts.

---

*Publication dates given in the text for Piaget's work refer to the date of first printing.
†See also Denis-Prinzhorn, Kamii, and Mounoud (1972) for a discussion of this point.
‡See Piaget (1941) for the details of this research.

1.3. Areas of Knowledge

Recognizing that the stages signified a new conception of intelligence, some educators have taken the areas of knowledge for which stages were demonstrated as the content of intelligence to be taught. This application is somewhat less direct than the others in the sense that it does not involve teaching the tasks themselves, but instead involves designing activities to foster indirectly the appearance of higher level reasoning in areas such as spatial and temporal relations, seriation, and classification. Although this approach reflects a degree of decentering from the tasks, it also suffers from the basic shortcomings of effectively reducing the theory to a limited content and to the structural aspects of the development of scientific knowledge.

1.4. Action

Direct application of Piaget's emphasis on the importance of action has been simply to cite Piaget as justification for the clichés that "children learn by doing" and that they must have many opportunities to manipulate objects. Advocates of play in the child-development tradition in early education have added Piaget's name as a general justification for such activities as block building and pretend play. These applications are not inconsistent with the implications of the role of action in Piaget's theory. Nevertheless, they have the effect of reducing it to a pale shadow of Piaget's meaning. For Piaget, action is at the core of the constructive process, and this aspect of the theory opens up implications far beyond the vague justification of play. This point is elaborated below in the discussion of the constructivist aspects of the theory.

1.5. Specific Practices

When educators begin to try to translate the foregoing aspects of Piaget's theory into specific teaching practices, they immediately confront the fact that these structural aspects with which they are working provide neither a theory of teaching nor a theory of learning. Educators are then left to create their practices on the basis of their own assumptions about how children get from one stage to the next or acquire specific knowledge.* The result is that the educator who starts out with

---

*See DeVries (1974) for a discussion of how different theoretical assumptions lead to different educational practices.

the theory of stages ends up with practices for which the theory provides no rationale. Weikart, for example, recognized this dilemma and
was led, in essence, to reject the theory. In efforts to foster higher levels
of reasoning in areas of scientific knowledge, he found that the
rationales which made sense to him and his collaborators could not be
reconciled with Piaget's theory. His solution, as indicated in the following passage from the preface to *The Cognitively Oriented Curriculum*
(Weikart, Rogers, Adcock, and McClelland, 1971) was to change the
theory:

> a theory . . . should be employed only as long as it seems to do the job, and
> it may be altered to meet differing situations when it seems advisable. This
> approach leads into trouble very easily, because it permits a flexibility
> which may circumvent the theory. For example, Piagetian child develop-
> ment theory does not use some of the terms of processes employed in this
> guide. In addition, the guide alters some of the terms such as "operations"
> to mesh with the recommended curriculum teaching patterns which have
> worked well. Yet, the basic thrust of the theory is present. Therefore, while
> there is a growing congregation of "high church" Piagetians in preschool
> education, I would classify this curriculum as the product of "store front"
> Piagetian theory utilization. (p. ix)

Although the authors of this curriculum claim that "the theory of Jean
Piaget provides the foundation for the Cognitively Oriented Curriculum
(Weikart *et al.*, p. 1)," they end up reducing Piaget's work to notions of
representation which bear no resemblance to Piaget's theory.

When educators take only the structural aspects of Piaget's theory
outside the context of the underlying constructive aspects, the assumptions about learning which they generally fall back on are empiricist ones
which are in basic contradiction to Piaget's work. That is, most of us
have grown up in an environment permeated by the empiricist view that
knowledge comes from outside the individual to the inside through the
senses. We tend to assimilate Piaget's ideas with our empiricist beliefs
without any awareness that we are doing so. These beliefs are in opposition to Piaget's position that knowledge is constructed from within the
individual by his actions.* An empiricist assimilation of Piaget's theory
often leads educators to unrecognized contradictions in their rationale
and practice. Three examples of such contradictions are given below.

Play versus structured training. One hard-core empiricist belief in
education is that children's learning must be organized and directed by

---

*For discussion of Piaget's position in relation to the empiricist and rationalist traditions,
see Kamii and DeVries (1977 or 1978).

the teacher. This idea conflicts with Piaget's emphasis on the importance of the child's spontaneous actions, and leads to an unreconcilable contradiction when the educator attempts to combine these ideas. Lavatelli, for example, recognized Piaget's emphasis on action and recommended that "a major part of the preschool day should be reserved for free choice of activity" (Lavatelli, 1970, p. 43). She insisted that "the teacher must have confidence in the child's ability to learn *on his own*" (Lavatelli, 1970, p. 48). However, when she focused on the objective of making children concrete operational, she isolated this part of the theory from the notion of play and developed training sessions to teach the tasks. In these sessions, the teacher structures the child's actions for him. For example, in a classification activity, Lavatelli's model teacher tells the child to "take the two rings and put them on the table so that the green square is not inside either ring. . . . Now, I'd like you to pick up one of the rings and place it so that the green square is inside the ring" (1973, p. 30). Throughout the lessons given in her *Teacher's Guide* (Lavatelli, 1973), initiative rests solely with the teacher.

In this application, lip service is given to the value of play, but, when it comes to what the teacher can do with the theory, it is the tasks that are emphasized, and play is mentioned specifically only as providing opportunities for the teacher to "reinforce the learning developed in the small group sessions" (Lavatelli, 1970, p. 4). The result is that the tasks are simply pasted on to "those preschool practices which have stood the test of time" (Lavatelli, 1970, p. 1), and the idea of spontaneous action in play remains undeveloped and juxtaposed to structured training on the tasks.

Operational development versus the learning of verbal concepts. Another empiricist belief in early education is that we can give children knowledge by giving them words. In opposition to this belief, research by Sinclair (Inhelder, Sinclair, and Bovet, 1974) demonstrates that training in language is insufficient for the development of conservation structures. A basic contradiction thus arises when educators attempt to combine notions of operational development with verbal methods. This can be found, for example, in *The Cognitively Oriented Curriculum* (Weikart *et al.*, 1971) where the child is said to use a verbal level of operation in learning. This leads to recommendations that the teacher bombard the child with language in order to promote development in the areas of classification, seriation, spatial relations, and temporal relations. In the area of spatial relations, children are taught words such as "up," "down," "over," and "under." Great effort is invested in the teaching of these words as can be seen in the following excerpt:

A. *Teacher provides the verbal stimulus:* In dealing with the concept *down,* the teacher might say, "Go down the slide." As the child is sliding, the teacher may say, "You are going down the slide."

B. *Teacher provides the verbal stimulus and the child responds in one of the following ways:*
   1. Child verbalizes *while performing* the action; e.g., "I am going down, down, down [the slide]"; "I am going up, up, up [the ladder]."
   2. Child interprets what he has done just *after* he has completed the task or action; e.g., "I went down the slide"; "I went up the ladder."
   3. Child tells what he is going to do before he does it; e.g., "I will go up the ladder and down the slide."
   4. Child interprets his actions from memory: after work time, the child tells what he has done; e.g., "I went up the ladder and down the slide."

C. *Child spontaneously verbalizes* about a task, action or event without requiring verbal stimulus from the teacher.* (Weikart *et al.,* p. 34)

In this application, empiricist assimilation of Piaget's theory of operations reduces the areas of knowledge studied by Piaget to a list of verbal concepts.†

Children's "wrong" ideas versus correct answers. Another empiricist belief in education is that knowledge is an accumulation of facts, an assumption which leads teachers to emphasize the importance of correct answers. Piaget's research, however, shows that children do not simply accumulate ideas which are correct from the adult point of view, but that they construct their knowledge by assimilations which often result in a long series of "wrong" ideas. These two contradictory ideas can be found in the work of Lavatelli. She recognized the importance of accepting children's "wrong" answers, and wrote that the teacher should "not correct wrong answers" (Lavatelli, 1970, p. 2). Nevertheless, throughout her lessons to teach the tasks, one finds that the teacher should not be satisfied with the child's wrong answers. Many procedures are given for what the teacher can do to get the child to correct himself. Both verbal and nonverbal methods can be found in her *Teacher's Guide* (Lavatelli, 1973), summarized as follows:

   1. *Ask leading questions:* If a child chooses a figure other than the green square in the classification task, the teacher should ask, "Is that a green square?" with emphasis on the word for the property the child has missed. (p. 30)

---

*When verbalizations described in B occur spontaneously, their significance in terms of the constructive process is very different from that of unspontaneous responses to stimuli.
†See Kamii (1975) for a discussion of the contradiction between teaching concepts and Piaget's theory.

2. *Give a verbal rule:* In a number, measurement, and space activity, the teacher is told to "Alternately add and take away (from a group of cubes): repeat a verbal formula each time, 'Adding makes things have more; taking one away makes things have less.'" (p. 44)

3. *Demonstrate actions the child should perform:* In a classification task, children are to make as many different pairs as they can with three types of cars. If they do not use a system of starting with one car and combining that car with itself and then with the other two, then starting with the next car, etc., the teacher is told to say, "Would it help if we used a system like this?" and to demonstrate the system. (p. 35)

4. *Provide figurative materials:* If a child does not conserve, the teacher is told to "Try gradual transformation of the visual correspondence." (p. 40)

These are only a few examples of the ways in which unconscious assimilations of Piaget's theory to empiricist beliefs result in practices which contradict the theory. Let us turn now to the crucial aspects of the theory which are missing in these applications and which lead to quite different educational implications.

2. Implications of Piaget's Constructivism

As pointed out, educational applications of isolated structuralist aspects of Piaget's theory result in reductions of the theory and lead to practices which are in basic contradiction to it. Essentially what is missing from these applications is the constructivist aspect of Piaget's work which deals with the process by which knowledge comes about. In the sketch which follows,* aspects of constructivism that are crucial to any educational use of the theory are outlined. The aspects discussed are (1) the types of experience, action, and knowledge, and (2) interest, autonomy, and the role of peer interaction.

2.1. Types of Experience, Action, and Knowledge

Piaget (1965, 1970a,b,c) distinguishes two kinds of experience—physical and logico-mathematical—each of which gives rise to a type of action by which the individual obtains knowledge. Physical experience consists of actions on objects which lead to knowledge of the objects themselves. For example, in picking up solids, the child can notice their weight by physical experience. In order to obtain this information, he

---

*For a fuller discussion of Piaget's contructivism, see Kamii and DeVries (1977, 1978).

must focus on this particular aspect of an object and ignore other properties such as color and shape. Piaget refers to this action as simple or empirical abstraction. Other examples include abstracting properties of objects by observing their reactions to being dropped or pushed. Knowledge which thus has its source mainly in objects is referred to as physical knowledge.

Logico-mathematical experience, in contrast, consists of actions on objects which introduce into the objects characteristics they do not have. For example, number is not a property of any group of objects but consists of relationships created by an individual. That is, the "twoness" of two objects does not exist in either object, but is a group of relationships coordinated by the individual who confers on them this characteristic of quantity. Piaget refers to this action as reflective abstraction. Knowledge which thus has its source mainly in the knower himself is logico-mathematical knowledge.

Although Piaget makes these important distinctions, he then goes on to point out that the different types of experience, action, and knowledge are really inseparable. For example, when the child looks at six blue blocks and two yellow ones and thinks about them as "blue ones and yellow ones," he is focusing on their specific properties on the one hand and also activating a whole network of relationships on the other. That is, to think of the blocks as blocks, he must distinguish their similarities and differences in relation to all other objects. In order to think of blueness, he must put this property in relation to all other colors. It is these networks of relationships which constitute the general framework that enables the child to recognize the blue and yellow blocks. There can be no physical experience without a logico-mathematical framework, and, for babies and young children, there can be no logico-mathematical experience without objects to put into relationship.

Piaget also discusses a third type of knowledge—social knowledge—which has as its source people. Social knowledge includes arbitrary truths agreed upon by convention (such as the fact that December 25 is Christmas Day) and moral rules agreed upon by coordination of points of view (such as the rules that one should not lie or steal). Arbitrary social knowledge and moral knowledge are similar to physical knowledge in that they require specific input from the external world. However, this content must also be structured with the logico-mathematical framework. For example, the fact that there is no school on Saturdays and Sundays can have meaning only in relation to every other day of the week, and days thus have to be structured into school days and nonschool days.

Knowledge begins in infancy as the child focuses mainly on specific, physical, observable content. In the course of constructing his knowledge of objects by empirical abstraction, he also constructs his logico-mathematical framework by reflective abstraction. The baby's actions on objects and people have two undifferentiated poles, one in which his attention is oriented toward the specificity of each object (such as the sound of a rattle when he shakes it) and one in which he is oriented toward what is general (such as the way he has to integrate smoothly the different actions of moving toward, grasping, and then shaking the object). The first aspect of the action is physical and the second is logico-mathematical. During the sensorimotor period, the baby constructs objects by observing what happens when he pushes, pulls, shakes, and drops objects, and by putting into relationship all the differences in the reactions of objects.

During the preoperational period, the physical-material-observable and logico-mathematical aspects of actions continue to be undifferentiated, with the former still dominating the child's thinking. The observable result of his actions is the child's main interest, rather than the structured system to which the action that produced the result belongs. Therefore, when actions modify the shape of a clay ball or the spatial arrangement of a number of objects, the young child views quantity (when he thinks about it at all) as changing along with shape or arrangement.

During the period of concrete operations, the logico-mathematical aspect develops into operational systems which enable the child to make logical deductions. As these systems become more powerful, he becomes able to arrive at conclusions with a feeling of logical necessity. These operational systems appear first with respect to contents that are easy to structure. Thus, the conservation of elementary number appears before the conservation of amount and weight of clay. In other words, the logico-mathematical aspect can be said to become partially dissociated from the physical aspect during this period.

With the attainment of formal operations, the logico-mathematical pole becomes independent of content (as can be seen in "pure" mathematics), and the further elaboration of all aspects of knowledge becomes more dependent on logico-mathematical structuring.

These aspects of Piaget's constructivism lead to two general educational implications in contrast with direct applications. First, the emphasis shifts from trying to foster directly the characteristics of a future stage of development to maximizing the child's opportunities to create and coordinate many relationships of which he is presently capable. This shift reflects the recognition that all future reasoning capacities arise from an evolution which can only be enhanced by exercising present reasoning capacities. Moreover, concrete operations are recognized as one indirect and, for normal children, inevitable result of a process which has broader ramifications. That is, when one focuses on facilitating the child's exercise of his intelligence, one not only fosters the eventual construction of operational capacities in the areas studied by Piaget, but capacities to coordinate relationships in many other areas as well.

The second implication is that the emphasis shifts from a narrow focus on logico-mathematical knowledge to a much broader one. *All the applications discussed above focus in an isolated way on logico-mathematical knowledge* without any recognition of the nature of reflective abstraction or the way in which the construction of this aspect of knowlege is connected with the construction of physical knowledge. Thus, in the empiricist applications, logico-mathematical knowledge often tends to be reduced to social knowledge which is taught directly. In contrast, recognition that logico-mathematical knowledge grows along with physical knowledge leads to an emphasis on activities in which the child has rich opportunities to act on objects and observe their reactions. By capitalizing on children's natural motivation to act on objects, teachers can develop classroom activities in which children exercise their initiative in creating and coordinating the basic relationships that will later become structured into operational systems. For example, in a game of target ball, children aim at constructions built with milk-carton blocks. In this situation, they do not need the teacher to give them the words "over," "down," "farther," or "ricochet" in order to be motivated to think about these spatial and logical relationships. Similarly, when children try to make Kleenex, wooden cubes, juice cans, and other objects move across the floor by blowing on them through a straw, they do not need the teacher to correct their wrong anticipations. Nor do they need the teacher to direct their thinking about the categories of objects that never move, always move, and sometimes move.* In physical-knowledge activities, the child's own actions and feedback from objects provide the content for the logico-mathematical coordination of relationships.

2.2. Interest, Autonomy, and the Role of Peer Interaction

The foregoing discussion centered primarily on what Piaget refers to as the "motor" of development. Now we turn to consider aspects of constructivism which include the "fuel" and the social context.

---

*These examples are taken from Kamii and DeVries (1978). In this book, the interested reader will find many more examples of physical-knowledge activities, along with an elaborated rationale, criteria and suggestions for developing activities, and principles of teaching.

Interest. Piaget (1965) refers to the element of interest as the "fuel" of the constructive process. Adults, whose interests are generally differentiated, coordinated, and unified, are often capable of constructive activity even when their interest is at a low level and they feel the pressure of some kind of coercion. Even for adults, however, the absence of interest can prevent effective effort. Certainly, it is when our interest is thoroughly engaged that our efforts are most productive. This condition is even more necessary for young children whose personalities are relatively undifferentiated.

The educational implication here is clear—to capitalize on those kinds of situations in which children's spontaneous interests can be aroused. This implication constitutes an additional reason for looking beyond the tasks for content with which to stimulate children's constructive energies. Piaget made this point in the following way:

> The child can certainly be interested in seriating for the sake of seriating, and classifying for the sake of classifying, etc., when the occasion presents itself. However, on the whole it is when he has events or phenomena to explain or goals to reach in an intriguing situation that operations are the most exercised. (Piaget and Garcia, 1971, p. 26)

The kinds of physical-knowledge activities described above are especially good for stimulating children's fascination with content which leads them to construct physical and logico-mathematical knowledge. Other activities appealing to children's spontaneous interests include many of those found in curricula in the child-development tradition, such as painting, block building, pretend play, singing, listening to stories, and climbing on a jungle gym.*

While interest is necessary to the constructive process, it should be noted that it is not sufficient to justify the educational value of an activity. Children may, for example, be fascinated with observing a battery-driven whale spouting water as it swims in a pan of water, but since they cannot possibly understand the mechanism that causes this event, the possibilities for creating and coordinating relationships are not very numerous. Certainly, the curiosity and wondering which the phenomenon arouses have some value, but when one selects educational activities from the constructivist point of view, those with the highest priority are those which engage the child's active interest in such a way that intelligence is most exercised. When children are interested in an activity, one must observe and try to figure out what is the focus of their

---

*Additional discussion of the child-development curriculum from the perspective of Piaget's theory may be found in Kamii and DeVries (1977; 1978).

interest and what possibilities the activity offers for the exercise of reasoning. Thus, many of the activities found in child-development curricula can be justified in terms of a much more solid and specific rationale than the general rationale usually given in terms of play and socioemotional development.

Autonomy. In his early research on moral development, Piaget (1932) demonstrated that knowledge and convictions about moral rules, too, are constructed by children. In discussing this research, he contrasted two types of adult-child relationships, one of which tends to promote and the other to retard the child's construction of knowledge and morality. These are briefly discussed below.

In a relationship characterized by adult constraint, or authority, the child is heteronomous—that is, he is governed by the adult and is not encouraged to regulate his behavior by his own decisions. To the extent that the child is externally controlled, he will be prevented from developing the ability to govern himself on the basis of convictions, values, and knowledge about which he has a feeling of necessity. When governed continually by the values, beliefs, and ideas of others, the child practices a submission which leads to mindless conformity in both moral and intellectual spheres.

Only in relationships characterized by cooperation, in contrast, can the child become autonomous—that is, be governed by knowledge, values, and convictions constructed by himself and not just accepted from others. In a relationship of cooperation, the adult minimizes his authority in relation to the child and gives him as much opportunity as possible to practice governing his behavior on the basis of his convictions.

The educational implication of this aspect of constructivism is that the child's opportunities for choice and voluntary action should be maximized. This perspective leads to practices in contrast with the teacher's direction of the child's actions or language. However, it is not possible for the teacher to relinquish adult authority completely, and the implication here is not to give the child complete freedom. Nevertheless, there are many ways in which, by reducing adult authority, children can be given opportunities for exercising and thereby developing their autonomy. For example, when a child spills something, the teacher can simply encourage the child to recognize the need to clean up (if he does not do so spontaneously) and to act on this recognition. Such an approach is significantly different in its effect on the child's motivation from telling him to clean up. Even when the teacher must coerce a child, the consideration of autonomy can lead to the use of authority in a way which still leaves room for the child's voluntary action. For example, if a child refuses to come inside after outdoor play, the teacher can still offer the child the option of walking or being carried (and in this situation most children preserve their autonomy by choosing to walk inside by themselves). It is by exercising his ability to govern his own beliefs and actions that the child gradually constructs internally coherent knowledge, morality, and personality. This implication of Piaget's theory is in contrast with applications in which teachers perpetuate heteronomous relationships and take initiative away from children.

Peer interaction. Piaget (1932, 1935, 1965) also emphasizes the importance of social interaction, especially with peers, for the development of intellectual objectivity and a morality characterized by social reciprocity. His research shows that in many domains of thought, young children only gradually become able to decenter from one point of view and to consider and coordinate a variety of perspectives. What is crucial to this evolution is a social context in which the child has many opportunities to confront other ideas, values, and opinions, to compare these, and to come to recognize the need for objective verification on the intellectual plane and social reciprocity on the moral plane.

When the significance of peer interaction is seen in terms of opportunities for the construction of children's own convictions, the teacher puts the emphasis on encouraging the kind of discussion which is an exchange of honest opinions and feelings. Such an emphasis leads even to valuing occasions of conflict for their potential as a context in which children can confront the opposing ideas and wishes of others. With this perspective, the teacher's goal leads to less concern with the specific outcome of an interaction (whether a child shares a toy, for example) than with the process of exchange between children. This aspect of constructivism is reflected in specific classroom practices such as voting to decide the name of the new goldfish, arranging cooking so that two cooks must decide together what they will make the next day, and asking children at group time whether they want to take the pendulum down to make room for target ball. Practices such as these are in contrast with those in which teachers emphasize the teacher-child relationship as the primary context for children's learning and development.

3. Conclusion

Piaget's work began with the hypothesis that knowledge is neither innate nor due solely to experience, but is a progressive construction through interaction. Although he had the idea of constructivism from the beginning and it appears even in early works, his emphasis first was on investigating the existence of structures in mental functions. His research focused specifically on the tasks which demonstrated empirical stages in a variety of areas of scientific knowledge and which then led to the theory of broad stages of development. After establishing that knowledge is a progressive construction by the individual, Piaget then turned to investigations of the relationship between the physical and logico-mathematical aspects of knowledge, that is, to more detailed consideration of interactionism. This work led to elaborations of the constructive aspects of the theory which was then followed by research on learning (Inhelder, Sinclair, and Bovet, 1974). Current work proceeds with investigations of the processes of invention or discovery (see, for example, Inhelder, Ackermann-Valladao, Blanchet, Karmiloff-Smith, Kilcher-Hagedorn, Montangero, and Robert, 1976; Karmiloff-Smith and Inhelder, 1975). The theory itself continues to evolve as Genevans follow each new elaboration with new research to provide further clarification of our knowledge about knowledge.

In early education, efforts to use this work have centered primarily on the early structural aspects and have not followed in the footsteps of the theory's further development. As a result of empiricist assimilations which failed to recognize the constructivist aspects of the theory, educational applications have been made which are in basic contradiction with constructivism. It is only very recently that efforts are just beginning in the direction of developing educational implications derived from the elaborations of constructivist aspects of the theory (see Kamii and De-Vries, 1977; DeVries and Kamii, 1975; and Kamii and DeVries, 1978). Because the theory is not a theory of teaching, educators must derive its implications rather than making direct applications. This work can only be carried out by teachers who experiment (perhaps in collaboration with psychologists) to find out what kinds of classroom procedures best engage children's active interests, stimulate their coordination of relationships, and foster autonomy and cooperation.

In other words, Piaget's theory offers a tool teachers can use to develop their practice, but it is a tool which itself must be constructed by teachers who actively engage in the task of figuring out how children are thinking in particular situations and who then modify their interventions and planning on the basis of these observations. In order for preschool educators to catch up with the development of Piaget's theory, we must follow the lead of researchers in Geneva who are focusing on the ways in which children construct their knowledge. Inhelder contrasts this with the earlier work on the structures of comprehension, stating: "now the time has come to interest ourselves more in the processes of invention or discovery of the subject in his research for a solution to particular well differentiated problems" (Inhelder *et al.*, 1976, p. 59; translated by the author of this chapter). In preschool education, too, the time has come for us to decenter from the structures of comprehension and focus on the construction of knowledge in life. It is only by making this shift that we can hope to develop the kinds of active methods that will facilitate the child's construction of his knowledge, morality, and personality.

ACKNOWLEDGMENTS

The author would like to thank Professors Hermina Sinclair and Marianne Denis-Prinzhorn of the University of Geneva for critically reading this manuscript and making helpful suggestions.

References

Denis-Prinzhorn, M., Kamii, C., and Mounoud, P., 1972. Pedagogical applications of Piaget's theory. *People Watching, 1(2)*, 68–71.
DeVries, R., 1974. Theory in educational practice. In R. Colvin and E. Zaffiro (Eds.), *Preschool education: A handbook for the training of early childhood educators*. New York: Springer Publishing.
DeVries, R., and Kamii, C., 1975. *Why group games: A Piagetian perspective*. Publication 132, Educational Resources Information Center/Eearly Childhood Education, Urbana, Ill.
Inhelder, B., Sinclair, H., and Bovet, M., 1974. *Learning and the development of cognition*. Cambridge: Harvard University Press.
Inhelder, B., Ackermann-Valladao, E., Blanchet, A., Karmiloff-Smith, A., Kilcher-Hagedorn, H., Montangero, J., and Robert, M., 1976. Des structures cognitives aux procédures de découverte: Esquisse de recherches en cours. *Archives de Psychologie, 44(171)*, 57–72.
Kamii, C., 1975. One intelligence indivisible. *Young Children, 30*, 228–238.
Kamii, C., and DeVries, R., 1977. Piaget for early education. In M. C. Day and R. K. Parker (Eds.), *Preschool in action* (2nd ed.). Boston: Allyn and Bacon.
Kamii, C., and DeVries, R., 1978. *Physical knowledge in preschool education: Implications of Piaget's theory*. Englewood Cliffs, N.J.: Prentice-Hall.
Karmiloff-Smith, A., and Inhelder, B., 1975. If you want to get ahead, get a theory. *Cognition, 3(3)*, 195–212.
Lavatelli, C., 1970. *Piaget's theory applied to an early childhood curriculum*. Boston: American Science and Engineering.
Lavatelli, C., 1973. *Teacher's guide to accompany early childhood curriculum: A Piaget program*. Boston: American Science and Engineering.
Piaget, J., 1952 *The child's conception of number*. London: Routledge and Kegan Paul, Ltd. (First published in 1941.)
Piaget, J., 1970a. *Genetic epistemology*. New York: Columbia University Press.

Piaget, J., 1965. *The moral judgment of the child*. New York: The Free Press. (First published in 1932).

Piaget, J., 1971. *Science of education and the psychology of the child*. New York: Viking Press. (First published in part in 1935; in its entirety in 1965).

Piaget, J., 1972a. *The principles of genetic epistemology*, New York: Basic Books. (First published in 1970b).

Piaget, J., 1972b. *Psychology and epistemology*. New York: Viking Press. (First published in 1970c).

Piaget, J., 1974. *Understanding causality*. New York: Norton. (First published in 1971.)

Piaget, J., and Garcia, R., 1974. Physico-geometric explanations and analysis. In J. Piaget, *Understanding causality*. New York: Norton. (First published in 1971.)

Sinclair, H., 1971. Piaget's theory of development: The main stages. In M. Rosskopf, L. Steffe, and S. Taback (Eds.), *Piagetian cognitive-development research and mathematical education*. Washington, D.C.: National Council of Teachers of Mathematics.

Weikart, D., Rogers, L., Adcock, C., and McClelland, D., 1971. *The cognitively oriented Curriculum*. Educational Resources Information Center-National Association for the Education of Young Children, Urbana, Illinois.

4

The Impact of the Work of Piaget on Science Curriculum Development

KENNETH LOVELL and MICHAEL SHAYER

1. Introduction

The Piagetian model of cognitive development involves a description of the growth of human thinking under certain conditions. The rate of development along the dimension sketched out by Piaget seems to depend upon the culture pattern in which the individual is reared and the quality of schooling. We recognize, of course, that the extent of the development will also depend upon the genetic make-up of the individual, in the sense that genetics will play a role in determining the extent to which he can develop those skills said to be indicative of intelligence in his culture pattern.

A brief description of some relevant aspects of the Piagetian theoretical system will be followed by the use that can be made of the system in coming to understand better the intellectual difficulties of pupils encountering work in physics, chemistry, and biology. Individuals differ greatly in their rate of cognitive growth and this is illustrated by discussion of a large-scale survey involving pupils between 9 and 14 years. This differential growth is germane for the curriculum builder. There are

KENNETH LOVELL • School of Education, University of Leeds, Leeds, England.
MICHAEL SHAYER • Chelsea College, University of London, London, England.

three science curricula in which deliberate attempts have been made to take into account Piaget's description of the genesis of thinking, either in deriving the course structure or in deciding on learning strategies. These curricula will be described in some detail. If an attempt is made to ensure that the intellectual demands made on the pupil are either on a par with, or slightly ahead of, intellectual skills available to him, his progress is likely to be maximized. But if, as was the case in the 1960s, curriculum building goes ahead regardless of the intellectual growth of pupils, we must not be surprised that many curricula, as elaborated in the 1960s and early 1970s, have been understood by a smaller proportion of the population than was intended.

2. Some Basic Points in Piagetian Developmental Theory

The writings of Piaget indicate that for him intellectual growth involves the building of semilogical and logical structures, these having to be actively constructed by the child as he interacts with his environment. The internal changes that occur within the child, resulting from biological control exercized in maturation, are integrated with the child's own action structures, the integration being carried out by means of a unique auto- or self-regulatory mechanism thus ensuring the natural process of the building of intellectual structures.

In recent years, the Geneva School has altered its views somewhat on the nature of the relationship between language and thought. It is now said that linguistic structures do not derive from cognitive structures or vice versa; rather, both sets of structures are said to derive from a more abstract system of regulating and organizing mechanisms that are common to language, cognition and other nonlinguistic domains. The Piagetian position on the question of the relationships between language and thought is of some consequence for it implies that if the pupil is unable to understand some aspect of science, it may not be sufficient merely to attempt to explain to him in words.

It is also important to note at the outset that Piaget makes a distinction between physical knowledge and logical-mathematical knowledge (Piaget, 1970, p.17), although he also makes clear that these are almost indissociable and are to be looked upon more as a continuum than as a dichotomy. In respect of physical knowledge, the individual abstracts or "takes from" things to which his knowing is directed. The child can determine whether or not a lump of lead floats or sinks in water by trial, and the result can be generalized empirically. By acting on objects, he can discover their properties. Against this, logical-mathematical knowledge is not derived from objects themselves but from his own mental actions on the objects. Thus, the concept of density, considered in an analytic sense, cannot be discovered empirically. It has to be invented or constructed by the child's own cognitive activity in combination, of course, with physical experience. To construct in this manner necessitates that he reflects on his coordinating activity in a self-regulatory manner. However, it must be stressed that physical knowledge is not a mere recording of phenomena. Although it is a simple abstraction, rather than a reflexive abstraction (Piaget, 1975), it always involves assimilation to logical-mathematical structures, as for example, when the differing weights of objects that have the same shape and size are compared and ranked according to their weights.

3. The Early Years

In Piaget's view, the infant, during the first 21 months of life, slowly becomes aware of his world through an increasing recognition of his own actions. The infant constructs a complex system of action-schemes, and organizes reality in terms of elementary temporal and causal structures. Since the semiotic function is not yet in evidence, these constructions depend only on movements and perceptions. And, with the genesis of the permanent object at around 21 months, the child attains the first level of abstraction or dissociation from reality, for he has separated the self from the not-self. There is a delay of some years between the interiorization of actions to give implicit mental actions at 21 months of age and the organization of these mental actions into coherent reversible systems around 7 years. Although his thinking to around 7 years is not exactly systematized or logical, the child has, nevertheless, been interacting with objects, persons, and situations and building up a great amount of specific knowledge of the world around him. This knowledge is taken directly from the situation and consists of a form of physical and social knowledge all obtained, of course, at the first level of abstraction. This knowledge, although laying the very foundation for his knowledge of the world, is of limited value from the strict scientific viewpoint.

4. Concrete Operational Thought and Understanding Science

By 6 to 7 years of age the pupil can, essentially, begin to look in on and monitor his own thinking, and he becomes aware of the sequences of action taking place in his mind. He has, in essence, reached the second level of abstraction or dissociation from reality for he is able to distinguish between his experiences and the order or categories he imposes on them. The mental operations that are subsequently elaborated are termed *concrete*, because they relate to data that are perceptible or that can be imaged, and not to verbally stated hypotheses. In Piaget's view, these operations represent a transitional state between action schemes and the general logical structures of adolescence, which are said to involve a combinatorial system and a "group" structure, thus fusing the two forms of reversibility, namely, negation and reciprocity (Inhelder and Piaget, 1958).

During the period of concrete operations, we find emerging groupings of classes and relations, that is, structures that include classification, seriations, correspondences (one-to-one or one-to-many) and double-entry tables or matrices (Inhelder and Piaget, 1964). These logico-arithmetic operations relate to discrete objects and are based on differences and similarities between the elements. Moreover, developing at the same time are what Piaget calls infralogical operations comprising a group of structures isomorphic to the logico-arithmetic operations, but relating to continuous objects and based on proximities and separations.

With age then, we see the child increasingly able to master the following: hierarchical classification, seriation, substitution or equivalence, symmetry, multiplication of classes, and multiplication of relations, although there is a time lag for some of them. These are the tools, so to speak, that allow him to organize his experience and make sense of his world. Thus equipped, he begins to build the basic concepts of science, for he can increasingly elaborate those concepts that involve the building of precise relations between mental actions bearing directly on things, whether real or imagined. Now the child can commence to systematize the relations between objects and events and build such basic concepts as class, series, number, length, weight, axes of reference, area, time, temperature, and so forth, for these all result from the coordination of mental actions that bear directly on reality.

Shayer (1972a) has carefully examined the evidence produced by Inhelder and Piaget (1958) with respect to pupil responses in the period of concrete operational thought. He categorized individuals' performance into five categories. Such categories (or lack of them) are of great importance to the science teacher. In the early part of the period, the pupil

> will investigate what happens in a haphazard way: argue that "this goes
> with that" (association only): order a series (e.g., length or weights) but is

unable to do so as part of a perception of a relationship in an investigation: is unable to use any model as theory.

During the latter part of the period when the thinking is more flexible and extends to greater areas of experience, the child

> will find out what happens, including the use of seriation and classification as tools of perception: can use ordering relations to partially quantify associative reasoning, e.g., "as this goes up, that comes down," "if you double this you must double that": can use seriation and the multiplication of two seriations as perceptual strategies: understand the rules of a simple model, but not in relation to the experiment in hand.

From all that has been said, it will be realized that at the level of concrete operational thought the pupil will not be able to understand force, work, energy, in a formal analytic sense, for these involve second-degree relations. But he can understand these ideas in an intuitive sense.

Consider, for example, force which is understood, at first, as push or pull, as when the child acts on some object. There are, of course, innumerable examples in everyday life that can be used as examples to illustrate force. Again, work can be grasped intuitively from 10 to 11 years of age onward. Everyday examples of work done can be shown through the arm muscles lifting an object from the floor to the table against the pull of the earth, and the wind blowing the sailboat along against the resistance offered by the water. A little more formally, pupils could consider deformation work, as when expanders are stretched to different lengths, lift work when various sandbags are lifted to varying heights, and acceleration work when different masses are given varying speeds.

Thus, if we define energy as the capacity for doing work, the pupil at this stage can grasp intuitively that muscle, fuels, and the wind are all sources of energy since they can do work. Pupils can understand that, with respect to mechanical energy, some agency may be a source of energy either by virtue of its position or by virtue of its movement. The water at the top of the waterfall has potential energy by virtue of its position; at the bottom it has movement energy by virtue of its motion and it can thus turn the turbine. The pupil at this stage can consider height energy; motion energy; motion energy converted to height energy using toy cars of differing masses and traveling at different speeds, moving up an inclined plane to a halt; and tension energy as in a compressed spring.

In the biological field consider the notion of respiration. At 5 or 6 years of age children can well understand respiration in the sense of breathing in-and-out as bellows go in and out. The chest can be seen to expand and contract. Then, at 10 years of age, pupils can grasp intuitively that the body uses up air much as a car burns petrol. With flexible concrete operational thought, pupils can understand that a gas called oxygen is taken from the air, that there are chemical changes in the body tissues, and that carbon dioxide is liberated. But the convertibility of energy from one form to another is only grasped intuitively.

5. The Move to Formal Operational Thought

In terms of the Piagetian model, the pupil begins to move forward to the early stages of formal operational thought at about 12 years of age, such thinking coming to maturity, so to speak, around 16 years. This may well be true of outstandingly able pupils in industrialized societies, but for pupils of average intellectual growth the early stages of formal operational thought are seen, at least in their application in formal school-type tasks, by about 16 years of age. The Geneva School does not say a great deal about the period immediately prior to the onset of formal operational thought (Inhelder and Piaget, 1958). It does seem, however, that new intellectual skills are slowly developing in the preformal operational period that seem to be necessary but are not in themselves sufficient for the elaboration of formal operations.

One of these skills seems to be the ability to weigh the evidence. To study this, Matalon (1962) carried out the following experiment. A red light and a green light were shown individually to each child, each light having to be inspected independently. The child was told, "Whenever the red light is on, the green light is on." The three questions that followed asked him in essence what would be the state of the other light when, "green is off," "red is off," and "green is on." If, to the first of these questions the child replied "green off implies red is off," he is correct, but we cannot be sure of his reasoning. The critical questions are the last two, for here the answer cannot be given since insufficient information is available. Matalon's study suggests that up to 11 years of age children tend to make the inference one way, generally in the direction of symmetry, thus treating implication as if it were an equivalence. Up to 11 years of age at least, pupils do not grasp that there is insufficient evidence to yield a definitive answer and they make a premature closure. In essence, they find great difficulty in weighing the evidence.

After 11 years of age there is slow improvement in the ability of the individual to accept lack of closure or weigh the evidence, but many adults and able university students fail to do so in a variety of situations. This is supported by the work of Shapiro and O'Brien (1970), and also by O'Brien (1972). In these studies, pupils over a wide age range, including older students, were given verbal tasks such as: "If the car is shiny, it is fast. The car is shiny. Is it fast?" (*modus ponens*). Although this form is easy at all ages, the contrapositive is more difficult, the inverse form much more so, and the converse form very difficult indeed. The relevance of implication to science teaching is illustrated by the work of Kuhn and Brannock (1977) involving a problem of controls in biology.

Another skill that appears to be necessary for more advanced strategies of thinking is that which enables a pupil to move from being able to handle a two-variable system to being able to handle a three-or-more-variable system. Even in a simple system there must be two variables, e.g., heights and speeds, or amount of moisture in the soil and yield, or there would be no system at all. It is, of course, only a convention that causes us to regard one as a dependent and the other as an independent variable. When we come to a three-variable system, there is now some dependent variable like "yield" covarying with amount of sunlight and amount of moisture. The ability to work with three or more variables as distinct from two variables, heralds a skill that seems to be a component of formal operational thought. The experiment by Inhelder and Piaget (1958) involving the inclined plane illustrates the point that has just been made.

Finally, there is an increasing ability to reach a third level of abstraction, the first having been reached at around 21 months of age and the second at about 7 years. At the third level, pupils can dissociate themselves from intuitable referents. Thus, while at 13 years of age it may well be possible to get an ordinary pupil to appreciate the properties of a mathematical group by suitably rotating an envelope, he will be perhaps 17 years of age before he can understand group structure without this concrete aid. It is this need to move to this third level of abstraction that delays the pupil's grasp of the conservation of displacement volume. When a piece of plasticine is placed in water and the former's shape changed (with no compression), the volume of the plasticine has to be dissociated from the plasticine itself before displacement volume can be conserved. Again, when objects of the same dimensions but differing weights are placed in water, weights and volumes have to be dissociated from the objects themselves and considered in their own right before displacement volume is conserved. Finally, weights and volumes of objects inserted in water have to be dissociated from the size of the containing vessel before the amount of water displaced for a given sized object is conserved regardless of the dimensions of the container.

Again, an intuitive notion of density is available at the level of advanced concrete operational thought, for it arises out of the idea that some objects are heavy or light for their size. However, it is not understood analytically until the advent of formal operations, for the pupil has to construct the notion of an equivalent amount of water and this cannot be derived from perceptible or imageable experience. The volume of water equal to the volume of an immersed solid has no visible contours; it can only be conceptualized by detachment from concrete referents.

6. Formal Operational Thought and Understanding Science

Inhelder and Piaget (1958, p. 282) suggest that the pupil has to forge new thinking skills to handle certain kinds of problems which he is certain to meet. For example, experience shows that most heavy objects sink in water, but some do not although some light objects do. Thus, the solution to a problem may result from several concomitant factors such as linear lengths and speeds, or a causal factor may be masked by several noncausal but concomitantly varying factors as may be the case in the pendulum experiment. Sooner or later the pupil meets a multifactorial situation when variables are mixed, and concrete operational thought cannot provide a solution. This issue has, of course, already been raised in our discussion of three or more variable systems or multiple interacting systems; the ability to handle such systems is seemingly an important ingredient for formal operational thinking, although not always required in problems for which formal operational thought is necessary.

For Inhelder and Piaget the essential property of formal thought resides in the reversal of direction, so to speak, between reality and possibility. While the pupil at the stage of concrete operational thought makes some simple extension of the present in the direction of the possible, formal operational thought begins the other way round. A hypothesis is elaborated implying that certain relationships exist, deductions from the hypothesis are made, and fresh data checked to see if they are consonant with the deductions. Thus, formal operational thought is characterized as hypothetico-deductive in nature, a type of thinking often employed by the scientist.

Again, since formal thought does not always deal with objects directly but often with verbal statements involving objects, in the Genevan view a new type of thinking, namely, propositional logic, is imposed on the logic of classes and relations relevant to these objects. Thus, formal operational thought is based on a logic of all possible combina-tions, whether the latter arise in experimental work or in verbally pre-sented problems. This combinatorial ability certainly needs inner verbal support, although the essential power of propositional logic lies not in such support but in the combinatorial power which allows the individual to set up more complex anticipations, in short, to feed reality into a set of hypotheses compatible with the data. It must be realized, however, that there is more to thinking than logic *per se*.

Two points may be made at this juncture. First, adolescents do not usually elaborate, systematically and spontaneously, all possible combi-nations. More recent studies have not confirmed that persons elaborate spontaneously the sixteen binary combinations of propositional logic as Inhelder and Piaget (1958) claim in the experiment involving the role of invisible magnetization. It has also been asked if propositional logic is even less valuable with respect to biology than the physical sciences. Second, much criticism has been made of Piaget for using propositional logic to model adolescent thought. It has been said that the other aspect of modern logic, namely, the predicate calculus, or the more complex modal logics, might have been employed with better effect.

Formal operational thought may also be considered as a system of second-degree operations. At the level of concrete operational thought we have already seen that the individual can elaborate first-degree oper-ations because he can structure relations between the elements of firsthand reality. With the advent of formal operations he can structure relations between relations or second-degree relations. This is seen in proportions, since in these there must be a recognition of the equiva-lence of two ratios, each of which is itself a first-degree operation. Again, as Inhelder and Piaget remind us, propositional logic itself pre-supposes second-degree operations because interpropositional oper-ations are carried out on statements whose intrapropositional content consists of class and relational operations. Or, as Inhelder and Piaget also indicate, when the individual is considering one hypothesis and its consequences in the pendulum experiment, he must also keep in mind alternative hypotheses and their consequences, so involving once more second-degree operations. Looking upon formal operational thought as second-degree operations is very helpful at times in science.

Finally, we reiterate the importance of the ability to move forward to third-level abstractions. In formal operational thinking, there is no longer the need to employ intuitable referents. That is not to deny that the individual who is able to work at the level of formal operations does not, some of the time, employ concrete situations and/or images to sup-port his thinking.

Shayer (1972a) also categorized the responses of individuals to the tasks set by Inhelder and Piaget (1958) when the individuals were showing evidence of formal operational thought. The headings under which responses were classified were the same as those used for the concrete operational period. In the early part of the formal operational period, the individual will

> show more interest in looking for *why:* see the point of making hypotheses if simplified to one variable, but cannot perform the simplification systematically himself: be able to establish causative necessity: use or perceive metric proportion in a concrete situation: make simple deductions from a model if the use of the latter is explained.

During the latter part of the formal operations period, the pupil will

> have an interest in checking a "why" solution: knows that in a system of several variables he must "hold all other things equal" while investigating one possible variable at a time: formulate abstract relations: use direct and inverse proportionality for both perceiving and formulating relationships: actively search for an explanatory model or extend one that is given.

With the development of the latter stages of formal operational thought, the pupil is capable of going beyond the organization of the surface features of reality. His understanding of science now involves:

1. The elaboration of concepts that may be categorized as second-degree operations and that are also at the third level of abstraction, e.g., momentum, latent heat, photosynthesis
2. The precise systematization of concepts in relation to one another, e.g., force, work, energy, mole
3. The construction of reference models to explain observed reality and the ability and willingness to shift from model to reality and vice versa; also the ability to manipulate relations as in calculations (thus involving mathematical concepts) without reference to either

7. An Analysis of Some Scientific Concepts

Piaget and his colleagues have examined in detail the development of many concepts relevant to science that are typically considered as first-order relations as far as their treatment in school is concerned. Such studies have extended into the fields of number, space, geometry, time, speed, and they will not be discussed further here. Rather, the attempt is being made to analyze some concepts that are met in high-school science curricula, and to see how the thinking skills involved in their understanding can be considered from the standpoint of Piagetian theory.

In order to have a good grasp of momentum at the General Certificate of Education (G.C.E.) "O" level examination in physics in England, there must be an analytic understanding that necessarily relates the concept to other concepts, such as force and time, in a precise manner. It has been shown at Leeds that such an understanding necessitates the ability to tackle seven broad types of tasks that can be arranged in order of difficulty. The simplest type of task needs only the ability to work $p = mv$ and simple calculations by rote. For this, the pupil requires only flexible concrete operational thought, because he merely finds the product of two variables which he takes as weight and speed, both first-order relations. The next most difficult type of task can also be worked by the use of flexible concrete operational thought, but pupil performance falls off rapidly thereafter since the later types of task require formal operational thought. Thus, the third most difficult task involves $p = $ constant type problem (excluding the class $p = 0$) together with the notion of inverse proportion so that if $mv = $ constant, $m = 1/v$. In the most difficult type of problem, the pupil must tackle vector p revealed as in problems involving $p = $ constant in rebound, and in calculations of p in rebound.

A principal components analysis of the data revealed three components which neatly partition the tasks into those that (1) could be solved by concrete operational thought; (2) involve the conservation of momentum law as it applies to linear momentum; and (3) involve the application of knowledge about the vector nature of momentum to the particular case of a collision when a reversal of direction takes place for one of the colliding bodies.

Next, consider some rather broad questions in biology. If we question a pupil regarding the necessity of transport mechanisms with reference to the surface area/volume ratio, we find answers of varying quality. For example, if the pupil only appreciates that any multicellular organism, whether a large organism or not, requires some means of getting food to the distant cells, only advanced concrete operational thought is needed. But if the notion of surface area/volume ratio can be used to explain the necessity for transport mechanisms, formal thought is demanded. Again, let us suppose we question the pupil on the function of meristematic cells in the growth pattern of plants. Only concrete operational thought is involved if the pupil shows only an understanding that wherever buds exist, growth results. But if his reply involves an understanding of the meristematic cells in the bud giving rise by cell modification to different tissues of the plant so that the bud can become a complete plant, then advanced formal thought is needed. A third example might question the general factors involved in the growth of an organism. If the pupil shows only an intuitive notion of some of the factors affecting growth but can offer no explanation as to how they act and interact, only concrete operational thinking is required. If he understands, however, that the genetic makeup of an organism is one factor limiting growth, and in addition can explain how other factors necessary for growth interact, then clearly the pupil can handle multiple interacting systems, and advanced formal operational thought is necessary. These examples help us to see pupil difficulties more clearly by using Piaget's conceptual framework.

His developmental psychology also helps the science teacher to understand why the logical order in which concepts are introduced does not necessarily indicate their relative difficulty. This is true in both the physical and biological sciences. For example, a concept of temperature is available to the pupil of 10 or 11 years of age because he has experienced differing sensations of hotness since birth; the idea of mercury expanding when warmed is intuitable (milk boils over) and the concept of measurement is understood. Essentially the term temperature, as used by pupils up to G.C.E. "O" level physics, involves a first-degree relation. But the concept of heat or thermal capacity is different, although the pupil of 10 to 11 years of age can certainly be helped to acquire an intuitive notion of this related to concrete referents. But unless he is outstandingly able, a formal analytic grasp of the term will be beyond him, for a formal conception will involve heat capacity as

$$Q = mc(T_1 - T_2)$$

where m is the mass, c the specific heat capacity, and $T_1 - T_2$ the temperature change. This involves a second-degree relation and third-level abstraction, for first-degree relations are now related precisely and without concrete referent. Again, the concept of entropy also involves a second-degree relation and third-level abstraction, although it is a more complex or higher order concept than heat, since a change in entropy in any system is given as

$$\Delta s = \int_{T_1}^{T_2} \frac{mc_p dT}{T}$$

in which c_p is the specific heat at constant pressure.

However, Piaget's developmental psychology makes clear why the more difficult step is from temperature to heat, from concrete to formal operational thought.

Karplus (1973) has indicated that, while the application of the ideal gas laws necessitates formal thought, there are aspects of atomic theory (which are taught later) which have a language that can be learned and used at the level of flexible concrete operational thought: for example, the conservation of atoms in a simple reaction. Finally, although a pupil with advanced concrete operational thought might well learn by rote that 1 mole of any gas at STP occupies 22.4 liters, it would not be possible for him to work the following problem unless he has been specifically trained on the precise type: If 1 liter of a gas weighs 1.52 g at STP, find the mass of 1 mole of the gas.

It was shown above that within second-degree relations there is a gradation of difficulty, although there have been few studies of this in science to date. One such study by Archenhold (1975) showed that there was little difference with respect to difficulty of understanding work done in a uniform field, work done in a nonuniform field, and work done as change in potential energy, but a grasp of electrostatic and gravitational potential was considerably more difficult. Incidentally, this study clearly indicated that some pupils work examples without much understanding of the concepts involved; presumably they recognize the example type.

Piaget (1975) summarized many detailed studies of the growth of the relation between physical causality and operational thought. His conclusion is that at every level the development of the understanding of causality proceeds through interacting with the development of thought. The two developments essentially aid and abet one another, there being only a one-way action on special and temporary occasions. His thesis is defended using the results of a large number of experiments on many diverse topics drawn from the general area of physics. In Piaget's book, there is much confirmation for the type of analysis expressed in this chapter: on pages 94–99, there is a discussion concerning the concept of work, in which it is maintained that this concept can only be elaborated when it is recognized that there are always two forces involved. One is the passive force or the one that is displaced, the other, the active force or the one that is used to displace it. In addition, there is the problem of the composition of a force and its displacement in terms of distance and often direction; for Piaget this involves a second-degree relation and is equivalent to a vector in psychological complexity. Now there must be a composition between this relation—already a second-order one—and the active force making possible the displacement of a passive one. Thus, for Piaget, work is a third-level abstraction but a higher order concept than vector, which is why its understanding comes later.

8. Some Difficulties with Piaget's Theory with Respect to Science Curricula

In considering curricula, one must recognize that the term *logical thinking* has often been employed synonymously with intellectual functioning more generally. This confusion can obscure the nature of many problems in science and mathematics, apart from those in other areas of the curriculum. If we define a reasoning task as logical in the strict sense such that deduction from given premises *alone* is sufficient to provide the solution to the problem and no further evidence is needed, then many tasks in science have a logical component, but they cannot be solved by strict logic alone. A background knowledge of facts is often necessary, while inductive reasoning and hypothesis construction are necessary. Logic alone, as defined above, does not enable the seven-year-old to distinguish even which relationships are transitive and which are not. When he is told that if rod A is longer than rod B, and rod B is longer than rod C, experience informs him that rod A is longer than rod C. But if he is told that A goes swimming with B, and B goes swimming with C, it does not follow that A goes swimming with C. He learns that "is longer than" carries over, "goes swimming with," does not, but logic alone (as just defined) does not show the transitivity or nontransitivity of these instances. Thus, in Piagetian type experiments, as in science more widely, the term logical thinking indicates intellectual functioning in a wider sense. Problems in science certainly have a logical component (as defined) but they also have components not strictly logical. However, although Piaget's broader concept of logic may be difficult to fathom, it is not quite as vague as the previous sentence might suggest (cf. Papert, 1963).

It is important to bear in mind that a number of problems remain when using Piaget's theoretical system in relation to science curricula. Take, for instance, the problem of stages. It might be inferred from what has been said that intellectual development is discontinuous rather than continuous. This is not necessarily so. Piaget has himself indicated that the number of identifiable intermediate steps is restricted by the limitation of the research techniques used. He thus concludes (e.g., Piaget, 1960) that the discovery of intermediate stages can never be so complete or exhaustive that we shall be able to decide unambiguously whether continuity or discontinuity of the phenomenon being considered can be regarded as absolute or relative. In keeping with this, he adopts Bertalanffy's notion that within an open system the phases of relative stability, like the concrete and formal operational stages, are punctuated by unstable phases of transition. Nevertheless, the stages of relative stability remain until conditions bring about further progress. It is in this light that the continuity–discontinuity issue might be regarded in relation to science curricula at the present time.

When a pupil has reached a given stage of intellectual development, it cannot be assumed that the strategies of thought appropriate to that stage will necessarily be invoked. Some tasks do not even demand the use of concrete operational thought. At other times, contextual issues are involved when attempting to solve a problem, and Piaget's developmental psychology can hardly allow for these.

It has long been known that familiarity with the content of a problem aids the pupil in eliciting the strategies of formal operational thought. The more facile he is with the relevant first-degree operations, the more readily will he elaborate second-degree operations. Again, Piaget's developmental theory cannot take into account a pupil's beliefs and preconceptions with which he approaches a task, and the effect these have on his thinking. When preconceptions are at variance with experimental findings, the adolescent is likely, at first, to put his faith in the former and not in logic, although he may well have the requisite logical thinking skills at his disposal. Indeed, it is not until he becomes experienced in seeing connections between phenomena that he is likely to reject his preconceptions and have faith in scientific methods (cf. Driver, 1973). Further, as Driver clearly shows, the language and forms of the latter may be quite familiar to the student before they are used with confidence as a natural preference.

Then there is the question of the pupil's comprehension of the language used by the teachers or experimenter. Within a given culture or subculture, assuming a developed society, there is no doubt that the language used makes some difference to the pupil's understanding and to the quality of his response. But it is equally certain that language is not all-important. For example, one may pour the contents of each of two identical soda bottles into two glasses of different size and shape, giving a glass to each of two five-year-olds without saying a word. When the soda was in the bottles each child seemed content, but after pouring, one child may complain "He has more than me."

However, the meaning that a particular task has for an individual is probably of great importance in some instances, less so in others. Many studies have shown that even the nature of the materials used in a specific task can affect pupil response to the task. Again, the meaning a given task in science (or other area of the curriculum) has for an individual depends on both his intellectual growth and on his sociocultural background. Luria (1966) made the point that higher mental functions are complex organized *functional systems* depending very much on social experience. There is no evidence today that there are cultural groups *per se* who lack the ability to categorize, abstract, or reason, although there are great individual differences between persons within such a group. Nevertheless, background experience may affect the way in which functional systems are organized for different purposes (Cole and Scribner, 1974), and thus we may get differences in performance across tasks that have the same structure but different meanings for the pupil. Piaget's developmental theory cannot easily cover this point.

The degree of structure of a problem is also of importance. When a task is loosely structured, then all the assumptions are not stated, the variables are not easily identified, or the universes of discourse of all the variables are not stated. In these circumstances, the individual must bring his own assumptions and universe of discourse drawn from his own experience. These may well structure the problem from the individuals viewpoint, but, if the assumptions are incorrect, the inference will be erroneous. Reynolds (1967), for example, set the following task to high school pupils:

> If all the men who are on Committee A are put on Committee B, which of the following statements are true, false, or cannot be decided:
>
> Every man who is on B is on A
> Any man who is not on B cannot be on A
> Every woman who is not on B is not on A

Some of the assumptions made by the pupils were:

> No woman is on both A and B
> There are no women on A
> There are no women on A or B
> Some women on B can be on A

Thus, although the individual may give the task more structure, gross errors in terms of the standard responses may be introduced. Piaget's developmental psychology does not readily deal with the introduction of incorrect assumptions in this type of problem, compared with the experiments of Inhelder and Piaget (1958) in which the individual had a far better opportunity to rectify wrong assumptions by direct manipulation of the variables.

The results of a number of studies also suggest that very often the adolescent does not recognize a hypothesis, as such, does not systematically construct hypotheses, and even when they are recognized or constructed, are not tested; whereas, in Piagetian theory, hypotheses should be constructed and tested together at the level of formal operational thought. Indeed, the adolescent should be able to exhaust the possibilities in a combinatorial analysis. Alas, there is much evidence that individuals do not do this over a wide range of problems (cf. Wason and Johnson-Laird, 1972). It will be seen then that there may well be a discrepancy between the response the individual is capable of giving and what he actually gives because of his interpretation of the situation.

We have already indicated that critics have suggested that Piaget might have used the predicate calculus, or modal logic, rather than the propositional calculus in order to model adolescent thinking. There are, of course, many logics, a logic being an axiomatization of the principles of valid inference.

In everyday life, an implication usually involves a cause and effect relation such as, "If it rains today I shall not play tennis," and it is generally without meaning to combine unrelated propositions into an implication such as, "If it is fine today, then $2 \times 5 = 10$." The person in everyday affairs wants to be able to infer the truth of the consequent from that of the antecedent. However, compared with natural thought in everyday life, the propositional calculus often combines quite unrelated propositions, in which no cause and effect are assumed to exist, into an implication. A set of rules, given in the logical truth table, interrelates the truth or falsity of propositions and the inferences made from them. The validity of the inferences are, of course, quite independent of the content or meaning of the propositions. An implication is meaningful if it is true or false according to the rules, not whether it is sensible from the viewpoint of everyday life.

However, in normal life, the individual wants to understand events and to reason about them, for the world contains many events in which cause and effect are clearly discernible. He may well be able to use truth-functional relations and formal deduction, but is unlikely to do so frequently (Wason and Johnson-Laird 1972). Normally, he will make assumptions about causal and temporal relationships which experience has taught him are sensible in relation to a given situation, so the meaning which the premises have for him are important. Thus, in everyday life, reasoning seems to depend upon relevant experience and on a number of skills not capable of being adequately characterized by the propositional calculus. True, the Genevans have admitted that formal operational thought could only be expected to be elicited by a suitable challenging deductive problem, but overall they say little about the relevance of a problem to a person's experience. In these circumstances it seems that if we confine the application of formal operational thought to problems in which a causal and logical analysis coincide, as is the case in the experiments of Inhelder and Piaget (1958), Piaget's model for formal operational thought fits individuals' responses much better. In science, a causal and logical analysis do generally coincide so that the model should have some relevance. But the forms of interaction of causal and logical analyses in Piaget's sense of those terms is a complex, unresolved problem.

In conclusion, reference is again made to the question of Piaget's notion of *structure d'ensemble*. There is certainly evidence that in pupils in kindergarten through Grade 2 the development of classificatory abilities may lag behind the development of relational abilities (cf. Hooper and Sipple, 1975) contrary to orthodox Piagetian theory. However, in pupils between ages 9 and 12, the evidence is not as certain. Hooper and Dihoff (1975) suggest from a study of multidimensional scaling of Piagetian task performance in this age range that the theoretical position of developmental synchrony cannot be abandoned. At the level of formal operational thought, however, the position remains unclear in the sense that even at age 17 or 18 there is no sure evidence as yet for a unitary concept. It may be that formal operational thought is best thought of as a number of formal operational skills (e.g., propositional logic, proportional reasoning) used by individuals when they are suitably motivated and appropriately cued into the task.

9. The Problem of the Existing Secondary Science Tradition

The secondary science tradition, as we know it, has considered none of the constraints hitherto mentioned. Its aim was the inculcation of the essential facts and principles of each science. No learning model was used, but by implication it was one of accommodation by the student to the course. The evolution of this art has been empirical, and limited to avoiding gross mismatches between the conceptual demand of the course and the abilities of the students. By such empiricism in the 1920s and 1930s, school physics, chemistry, and biology for the 13- to 17-year-olds in Europe and the elective high school science for the 16- to 18-year-olds in the United States, came out remarkably similar. But this need not be taken as confirming suitability. Bloom has described this evolution (Bloom *et al.*, 1971):

> The culmination of the public education system has been conceived of as entrance into or completion of a university program. Thus, of 100 students entering into formal education . . . 5 . . . were regarded as fitted by nature or

nurture for the rigors of higher education. Little interest was felt by educators in the 95% to be dropped at the different stages of the education system.

To empiricism, no scientist can object, but the "hard" scientists, still to be found, who pride themselves on ignoring educational theory, need reminding that their own empiricism is a highly structured and informed one, and no lesser sophistication can be tolerated in the science of science education. The empiricism that Bloom describes has led in Europe to a secondary education confined to the top 15 to 25 % of the population, and, when the traditional science courses are applied to them, it is found, as though it were a fact of nature, that only about a quarter of even such a select population as this can "really think." Later, it will be argued that this judgment is merely a social artifact of the school system: for the present, the quality of the science taught requires comment.

Although science is a technique of discovery with chance favoring the trained mind, it has unfortunately been taught in universities as though its theories were a body of received fact. So massive and ever-increasing is the bulk of each science, that the role of the school course has been essentially of apprenticeship to what is done in the university. Thus, the chemistry textbook came to resemble the Latin grammar of an earlier educational world, for this would be the most economical way of reducing the university teaching load.

The lesser objection to the tradition is that it falsified understanding. Shayer (1972b) found that the traditional science course utilized concepts of the level of early formal operational (Stage 3A) thought. It is inevitable that empiricism would produce this result for the top 20% of the 14- and 15-year-olds. Yet, the concepts introduced, like those of quantitative analysis or kinetic/atomic theory in chemistry, and simple harmonic motion and the interconnection of Newton's laws in physics, required for understanding the fullest subtlety that Piaget describes in any of his chapters relating to late formal operational thinking (Stage 3B). Thus, generations of students who "didn't get it" were taught mnemonics like $m_1v_1 = m_2v_2$ and algorithms with which to solve Newton's Laws problems. Perhaps it would have been better to avoid evolving this tradition of pseudoscience and leave difficult thinking to pupils of an age and ability high enough to cope with it, or to teach physics in a more qualitative manner.

The greater objection to the tradition is that it falsified the spirit in which students were to work and learn. Both these objections contain a paradox: it is being asserted that the traditional courses are suited ideally only for the top 5% of the population, and yet objections are also raised that the level at which understanding was pitched did not do justice to the concepts involved. This paradox disappears only when the process of science is distinguished from its body of theory. It may very well be that to teach the process of science in the context of elementary chemical thermodynamics requires a student population of the top 2% in the age range 18 to 20. Yet experience of the SCIS program in the United States and the Science 5–13 materials in Great Britain has shown that science process, in suitable contexts, can be handled by average 10-year-olds. If a context is chosen in which understanding of the process of science involves an intellectual level beyond that to which most of the students have developed, teachers will not be able to provide a process approach by which their students can experience the spirit of scientific inquiry and exploration. Instead, they will have to spoonfeed their students with algorithms and cram their memories. Thus, a false world is created in which theory, that is, useful metaphors, become treated as fact. Perhaps a 15-year-old is safe in asserting that water is H_2O, or that "space is an empty three-dimensional continuum in which an object maintains constant velocity unless acted on by a force," only if his general process of education has shown him the limits within which such correlating concepts are useful. That it is possible to choose contexts, such that students even of early secondary age are allowed to develop their judgments to the extent to which the theory they use is valid, is shown by the Australian Science Education Programme materials to be discussed later.

So far, mention has been made only of the older tradition of secondary science teaching. What of the new secondary curricula of the 1960s? Both the American and the British examples can be said to improve the quality of understanding. Chemstudy, PSSC, and BSSC materials for the 15- to 18-year-olds in the United States, and Nuffield O-level courses for the 11- to 16-year-olds in England and Wales have in common that the learning experiences are structured so that the concepts introduced are understood in depth. Although it cannot be claimed that Piaget's work had any influence on these, their strategy would surely meet with his approval. In British courses, the relevant practical or demonstrated work comes before the concept that order or elucidate such work; in American courses, the practical or demonstrated work goes alongside the theory. Thus, for the falsely ordered world of the traditional textbook is substituted something of the messiness of experimental reality, and the concepts are seen to be justified by their usefulness, rather than as descriptions of the work as it is. The virtue of these courses turns out to be also their vice. A generation of highly intelligent students will already be clearing the universities whose school experience of science will have been more favorable to their ultimate future as research scientists. Yet, this will have been obtained at the expense of increasing the level of intellectual demand in the content of the school courses themselves, thereby reducing the proportion of the population that has benefited from the change. Indeed, the growing elitism of secondary school science is documented in Stake *et al.* (1978).

These new courses have in common with the traditional ones that the actual activity of being a scientist is the ultimate end in view. In the traditional courses, this end is, by implication, deferred until the end of a first-degree university course. In the post-Sputnik and Nuffield courses this activity is, as far as possible, to be enjoyed from the beginning. Thus, either form of the existing secondary science tradition makes the practice of university science the justification of their being included in the school curriculum. The new courses do this better, but at the expense of producing a self-contained world of pure science: they come from no vision of what balanced place science activity should have within the total spectrum of any person's life, nor from any model of human development in adolescence from childhood to young adulthood. It is as though, after deciding that some musical experience is good for everyone, schools were to give everyone a training suitable for a future composer or concert soloist.

For some of the assertations hitherto made, evidence is needed. For the British Nuffield courses, for the 11- to 16-year-old group, this was done by a painstaking analysis for each experiment or lesson in a course of the Piagetian level of conceptual demand (Shayer, 1972a, 1974; Ingle and Shayer, 1971). The implied experimental test was to match the level of conceptual demand of the course, for example, for the 13-year-olds, with the proportion of the school population capable of thinking at that level. If the level of demand was early formal Stage 3A only and the course was designed for the top 20% of the population, then, if the proportion of the population at 13 thinking at the Stage 3A level or above was 20 %, the course would be well adapted to that population. If the latter proportion was only 5 %, the assumption would be that about three quarters of the target population would not cope with the course.

The analysis of conceptual demand was an analogy of case-law. Two taxonomies were drawn up. The first was a behavioral description of early concrete Stage 2A, late concrete Stage 2B, early formal Stage 3A and late formal operational thinking Stage 3B performance for each of the chapters in *The Growth of Logical Thinking.* If the lesson material was directly or by analogy similar to one of the chapters, the level of demand would be estimated by matching with one of the levels described by Piaget. The other taxonomy has been referred to earlier in this chapter.

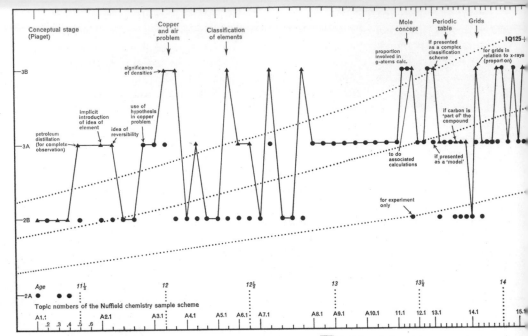

Figure 1.   Conceptual demands in Nuffield O-level chemistry.

By abstracting from Inhelder and Piaget's descriptions under five headings, Shayer produced behavioral descriptions of Stages 2A, 2B, 3A, and
3B performance. These headings were "investigating style," "quality of
interest," "the reason is," "relationships," and "the use of model as
theory." Where the lesson material was far removed from any of the test
situations in *The Growth of Logical Thinking*, the second taxonomy was
used for matching. Since the Nuffield courses in chemistry, physics, and
biology were described in detail for each of the five years for which they
would be taught, it was then possible to construct for each course a
diagram showing the variation of level of conceptual demand with the
age of the pupil studying the course. This is shown in Figure 1 for the
chemistry course. (The diagrams for physics and biology have a similar
developmental pattern.) As can be seen, the level of demand in the first
two years (11 to 13) is mainly late concrete or early formal. But, as the
courses develop the interconnections of concepts become more important. Thus, on the diagrams, the level of thinking required for the pupil
to show interest in the lesson material is sometimes shown at a different
level from that required to see the connection between that lesson and
the ones to come. The course structure on the diagram is shown by the
path through the latter points, and it will be seen that in the third year

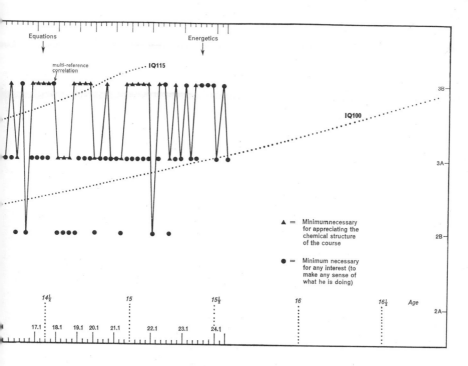

there is an abrupt steepening of conceptual demand, about half-way through, to the Stage 3B level. Whether the course, then, is suitable will depend on whether its target population is capable of late formal thinking at 13½.

No criticism is here intended either of the logic of the course structure or of the strategy by which experimental experience is related to chemical theory. This course, indeed, is already a classic among curriculum models. In Stage 1 those experiences of chemistry that can be conceptualized in the semiquantitative schemes of classification and seriation characteristic of late concrete operational thinking are introduced. Thus reactivity, series of elements, oxidation and reduction, acidity and alkalinity in terms of the pH scale are introduced before any work in formulas and equations or in terms of atoms is attempted. At the same level of treatment, changes of state are experienced in enough detail to give an experimental definition of the differences between chemical changes, and reversible physical changes. Then comes the problem that confronts anyone attempting to construct a chemistry curriculum: at what point and how will the concept of "an-element-within-a-compound" be introduced? In the Nuffield course, as in Chemstudy, this is done by the mole concept. The gram-atom is shown to convert the apparently arbitrary reacting weights of elements to simple whole-number relationships. Thereafter, the mole concept is used to make connections between latent heats of evaporation of related substances and, later still, to impose whole-number relationships on reacting quantities of compounds and hence establish a rational basis for chemical equations. The virtue of this approach is that formulas and equations are deferred until the pupil can understand their essential experimental basis, rather than treat them as a variant of pencil and paper algebra. Moreover, the whole of Stage 2 is presented as an interplay of three major concepts: the mole, the periodic table, and the fine structure of compounds as explaining their physical properties. It was the intention of the curriculum developers that, even if the pupil did no more chemistry beyond the age of 16 and forgot all the chemistry facts he had learned, what would remain would be a feel for what a scientific theory was, how it differs from a dogmatic assertion, and how experimental investigation and theory are related. In this way, he would be in a better position to judge scientific evidence; in this way, he would get the best introduction to further training in science if this was the direction he would decide to go.

These intentions are clearly admirable. But for what proportion of students in this age-range is the realization of these intentions possible by the context of this course? As the first part of a five-year research program Concepts in Secondary Mathematics and Science (CSMS), based at Chelsea College in the University of London, an experimental measure was made of the proportion of boys and girls in the age range from 9 to 14 showing thinking performance characteristic of the four Piagetian levels referred to (Shayer, Küchemann, and Wylam, 1976). To obtain a representative sample of British children, it was necessary to test about 2,000 in each year of age, making a total sample of 10,000. Cognitive representativeness was obtained by choosing from each year-group a sample of schools such that the distribution of the children's performance on a psychometric test standardized by the National Foundation of Educational Research (Calvert Non-Verbal DH) matched the standardizing population used by the NFER for calibrating the test. In order to measure the whole range of thinking to be found in such a wide age-range, it was necessary to develop measurement techniques from preconceptual thinking right through to late formal operational thinking.

For this purpose three tasks were devised: the first went from preoperational thinking to Stage 2B, and was based on *The Child's Conception of Space*; the second went from Stages 2A to 3A, based on *The Child's Construction of Quantities*, and tested the development of the analytic concept of density from the primitive concept of "bigness"; and the third was the pendulum problem, from Chapter 4 of *The Growth of Logical Thinking* and measured in the range Stages 2B to 3B. In order to carry out such a measurement on so many children, a novel form of test, called a Class-Task, was used. As far as possible, the original interview situation and apparatus used by Piaget and his co-workers was demonstrated to a class by the teacher, and a series of questions was asked. These questions were repeated on the students' individual response sheets and were assessed by grouping the items according to the Piagetian level required for a correct response. The student's level would be the highest group in which he still achieved at least two-thirds success. In this way the curves shown in Figure 2 were obtained. If these are now compared with the conceptual analysis of the Nuffield O-level chemistry course, it will be seen that a Stage 3B level of demand by the age of 14 is likely to be appropriate only for the top 5% of the pupil population as a whole. For comparison, the traditional British O-level courses in science were designed for the selective school population, which is approximately the

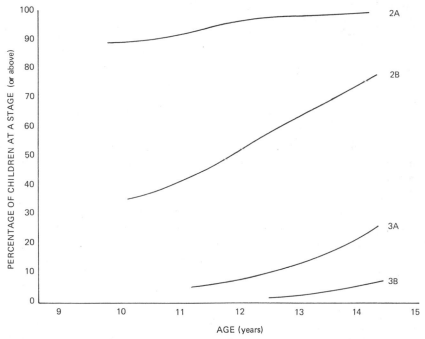

Figure 2.   Proportion of children at different Piagetian stages in a representative British child population: 2A = Early Concrete; 2B = Late Concrete; 3A = Early Formal; 3B = Late Formal.

top 20%. Since the level of conceptual demand in them was Stage 3A, from the age of 13½ to 16½, and since 20% of the population as a whole is showing Stage 3A thinking by the age of 14, it follows that the traditional courses were well-adapted to their target population. In improving the intellectual quality of the science course, the British Nuffield teams had at the same time stiffened the conceptual demand so that their ends could be achieved in the context of chemistry only by about the top quarter of the target selective school population. A similar observation applied to the Nuffield O-level physics and biology courses.

It appears, therefore, that the empiricism with which our educational systems produce their attempted solutions may not always guarantee a match between course and students. With hindsight, the reason now seems to be the classic pitfall of the sampling theory. There is no reason to doubt the success of the Nuffield courses for the classes on which they were tested in the trial schools. The problem is: undoubtedly empiricism in the hands of experienced subject specialist teachers will produce good curricula for the classes which they are accustomed to teach, but how does one then know that the trial population is characteristic of the target population for which the curriculum is designed? Put in this way the question would not be difficult to test experimentally, but such experimental tests were not a feature of the curriculum development of the 1960s. The 1974/1975 CSMS study (Shayer et al., 1976) shows how a mismatch may have occurred in the case of the Nuffield courses. It appears that the actual spread of ability in the secondary population is far wider than anyone in secondary education imagined. If one assumes that 7½, 11½, and 16 are the ages at which the average child attains Stages 2A, 2B, and 3A, respectively, it follows from Figure 2 that a cross-section of the 13-year-old population will consist of 20% at the level of the average 16-year-old or above, 45% between the level of the average 16- and 11½-year-old, and 30% between the level of the average 11½ and 7½-year-old. Even in the target populations for the Nuffield courses, the spread is wide enough to be a problem. From Figure 2 it can be seen that the gap between Stages 3A and 3B population growth curves is about three years. Thus, a course that fits well the top 5% at 13½ will not fit the 80th percentile until 16½, if the essential concepts are Stage 3B in demand. In this way, the gap between the very able and average selective school pupil was underestimated, by the assumption that the population was fairly homogenous.

It therefore seems that the empirical approach could never have been a satisfactory method of curriculum development for the secondary school student, at least not in activities with a severe conceptual demand such as science and mathematics. Such a test of match between curriculum and target population requires an appropriate experimental test of its own validity. That test is possible within the methodology already referred to. The same class tasks that served to measure the Piagetian levels of the 9- to 14-year-old population can serve to measure the levels of the pupils in a class about to be taught a well-defined course. In response to the demand for a general science course for the first two years of British secondary education (11½ to 13½), parts of the first two years work in the separate Nuffield O-level courses in chemistry, physics, and biology were integrated to make a combined science course. This consists of 10 sections, each of about six weeks work, with section headings such as How Living Things Begin, or Earth. An analysis of each lesson within a section can give a diagram of the rises and falls of conceptual demand within the six-week period. Such an analysis, combined with the class-task measure, allows one to predict which concepts within a section each pupil should be able to understand and which should be beyond his understanding. The prediction of failure or success for each student can then be correlated with their understanding, or otherwise, of each concept as revealed by their performance on a science examination constructed to test for understanding rather than rote success.

This test was carried out in 1976–1977 as part of the CSMS program, and is an extension of Piagetian studies to the field of formative evaluation (even though this application is summative rather than formative). It has the interesting feature of being potentially applicable rather widely to curriculum development in Western nations (Shayer, 1978). Since the British population of early secondary students studied by CSMS was fully representative, and since there is no reason to expect the spread of mental ability in the 9- to 14-year-old British student to be much different from any of the larger Western nations, any conclusions about the limits within which science and mathematics curricula should operate for students of each year should be generalizable. In this case, the conceptual demand of each section oscillates between Stages 2B and 3A, with occasional excursions up to Stage 3B. Reference to Figure 2 shows that a course with this level of demand should be within the understanding of about half of its target population of 12-year-olds in selective schools (i.e., about half of the top 20% of the total secondary population). However, the experimental test was carried out on first and second year comprehensive classes, because the Nuffield combined science course is being attempted by many such schools. The test showed that the same wide spread of levels of understanding in secondary schools, already found by the use of Piagetian class tasks, was also mirrored in the spread of understanding shown by the pupils in these mixed-ability classes on an examination based on the course material. When the examination items were classified according to their Piagetian level, the crossbreak of pupils' facilities ($N = 90$) on the examination items against Piagetian level of each group of pupils was:

Level of pupils	Level of examination items (%)		
	Stage 2B	Stage 3A	Stage 3B
Stage 3A	77	47	14
Stage 2B	35	12	2

Thus the proportion of material in the course requiring a Stage 3A level of understanding or above was ill-matched to such a population of pupils. From these results the course material can immediately be modified to suit any target population.

10. Curricula Which Have Used Piagetian Principles

The examples that can be quoted where the insights given by Piaget's developmental theory of thought have been explicitly used in curriculum development are only in primary and early secondary schooling. These are the British Science 5-13, the Australian ASEP, and the American SCIS.

10.1. Science 5–13

The team that produced these materials was commissioned in the mid-1960s by the School Council, the Nuffield Foundation, and by the Scottish Education Department to investigate both what science was suitable for children in this age range, and what methods of learning were appropriate for it. The result is radically unfamiliar, even alien, to those who have already learned their teaching habits in secondary education.

One may say, indeed, that a general movement in teacher training, beginning in the 1930s and drawing on the work of Dewey, early Piaget, and others has produced an orthodoxy (yet to penetrate secondary education) on how to teach younger children. This may be read, in Piagetian terms, as an attempt to accommodate to pupils in the transition from preoperational to concrete operational thinking. Those who have long since learned to generalize and abstract can find themselves curiously ill

at ease in this world of activity. American readers in particular, unfamiliar with the style of the British primary school, may find themselves
baffled at the lack of direction provided for the teachers. However, in the
5 to 13 age range, it must be appreciated that one cannot produce any
kind of structured science familiar to those who are used to teaching
intellectually able secondary school children, for the connective tissue of
such courses, being that of second-degree concepts, is barred because of
the absence of corresponding schemes in the children's minds.

It is difficult, therefore, for some science teachers to see anything
valuable at all in this style of teaching. The Science 5–13 team, then, has
done us all a considerable service in showing that it *is* a valid method,
and it is rather humbling to realize that to think constructively about it
makes an intellectual demand that is rather higher than lower to that
which one is used to for secondary science. It is clear, in fact, that one
needs what Piaget calls "reflective abstraction" (Piaget, 1971, p. 19)
characteristic of analysis of experience by group structure; for example,
if experimenting with different materials is done aimlessly, children and
teacher do indeed find themselves lost and insecure. So, in a *Science 5–13*
publication we read:

> To turn this aim into an objective requires a little more thinking in order to
> decide just why we wish our children to experiment with materials. What
> do we hope they will achieve through doing so? According to the previous
> experience and stage of development of the children, the answer might be
> that we hope they will gain:
>> Appreciation of the variety of materials in the environment.
>> or Ability to discriminate between different materials.
>> or Awareness that there are various ways of testing out ideas and making
>> observations.
>> or Appreciation that the properties of materials influence their uses.
> *(With Objectives in Mind, p. 22)*

But these objectives are abstract, that is, "indicate the outcome, but
do not prescribe the means of reaching it." Because they are abstract,
"there is a wide range of activities through which a particular objective
can be achieved." Moreover there is not a one-to-one correspondence
between any one activity and an objective, so "there is a wide range of
activities through which a particular objective can be achieved."

The relationship is shown diagrammatically in Figure 3. Such an
approach to finding direction in the process of pupil–teacher interaction
is allied to the following general convictions:

> In general, children work best when trying to find answers to problems that
> they have themselves chosen to investigate. These problems are best drawn
> from their own environment and tackled largely by practical investigations.

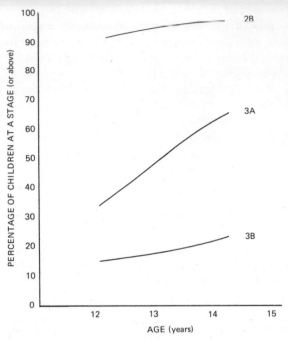

Figure 3.   Selective school population (top 20%): 2B = Late Concrete; 3A = Early Formal; 3B = Late Formal.

Teachers should be responsible for thinking out and putting into practise the work of their own classes. In order to do so they should be able to find help where they need it.

The last of these is the purpose of the *Science 5–13* materials.

While aiding and encouraging children to find out for themselves, the teacher is to "read" their activity both for its immediate success and for the extent to which it helps them realize the objectives listed above. Now this approach is not so unfamiliar to teachers of physical science as might seem at first sight. Suppose one wishes to teach thermodynamics to very able 17-year-olds or to university undergraduates. One knows quite well that, being a system whereby the student has to learn to relate concrete measurements, like those of mass or concentration or temperature, to abstract concepts such as enthalpy or free energy, thermodynamics can be started anywhere, and will probably not be completed until the student has gone through all the territory by two or three different routes. Thus, the teacher will have vaguely formulated objectives such as "appreciating that activity changes can be interpreted in terms of kinetic-molecular theory," or "realizing that colligative properties can be handled in terms of activity changes" and mentally ticks off the extent to which the pupil has progressed toward each objective, giving him further relevant work where the progress is deficient. The difference, however, is that thermodynamics is a well-structured system of concepts, and the students envisaged have the formal operational schemes required to integrate their experiences. Thus, it is reasonable for their teacher to survey the ground they are to cover, as with an eagle's eye, and choose routes, any of which his students are capable of treading. Not so when planning for young children. Here the conceptual links a teacher may see are not available paths for the children to use. The recommendation to the teachers is that they choose a general area of investigation but, within that, make use of the children's own interests and suggestions. Thus, for activities in which objectives can be realized, the published materials contain detailed suggestions for teachers under the titles, *Working with Wood, Time, Structure and Forces, Science from Toys, Minibeasts, Holes, Gaps and Cavities, Change, Metals, Trees, Colored Things, Ourselves,* and *Like and Unlike.*

The objectives themselves are grouped under these broad aims:

Developing interests, attitudes and aesthetic awareness	Observing, exploring, and ordering observations	Developing basic concepts and logical thinking	Posing questions and devising experiments or investigations to answer them
Acquiring knowledge and learning skills	Communicating	Appreciating patterns and relationships	Interpreting findings critically

Under each broad aim the objectives are not only listed, but they are also cross-classified under four Piagetian substages: intuitive; early concrete; late concrete, and early formal (this list is not exhaustive). This can be illustrated in the case of the broad aim of *developing basic concepts and logical thinking:*

Intuitive:	Appreciation that things which are different may have features in common
Early concrete:	Development of conservation of length and substance
Late concrete:	Appreciation of measurement as division into regular parts and repeated comparison with a unit
	Understanding the speed-time-distance relation
Early formal:	Ability to formulate hypotheses not dependent on direct observation
	Ability to extend reasoning beyond the actual to the possible

In this way the teacher is made to recognize in a rough way in their pupils' behaviors, under the nine broad aims, the Piagetian level at which they are functioning, and hence be guided to what other activities might be suitable and to recognize the relevance of other objectives.

How this may work in practice can be illustrated by the activity of *Change*. There are two teachers' books for this activity, the first going up to late concrete in general scope, and intended mainly for 7- to 11-year-olds, and the other dealing with work suitable for those in transition from late concrete Stage 2B to early formal Stage 3A, and intended for the 11- to 13-year-olds. In the first book science has to be discovered in situations that are not themselves obviously scientific. In the kitchen, changes may be seen in processes of washing. A possible early concrete activity is three boys with dirty hands washing them in (1) cold water, no soap, (2) cold water, with soap, and (3) warm water, with soap, and then comparing their hands. Discussion ensues on whether the comparison was fair. At the late concrete level, in investigating dishwashing, the question might be asked, "Does twice as much detergent wash plates twice as clean?" This in turn leads to the problem of devising a standard dirty plate. In the text, alongside each example of activity, references to objectives involved are listed. Similarly, decay as a process of change offers many investigations at different levels of approach. By contrast to this kind of opportunistic imposition of the ordering eye of structured observation, as one aspect of the child's interaction with the world, the Stage 3 work on Change is more recognizably that of the specialized world of science. Chapter headings are *Energy for children*, *Investigations involving energy and change*, *Chemical change: What is going on?*, and *Heat and electricity as tools of investigation*. One may indeed ask: If the objectives now become, because of the level of thinking to which the students have attained, actually phrased in terms of the specialized language of science, such as *awareness of the universal nature of gravity*, or *knowledge that chemical change results from interaction*, why still hand over to the teacher the job of finding routes by which such objectives may be achieved? If the children are now programmable, why not provide economic programs for the teacher to use?

It will be seen that the invention in the *Science 5-13* materials lies in the exemplification of how to introduce the aspect of scientific inquiry into the world of children, when their level of thinking is at the concrete stage only and thus does not permit the economy of understanding possible to those who have become able to use third-level abstractions. The Piagetian contribution lies more in the area of pupil assessment than in course structure (it may fairly be said that these materials only make the very first step toward the ordering of science experiences by Piagetian criteria, and no evidence is provided). The listing and classification of objectives by Piagetian level obviously leads in the direction of making records of pupil progress containing far more information than the numbers or grades by which, at best, the pupils are put in a rough ordinal scale in relation to each other (at present the universal method). Thus, Dr. W. Harlen, who was the team's evaluator, has carried this aspect further in a two-year research project, Progress in Learning Science. Drawing on the whole corpus of Piaget's work and not just on that pertaining to science, she has developed record sheets for pupils which make use of the accumulated but nonverbalized experience which a class teacher builds up of her pupils. Under 24 headings such as Communicating Nonverbally, Proposing Inquiries and Curiosity, she has provided behavioral descriptions, at three different levels for each, of pupil activity. Perhaps four or five times a year the teacher goes through the headings, and for each child checks off the most appropriate description. The resulting list not only provides a kind of pupil profile, at any moment, but also serves to highlight rapid progress or to direct attention to areas where children are standing still and may need provision of stimulating activity. It should also, incidentally, provide one way of gathering research on how children do progress from one Piagetian stage to another, although that was not the intention of the project.

10.2. Australian Science Education Project (ASEP)

Whereas the Science 5–13 approach was nondirective for the younger children assumed to be concrete thinkers but tended to become more directed for those assumed to be capable of formal thinking, ASEP reverses the order. Designed for the 7th to 10th graders (age 12 to 15), ASEP materials are highly directed for pupils assumed to be at the concrete stage only, and become open-ended for those at the formal stage. It is clear that noncognitive factors have influenced both curriculum developers to avoid too much open-endedness for early adolescents (age 11 to 13). Many secondary curricula have been developed on the assumption that if students are older and more intelligent, this is an argument for giving them more structured and directed science teaching. It seems that a Piagetian approach calls this in question. Again, as with Science 5–13, no evidence is provided of validity, but Piaget's work is used both to order the ASEP teaching materials according to whether their demand is concrete, transitional or formal, and also to provide the whole project strategy. An estimate was made of the distribution of Piagetian levels in the target population. Since the number of units provided (each of 10 to 15 hours class work) was based on that estimate (12 at Stage 3, 13 at Stage 2, and 16 at Stage 1), there is now some interest in looking at the history of school experience of these materials. The CSMS 1974/1975 results (Fig. 2) suggest that the relative proportion of concrete and transitional material should have been much higher. Moreover, since the whole school population was being provided for, it is to be expected that the problems involved in the logistics of using these materials, over the wide ability range to be expected, will have shone fresh light on the project's planning assumptions.

ASEP was funded from 1969 to 1974 jointly by the Commonwealth and state governments in Australia to provide materials from which teachers could choose when planning courses and to allow for individual differences between students. ASEP chose to concentrate on the processes of science, considered in relation to the students' intellectual, social, and emotional development. For content, they ignored any conjectured needs for pretraining future university students and produced a set of ideas concerned with man in relationship with the environment. Each unit had a central part, the core, in which the student could attain minimal competence. This was followed by a range of options to cater to different interests, skills, and abilities.

Since planning was focused on students' development, the style of teaching and student activity was also derived from Piaget's work. The following principles were enunciated (ASEP, 1974, p. 97):

1. New ideas and knowledge should be presented at a level consistent with the child's state of development of thinking and language.
2. A major source of learning is the activity of the child.
3. Classroom practise should be tailored to the needs of individual children and should present moderately novel situations.
4. Children learn by social interaction.
5. Children should have considerable control over their own learning.

These principles are very similar to the assumptions made by the *Science 5–13* team, so it seems wotth speculating why their use resulted in such different styles of working. Both the team experience and the teachers provided for in *Science 5–13* were in primary education. In the British primary classroom it is to be expected that the class teacher is in contact with her own class at least two thirds of each day. By contrast, the ASEP materials assume that classes come to specialist teachers and workrooms for only a small proportion of the week, perhaps for six lessons. So the same principles can lead to two different outcomes. The British teacher can afford to scorn the prepared course, because, by virtue of the time she spends with her pupils, she can skilfully follow and respond to their own interests. The Australian teacher, on the other hand, requires the provision of highly detailed units, among which the student makes his own selection. It is probably fair to guess that the Australian secondary science teacher also scorns what would appear to be the lack of detailed instruction in the British materials. Both these courses would repay investigation and comparison for their effect on 11- to 13-year-old pupils. But ASEP deduces, from these principles, that class teaching is no longer valid, since children develop at different rates, and thus units of work must be provided which are different overall in level of thinking involved and which also allow within the unit for differences in interest and speed of working. The instructions should be provided in writing to relieve the class teacher from telling the same thing to each pupil, and accommodation to the pupils is attempted by writing at a reading level about two grades below the average level of the class to ensure that at least 90% of the class could understand them. The teacher's skill is to organize, encourage, control, and facilitate the student's work. This includes encouraging the students to work in small groups and to learn by discussion and argument with each other. *A Guide to ASEP* (1974, p. 70) contains a nice statement of position on this:

> Many teachers object that children would waste their time if they were not required to do a certain amount of compulsory work. Piaget argues that the secret of motivation is neither to allow children to do only what they like, nor to select only "interesting" topics to please them and keep them occupied. He argues that if the material is either so new or is so much in advance of the child's understanding that he experiences great difficulty in understanding it, then it is not motivating. Interest is aroused when the material is moderately novel. This means that the teacher who knows the experiential background of the child and his stage of mental development can lead the child to interesting activities, provided that the experiences are moderately new.

10.3. Science Curriculum Improvement Study (SCIS)

This American program, begun as long ago as 1958 and published finally in 1974, for primary school children from 6 to 12 years of age, has both learning strategy and evaluation techniques derived from Piaget. We who have heard average British (i.e., not unintelligent for their age) 14 year-olds tell us very firmly not to use long words, when we either have used long words or monosyllables conveying the same message, find it very difficult to believe we are on the same planet as the second-year children whom this course assumes may, at the age of 7 or 8, be introduced to the physical science concepts of interaction, system and interaction at a distance, and to the biological concepts of generation, biotic potential, and genetic identity. The third year continues with subsystems and variables, populations, food webs and food chains, and the fourth year with reference objects, rectangular coordinates, polar coordinates and relative motion, environment, and range. The world of science is clearly treated as one with its own language and language referents, and the young children are taken in it by hand as into any other rich domain of fantasy. Perhaps this is well and fine. If it is, much British thinking on primary education has got to be wrong.

To be fair to the course, when an experiment heading reads "thermometers interact with water," it is obviously not intended that the pupils use the word "interact" as other than a pointing or a context word. It is all part of a process of getting them familiarized early with the strange and specialized language of the science world. If one reads the accounts of the study materials, one gets the impression (which is a true one) that the authors were highly intelligent, humane people with great good will and the willingness to go right back to first principles. They have, nevertheless, had almost no experience of other than tertiary education to start from. This is to be distinguished from the starting point of the designers of the British Nuffield O-level courses, who obviously have had very considerable firsthand experience of how to interact with very highly intelligent adolescents, and designed their courses empirically. The American authors of SCIS appear to have drawn on no institutionalized empirical experience, and herein may lie their great advantage and the long-term value of the thinking they have done about science education. It seems there are three achievements of particular note in their work: They have produced a novel learning cycle theory of scientific activity, which is quite general and has been applied at all levels up to and including college; they have applied Piaget's account of the preoperational, concrete, and formal operational stages in producing the developing structure and evaluation of the course through elementary school; and they have produced an integrated course of science (broadly differentiated between physical and life sciences) which breaks totally away from the tradition of specialized single science subject teaching. Piaget's work features in the first two of these.

But before describing them, a comment must be made on the very great difference between the assumptions about elementary school children made in the SCIS course and by the British authors of the *Science 5-13* materials. The British authors assume by implication that children are excluded from what we as adults have experienced as the world of science. They assume, moreover, that children must be allowed to be children and not be imitation young adults. They also have arrived at their position empirically, from long experience of teaching primary-age children. In common with all Piagetians (including SCIS) they insist on the primacy of direct experience in the learning process. But this leads them to put emphasis on direct observation and inquiry of any features of the child's own world as a way of inculcating habits which will eventually lead them as young adults to take to specialized science more readily. The American authors, by contrast, assume that science is a world of its own, where its language and its rules of behavior are inseparable; therefore the children are to be introduced to both if they are to get anything of value from time spent on its study. This applies, even if the children are only eight years old. One would like to see a test of the SCIS materials on British children.

The learning cycle is a cyclical pattern of three phases, called exploration, invention, and discovery. The first step, that of direct handling and observation, is assumed to be essential if real activity of the mind is to follow, rather than book learning. At the same time part of the reason for it is Piagetian in nature, as: "It allows the learner to impose his own ideas and preconceptions on the subject-matter to be investigated. If he comes up with a successful new idea, more power to him. At the same time the exploration should create some disequilibrium as students are challenged by new experiences" (SCIS Final Report, 1976 ch. 6, p. 7).

The invention phase is oddly named, for its concepts are introduced by the teacher rather than produced by the students. It is assumed that motivation will occur by the student having some of his conscious "disequilibration" resolved by seeing that the invented concept works better than the self-contradictory account which he tried to impose upon (assimilate) the experimental experience. Finally, the discovery phase has the student apply the new concept in a variety of situations, and this is held also to fit with "learning by equilibration," because it continues the satisfaction the student has had in his first successful use of the concept. Naturally the nature of the disequilibration introduced will vary with the conceptual level of the class the work is designed for.

When the SCIS materials were first planned, *The Growth of Logical Thinking* had only just been published, and, while planning the structure of the whole elementary school course the authors correctly assumed that the earlier years would involve preoperational and concrete operational thinking, "the trials involved in the development of the upper grade units were more numerous" (being designed to promote the transition from concrete to formal thought) "and tended to overestimate the children's capacities " (SCIS Final Report, ch. 6, p. 8). From this stemmed the already well-known work of Karplus with paper and pencil tests, showing not only that American 11 and 12-year-olds had been overestimated (by taking the ages that Piaget gives as typical), but that older American students and European students had a much smaller proportion of formal thinkers than had been thought (Karplus, 1975).

Karplus was also the source of many of the basic planning ideas, which he evolved while learning from the experience of teaching a second grade class (Karplus and Thier, 1967, p. 11). There is a sense in which Piaget's work could be called prescriptive rather than descriptive, that is, it describes the evolution of a particular kind of flexible thinking (assumed to be that of health) which is scientific literacy. The SCIS program identifies with that evolution (*SCIS Final Report*, 1974, p. 72.) Under the general heading of Interaction there is the attempt to promote at different levels the development Piaget describes. Under *Reference Frame*, there are activities at each grade which gradually lead the child out of observational egocentricity; under *System* comes, first, the development of classificatory thinking which is part of Piaget's description of concrete operational thinking, and then the concept of an interacting system which involves formal operational thinking, for at least two independent variables need to be related as in the loading of a spring there is only one independent variable. *Property* is one of the contexts of relational thinking, and *Model* leads from mechanistic thinking to hypothetico-deductive thinking. These process concepts are realized in the major scientific contexts of matter, energy, organism and ecosystem. In the words of the *SCIS Final Report* (ch. 6, pp. 8–9):

> consider the pulley sets included in a second year unit. Some children may assemble a pulley system and try to make the pulleys turn as fast as they can (preoperational), others may compare the turning rates of pulleys of various sizes (concrete operational), while still others may carefully observe the relative turning rates of two different-sized pulleys and then predict the outcome of as yet untried combinations (formal operational). Though extremely few formal operational students are likely to come into contact with these activities, the existence of these challenges will be a source of intellectual stimulation for the concrete operational children using them.

and

> the school science program can contribute to learning and development in these ways: (1) observations and investigations provide children with experience of the physical world, extending their knowledge and acquainting them with certain regular patterns of behavior of the natural universe; (2) the social environment in the classroom allows children to learn from one another and from the teacher by asking questions, observing others, and listening to explanations; (3) the content and form of the activities lead

children to reorganize their reasoning as they recognize its limitations, discover more fruitful procedures, and apply their ideas autonomously to a variety of situations. These three contributions, taken together, result in what Piaget has called equilibration, the active process whereby a person responds to inadequacies in his own thinking through the formation, trial, and evaluation of new approaches.

The final structure of the program is shown in Figure 4.

Thus, there are three science curricula, each explicitly based on Piaget's work, yet with very different outcomes. Of the three, it has been implied that the SCIS program is probably most out of phase with the general child population. Yet it is the only science curriculum program known to the authors in which the development phase has been planned to take place in a sufficiently leisurely way for formative evaluation to take place, and this apparently adverse comment is prompted by the evidence that the directors have themselves provided (see page 129). Not only did they commit themselves to a long-term process of teacher education, in which the teacher learned about the pupil–pupil and pupil–teacher interactions most favorable to the development of scien-

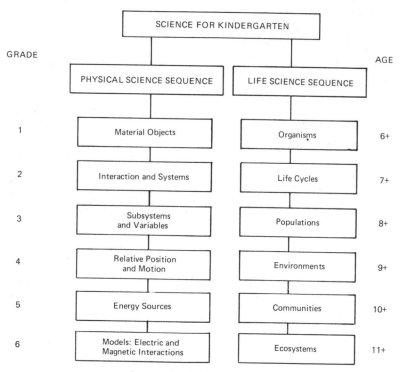

Figure 4.   SCIS Program.

tific thinking, they were also part of the team and associates committed
to evaluating both course effectiveness and pupil outcome. They provided advice for teachers, as with *Science 5–13*, on how to recognize
different Piagetian stage levels in pupils' behaviors in different learning
contexts; they also provided test material for evaluating the level of
pupils' understanding on the concepts. Feedback from schools has resulted in further research (see various papers under the heading of
AESOP) both at Lawrence Hall and elsewhere (see references quoted in
Brown, Weber, and Renner, 1975). A truly Piagetian process of adaptation of curriculum to population has thus been set in train, with part of
the accommodation already accomplished.

All three curricula take in common from Piaget's work a model of
the right relationship between pupil activity and conceptual development, and the way this is aided by pupils' social relationships and opportunity to verbalize. ASEP, for older pupils, is the one most immediately geared for use and evaluation of its use. SCIS and Science
5–13 are more dependent on the evolution of teacher styles appropriate
to their materials.

11. Possible Uses of Piaget's Work Suggested by the 1974/1975 CSMS Study

It can be seen, then, that the curriculum development of the 1960s,
even if related to Piaget's work, has left problems that only research can
solve.

From Figure 2 the developing spread of Piagetian levels in children
of secondary age can be seen. If one bears in mind the largely empirical
development of secondary education in the West in the second two
quarters of this century, one can see how the nature of the secondary
education which most of the readers of this book will have had, and
which will have seemed to them to be essentially immutable, even
though suspectable of improvement, can be asserted to be merely a
social artefact. If, by various processes of social and intellectual selection, only the top 15% to 20% of the child population have been considered worthy of education, and if one grants that most teachers, most of
the time, try to lead their pupils near the limit of their capacity, then the
intellectual style of science and mathematics courses evolved would be
expected to have arrived by a process of teacher-pupil accommodation
governed by the curves of Figure 3. In the first two years of secondary
education (11 to 13), the top one fifth of the population is showing a

change from 35% at level 3A or above to 65% at level 3A or above. One would expect, therefore, the nature of the conceptual demand to be transitional in the sense of laying the groundwork for the second three years of secondary education (13 to 16) where the structure of the course consists of concepts making a 3A level of demand. Only above the age of 16 (in British schools, for what is called sixth formers) would one expect a substantial amount of 3B level of demand to be introduced.

Suppose one now wishes to construct a course for the part of the population between the 80th and 50th percentiles, and suppose, further, that one chooses not to make a radically new course structure but to use traditional science materials. Then, from Figure 2 it follows that the experiences that were appropriate for the top 20% from 11½ to 13½ years of age should be appropriate for this different population from 14½ to 16½, and that what was begun at 13½ for the top 20% should be begun at 16½ for the next 30% with a fair expectation of success. The type of courses developed in tertiary technical education in Britain for students of 16+, again empirically, do indeed conform to this pattern. Similarly, one could predict that for the part of the secondary population below the top 5%, but above the top 20%, the ages of 16 to 18 would be more appropriate for courses making the level of demand of the Nuffield O-level courses (or the American Chemstudy).

The analysis of the Nuffield O-level chemistry course (Ingle and Shayer, 1971) referred to earlier was carried out as part of a process of revision of course materials in the light of five years experience in schools for the Nuffield Foundation at Chelsea College. Many teachers, in response to detailed questionnaires mentioned that the backbone of course structure, for the 13½- to 16½-year-old students, of the mole concept in various applications gave their students a lot of trouble. Would a detailed analysis of the conceptual demand of the course reveal the source of difficulty and suggest possible changes? Extrapolation of Figure 2 suggests that if the concepts making a Stage 3B level of demand are deferred until the students are 15½, a substantially higher proportion should be able to understand the unity of the course. Accordingly, an alternative sample scheme for Stage 2 was prepared, using the spiral curriculum development principle. At 13½, instead of the mole concept being introduced to the students, formulae are given qualitatively; a year later work on structure is used to connect up atom ratios in compounds to their physical and chemical properties, and only two years later is the development integrated by applying the mole concept to reacting quantities in reactions leading to equations. In this way it is hoped to accommodate to a higher proportion of the selective school population than had originally been the case.

12. Curricula for the 80th to 20th Percentile of Population

If the assertion is granted that the structured secondary science course as we have known it is a social artifact, it should then be possible, from Figure 2, to deduce the ground rules within which the invention of new courses more appropriate to their target populations should be confined. Perhaps no section of the student population has had less thought given to their science education, both in the States and in Europe, than the middle 60% between the ages of 11 and 14. Too old to come within the scope of new thinking on primary education, and below the age at which much serious science teaching was given, they are, in their critical period from childhood to young adulthood, in need of the widest range of relevant educational expertize. Here only the cognitive aspect of their problem can be considered. In this period, those between the 20th and 40th percentiles will develop from a partial operational thinking (Stages 2A/2B) to a more consistent concrete operational thinking (Stage 2B); those between the 40th and 60th percentiles will remain basically at the Stage 2B level, but will show toward the age of 14 occasional performances which would lead to their being classified on Piagetian tests as Stages 2B/3A, and some of those between the 60th and 80th percentiles may develop as far as Stage 3A (early formal operational). It follows that, in Piagetian terms, the activities for such students should not only remain within the limits of concrete operational thinking, but should also be deliberately designed to promote such thinking, since a substantial proportion of such students will not have developed such thinking over much of a range of their life experiences.

There is no science curriculum known to the authors for this age range that fulfills these conditions. The construction of one will be a very interesting exercise. It will be necessary to forget the science games that are familiar, because they operate at the early formal operational level at least, and make use of the programmability of highly intelligent students. Here the students will be by definition not programmable in this sense. One will not be able to feed them the essential ideas and the connections between them and then set them to practice many examples. Concrete operational thinking is the imposition or discovery, on the world of immediate or remembered experience, of the varieties of classifications and orderings which Piaget describes in his eight groupings. It does not encompass the step of abstraction needed to look at the relations between one set of conceptually structured experiences and another. Yet, it is most definitely a powerful and valuable level of thinking, and its confident establishment should provide for the adolescent a better basis for further intellectual development than an attempt to use a level of thinking which mystifies him or her. A generation of science teachers need consciously to forget the style by which they were themselves taught. Among the many possible activities by which science process can be experienced, and for which the SCIS and *Science 5–13* materials give valuable pointers, those which keep within the limits suggested need listing, and from among them, by an imaginative step, new patterns of content which make sense scientifically will need to be formed and tested on this range of pupils. And again, new games of transition will need to be worked out between this section of the secondary curriculum and what would be appropriate science activity for the same population between the ages of 14 and 16.

Detail cannot be given here, but there is only one curriculum known to the authors which does attempt to cater for the 80th to the 40th percentile of 14- to 16-year-olds: the British Nuffield secondary science course. Again, no explicit use was made of Piaget's work, but some of its authors had developed their teaching empirically on such a population in British secondary modern schools (schools which largely catered for those leaving school at 15+). A *post hoc* Piagetian analysis (Shayer, 1972a) showed that most of the routines developed kept within the conceptual range of Stages 2B to 3A and were hierarchically ordered in sequence. Reference to Figure 2 shows, by extrapolation, that this would be the correct strategy. And, as a pointer to science teaching styles to come, it is worth noting that this project abandoned the customary subject-logical ordering of its materials (presumably because they knew their pupils would not connect them abstractly anyway), produced an ordering within topics only, and developed new examination techniques for testing students achievement in whatever route the student had taken through the course materials.

13. Life Style and Formal Operational Thought

It might well be asked if more could be done to facilitate the development of formal operational thought and raise the levels of thinking that research has shown. While much experimentation has taken place to see to what extent and in what sense a move from preoperational to concrete operational thought can be facilitated by means of short-term training, far less has been done to see if such means can aid the growth of formal operational thought. In any case we do not know the long-term effects of short-term training. However, it is known, in general terms, that life style, culture, and schooling do aid the growth of operational thinking.

The point made here is that the life style of the home affects the facility with which available modes of thinking can be applied to particular problems and contents of discourse. In certain kinds of life style children's thinking tends to be dominated by the perceptual, the immediate, and the concrete, and in these conditions concept formation and reasoning is more difficult when form is separated from content (cf. Lévi-Strauss, 1966; Luria, 1976). In other life styles children are more encouraged to think of possibilities and hypothetical situations, thus divorcing themselves more often from the tangible and concrete, to subject themselves to more long-term planning, and to think and find solutions to problems for themselves rather than have solutions transmitted to them by rule and routine. It should also be added that there is by no means a simple relationship between life style, as used in this sense, and family income.

Children who tend to focus their thinking on the immediate and concrete may well be better at assessing perceptual cues as indicators of the properties of objects or situations, but they have less facility in handling verbal logical relations that are independent of content. This does not, of course, imply that these pupils are necessarily less "intelligent," but it does mean that their thinking is more dominated by their own practical experience compared with other children. There is much cross-cultural experience to support this argument. Tulkin and Konner (1973) indicate hypothetico-deductive thinking in Kalahari Bushmen when concerned with tracking animals. It is doubtful if such bushmen would immediately show such thinking if presented with the simple pendulum that involves much the same kind of task, namely the exclusion of variables.

References

Archenhold, W. F., *A study of the understanding of the concept of potential in sixth form students*. Unpublished masters thesis, University of Leeds.
ASEP, 1974. *A guide to ASEP*. Melbourne: Australian Science Education Project.
Bloom, B. S., Hastings, J. T., and Madeus, G. F., 1971. *Handbook of formative and summative evaluation of student learning*. New York: McGraw-Hill.
Brown, T. W., Weber, M. C., and Renner, J. R. 1975. Research on the development of scientific literacy. *Science and children*, January.
Cole, M., and Scribner, S. 1974. *Culture and thought*. New York: Wiley.
Driver, R., 1973. *The representation of conceptual frameworks in young adolescent science students*. Unpublished doctoral dissertation, University of Illinois.

Hooper, F., and Dihoff, R. E., 1975. *Multidimensional scaling of Piagetian task performance.* Madison: Wisconsin Research and Development Centre for Cognitive Learning.

Hooper, F., and Sipple, T. S., 1975. *An investigation of matrix task classificatory and seriation abilities.* Madison: Wisconsin Research and Development Centre for Cognitive Learning.

Ingle, R. B., and Shayer, M., 1971. Conceptual demands in Nuffield O-level chemistry. *Education in Chemistry, 8,* 182–83.

Inhelder, B., and Piaget, J., 1958. *The growth of logical thinking from childhood to adolescence.* London: Routledge and Kegan Paul.

Inhelder, B., and Piaget, J., 1964. *The early growth of logic in the child.* London: Routledge and Kegan Paul.

Karplus, R., 1973. *Opportunities for concrete and formal thinking in science tasks.* Paper given at the third annual meeting of the Jean Piaget Society, Philadelphia.

Karplus, R., 1975. *Proportional reasoning and control of variables in seven countries.* Berkeley, Calif.: Lawrence Hall of Science.

Karplus, R., and Thier, H. D., 1967. *A new look at elementary school science.* Chicago: Rand McNally.

Kuhn, D., and Brannock, J., 1977. Development of the isolation of variables scheme in experimental and "natural experiment" contexts. *Developmental Psychology, 13,* 9–14.

Lévi-Strauss, C., 1966. *The savage mind.* Chicago: University of Chicago Press.

Luria, A. R., 1966. *Higher cortical functions in man.* New York: Basic Books.

Luria, A. R., 1976. *Cognitive development.* London: Harvard University Press.

Metalon, B., 1962. Étude génétique de l'implication. In E. W. Beth et al., *Implication, formalisation et logique naturelle: Etudes d'épistémologie génétique.* Paris: Presses Universitaires de France, *16,* 69–93.

O'Brien, T. C., 1972. Logical thinking in adolescents. *Educational Studies in Mathematics, 4,* 401–428.

Papert, S., 1963. Sur la logique Piagétianne. *Etudes d'épistemologie génétique, 15,* 107–129.

Piaget, J., 1960. The general problems of the psychobiological development of the child. In J. M. Tanner and B. Inhelder (Eds.), *Discussions on child development* (Vol. 4). London: Tavistock Publications.

Piaget, J., 1970. *Genetic epistemology.* New York: Columbia University Press.

Piaget, J., 1971. *Structuralism.* London: Routledge and Kegan Paul.

Piaget, J., and Garcia, R., 1975. *Understanding causality.* New York: Norton.

Reynolds, J., 1967. *The development of the concept of mathematical proof in grammar school pupils.* Unpublished doctoral dissertation, University of Nottingham.

Science 5–13, 1972. With objectives in mind. London: Macdonald Educational.

SCIS, 1974. *SCIS Teachers' Handbook.* Berkeley, Calif.: Lawrence Hall of Science.

SCIS, 1976. *SCIS Final Report.* Berkeley, Calif.: Lawrence Hall of Science.

Shapiro, B. J., and O'Brien, T. C., 1970. Logical thinking in children aged six through thirteen. *Child Development, 41,* 823–829.

Shayer, M., 1972a. *Piaget's work and science teaching.* Unpublished masters thesis, University of Leicester.

Shayer, M., 1972b. Conceptual demands in Nuffield O-level physics. *School Science Review, 186,* 26–34.

Shayer, M., 1974. Conceptual demands in Nuffield O-level biology course. *School Science Review, 56,* No. 195, 381–388.

Shayer, M., 1978. The analysis of science curricula for Piagetian level of demand. *Studies in Science Education, 5,* 115–130.

Shayer, M., Küchemann, D. E., and Wylam, H., 1976. The distribution of Piagetian stages
    of thinking in British middle and secondary school children. *British Journal of Educational Psychology*, 46, 164–173.
Stake, R. E., *et al.* 1978. Final report on case studies in science education. (NSF Project
    C7621134).
Tulkin, S. R., and Konner, M. J., 1973. Alternative conceptions of intellectual functioning.
    Human Development, 16, 33–52.
Wason, P. C., and Johnson-Laird, P. N., 1972. *Psychology of reasoning: Structure and content.*
    London: Batsford.

5

Four Decades of Conservation Research

What Do They Mean for Mathematics Education?

J. A. EASLEY, JR.

1. Overview

The context of this chapter is well put by Erich Wittmann in introducing one of his own papers:

> The *epistemology* of natural numbers has been a subject of discussion since Helmholtz, Frege, Russell, Poincaré up to Hilbert, Brouwer and Weyl. This includes questions as to whether the ordinal or cardinal aspect is constitutive for number, whether number is an a priori entity as believed by Poincaré and the intuitionists, or reducible to logic as claimed by Frege and Russell. As a paradigm of long standing for the epistemological problem, that of natural number kept the status of a controversial question depending on different philosophical views, as long as it remained within philosophy—indeed philosophy does not know means to remove these differences. A way out was shown by J. Piaget's genetic epistemology, which is based on the equality of developmental mechanisms both in the genesis of science and the individual, and consequently transforms the *epistemological* problem of natural number into an empirical problem,

J. A. EASLEY, JR. • Committee on Culture and Cognition, University of Illinois, Urbana, Illinois. Some of the research here was supported by NIE contract.

namely that of exploring the psychogenesis of the number concept. (Wittmann, 1975, p. 53)

1.1. Two Questions

In comparing the dozens of books and many more papers dealing with the conservation of number and physical quantities by Piaget and his colleagues in Geneva with the even more numerous books and other studies of the same subject by non-Genevan writers, two questions strike me: (1) Why have Piaget and his colleagues persisted in trying to find new theoretical mechanisms to explain the development of conservation, when only a few psychologists or educators not based in Geneva have shown any such interest? (2) Why is the phenomenon of the non-conserver so much more challenging to most non-Genevan writers and audiences than it is to Genevan writers? These two questions arise from my impression that about 90% of the literature from Geneva raises fundamental epistemological questions and only about 10% attempts to apply the theory. In other countries 90% of the literature on conservation appears to be still based on the first decade of the Geneva work and pays little or no attention to the kinds of questions that have motivated Genevan writers to look beyond their early theoretical models. These observations suggest a fundamental difference of purpose and/or perspective; hence the first question. With respect to the second question, it is my observation that, even today, reports that young children often do not believe a quantity of material remains the same when it is rearranged spatially raise serious questions in the minds of most non-Geneva trained psychologists and educators—especially the question of adequacy of controls for semantic confusion in nonconserving subjects.

Meanwhile, Piaget and his colleagues remain steadfastly interested in the conservers. In particular, they ask how it is possible for such quantitative concepts, with invariant properties, to arise spontaneously in children apart from instruction. That is, the Genevans are unwilling to take for granted what most non-Genevans want to assume that every child already knows. Epistemologically, this means that Genevans challenge both Platonism, which assumes that certain ideas are automatically and universally available to all intelligent beings, and empiricism, the belief that certain ideas are passively copied from the environment. They propose, instead of either of these epistemologies, an interactivist constructionism which postulates that a spontaneous, autonomous process of *a priori* ideas necessary for learning mathematics are universally developed by interaction of the subject with its environment, in which, starting with the primitive reflexes of the newborn child, one system of action scheme is used to develop the next. This "genetic epistemology" is proposed as a natural science, employing both theoretical and experimental inquiries.

It is my hope that, by raising these two questions and by comparing and contrasting the epistemologies of Platonists, logical empiricists, and the Genevans, some new light may be thrown on the relevance of the conservation studies to mathematics education. The relevance will then be seen to lie in the option it provides mathematics teachers of adopting a new epistemology to replace the ones implicit in current practice.

1.2. Genetic Epistemology of Number

A problem in the application of Piaget's work to mathematics education arises from the assimilation of genetic epistemology to conventional educational psychology, characterized as it is by learning goals, methods of instruction, goal-based evaluation, and in general a rational and operationalist philosophy. This assimilation, which Piaget's theory should prepare us to expect, leads to the interpretation of the tasks Geneva-based researchers invented for use in their clinical interviews as criterion-referenced tests (Renner, Stafford, Lawson, McKinnon, Friot, and Kellogg, 1977), "absolute measures of intellectual ability" (Cronbach, 1972), or "check-ups" (Nuffield Mathematics Project, 1970). That interpretation leads to the concept of readiness and to readiness training programs.

Having once made that kind of assimilation myself, I recall how gratifying it seemed to have a way to explain Piaget's work to my colleagues and students in terms of ideas familiar to them, and how unconscious I was that in doing so I was overlooking certain clear statements I had once read and even tried to teach.

Consider, for example, this statement from the foreword to *La Genèse du nombre chez l'enfant:**

> Discussion as to the relationship between number and logic has, as we know, been endless. The logisticians, with Russell, have tried to reduce cardinal number to the notion of "class of classes," and ordinal number, dissociated from cardinal number, to the notion of "class of relationships," while their opponents maintained, with Poincaré and Brunschvig, that the

---

*This book, which, except for the title, is one of the better translations of Piaget's work, draws together work published as early as 1937. (See p. ix.) The recent publication of Piaget's new theory (1977) thus culminates 40 years of research on conservation.

whole number is essentially synthetic and irreducible. Our hypothesis seems to obviate the necessity for this alternative, for if number is at the same time both class and asymmetrical relation, it does not derive from one or the other of the logical operations, but from their union, continuity thus being reconciled with irreducibility, and the relationship between logic and arithmetic being regarded not as unilateral but as reciprocal. (Piaget and Szeminska, 1941, pp. viii–ix)

The statement just quoted provides a clear purpose for the work in Geneva: to unite the quarreling factions among philosophers of mathematics by demonstrating the scientific hypothesis that number is not reducible either to classes or relations because, and just because, it is a fusion of both ideas. If this is the goal of the Genevan studies on conservation of number and continuous quantity, then confusion of the clinical method employed for these studies with that of tests (i.e., assimilation of Genevan tasks to the method of testing) should be resisted, even if it is predictable and understandable. In the same forward, the authors say this about their methods:

We shall still keep our original procedure of free conversation with the child, conversation which is governed by the questions put, but which is compelled to follow the direction indicated by the child's spontaneous answer.

It is clear that they are treating children's mathematical ideas as natural phenomena whose organization they want to explore. But that exploration is motivated by the goal of solving philosophical problems by making scientific discoveries.

Their procedure is reminiscent of that of an anatomist dissecting the delicate tissues of a snail to see how its reproductive organs are arranged. As a taxonomist, on the other hand, the very same scientist might later decide that certain differences in the size and form of the genitalia could prevent two particular individuals from mating, and he might declare therefore that they belong to different species. As a taxonomist, he might then publish criteria for classifying such specimens, thus changing his role from that of a student of structural relationships to that of the maker of keys for the classification of specimens. While Piaget has been called a collector and classifier of children's explanations. (Claparède, 1932), and has established stages for the classification of the underlying structures of children's thought, his taxonomic interests are different from those of most educational psychologists. As he remarked at a conference on "Measurement and Piaget," he had never been interested in individual differences (Green, Ford, and Flamer, 1971, p. 211).

Educational psychologists *are* interested in individual differences, and they have quite naturally seized on Piaget's discoveries to make tests for the identification of children who have not attained the concepts that their teachers and school programs assume they already have. This not only results in paper-and-pencil tests but even interviews which have abandoned a great deal of the flexibility and freedom to discover the natural organization of children's thought. The next step, naturally, is the creation of readiness training programs to bring children up to the intellectual level at which they are supposed to be, if they are going to learn. But this is not Piaget's goal but the goal of educational psychology and of most research in mathematics education.

1.3. Epistemological Issues in Mathematics Education

Many mathematics educators seem to start with the assumption that the nature of the mathematics to be taught is clearly understood and the only problem is to bring students into a condition in which they can learn it. But philosophers of mathematics, from Socrates to Lakatos (1963), have been quite aware that there are problems about the nature of mathematics that are very difficult to solve: for example is mathematics purely abstract? If so, how is it learned and how does it help solve real-world problems? Are mathematical principles and concepts realities to be discovered, or are they inventions of man for practical or aesthetic purposes? Is there one foundation of all mathematics, or are the various branches, relatively autonomous, relating to each other by analogy? These questions may not seem relevant to education, yet it was issues of this sort that mathematicians have fought over in what have been called "the math wars" (DeMott, 1962). Mathematicians and educators chose sides in those battles, and eventually teachers and parents wished new math, whatever its philosophy, good riddance. But what is the epistemology of the old math? Are there any epistemological issues now left, or is the present truce a stalemate?

Piaget (1975) argues for the relevance to mathematics education of an understanding of the natural way mathematical ideas develop in children, and those who support him may conceivably launch a new set of math wars against the authoritarianism of most mathematics teaching. Clearly, most teachers, parents, and educational psychologists, let alone empiricist mathematics education researchers, see mathematics as something that must be taught didactically, not something that all children can figure out on their own. Atkin and Karplus (1962), writing about science teaching, expressed their doubts about the possibility of children discovering (or reinventing) modern scientific concepts. After defining discovery and invention, they wrote:

> [The child] makes observations all the time, and he invents concepts that interpret the observations as well. He also makes discoveries that enable him to refine his concepts. Most of the discoveries and inventions reveal a type of natural philosophy—a "common-sense" orientation popular in the culture at a given point in history.
>
> If the children are not able to *invent* the modern scientific concepts, it is necessary for the teacher to *introduce* the modern scientific concepts. . . .

For these writers, as for most educators, Piaget's notion that universal mathematical and scientific concepts develop in nearly all children in all cultures and in all times (except of course many millions of years in the past or in the future when because of evolution the human species is quite different) seems to have little chance of acceptance.

Most evolutionists do not believe that major new forms of life spring out of one or two individuals without the preexistence of genes or prior homogenous structures in the population. For Piaget, mathematical inventions must also originate from structures in the population. The inner bones of the mammalian ear did not appear from nowhere but were adapted from ancestral bones of the lower jaw. Analogously, Piaget's life-long search to identify conceptual seeds of key ideas that talented mathematicians employ in their work, and his claim to have found such seeds in all children, is a fundamental part of this program of genetic epistemology. This discovery that children spontaneously acquire unquestioned belief in conservation of numerical and physical quantities over various transformations, like any surprising scientific discovery, is persuasive evidence for the theory that led to the discovery.

However, the mechanism of the formation of such concepts in children needs to be understood in a way that philosophers of mathematics would recognize as an epistemological solution. Axiom systems for Piaget's theory were attempted by Piaget, Grize, Papert, Witz, and Wittman for this reason (cf. Greco *et al.*, 1960; Greco and Morf, 1962; Grize, 1963; Witz, 1966–69; Wittman, 1975). Likewise, to help connect mathematics with children's thought, Piaget treasured Einstein's expression of interest in the question whether conservation of speed develops before conservation of length and time. The mathematician Dieudonné, and logicians like Apostel, Beth, and Nowinski have had similar interests in Piaget's research. In the past decade Piaget has been studying category theory with a view to relating his research to the deeper understanding of mathematics which that theory makes possible.

Note that Piaget's goal is not mathematical psychology, such as Simon (1962) and Pascual-Leone (1970) have urged on him. Rather it is to reach philosophers on their own terrain with arguments they should recognize and respect but with a psychological basis in child study. This concern was expressed early when Piaget and Szeminska wrote (1941; English translation, 1952) continuing their remarks first quoted:

> Nevertheless, the connections established in the field of experimental psychology needed to be verified in the field of logistics, and we proceeded to attempt this verification.
>
> In studying the literature on the subject we were surprised to find to what extent the usual point of view was "realist" (i.e., Platonist) rather than "operational," with the exception of the interesting work of A. Reymond. This fact accounts for the connections, many of them artificial, established by Russell, which forcibly separated logistic investigation from psychological analysis, whereas each should be a support for the other in the same way as mathematics and experimental physics. (p. ix)*

The Platonistic character of much mathematical thought has been a surprise to empiricist educators. The University of Illinois Committee on School Mathematics (UICSM), for example, was committed to having children discover mathematical concepts as patterns evident in their experience with numbers, and to teach them a meta-language derived from Gentzen's (1969, original German, 1938) natural deduction with which to write and prove theorems about sets of numbers. Opponents like Polya, Klein, and Wittenbrug took a more intuitionist view of the nature of mathematics (Easley, 1967). Teachers by and large may take a moralistic view—math must be done the right way! If mathematical rules are challenged, the weaker societal rules will fail (Stake and Easley, 1978, Ch. 16). Few but Piaget took a constructivist approach to mathematics. Perhaps most mathematics educators are very interested in the epistemology they employ, but not in considering a new one. Even to discuss epistemology may be to pull out the props for doing mathematics education. People sometimes become very angry when their epistemology is not accepted. However, peacemakers, who, like Piaget, would attempt to synthesize opposing views, naturally become the enemies of both sides. When someone on either side wants to assimilate Piaget's work to their view, if Piaget accepts it, the opposition is an-

---

*This statement, published in 1941, foretold the publication of *Traité de logique* in 1950. On Russell's Platonism, see Lakatos (1962).

noyed; but, if he refutes the assimilation, it angers those who embraced his view.

1.4. A Logical Empiricist's View

Although the literature on conservation often appears to address specific, factual questions (Can conservation be taught? Would any damage result? What methods of training are most effective? Is the order of conservation of different quantities uniform? Is the rate of development uniform across cultures?), epistemological positions are often simply assumed and not addressed directly. If one is insensitive to the uses being made of logical concepts, it is difficult to notice the empiricist assumptions made by writers using more or less the same words Piaget uses.

Murray (1977) is particularly clear about children's uses of logical ideas:

> Operational responses to conservation tasks . . . are logical deductions from four premises, two of which are given in the experimental paradigm and two of which the child supplies.

His phrase, "given in the experimental paradigm," appears to assume both that the actions of the experimenter have been represented for the subjects by premises that can be read out directly and accurately from their observation and that they can already employ deductive logic. These are traceable to the two key ideas that logical empiricists proposed for scientific inquiry. Murray (1977) goes on to say:

> The premises explicit in the procedure, and about which there must be experimental guarantees, are the child's understanding that (1) Object A equals Object B in two respects, say weight and shape, and (2) Object B is transformed to Object B_1 with respect to only one attribute, say shape. (p. 9)

Here also he supports the two central ideas of logical empiricism. He requires guaranteed data premises for the psychologist's inferences and, in formulating these premises, he assumes with the word "only" an exhaustive universe of attributes, an essential component of deductive logic. This assimilation of Piaget's concept of natural logic to a copy view of perception and an artificial, mechanical logic leads naturally to Murray's focus on methods of preventing misunderstanding of the conservation question by the nonconserver. There is a Catch 22, however. Once the second premise has been accepted, conservation of weight (or whatever second variable is involved) is deductively certain.

A scientific study of the natural development of mathematical knowledge should be one that is open to criticism from all quarters. Assuming that children already function with the basic assumptions of logical empiricism is a poor strategy either for producing an alternative epistemology or explaining the origins of mathematics. Such criticism or reformulation of Piaget's work should, however, be recognized as an open, if unsuccessful, attempt to defeat his epistemology by assimilating whatever he does to a system of thought that makes the evaluation of knowledge claims purely mechanical in nature.

The assumption that all knowledge is linguistically formulatable and can be given to a person exactly by events in his environment is referred to by Piaget as the *copy theory* or as *empiricism*. In the form of *observation sentences*, it was an explicit premise of the philosophy of logical positivism (Carnap, 1963), which assumed that such positive forms of knowledge, together with the principles of deductive logic, could be used to construct scientific theories. While the literature on the philosophy of science today has largely turned away from this as a naive view, some version of it (operationalism, logical empiricism, or behaviorism) is still widely accepted in the natural and social sciences. Many writers in mathematics education may suppose that, when Piaget speaks of logico-mathematical reasoning, he is speaking of deductive logic, since that is the dominant view of how mathematics is done. The opposition provided by Polya (1954), Lakatos (1963), Wittgenstein (1956), and numerous other philosophers of mathematics (cf. Benacerraf and Putnam, 1964), is easy to overlook if one has never questioned one's own epistemological sources.

1.5. Dynamic Structuralism in Piaget's Genetic Epistemology

Consider now how Piaget and Szeminska (1941) discuss a question similar to Murray's. Speaking of the famous liquid pouring experiment and the nonconserving child, they wrote:

> The child might simply be comparing one level with another or one width with another, without considering the total quantity of liquid, but that would not necessarily prove that he was incapable of so doing. If this were so, as soon as the idea of the whole quantity made its appearance, the child would suddenly discover conservation; he would at once understand that the liquid remains the same since nothing is added to or subtracted from it. . . . If the child hesitates, if he gives a correct answer when the variations are slight but does not assume conservation when the variation in shape is

148J. A. Easley, Jr.

greater, it is obvious that he understands the question but is not convinced *a priori* of the constancy of the whole quantity. (pp. 14–15)

Clearly, in this passage, the knowledge of whether or not the quantity in question has changed is not subject to experimental guarantees. It is not something which can be read from the experimental procedure, but has a dynamic quality, full of uncertainty, until the child attains an *a priori* conviction that the quantity is conserved in such transformations. This is reminiscent of Kant's synthetic analytic knowledge, knowledge of facts about the world that is not dependent on having observed that the world is that way and thus is *a priori*.

The difference is that, for Piaget and Szeminska, such *a priori* knowledge is not always there but emerges hesitantly and gradually during child development by a mechanism that may be elusive but is clearly not a direct reading out of the environmental regularities. Children do not go around testing whether changing the shape of their collections of mud, water, sticks, and stones changes their quantity. In fact, as Piaget points out repeatedly, there is no other way to measure the continuous quantity of substance whose conservation most children solidly believe in by the time they are seven. Weight and volume by construction or displacement can be measured, but these quantities are typically not conserved until several years later.

Murray's (1977) reference to logical deduction can be compared to what Piaget and Szeminska (1941) wrote about the child's acquisition of conservation of continuous quantities:

> He begins... by considering only un-coordinated perceptual relationships of qualitative equality or difference, thus acquiring the notions of gross quantities and qualities not susceptible of composition. During the second stage, there begins a process of logical coordination, which is completed at the third stage and leads to classification when there is equality and to seriation when there is difference, this seriation resulting in intensive quantities. Finally, the third stage is characterized by the construction of extensive quantities through the equating of intensive differences and therefore through the arithmetization of logical groupings. (pp. 23–24)

The word "logical" appears twice in this passage and is used freely on a large number of pages throughout the book, but nowhere does "logical deduction" appear. What is it to be logical if not deductive? The frequent reference to logical multiplication and logical composition in which elements of classes and relations are put together in various combinations makes it clear that Piaget is making use of Boolean algebra that used to be called Boolean logic (cf. Boole, 1854) and might be more recognizable today as the elementary concepts of set theory—a theory which has the same mathematical structure as the first order predicate calculus, a branch of logic used to test the validity of many kinds of deductive inferences. But Piaget is not talking about deductive inferences from premises to conclusions or logical consequences of premises. He is postulating a mechanism of the formation of quantitative concepts that uses Boolean algebra (or set theory) in much the same way that geneticists use probability theory or economists use algebra. There is no assumption that children, fruit flies, or buyers and sellers are using the mathematical theory that the scientist uses to describe their behavior. Furthermore, such scientists assume mechanisms composed of interacting units that justify the particular mathematical system they employed. The geneticist speaks of genes segregating and recombining, producing enzymes which under certain conditions are expressed as characteristic growth formations. The economist speaks of decisions that buyers and sellers make which are functions of supply and demand. Piaget speaks of relations which are coordinated in various ways yielding intensive and extensive quantitative concepts. The term *logical* is applied by Piaget to some of these coordinations in the same way as the term *probabilistic* is applied by geneticists to gene recombination in a fruit fly, or *function* is applied by economists in stating the law of supply and demand. The child is not performing logical deduction, the fruit fly is not calculating probabilities, and the average buyer or seller has no use for the concept of function in his activities.

1.6. Other Empiricist Views

What Murray (1977) makes so clear for us is the common assumption that knowledge of conservation is acquired by using logic to deduce conclusions from "data," a word meaning facts that are *given* in the situation. Similar epistemological assumptions have been adopted by many psychologists studying conservation. For example, Lovell and Shayer (in this volume) interpret the process of cognitive development investigated by Piaget and his associates as one of progressive levels of abstraction using another fundamental concept of logical empiricism. Bruner, Olver, and Greenfield (1966), like Murray and most experimental psychologists, refer to attributes as objective properties of objects and to variables as classes of alternative attributes. Lunzer (1973) states that solving problems of deductive logic is the clearest example of formal operational thinking. Renner *et al.* (1977) give behavioral criteria for concrete and formal operations for numerous tasks.

All of these and many other writers seem to take Piaget's use of the language and symbols of logic literally and miss the metaphoric way he uses a variety of basic concepts that mathematicians and logicians have developed. However, the work of such psychologists cannot contribute to Piaget's program and vice versa. (See Papert's essay, "Sur la logique Piagétienne," 1963, which praises Piaget for adapting such structures and such notation to new conceptions of human thought; cf. Easley, 1973, 1978a, and Emerick and Easley, 1978, for criticism of empiricists' misinterpretations.) But this is predictable, as I have already observed, since without extensive philosophical training it is difficult to put aside one's habitual epistemology and consider others. Even philosophers such as Toulmin (1972) appear to have difficulty putting aside the fundamental role of logic and employing the inductive and constructionist theory building of Piaget. Piaget is not a philosopher; he disavows its methods (1965) and seeks a biological epistemology. Unfortunately, few biologists are interested. (Exceptions include Lorenz, 1962, and Maturana, 1970, who have their own biological epistemologies.) Meanwhile, Anglo-American psychologists and others remain unaware of the distortions they have introduced.

Other possibilities for interpreting what I have called a distorted assimilation are found in Kuhn (1962), Conant (1947), Burtt (1965), Pepper (1942), and many others. Essentially, these writers are saying that the conceptual frameworks, methodologies, world views, and epistemologies taken from the community of scholars to which the scientist belongs so guide the perceptions and interpretations of phenomena in his laboratory (even deciding what data are relevant and what are irrelevant) that a direct confrontation between two such general frameworks is not to be expected. Bohm (1974), who likens the overthrow of an established conceptual framework to a political revolution (in which the revolutionary ideology becomes the new orthodoxy), goes so far as to suggest that choosing a conceptual framework is like making an esthetic judgment of how well an abstract system represents a complex experience (personal communication). Bridgman (1936, p. 5) suggested that scientific revolutions like the one that shook physics in the 1920s, could be prevented by his program of operational definitions. Popper (1970), inspired by Einstein's accomplishments, argues that science should be in a perpetual state of revolution. Lakatos (1963) argues that Popper's view of the growth of scientific knowledge and Polya's conception of heuristics (1945) provide an open view of mathematics and the way mathematical concepts in all areas change. Scheffler (1967) takes exception to the apparent subjectivity of many of these views and argues that there is a basis for scientific objectivity.

In the social sciences, unlike the natural sciences, many perspectives compete at once and to a considerable extent experiments are an attack from one perspective on another. Many researchers, however, seem to see things primarily from one perspective and seem to have difficulty in adopting another perspective even for the sake of making an argument with a colleague who accepts it. Easley (1977a) discusses seven metaphorical perspectives on teaching and learning and some cooperative interrelations, as well as competition between them. The discussion of the epistemologies in this and previous sections has revealed some of the profound differences between Piaget's views and those held by psychologists who are logical empiricists, which may prevent effective communication. These differences are also important when trying to relate Piaget's work to mathematics education. They also seem to make communication or interaction difficult, as will be seen later. Although mathematics educators might be expected to have more interest in the question of the natural origins in childhood of mathematical concepts than would psychologists, there are strongly competing views. A more detailed discussion of genetic epistemology and of Piaget's research on conservation will be taken up after that. In this discussion, his continued use of fundamental mathematical ideas to develop and to extend his theory of conservation will be illustrated. Finally, looking at the views of some mathematics educators in relation to Piaget's program for genetic epistemology, we will consider what the conditions might be either for an effective use of Piaget's theory or for an effective challenge of it. The futility of continuing to focus so much attention on the existence of the nonconserver (either to prove it, to rationalize it, or to remove it by training) should become apparent.

2. The Logistics of Genetic Epistemology

2.1. The First Conceptualization

Piaget and Szeminska (1941) advanced a picture, whose complexities are still not generally appreciated, of a progressive organization of relations between relations in which the concept of number emerged finally in a form sufficiently well developed to permit operations like addition, subtraction, multiplication, and division. One-to-one correspondences between elements of sets (eggs and egg cups, hikers and hiking sticks, etc.) were studied, but found to be insufficient to establish the cardinality of a set, that is, the concept of a number of elements that did not change with rearrangements of the set. Ordinal relations were

explored both in terms of discrete quantities (one more than, one less
than, etc.) and in terms of length or height of sticks and dolls (longer
than, taller than, etc.). Arranging a series of sticks or dolls ordered by
height turned out, in many cases, to involve a process of coordinating
pair-wise judgments so as to establish a complete series. Making a one-
to-one correspondence between the elements of two such ordered series
was even more difficult; yet that was exactly what true counting involved, it was argued.

Piaget and Szeminska, however, never let go of the epistemological
problem of what numbers are when viewed in terms of their natural
origins. This statement (1941, Ch. VII) summarizes their argument
against Russell's definition of number (1903):

> As we saw in Chapters III–IV, Russell's solution to this problem is too
> simple. For him and his followers, two classes have the same number when
> there is a one-one correspondence between their elements . . . [however], as
> we saw in Chapters III–IV, there are various kinds of qualitative corre-
> spondence, which depend on the spatial position of the elements and have
> no numerical significance. When an anatomist compares the bones in the
> skeleton of mammals with those of other classes of vertebrates, the corre-
> spondence he makes is qualitative, and not mathematical, whereas in our
> case, if we assert that any element in F can correspond to any element in F_1,
> we have the right to conclude that F and F_1 correspond numerically term for
> term, and that this correspondence defines the number six. This number is
> not a "class of classes," but the result of a new operation brought in from
> outside, which is not contained in the logic of classes as such. In fact, this
> "quantifying" correspondence is only achieved by disregarding all the at-
> tributes in question, i.e. by disregarding the classes. (1952, pp. 182–183)

In contrast, we have studies such as that of Bearison (1969), in
which children were taught to divide two continuous quantities into
many equal parts and count them. He showed that nonconservers were
able to give apparently conserving answers to the usual questions of the
conservation tasks ("Is there the same amount to drink or does one
container now have more?"). From the Geneva perspective, however,
such studies simply ignore the many interviews in which children were
found to count rows of counters correctly but still insist that the one that
had been spread out had more counters.

In the final chapter of their book, Piaget and Szeminska (1941) return to the task of pouring of liquids treated in the first chapter, but this
time they explicitly test the ability of children to measure quantity of
liquid by dividing it into equivalent portions. Already the Genevan
trend to elaboration of experimental technique is in evidence, for this
procedure has six sequential problems. Later studies followed this point

further. Note, for example, the experiments of Greco (1962) which led him to propose a general, global idea of quantity he called "quotité," and Inhelder *et al.* (1974, Ch. 6). In other words, many children who can say the counting words in correct order and make an attachment of some kind of each word to each object, do not take the last word used as an indicator of the quantity of objects in the collection. In Bearison's (1969) experiment, Genevans would have to argue, the subjects learned that the experimenter would be satisfied with the last number reached in their counting, whether they were or not, as representing the total quantity involved. From the operationalist point of view, of course, that is what a total, discrete quantity means. The fact that counting may be performed correctly but not generate the idea of the whole quantity is one which probably cannot be perceived if one takes operational definitions seriously.

To the empiricist researcher the responses given to questions are the only evidence acceptable as evidence. To the Genevan, however, a probing, clinical interview is necessary to establish whether the child is a true conserver or whether some form of psuedoconservation is involved in his answer. To the empiricist, often, the probing of the interviewer is seen as cueing the child that his first answer was not acceptable and he must come up with another. This possibility is admitted by the clinical interviewer, but he continues to probe to eliminate the contradictions, if possible. If he cannot, he may drop the child from his study or decide that the child is in a transitional state. The empirical researcher usually wants his sample drawn randomly so he can use a statistical inference model; therefore, he cannot drop any subjects. The non-Genevan study shows additional difficulties arising from epistemological differences from the Genevan researchers.

Other conservation studies during the 1940s in Geneva (Piaget and Inhelder, 1941; Piaget, 1946a,b; Piaget *et al.*, 1948) continued to elaborate and refine the tasks used and to expand the epistemological problems addressed. The use of fundamental mathematical ideas continued in the same manner as Piaget and Szeminska had illustrated in their first work.

Consider two passages from their conclusions to illustrate further the use Piaget and Szeminska (1941) make of logical and mathematical systems in explaining number and its natural and spontaneous development in children:

> It seems that the third stage only becomes possible with the constitution of two interdependent systems, the "grouping" of multiplications of relations, and the "group" of numerical multiplications, both of which coordinate into a closed and reversible whole the operations involved, the one on the qualitative plane and the other on the numerical plane. (pp. 241–242)

Here, they do not refer to the rational numbers, which are closed under multiplication, but to systems of transformations, including identity and reversible transformations, somewhat like mathematical groups. These Piaget (1964) linked with the so-called "mother structures" of the Bourbaki integration of mathematics (1939–1940):

> while multiplication of classes and multiplication of relations are two distinct operations, the one bringing into correspondence terms that are qualitatively equivalent, and the other asymmetrical relations between nonequivalent terms, all that is necessary in order to make the terms of the relations equivalent and thus to fuse multiplication of relations and that of classes into a single operational whole, is that the differences shall be equalized. We then have multiplication of numbers. Once again, therefore, number is seen to be the synthesis of class and asymmetrical relation. (p. 243)

One has to recognize these two operations as belonging to what Piaget often calls *logical operations* or, more specifically, *logical multiplication*, thus leaning on the isomorphism between elementary set theory and logic.

2.2. Mental Imagery and Mental Operations

In the 1960s, studies were conducted in which perceptual cues were controlled by partially screening the objects or containers from sight while transformations were being carried out (Piaget and Inhelder, 1966). In the case of conservation of number, counters were placed on a fan arrangement of lines drawn on paper (or beads were strung on wires). This arrangement was used to strengthen the visual one-to-one correspondence between the two sets of counters. Other variations were tried exhaustively in the spatial conservation studies of Bang and Lunzer (1965) and the training experiments by Inhelder, Sinclair and Bovet (1974). Throughout all this research, the general idea persisted that physical acts of transformation were the basic elements of logico-mathematical thought. The cognitive structures these transformations formed, called *identity, negation, reciprocity,* and *correlative* were themselves thought to organize into a still higher level structure, the INRC group, around the age of 12. Thus, a physical transformation such as flattening a ball of plasticine into a pancake may be immediately seen by a conserving child as reversible in the sense that seeing it immediately suggests the inverse transformation of balling up the pancake. Research for many years attempted to find sufficient criteria in terms of these theoretical constructs. That is, whether the appearance of identity arguments or arguments based on one form of reversibility or another were sufficient to conclude that a child was a genuine conserver. [Easley (1974) and Kamara and Easley (1977) develop the argument that Piaget's assimilation-accommodation model provides an interpretation of the functioning of systems of operations in just this way. Witz's notion (1973) of many-many relations between molar observable behavior and aspects of cognitive structures is used to develop diagrams of relations between cognitive structures.]

Intensive research based in Geneva on alternative centerings, aspects of mental imagery, interactions among operations, and linguistic correlates of cognitive development was carried on. Despite this work, the essential problem of finding a mechanism by which the origin of conservation of number and structurally similar concepts of various physical quantities could be adequately explained remained unsolved.

Contradictions of various kinds inherent in the nonconserving child's cognitive structures had been considered in Geneva: Piaget (1974b), Smedslund (1961), and Halford (1970) devised training programs to teach conservation based on bringing contradictions into clearer focus. However, none of the training studies (Geneva-based or otherwise) really solved the problem of how children in the absence of any training at all rather uniformly come to acquire conservation concepts in the appropriate sequence. In short, not only were the empiricists unconvinced by the Geneva-based research to drop their empiricism and adopt a structuralist epistemology, but Piaget himself continued his quest for a more adequate explanation than the rather loose theory that transformations and operations on transformations provided. (For a fresh mathematical picture of one of the structures underlying transformations, grouping I, see Witz, 1966–1969 and Grize, 1966–1969).

2.3. Category Theory and Genetic Epistemology

A new set of ideas, however, emerged in Geneva within the past decade. These ideas, like the earlier ideas of transformation groups, came from studies in mathematics of a very general nature. In 1975, in his address to the Jean Piaget Society, Piaget called attention to category theory, a relatively recent development in mathematics that has great unifying power (MacLane, 1971). A category is a system of morphisms, and a morphism is a system of one-to-one correspondence (a mapping) that preserves the structure one is interested in. For example, a photographic enlargement is a morphism. A category, or system of morphisms, is like a system for making enlargements of enlargements. If there are alternative ways of getting the same result, a category is said to be commutative. In category theory, a major difference can be seen from that of transformation groups. Any group can be defined so that its elements are transformations, and Piaget often chose to look at groups (like the integers and the operation of addition) as though each element were an operator increasing or decreasing whatever one had to start with a given amount. Thus "+2" is seen as "adding two" and " −4" is seen as "subtracting four". If these are the elements of the group, then the general operation that unites them into a mathematical structure, successive application of any two transformations, defines a closed set—every combination is equivalent to one of the set. A category is a more general concept than a group because any transformation or mapping between sets of elements (e.g., the set of integers mapped into itself by doubling) does not have to be composable with any other (perhaps only with tripling integers). It thereby can express lower degrees of organization. Flattening a ball of plasticine into a thick pancake can be seen as the mapping (or correspondence) between the positions of every element of plasticine before and after flattening, a morphism that preserves the continuity of the whole mass. Futher flattening is another morphism. Attention is drawn to how the different parts of the plasticine ball move to arrive at new positions in the pancake, and a single transformation is thus seen as composite rather than elemental. This provides a definite theory to accompany the idea of *atomism* discussed in Piaget and Inhelder (1941) which could not, by itself, function clearly. However, a closed system is not required. Piaget (1977) reports new developments in the formulation of groupings relating them to categories (see Steiner, 1974; Wittmann, 1975; Easley, 1978b).

The point of bringing in this new piece of mathematical theory is not to make an already accepted idea (conservation) seem obtuse, but rather to establish connections between loosely connected theoretical concepts and to strengthen the connection between child development and mathematics to help solve the epistemological puzzle of how mathematical thinking is possible in the first place. Piaget's interest in such connections had led Freudenthal (personal communication) to predict that, since mathematicians were turning from the structural ideas of Felix Klein (1939) and Nicholas Bourbaki (1939–1940) (on which Piaget had based his theory) to category theory (MacLane, 1971; Papert, 1967), another psychologist would have to work out a theory that related children's ideas to category theory. Freudenthal was really surprised to learn that Piaget was hard at work at doing so himself.

3. Piaget's Overall Strategy

The effect of Piaget's program is that he is trying to use the newest insights of mathematicians to guide his study of children's thinking about quite traditional mathematical topics like number, operations on number, length, area and volume, and other measurable quantities. His purpose is not purely psychological—genetic epistemology is not just another name for child psychology—but he has created a kind of psychology related to traditional knowledge areas like mathematics and physics that aims to solve philosophical problems by nonphilosophical methods. It is easily confused with educational psychology because it treats school subjects, but Piaget explicitly says it is not the same thing. It is widely recognized as one of the leading developmental psychologies, but, because of his advanced mathematical interests, most developmental psychologists have difficulty following Piaget's thinking. It may be that their interests are not sufficiently epistemological to want to follow Piaget's program into new developments in mathematical theory.

However, mathematics educators of all kinds do have to make some assumptions about the nature of their subject matter, for their practices imply such assumptions whether they are interested in discussing them or not. Furthermore, some of them might be interested in keeping abreast of mathematical theory. Most appear to have assumed that mathematical ideas do not arise spontaneously in children but have to be instilled in them by teachers or parents.

The possibility that a significant number of key mathematical ideas do arise naturally from the spontaneous organization of the actions of children on manipulable objects like sticks, stones, mud, and water may fundamentally challenge most educational theory. If Piaget's efforts to keep the nature of contemporary mathematical thought clearly in view leave educators behind, there is the possibility that educators might carry out separate investigations from their own point of view. However, another possibility exists (Easley, 1977b). Piaget may have inadvertently discovered a masterfully heuristic strategy for studying the development of mathematical thought in children by applying deep mathematical concepts. The ingenuity of his experiments and the elegance of his explanations generally exceed what other psychologists of a less philosophical bent have been able to produce. In this author's opinion, however, the experiments have to be repeated to discover the generality and stability of each of the phenomena described.

Piaget not only rejects the prevalent empirical philosophy of science as a basis for children's development, but also as a guide for his own research methods. His structuralism, deriving from Kant (cf. Kemp, 1968), Meyerson (1912, 1921, 1925), Brunschwig (1912, 1922), Baldwin (1895), Bergson and Spencer (Čapek, 1971), also bears some relation to that of Levi-Strauss (1969), an apparently independent development. Methodologically, Piaget looks for the appearance of fundamental structures of adult logico-mathematical knowledge within the natural, and especially the provoked, behavior of children. He defines the transition to new stages of development by the first appearance of such structures, provided they can be fitted to a developmental sequence of explanatory constructions by the child.

This dynamic constructivism faces numerous questions. For example, why is the pathway of intellectual development so similar in individuals who are raised in very different environments (Kamara and Easley, 1977)? What is the integrative process that progressively, but never totally, eliminates contradictions in thought? What is the process of progressive differentiation of global ideas? It is evidently the questions Piaget faces with his own work that motivate his further study. With this picture in mind, some of the latest ideas from Geneva will now be discussed.

4. Toward a New Theory of Conservation

4.1. Geneva and the Nonconserver

Children who do not give a conservation answer to tasks involving transformations of form are said to be nonconservers and thus in a preoperational stage. However, it would be interesting to have a more positive description of how they do think of number or quantity of matter, or length, for example, in such a way that it makes sense for these quantities to change when there is just a rearrangement of relative position. In a recent report, Inhelder et al. (1975) advanced the idea that the nonconserver sees a collection of counters as a totality, in terms of its overall form which the authors call an envelope, borrowing an expression from mathematics used to refer to a smooth curve just touching a set of lines or vertices (see Figs. 1a, 1b, and 1c). However, by *envelope* these authors refer not only to the outer form but to the contents as well, including both counters (or other elements) and the spaces that separate them. The envelope is the collection for the nonconserving child and is judged as a whole to be equal in quantity or not equal to another envelope. This explains why a row of counters that is spread apart is judged to be more numerous, or to have more candies to eat, than another row with which it is evidently in one-to-one correspondence, even though when counted the counting stops at the same number in each case. However, it does not explain why two rows initially in clear one-to-one correspondence are judged unequal when one counter has been removed from one end of a row and placed at the other end of the

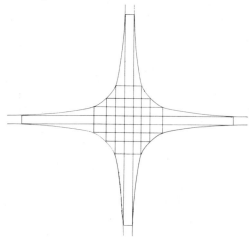

Figure 1A. Hyperbolas forming the envelope of concentric rectangles of equal areas.

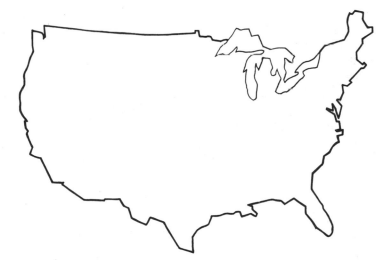

Figure 1B. The envelope as a territorial boundary.

Figure 1C.   Envelopes as outlines representing the whole of familiar objects.

same row (see Fig. 2). For now each row has the same size envelope. This case, however, resembles one of the conservation of length tasks (comparing two sticks of equal length). There the comparison is said not to involve whole objects, but just to focus on the displacement at one end or the other. This is not inconsistent with other discussions of displacement in the same paper, in which the counter removed is replaced elsewhere than at the other end of the same row. In moving a counter, there is a tendency to see what is added or what is taken away but not to see the two actions as being in a necessary correspondence. That explanation focuses on the failure of the child to see the transformation as a unity. Instead he sees only a part of it.

A more positive version of the explanation is that the nonconserver of numbers of counters (where the task involves moving a counter from one end to another) is like the nonconserver of length of sticks because he is seeing one envelope as surpassing another. The surpassing or overtaking phenomenon is a familiar one to children engaged in any kind of race, racing toy cars, running, or riding vehicles of some kind.

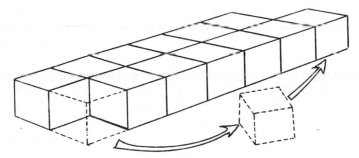

Figure 2. Rows of blocks with a transformation broken into two actions in correspondence.

As Piaget has made clear in research on movement (1946b), the surpassing element is judged to have gone farther and faster than the one surpassed, regardless of where they started. Similarly, the nonconservation over the displacement of counters from one end of a row to the other can be regarded as an *overtaking*. A similar case is the arrangement of blocks in serial order, not by length but by forming a "staircase" with one end of each block (see Fig. 3). In a few trials with kindergarten children, I found no easy overcoming of the overtaking idea of length by calling attention to the correspondence between the block that is first removed from one end of a compact row of cubes and then added to the other end. More detailed reports on these new experiments will be forthcoming soon.

4.2. The "Operational Envelope"

From one point of view, the disappearance of the envelope form and the space between the elements would seem to be involved in the

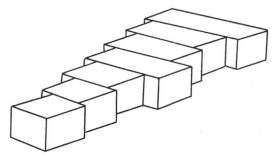

Figure 3. A staircase constructed from blocks of irregular lengths.

acquisition of operational conservation. However, there is another aspect mentioned earlier which applies here, namely, the correspondence between positive and negative actions making up a whole transformation. If one is only moving one piece from one end of a compact row of cubes to another, thus disturbing the rectangular envelope of the two adjacent rows in their original position, no new envelope seems necessary to make the correspondence between removing one cube here and adding it on there.

However, in the case of plasticine balls or containers of liquid, the quantity of matter transformed needs an envelope to represent the fact that nothing is added and nothing is taken away. A plastic skin impervious to matter might help, and water-filled plastic bags or balloons should be tried in the conservation of liquid task.

The task with a sheet of paper used as a competing envelope (Inhelder *et al.*, 1975; see Fig. 4), also suggests putting rubber bands around rows of blocks before one of them is displaced. Picking up a cube and putting it down elsewhere suggests the idea of gluing semicircular bits of white paper on the bottom of each block to form a continuous outline around the whole array. This also should be tried, both with closely packed rows of cubes and with a small space in between.

The question of correspondence, in the sense of morphism, could be investigated by using a piece of string attached to the block to be moved (see Fig. 5a) which would label that block as identical. A unique color also might help establish the correspondence. The water pouring

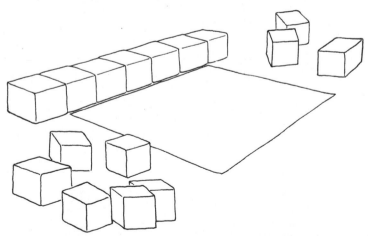

Figure 4.   Apparatus for the task of forming a second set of blocks on the sheet of paper that will be "just as many" as the first set.

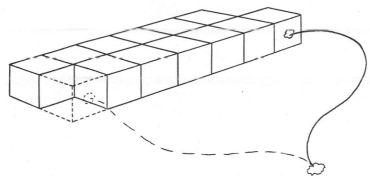

Figure 5A. Emphasizing the correspondence between the subtraction and the addition of a block by means of an attached string.

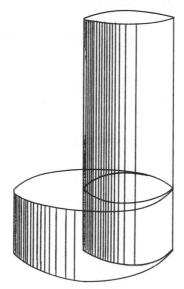

Figure 5B. Cylinders of equal volume, showing changed and unchanged parts in water pouring task.

could also be simulated with crescent and cylindrical blocks of wood (see Fig. 5b).

The plasticine ball experiment was repeated by Inhelder *et al.* (1975) using different colored bits of plasticine pressed together in a ball but still identifiable by color. Conservation here did not transfer to the case with plasticine of one color. However, when separate pieces of plasticine

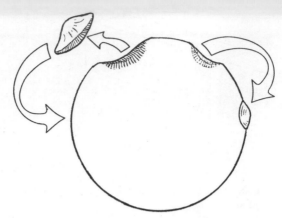

Figure 6.   Beginning the transformation of a ball of plasticine into a sausage bit by bit, showing the corresponding subtraction and addition of each piece.

of uniform color were moved from one place to another—where the action of moving each piece was divided into two discrete but corresponding steps, removing and adding on (Fig. 6)—true conservation was achieved, advancing children even three years in some cases.

4.3. Discrete and Continuous Quantities

The empirical conclusion that conservation over discrete transformations has the same structure as conservation over continuous transformations makes plausible the general envelope theory, because it provides a connecting link not previously available. What is interesting here, as in the case of formal operations, is that there is a tendency to see each different task in terms of various theoretical constructs—here, various conceptions of envelope.

We note these different concepts: (1) the mathematician's conception of the limiting form as parts are reduced in size; (2) the concept of a container that is impervious to gaining or losing matter; (3) the outline or overall form with elements contained between spaces; and (4) the operational concept of envelope, in which paths of correspondence between actions of removal and actions of adding on are preserved within the envelope. The earlier conceptions of partitions now seem less important, and likewise reversibility. Identity becomes more important but with new meanings. The multiplication of relations, which always seemed to have a doubtful or even ambiguous role, now appears to fade out of the picture altogether.

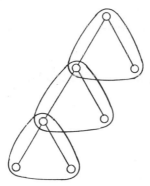

Figure 7. Grouping I representing unity of each composition by an abstract envelope (after Witz, 1966–1969).

The groupings, which played a major role in seriation and class inclusion explanations and were seriously involved in the concept of number, now have faded into the background psychologically. However, Witz's interpretation of grouping I (1966–1969), which uses an abstract envelope (Fig. 7), remains as a potentially useful theoretical concept. However, the original goal of replacing Russell's definition of number seems less important now than the goal of preserving the continuity of development from sensory-motor schemes through logico-mathematical reasoning.

5. Mathematics Education and Conservation

What would it mean for educators to examine the phenomena the Geneva conservation studies have revealed which connect children and mathematics from various epistemological points of view? This is the question that concerns us in the remainder of this chapter.

First, we may consider the linguistic point of view in mathematics, since it can be dealt with most briefly and succinctly. This is represented by the work of Suppes (1966), the early work of Beberman and Vaughan (1964), and the many followers of these pioneers who introduced the notation of sets and the manipulations of symbolic logic into elementary and secondary school mathematics. The revolution due to Frege (1950) and Boole (1854) in the standard ways of formulating mathematical arguments is accepted as a powerful tool of research and teaching at advanced levels. However, the replacement of so-called intuitive approaches to elementary topics in schools by concepts and principles formulated in terms of (1) sets of objects, sets of numbers, sets of points, and (2) carrying out arguments by a mechanical application of patterns for commutativity, associativity, etc. (together with substitution rules) treats elementary mathematics strictly as a language. In fact, Suppes (personal communications) makes the point that the assumption that sets can provide semantic referents for abstract notation fails in practice, for strings of symbols of all kinds are learned syntactically. That is, mathematics is reduced to rules as to what symbol can follow what in a string. The only relevant aspect of Piaget and Inhelder's work would seem to be the studies of conservation of order of colored beads on a wire (1946b) when the wire is screened from view and rotated 180°, 360°, or multiples thereof. For example, if $2 + 4 = 4 + 2$ is treated as two strings linked by the equals sign, then there is a rotation of one string that would produce the other.* It is the "ferris wheel" half-rotation, in which the "seats" remain vertical.

That children at the age of 9 (Piaget, 1946b) are capable of such transformations of rows of beads is interesting. They can be applied to mathematical symbols, as when a sixth-grade boy invented the Ferris wheel half-rotation as an improvement over his teacher's "pancake-flipping" rule for dividing by a fraction. The question of what children think numbers are was touched on by Suppes when he considered sets as semantic references but later found that they functioned syntactically as children actually worked with the materials. Beberman and Vaughan (1964) treated numbers as imaginary quantities that obey the axioms of arithmetic. The trouble is, as Waismann (1951) pointed out, no one has developed a set of axioms of arithmetic that apply just to numbers and not to numerous other kinds of systems. Furthermore, there is very little that linguistically oriented mathematics teachers can look at in the Geneva studies that would relate to their view. If these teachers happen to be Chomsky-like nativists, they might look at Piaget and Sinclair's claim that the deep structures Chomsky (1957) postulates as precursors of any language acquisition are simply sensory-motor schemes of infancy. However, it is difficult to move from studies of infancy to Piaget's theory of operations. The hypothesis that mathematical structures are analogous to biological structures intervenes, and a linguistically oriented mathematics educator would probably reject that idea.

Another view that appears closely related to Piaget's is that of Dienes (1960, 1963, 1973; cf. Easley, 1965). He has devised materials and

---

*Whether the string is vertical or horizontal really doesn't matter, but the innovators referred to went in mainly for the horizontal.

numerous games and activities that embody mathematical structures. Further, he advanced the thesis that through the practical activities involving many of these multiple embodiments the child will acquire the structures. Thus, groups, fields, vector spaces, Boolean algebras, and various number bases have been embodied in his many materials and activities. The implicit assumption of Dienes's work is that children learn by constructing such structures by abstraction from active involvement in systems that possess these structures. The possibility that other structures than the ones intended might be abstracted is to be reduced by employing multiple embodiments of the same structure.

The fact that Piaget tries to find relationships between mathematical structures, children's actions, and actions of others which they perceive, is the only direct connection between his work and that of Dienes. The fact that children conserve number, length, or other quantities at certain ages seems to be of little concern in Dienes's approach. The theory that children develop through stages which form a logical progression, without being exposed to environmental systems that embody those structures, is quite different from Dienes's idea of creating an environment with a given mathematical structure. The major emphasis in Dienes's approach is the induced acquisition of mathematical structures of a modern character, whereas the experiments of Piaget all have to do with the spontaneous development of quite traditional mathematical structures which is explained in terms of modern structures.

The British Infant and Primary Schools have evolved certain informal approaches to mathematics education which are often said to have a close relation with Piagetian theory. Characteristic of these approaches is the encouragement of young children to deal with their immediate environment quantitatively. For example, they may measure body dimensions, foot-sole areas, or dimensions of the school building, compute ratios of measured quantities, plot graphs, construct geometric designs in planes and solids, and use quantities of all kinds in connection with constructing models, planning excursions, etc. These activities in school seemed, by dint of considerable imagination on the part of both teachers and students, to give the lie to the old complaint that "incidental arithmetic" could not cover the essentials of the subject well enough. In schools connected with the Nuffield Mathematics Project, Geneva-trained scholars interviewed children to report their rate of progress in Piagetian stages. However, the booklets for training teachers in such check-ups, as they were called, deemphasized their use as assessment of educational achievement and stressed the character of the child's thinking that can be revealed in Piagetian tasks by a sensitive interviewer. Teachers were thus encouraged to become their own clinical psychologists, not to test progress, but to get to know their students' minds better.

The author knows of no reports of what teachers who do such checkups think of children who do not conserve length (either of sticks or of the rulers that might be used to measure them) and yet who can measure lengths and make scale maps of their schoolroom or scale models of nearby buildings. This would seem to give a lie to the argument that arithmetic cannot be learned meaningfully unless the child is conserving the quantities involved. If teachers in such schools find no relevance of the results of the clinical interviews in terms of conservation or seriation, but rather look only at the children's quality of mind, then it is possible that such teachers may well be open to Piaget's epistemology which looks for the development of mathematical thought out of reflections on actions the child performs. While teachers may not be technically interested in whether transformation groups or correspondences and morphisms best explain the natural development of logico-mathematical thought, they may have overcome the empiricists' epistemology which supposes that mathematical ideas have to be taught and cannot be reasonably expected to be created by individual children (Atkin and Karplus, 1962). To believe the enthusiasts of this kind of open education, the technical questions that concern Piaget in his research are of little interest, for these teachers already believe in a constructivistic structuralism based on their own experience of children's thinking.

Mathematics teachers, textbook writers, and specialists who look at mathematics as a skill subject should, one might think, have the greatest concern to understand the natural development of mathematical reasoning (Easley and Witz, 1972; Easley and Zwoyer, 1975). There are, however, many different versions of mathematics as skill: data-processing for decision making, memorization of facts, hierarchical task-analysis, motivation through competition and tangible rewards, following rules and procedures as moral training, and various combinations of the above. All of them treat mathematics problems as requiring skill in solving them and differ only in the format and recommendations for training in the composite skills.

If Genevan theory about conservation has aroused little interest, the seriation skills may seem to be more important as components of mathematical skills. Thus there are computer programs that simulate seriation and a Geneva group that studies information processing and works on advanced seriation tasks. However, information processing theorists tend to take their epistemological positions more seriously than most, for the differences between the different versions are tied to epistemological differences. For example, simulation data processors, like

Newell and Simon (1972) model human problem solving by heuristic programs representing internal processes, but task analysis psychologists like Gagné treat behavior as sequenced externally. (See Erlwanger, 1973, for conceptual problems arising from such approaches.) Memorization can be treated as a matter of drill and practice as Suppes does or as a matter of extrinsic motivation like math games developers do. Intrinsic motivation can be associated with some discovery process, as Bruner does. For these thinkers, Piaget's research is apparently just Piaget's research, not a particularly challenging epistemology they have to defeat or defend. But knowing the epistemological differences should help educators communicate.

The chief defender of Piaget's theory as relevant to mathematics education is Copeland (1970, 1974) who takes the view that the symbols of mathematical notation must have meaningful concepts to refer to or the memorization that results in studying mathematics is worse than useless (see Easley, 1971). While meaningful learning of mathematics is not a new idea, there has always been a problem as to the meaning of meaning. This gap is precisely what Piaget's theory seems to fill (Easley, 1975). Yet, he himself is interested in epistemological questions like: "Where does necessity come from? What produces the new synthesis out of a conflict?" For Piaget, the problem of meaning is taken care of by the concept of assimilation. So, in fact, the difference between the purposes of Piaget and the meaningful teaching of mathematics provides little basis for communication between Geneva and those educators who divide mathematics teaching practices into "meaningful" and "rote" learning.

Now Piaget himself urges mathematics teachers to pay attention to the developmental process in their pupils. However, among mathematics teachers we might also find a majority of teachers who see math teaching and skill drill as having the function of developing such general societal values as attention to instructions, careful detailed work, neatness, responsibility for working on schedule, checking one's own work, and an attitude of not giving up when faced with difficult or confusing tasks (Stake and Easley, 1978). Here again, there is little connection with Piaget's work on operations. (His studies of moral judgment might be more relevant.) There might be articulated, however, an epistemology of mathematics as disciplined work, progressing from the known to the unknown (see Perry, 1970). How different from Piaget's view now!

Therefore, the conclusions in which Genevan writers often express their findings can be confusing to educational psychologists who are used to statistical conclusions that could be derived from tests administered to random samples of well-defined populations. Not being trained in dialectics, they do not understand the study of relations between concepts except as an examination of their joint distribution in a population. That anyone could interview lots of children on many different concepts and not be interested in the relative frequencies of their various conjunctions would seem odd indeed. That would be taxonomic thinking. However, the continuing use of nonstandardized interviews, informal selection of subjects, and even on occasion very detailed study of individuals (Piaget, 1936, 1937, 1946c; Robert *et al.*, 1972) makes it clear that Genevan researchers have not been content with the conclusions reached in their earlier studies. In fact, the epistemological problems—the quest "to discover the mechanisms that determine thought, to investigate how the sensory-motor schemata of assimilating intelligence are organized in operational systems on the plane of thought" (Piaget and Szeminska, 1941, p. vii)—continue to motivate the almost uninterrupted series of studies published on conservation from 1937 to 1977. By and large, educational psychologists are not following this quest and continue their investigations into the correlations, regression lines and planes, and other statistical models of populations of individuals classified according to what are now for them standard conservation tests. It is as though the malacological taxonomists had ceased reading the anatomical and physiological literature about the organisms they are classifying.

6. Two New Questions

On the first page of this chapter, I raised two questions which seem now to be clearly answered. Piaget and his Geneva colleagues have maintained a steady interest in trying to answer Kant's question, "How is pure mathematics possible?" (cf. Kant, 1951). To answer how conservation of number and continuous quantities arise would constitute a big step in answering that question from an evolutionary biological perspective Kant could not have known. In contrast, most psychologists and mathematics educators interested in Piaget's work, taking the existence of mathematical knowledge for granted and feeling no need for a new epistemology, are instead trying to incorporate Piaget's disturbing revelation of the nonconserving children into the philosophically outmoded logical empiricist's epistemology. Meanwhile, Piaget's quest, stimulated by the development of mathematical category theory, has led him to new theoretical formulations which explain better both the conserver and the nonconserver than he could with a theory based primarily on transformational thinking.

Now that the Genevans have taken the question of the nonconserver very seriously, I am left with two new questions. The first is: Why does Piaget's genetic epistemology still have such great fascination for mathematics educators? I have already suggested the first answer, that Piaget shows that the conservation assumptions they have been making in curriculum planning can be challenged. But why wouldn't it be acceptable to wait a year or so until the nonconserving children begin to conserve particular quantities before teaching these quantities in school, as Copeland suggests? The answer seems to be, not that this misses (as it does) Piaget's (1974b) view of the useful function of various contradictions in cognitive development. Rather it would appear that the spontaneous appearance of conservation concepts in children is now philosophically unacceptable. Piaget's program for discovering the roots of advanced thought in childhood goes unrecognized in the flurry of activity of all kinds to promote conservation training and demonstrate the cultural origins of conservation (cf. Dasen, 1977).

Piaget gets little help from mathematics educators (not even a vigorous counterattack) for his program of genetic epistemology. The long-range benefits to education of a naturalistic epistemology go unexplored (now that Dewey's philosophy has largely been dropped), as do the more practical questions of how entrenched epistemologies could be loosened so as to make room for new ones. If mathematics teaching, like scientific research, cannot function without making assumptions about the nature of knowledge, it appears that neither of them can function when their basic assumptions are being questioned. The response to such questions typically seems to be a defensive one. It seems to be feared that if epistemological questions were taken as real questions, they could paralyze action as the proverbial centipede asked to tell how he moves his legs. My second question is this: Does epistemology have to paralyze action? For the results of asking children how they move their legs and arms when they go on all fours, see Piaget (1974a).

ACKNOWLEDGMENTS

The author is indebted to Linda Brandau, Peter Braunfeld, and Hans Steiner for helpful criticism.

References

Atkin, J. M., and Karplus, R., 1962. Discovery or invention? *The Science Teacher, 29(5)*, 45–51.
Baldwin, J. M., 1895. *Mental development in the child and in the race.* New York: Macmillan.
Bang, V., and Lunzer, E., 1965. Conservations spatiales. *Etudes d'Epistémologie Génétique, 19.*

Bearison, D. J., 1969. Role of measurement operations in the acquisition of conservation. *Developmental Psychology, 1,* 653–660.
Beberman, M., and Vaughan, H. E., 1964. *High school mathematics* (Teachers Ed.). Boston: D. C. Heath.
Benacerraf, P., and Putnam, H., 1964. *Philosophy of mathematics* (selected readings). New York: Prentice-Hall.
Beth, E. W., and Piaget, J., 1961. *Epistémologie mathématique et psychologique.* Paris: Presses Universitaires de France.
Bohm, D., 1974. Science as perception-communication. In F. Suppe (Ed.), *The structure of scientific theories.* Urbana: University of Illinois Press.
Boole, G., 1854. *An investigation of the laws of thought.* London: Walton and Maberly. (Reprinted, New York: Dover, 1951).
Bourbaki, N., 1939–1940. *Eléments de mathématiques.* Paris: Hermann. (English translation: *Elements of mathematics.* Reading, Mass.: Addison-Wesley, 1966.)
Bridgman, P. W., 1936. *The nature of physical theory.* New York: Dover.
Bruner, J. S., Olver, R. R., and Greenfield, P. M., 1966. *Studies in cognitive growth.* New York: Wiley.
Brunschvicg, L., 1912. *Les étapes de la philosophie mathématique.* Paris: Alcan.
Brunschvicg, L., 1922. *L'Expérience humaine et la causalité physique.* Paris: Alcan.
Burtt, E. A., 1965. *In search of philosophic understanding.* New York: New American Library.
Čapek, M., 1971. Bergson and modern physics. *Boston Studies in the Philosophy of Science* (Vol. VII). Dordrecht-Holland: D. Reidel Publishing Co.
Carnap, R., 1963. Autobiography. In P. Schilpp (Ed.), The philosophy of Rudolph Carnap: *The library of living philosophies* (Vol. XI). LaSalles, Ill.: Open Court.
Chomsky, N., 1957. *Syntactic structures.* The Hague: Mouton and Co.
Claparède, E., 1932. Foreword. In J. Piaget, *The language and thought of the child.* New York: Harcourt, Brace. (Reprinted, New York: Meridian Books, 1955.)
Conant, J. B., 1947. On understanding science. New Haven: Yale University Press.
Copeland, R. W., 1970. *How children learn mathematics: Teaching implications of Piaget's research* (2nd ed., 1974). New York: Macmillan.
Cronbach, L. J., 1972. Judging how well a test measures, new concepts, new analysis. In L. J. Cronbach and P. J. D. Drenth (Eds.), *Mental tests and cultural adaptation.* The Hague: Mouton Publishers, pp. 413–426.
Dasen, P. R. (Ed.), 1977. *Piagetian psychology: Cross-cultural contributions.* New York: Gardner Press.
DeMott, B., 1962. The math wars. *The American Scholar, 31,* 296–310. (Reprinted in B. DeMott, *Hells and benefits.* New York: Basic Books and in R. W. Heath (Ed.), *New curricula.* New York: Harper and Row, 1964.)
Dienes, Z. P., 1960. *Building up Mathematics.* London: Hutchinson.
Dienes, Z. P., 1963. *An experimental study of mathematics learning.* London: Hutchinson.
Dienes, Z. P., 1973. *Mathematics through the senses, games, dance and art.* Slough, Bucks., England: NFER Publishing Co., Ltd.
Easley, J. A., Jr., 1965. New math and new ideas: A review of Z. P. Dienes, "An experimental study of mathematics learning." *Contemporary Psychology, 10,* 328–329.
Easley, J. A., Jr., 1967. Logic and heuristic in mathematics curriculum reform. In I. Lakatos (Ed.), *Problems in the philosophy of mathematics.* Amsterdam: North-Holland Publishing Co., pp. 208–241.
Easley, J. A., Jr., 1971. A review of R. W. Copeland, "How Children Learn Mathematics." *The Educational Forum, 35,* 564–565.
Easley, J. A., Jr., 1973. Levels of abstraction and intellectual development. *The Journal of*

Children's Mathematical Behavior, 1(2), 76–83. (Urbana: Curriculum Laboratory, University of Illinois.)

Easley, J. A., Jr., 1974. The structural paradigm in protocol analysis. *Journal of Research in Science Teaching, 11*, 281–290.

Easley, J. A., Jr., 1975. Thoughts on individualized instruction in mathematics. *Schriftenreihe des IDM, 5*, 21–48 (Institut für Didaktik der Mathematik der Universität Bielefeld).

Easley, J. A., Jr., 1977a. Seven modelling perspectives on teaching and learning their interrelations and cognitive effects. *Instructional Science, 6*, 319–367.

Easley, J. A., Jr., 1977b. *Piaget and education*. Paper presented at the Jean Piaget Society Seventh Annual Symposium, Philadelphia.

Easley, J. A., Jr., 1978a. Symbol manipulation reexamined: An approach to bridging a chasm. In B. Z. Presseisen, D. Goldstein, and M. H. Appel (Eds.), *Topics in cognitive development* (Vol. 2). New York: Plenum.

Easley, J. A., Jr., 1978b. *Mathematical foundations of Piaget's research on conservation*. Paper presented at the presession of the National Council of Teachers of Mathematics, San Diego.

Easley, J. A., Jr., and Witz, K. G., 1972. Individualized instruction: Some observations from the ivory tower. *Educational Technology, 12(3)*, 50–52.

Easley, J. A., Jr., and Zwoyer, R. E., 1975. Teaching by listening: New hope for mathematics classes. *Contemporary Education, 47(1)*, 19–25.

Emerick, B., and Easley, J. A., Jr., 1978. *Fundamental challenges to the validity of formal operational tests*. Paper presented at the American Educational Research Association, Toronto.

Erlwanger, S. H., 1973. Benny's conception of rules and answers in IPI mathematics. *The Journal of Children's Mathematical Behavior, 1(2)*, 7–26. (Urbana: Curriculum Laboratory, University of Illinois.)

Frege, G., 1950. *The foundations of arithmetic*. Oxford: Blackwell.

Gentzen, G., 1969. Investigations into logical deduction. In M. E. Szabo (Ed.), *The collected papers of Gerhard Gentzen*. Amsterdam: North-Holland Publishing Company, pp. 68–131.

Greco, P., 1962. Quantité et quotité. *Etudes d'Espistémologie Génétique, 13*, 1–70.

Greco, P., and Morf, A., 1962. Structures numériques élémentaires. *Etudes d'Epistémologie Génétique, 12*, 000–000.

Greco, P., Grize, J. B., Papert, S., and Piaget, J., 1960. Problèmes de la construction du nombre. *Etudes d'Epistémologie Génétique, 11*.

Green, D. R., Ford, M. P., and Flamer, G. B. (Eds.), 1971. *Measurement and Piaget*. New York: McGraw-Hill.

Grize, J. B., 1963. Des groupements à l'algèbre de Boole: Essai de filiation des structures logiques. *Etudes d'Epistémologie Génétique, 15*, 25–63.

Grize, J. B., 1967. Remarques sur l'epistémologie mathématique des nombres naturels. In J. Piaget (Ed.), *Logique et connaissance scientifique, Encyclopédie de la Pléiade*. Paris: Gallimard, pp. 512–525.

Grize, J. B., 1966–1969. Note sur la notion de groupement. *Archives de Psychologie, 40(159)*, 51–54.

Halford, G. S., 1970. A theory of the acquisition of conservation. *Psychological Review, 77*, 302–316.

Inhelder, B., Sinclair, H., and Bovet, M., 1974. *Apprentissage et structures de la connaissance*. Paris: Presses Universitaires de France. (English translation: *Learning and the development of cognition*. Cambridge: Harvard University Press, 1974.)

Inhelder, B., Blanchet, A., Sinclair, A., and Piaget, J., 1975. Relations entre les conservations d'ensembles d'éléments discrêts et celles des quantités continués. *Année Psychologie, 75,* 23–60.

Kamara, A. I., and Easley, J. A., Jr., 1977. Is the rate of cognitive development uniform across cultures? A methodological critique with new evidence from Themne children. In P. R. Dasen (Ed.), *Piagetian psychology: Cross-cultural contributions.* New York: Gardner Press.

Kant, I., 1951. *Prolegomena to any future metaphysics.* Indianapolis: Bobbs-Merrill.

Kemp, J., 1968. *The philosophy of Kant.* London: Oxford University Press.

Klein, F., 1939. *Elementary mathematics from an advanced standpoint* (Vol. II). New York: Macmillan.

Kuhn, T. S., 1962. *The structure of scientific revolutions.* Chicago: The University of Chicago Press.

Lakatos, I., 1962. The foundations of mathematics. *Aristotelian Society Supplements, 36,* 155–184.

Lakatos, I., 1963, Proofs and refutations. *British Journal for the Philosophy of Science, 14,* 1–25, 120–139, 221–245, and 296–342. (Reprinted in book form by Cambridge University Press, 1976.)

Levi-Strauss, C., 1969. *The raw and the cooked: Introduction to a science of mythology* (Vol. 1). New York: Harper and Row.

Lorenz, Konrad, 1962. Kant's doctrine of the *a priori* in the light of contemporary biology. *General Systems, 7,* 23–25.

Lunzer, E. A., 1978. Formal reasoning: A reappraisal. In B. Z. Presseisen, D. Goldstein, and M. Appel (Eds.), *Topics in cognitive development* (Vol. 2). New York: Plenum.

MacLane, S., 1971. *Categories for the working mathematician.* New York: Springer-Verlag.

Maturana, H., 1970. Neurophysiology of cognition. In P. L. Garvin (Ed.), *Cognition: A multiple view.* New York: Spartan Books.

Meyerson, E., 1912. Identité et réalité (2nd ed.). Paris: Alcan. (English translation: *Identity and Reality.* London: G. Allen and Unwin, Ltd., 1930.)

Meyerson, E., 1921. *De l'explication dans les sciences.* Paris: Payot.

Meyerson, E., 1925. *La déduction relativiste.* Paris: Payot.

Murray, F. B., 1977. *Logic of nonconservation.* Presidential address (May). Abstracted in *The Genetic Epistemologist, 6(5),* 10–11.

Newell, A., and Simon, H. A., 1972. *Human problem solving.* Englewood Cliffs, N. J.: Prentice-Hall.

Nuffield Mathematics Project, 1972. *Checking up 2.* New York: Wiley.

Papert, S., 1963. Sur la logique Piagetienne. *Etudes d'Epistémologie Génétique, 15,* 107–129.

Papert, S., 1967. Structures et catégories. In J. Piaget (Ed.), *Logique et connaissance scientifique, Encyclopédie de la Pléiade.* Paris: Gallimard, pp. 486–511.

Pascual-Leone, J., 1970. A mathematical model for the transition rule in Piaget's developmental stages. *Acta Psychologia, 32,* 301–345.

Pepper, S. C., 1942. *World hypotheses: A study in evidence.* Berkeley and Los Angeles: University of California Press.

Perry, W. G., 1970. *Forms of intellectual and ethical development in the college years.* New York: Holt.

Piaget, J., 1936. *La naissance de l'intelligence chez l'enfant.* Neuchâtel and Paris: Delachaux et Niestlé. (English translation: *The origins of intelligence in children.* New York: International Universities Press, 1952. Reprinted New York: W. W. Norton, 1963.)

Piaget, J., 1937. *La construction du réal chez l'enfant.* Neuchâtel and Paris: Delachaux et Niestlé. (English translation: *The construction of reality in the child.* New York: Basic Books, 1954. Reprinted New York: Ballantine Books, 1971.)

Piaget, J., 1946a. *Le développement de la notion du temps chez l'enfant.* Paris: Presses Universitaires de France. (English translation: *The child's conception of time*. New York: Basic Books, 1970.)

Piaget, J., 1946b. *Les notions de mouvement et de vitesse chez l'enfant*. Paris: Presses Universitaires de France. (English translation: *The child's conception of movement and speed*. New York: Basic Books, 1969.)

Piaget, J., 1946c. *La formation de symbole chez l'enfant*. Neuchâtel and Paris: Delachaux et Niestlé. (English translation: *Play, dreams and imitation in childhood*. New York: W. W. Norton, 1951.)

Piaget, J., 1964. Relations between the notions of time and speed in children. In R. E. Ripple and V. N. Rockcastle (Eds.), *Piaget rediscovered*. Ithaca, New York: Cornell University School of Education.

Piaget, J., 1965. *Sagesse et illusion de la philosophie*. Paris: Presses Universitaires de France. (English translation: *Insights and illusions of philosophy*. New York and Cleveland: World, 1971.)

Piaget, J., 1974a. *La prise de conscience*. Paris: Presses Universitaires de France. (English translation: *The grasp of consciousness*. Cambridge: Harvard University Press, 1976.)

Piaget, J., 1974b. Recherches sur la contradiction. *Etudes d'Epistémologie Génétique*, 32.

Piaget, J., 1975. Comments on mathematics education. *Contemporary Education*, 47(1), 5–10.

Piaget, J., 1976. Transformations and correspondences. *Newsletter of the Jean Piaget Society*, 5(3).

Piaget, J., 1977. Some recent research and its link with a new theory of groupings and conservations based on commutability. *Annals of the New York Academy of Sciences*, 291, 350–357.

Piaget, J., and Inhelder, B., 1941. *Le développement des quantités physique chez l'enfant*. Neuchâtel and Paris: Delachaux et Niestlé. (English translation: *The child's construction of quantities: Conservation and atomism*. London: Routledge and Kegan Paul, 1974.)

Piaget, J., and Inhelder, B., 1966. *L'image mentale chez l'enfant*. Paris: Presses Universitaires de France. (English translation: *Mental imagery in the child*. New York: Basic Books, 1971.)

Piaget, J., and Szeminska, A., 1941. *La genèse du nombre chez l'enfant*. Neuchâtel and Paris: Delachaux et Niestlé. (English translation: *The child's conception of number*. New York: Humanities Press, 1952.)

Piaget, J., Inhelder, B., and Szeminska, A., 1948. *La géometrie spontanée de l'enfant*. Paris: Presses Universitaires de France. (English translation: *The child's conception of geometry*. New York: Basic Books, 1960.)

Polya, G., 1945. *How to solve it*. Princeton: Princeton University Press.

Polya, G., 1954. *Mathematics and plausible reasoning* (2 vols.). Princeton: Princeton University Press.

Popper, K., 1970. Normal science and its dangers. In I. Lakatos and A. Musgrave (Eds.), *Criticism and the growth of knowledge*. Cambridge University Press.

Renner, J. W., Stafford, D. G., Lawson, A. E., McKinnon, J. W., Friot, F. E., and Kellogg, D. H., 1977. *Research, teaching, and learning with the Piaget model*. Norman: University of Oklahoma Press.

Robert, M., Cellerier, G., and Sinclair, H., 1972. Une observation de la genèse du nombre, *Archives de Psychologie*, 51, 289–301.

Russell, B., 1903. *Principles of mathematics*. Cambridge, England: University Press.

Scheffler, I., 1967. *Science and subjectivity*. Indianapolis: Bobbs-Merrill.

Simon, H. A., 1962. An information-processing theory of intellectual development. In W. Kessen and C. Kuhlman (Eds.), *Thought in the young child*. Monograph of the Society for Research in Child Development, 27, 150–161.

Smedslund, J., 1961. The acquisition of conservation of substance and weight in children,

I–VII. *Scandinavian Journal of Psychology*, 2, 11–20, 71–87, 153–160, 203–210, and 4, 257–264. (Partially reprinted in I. E. Siegel and F. H. Hooper (Eds.), *Logical thinking in children*. New York: Holt, Rinehart and Winston, 1968.)

Stake, R. E., and Easley, J. A., Jr., 1978. *Case studies in science education*. Washington: Final Report, National Science Foundation Contract C7621134.

Steiner, H. G., 1974. Mathematical analysis of Piaget's grouping concept: Papy's minicomputer as a grouping. *International Journal of Mathematical Education in Science and Technology*, 5, 241–250.

Suppes, P., 1966. Towards a behavioral psychology of mathematical thinking. In J. Bruner (Ed.), *Learning about learning: A conference report*. Washington: U. S. Department of Health, Education and Welfare.

Toulmin, S. E., 1972. *Human understanding*. Princeton: Princeton University Press.

Waismann, F., 1951. *Introduction to mathematical thinking*. New York: Frederick Ungar. (Reprinted, Harper Torch-Books, 1959.)

Wittgenstein, L., 1956. *Remarks on the foundations of mathematics*. New York: Macmillan. (Reprinted: Cambridge, Mass.: M.I.T. Press, 1967.)

Wittmann, E., 1975. Natural numbers and groupings, *Educational Studies in Mathematics*, 6, 53–75.

Witz, K. G., 1966–1969. On the structure of Piaget's Grouping I, *Archives de Psychologie*, 40, 37–49.

Witz, K. G., 1970. Representation of cognitive processes and cognitive structure in children (I). *Archives de Psychologie*, 40(160), 61–95.

Witz, K. G., 1973. Analysis of "frameworks" in young children. *The Journal of Children's Mathematical Behavior*, 1(2), 46–66. (Urbana, Ill.: Curriculum Laboratory, University of Illinois.)

6

Two Models of Human Behavior and Reading Instruction

FRANK B. MURRAY

1. Introduction to the Two Models

All psychology is behavioristic, in the sense that it is concerned with the description, prediction, explanation, and even control of human and other animal behavior. The various psychologies differ primarily in their description of the place of the events and mechanisms which each supposes controls human behavior. There are at present three principal models or theories of human behavior: the operant or S–R model, the cognitive-constructivist model which is the focus of this volume, and the psychoanalytic model. The operant theorist places the control of human behavior in the environmental consequences of the behavior itself. The locus of control, therefore, is external to the person and is public. Cognitive theorists, while accepting quite fully that environmental events or reinforcements are powerful determiners of human behavior, suppose in addition the existence of a mind and argue that behavior is controlled by a structure or system of rules, of plans, and of cognitions that reside within that mind. The psychoanalytic model supposes the existence not

FRANK B. MURRAY • Department of Educational Foundations, University of Delaware, Newark, Delaware.

simply of a mind but of an unconscious mind, and attributes the control and the motivation of all behavior to it.

All scientists agree that the operant model is the most parsimonious and scientifically elegant because, unlike the others, it does not have to invent or suppose the existence of factors or mechanisms that cannot be known directly. If the operant model explained all behavior adequately, there would be no justification or basis for the other models and theories of human behavior. However, in the opinion of many theorists, the operant and other conditioning mechanisms are simply not sufficient to account for some very important aspects of human behavior. These are the development of language, logical thinking, and certain abnormal personality patterns which in themselves seem to defy any natural reinforcement history in which they certainly would have been extinguished or punished. In the case of language and logic, it becomes very hard to imagine, without inventing some tremendous innate capacity, what kind of almost universal reinforcement pattern could produce such sophisticated systems as language in about two years, and logical thinking, if Piaget is right, in about seven years. In the case of language, the child produces a language system that he has never really heard since virtually no one speaks the language that a young child speaks. The language system is not just imitated and as it has to come from some place its acquisition has become a major problem for psychologists. The cognitive models have been invented to account largely for language and logical reasoning. The psychoanalytic model was invented to account for various neurotic and psychotic personality characteristics.

Another way of looking at the differences between these models is to consider how one would go about simulating a human being's behavior. With what mechanisms would one need to endow a robot, for example, so that it would do or could do all that human beings do? With what would you need to endow a machine so that after it was turned loose in the world, it would end up after some reasonable amount of time doing things that are indistinguishable from the things human beings do? Would it simply be the ability to be conditioned? Is that a sufficient mechanism? Can one dream up a gadget such that, if it had the plasticity of being conditioned, and if it were to run around in the world man runs around in, one would end up with something that could do all the things human beings do? This hypothetical question separates the various models from each other. Piaget and cognitive constructivists argue that conditionability is insufficient and that one would need to program or endow the machine with an initial system of responses to stimuli and to provide in addition a mechanism for preserving the system (assimilation) and one for modifying it (accommodation). Given these two mechanisms and the capacity to balance one against the other (equilibration), and given also an appropriate set of sensorimotor responses and the opportunity to sample a number of experiences in the environment, one would find that a cognitive structure would be constructed. If a machine were built that had these two mechanisms, assimilation and accommodation, and a way of trading one off against the other (equilibration), one would have a machine that presumably could simulate human intellectual behavior.* This contrasts nicely with the operant model, which assumes merely an external control mechanism. It would be more widely accepted if it could account for some of the more remarkable things that human beings do and also if it had introspective and intuitive validity. This limitation of the operant model enhances the credibility of the other models considerably.

The models may also be contrasted in terms of the aspects of human behavior which each attempts to explain. Learning is the principal phenomenon of the operant model while intellectual development and pathology are the principal phenomena of the constructivist and psychoanalytic models, respectively. In this sense, none is a complete model and all are provisional.

2. The Constructivist Position

Constructivism is a neo-Kantian epistemological point of view which claims that what we take for reality is something we have constructed for ourselves. It claims such major intellectual notions, as the world existing independently of perception or that events are caused or that there is time and space, are mental constructions and not features of the universe itself. The process of this construction and its result is the focus of constructivist inquiry. Take a very simple idea, one with which virtually no one would disagree, that objects exist whether or not anybody is perceiving them. This notion takes apparently about two years to construct. On this point there is some evidence—Piaget thinks there is good evidence although not everyone agrees—that the child in the first months of life quite clearly acts as though he thought the world was being continually made and unmade. One cannot presume what is later presumed: that the world is populated by stable objects. Piaget's evi-

---

*For an explanation of why it is difficult to interpret Piaget's theory within such a mechanistic framework, see J. Piaget (1971), *Biology and knowledge.* Chicago: University of Chicago Press. [Eds.]

dence for this is something on the order of the following: a child is given a toy, and then as the child is in the process of reaching for the toy, it is covered up, and it is found that the child stops reaching for it. Piaget deduces from this that the child for all intents and purposes has figured that when the toy has disappeared, it does not exist anymore. And when it reappears, it is not *that* toy reappearing, it is a new object, a new thing. This at least is a plausible explanation for what is going on with the toy. By the end of his second year, the child acts very much as an adult would act. That is, the child makes the extravagant assumption that it is the same object that reappears and not an identical but different object. The dependence of existence upon perception is an old philosophical question, and is, in fact, the kind of question at the heart of Piagetian and other constructivists inquiries. The inquiry seeks to work out some difficult epistemological problems, and attempts and effects a resolution of them by observing how human beings constructed them in the first place. This essentially is the logic of the constructivist program of research which inevitably turns on some philosophical problem. The focus is upon children, not so much because of an interest in children, but because there may be a clue to the resolution of a philosophical problem in children's development and thinking. Piaget's theory is part of the discipline of genetic epistemology; it is not a psychological theory, although certain claims about human behavior are made in it. As will be clear later, implications of the theory for education must be made tenuously.

The theory does make claims and statements about cognitive structure and intellectual development. It claims that intellectual development proceeds in qualitatively distinct stages. This means that the basic way of knowing and interacting with the world changes as the child develops and that each of these stages is necessary and sufficient for the one that comes after it. It is not just that there are stages but that the stages are hierarchically linked and that each sets the conditions for the next. While it is obviously true that adults have more information than children, this is not the important intellectual difference between them in this account of intellectual development. It is rather that adolescents' and adults' basic way of organizing that information is qualitatively different from the way the child organizes it. This claim of the theory has led to a number of educational and curriculum and instructional design revisions.

Another important claim in this theory is that the roots of knowledge are based in action and not in language. In this theory, language is a poor medium for conveying knowledge, especially before adolescence.

The argument is an ancient one (e.g., Plato in *Phaedrus*) and has been phrased by St. Augustine as follows:

> There is nothing that is learned by the signs or the words that are proper to it, for when the sign is presented to me, if it finds me ignorant of the reality of which it is a sign it cannot teach me anything. But if it finds me knowing the reality, what can I learn by means of the word? It is a case of the sign being learned from the thing cognized, rather than the other way around. . . . What I am, above all, trying to convince you of is that we do not learn anything by means of the signs called words. We learn the meaning of the word (that is, the thing which it stands for) that is hidden in the sound, only after the reality itself which is signified by it is recognized rather than perceiving that reality by means of such a signification. (Price, 1962, pp. 153–154)

Piaget very clearly embraces this viewpoint of the relationship between language and thought. What is known is acquired through some non-language system. The fact that it can be expressed in language signifies really nothing more than the fact that one can express something previously acquired in some other way. Such a position would have the obvious educational implication that teaching by telling is inadequate unless a provision for the acquisition of the linguistic referents has been made previously.

Finally, this theory is a theory of knowledge (as opposed to information); it is a theory of things that are necessarily true, that have to be true and not merely of the things that simply are true. It is about the things which can be deduced from other things, and the process by which they are deduced.

3. Implications of Piaget's Theory for Reading Instruction

As has been said Piaget's theory of the development of intellectual competence is, strictly speaking, neither a psychological nor an educational theory, but rather a theory which makes a contribution to the constructivist discipline of genetic epistemology (the discipline that treats the development and structure of knowledge). Consequently the recommendations from the theory for educational practice are quite indirect and loose. In the main, the practical implications of the theory for education have already been made by others, and in fact what has really happened is that the theory has provided a theoretical justification for a number of long-standing educational innovations. Any instructional innovation, like progressive education, Montessori, open education, discovery learning, etc., which makes a major provision for the self-initiated activity of the pupil can be justified in the theory. The overriding curricular recommendation from the theory, on the other hand, is that the curriculum sequence should match or reflect the stage of cognitive development of the child. That the curriculum sequence should be based upon the psychology of the developing child is not a novel idea, of course, but what makes it interesting in this case is that Piaget has been able to be specific about the order in which specific curricular concepts and competencies develop.

The recommendations for reading instruction are limited somewhat by Piaget's view of the relationship between the development of language and thought in which, as has been noted, the former is dominated by the latter. The educational implications of this position are not limited simply to reading instruction. They constitute a general pedagogical recommendation that teaching by telling is inherently ineffective unless, as has been said, a provision has been made for the child to construct the meaning behind the word. The specific recommendation for reading instruction is that a smaller portion of the primary school curriculum could be devoted to reading than is presently the case, since reading is not critical for early cognitive development. Of course, this is a controversial recommendation, but one that has been put forth by Furth (1970) in the following manner:

> The average five to nine year old child from any environment is unlikely, when busy with reading or writing to engage his intellectual powers to any substantial degree.... A school that in the earliest grades focuses on reading cannot also focus on thinking. It must choose to foster one or the other. Historically it has chosen reading ... the first job of our elementary schools today should be to strengthen the thinking foundation on which any particular learning is grounded.... if early schooling aims to emphasize and purposefully nourish the thinking capacity of the child, it cannot look to performance in reading and writing as the immediate criterion of success.... My whole contention is that early reading does not have an intrinsic relation to intelligence and that its one-sided emphasis implies an underemphasis of intellectual development. (pp. 4–6)

Furth's argument is not that children cannot learn to read in the primary school or earlier, but that the instructional effort needed to teach reading is too great and should be placed instead in activities which directly promote cognitive development. The argument can be countered to some extent by the fact that cognitive development of children at this general age seems to proceed quite independently of schooling (Goodnow and Bethon, 1966; Mermelstein and Shulman, 1967), and that the effects of many training procedures for cognitive structure on children of this age are equivocal (Brainerd and Allen, 1971; Beilin, 1971, 1977).

Furth's argument is also not one against the eventual teaching of reading. The positive implications of Piaget's theory for the teaching of reading center upon the limitations cognitive structure may place upon decoding and comprehension. The general hypothesis is that concrete operational thought may be a prerequisite for reading. It seems to be a sufficient condition for reading, but not a necessary one because preoperational children, in fact, do learn to read. Presumably in these cases the preoperational reading skill is supported by some competence system other than the one Piaget has described for intelligence.

By the time children are 7 years old, they can respond to a number of problems more or less as an adult would respond to them. Before that time children tend to give quite surprising responses, such as that their brother has no brother (egocentrism), that a flattened clay ball has more clay, weighs more, and takes up more space than it did before it was flattened (conservation), that the water level in a tilted glass is parallel to the bottom of the glass rather than the horizon (absolute space), that there are more girls in the class than children (class inclusion), that if John is older than Jim, and Jim is older than Bob, John may or may not be older than Bob (transitivity), that a person cannot be two things at the same time, like an American and a Catholic (centration), or that a rearranged group of objects has more objects than it had before the objects were moved about (number conservation). These children under 7 tend also to focus their attention on only one aspect of a situation, such as noticing that a milk bottle and juice glass differ only in height while ignoring the difference in width. Similarly, they seem incapable of ordering a set of 10 or so sticks according to their lengths (seriation) because presumably this would require thinking of the same stick as both longer than the stick to its right and shorter than the one to its left. As well, all kinds of sorting and classification tasks from simple sorting on one dimension to more complex two by two (or more) classifications, are incorrectly performed by these children. Moreover, when they are pressed for their reasons for responding as they do, they resort finally to what appear to be elaborate and preposterous justifications (justification at any price). All of these pecularities in the young child's responses are characteristic of the preoperational stage of reasoning or cognitive structure and, as will become clear, could presumably provide obstacles to decoding the structure of written language and almost certainly place limitations upon the comprehension of it. In the space of three or four years, however, the child's responses in these areas become very much like the adult's.

Piaget hypothesizes that the ability to give adult-like responses in these instances rests upon the development of a system of operations. It is a system of reversible internalized actions that allows the child to mentally reconstruct the flattened ball as the original round ball (i.e., to reverse mentally the flattening transformation), to see himself as his brother's brother, to view the same object from more than one perspective or as on more than one dimension, etc. This system of operations, furthermore, has the properties of a mathematical group (viz., closure, associativity, identity, and inversion) and is both Piaget's description and explanation of the qualitative changes in the child's thinking that are found between 5 and 10 years of age. These operations are taken to operate distinctly upon different content areas so that there appears to be little transfer between the child's solutions to problems. Thus, the child typically knows that the number of objects in a set is unaffected by their spatial arrangement before he conserves their weight or volume, or he may be able to classify animals before vehicles although the principles of classification and deduction are the same in each case. The operations are said to be concrete because they are bound to specific situations and objects. That these operations function in various aspects of the reading task is a major implication of Piaget's theory for reading.

Virtually all task analyses of the reading skill (e.g., Gibson, 1968, or Carroll, 1970) acknowledge that the child must first know or speak a language to read it. According to Piaget, this acquisition is made possible by the development of representation (the ability to respond to stimuli that are no longer tangibly present), which signals the transition between sensorimotor knowing and the next stage (preoperational knowing). It is also generally acknowledged that reading requires the competence to dissect spoken words into sounds, to recognize and discriminate letters and graphemes, to decode graphemes to phonemes, to process more than one letter at a time, to process in left to right and top to bottom order, to know that written words are analogous to spoken words, to recognize words from such cues as configuration of letters, parts of the word, word context and sequence probabilities, and finally to reason, think, and make inferences about what was decoded. A main implication of Piaget's theory is that the competence to do all these things rests upon the development of concrete operations. The corollary of this implication is that reading readiness should be viewed from this perspective.

It would appear that the construction of the concept of number, which Piaget views as a fusion of the development of cardinality (that a numeral stands for a class of things) and ordinality (that a numeral has a position in a series—seriation), should be no less difficult a construction, for example, than the construction of the concept of letter, which has a kind of cardinality (t is the name of a class of things) and ordinality (t follows s) of its own and a place in a rule-governed system. Like conservation of number, which results from various spatial transformations on a set of objects, it makes sense to speak of the conservation of letter under various form transformations of case, size, and font. The notion is that the construction of the concept of letter is as dependent upon concrete operativity as are the construction of the concepts of number, length, substance, etc. Conservation of the meaning of a word (across transformations to other form classes, synonyms, homonyms) and conservation of the meaning of a sentence (across transformations from active to passive, for example) presumably represent similar, but also untested, relationships between reading and operativity.

In a similar way, it is possible to conceptualize the dissection of spoken words into sounds and the dissection of words into letters as a class inclusion problem in which the whole and a part must be compared. The recognition that words have both spoken and written forms can be seen as another decentration problem. Moreover, the all-important letter-sound correspondences may be viewed as instances of bi-univocal (square matrix) or co-univocal (triangular matrix) multiplications of classes and relations of sounds and letters. Indeed, Grant (1972) found that operativity and, in particular, performance on bi-univocal multiplication of classes, predicted reading achievement (NFER Reading Test) quite well ($R^2 = 0.5023$) and, in fact, as well as language development measures predicted it ($R^2 = 0.4993$).

Without quantity conservation it should be impossible, for example, to comprehend the point of the sentence, "Because he was on a diet, the fat man asked the waitress to cut his pie into four rather than eight pieces." The understanding of prose passages, the reasoning and making of inferences that define reading comprehension, also define comprehension in general and seem critically dependent upon such competencies as transitivity and formal operativity.

The evidence for the relationship between operativity and reading is largely correlational or limited to studies in which it is shown that conservers read better than nonconservers, or that good readers are better conservers than poor readers of the same age and IQ (see Waller, 1977). There seems to be a reliable low-positive correlation (about .40) between conservation and reading performance as measured by such standardized tests as the Metropolitan Reading Readiness Test (Brekke, Williams, and Harlow, 1973; Heatherly, 1972; Rausher, 1970), Stanford

Achievement Test (Kaufman and Kaufman, 1972), and individually designed reading tasks (Goldschmid and Bentler, 1968; DeVries, 1974; Stack and Murray, 1976). The correlation between reading and conservation is reduced somewhat, but usually not appreciably, by partialling out general intelligence; in these studies conservation is often more highly correlated with reading than IQ is correlated with reading. Performance on other operativity tasks is also positively related to reading, such as class inclusion (DeVries, 1974; Smith, 1971), seriation (Scott, 1969; Kaufman and Kaufman, 1972), absolute space horizontality (Lovell, Shapton, and Warren, 1964), generic identity conservation, and transitivity (DeVries, 1974). Moreover, Briggs and Elkind (1973, 1974) have found that early readers score significantly higher on conservation than normal-age readers of the same IQ. Of course early readers also score higher than normal-age readers on other tasks that are unrelated to reading.

Elkind and his colleagues have further identified a number of perceptual decentration abilities (systematic exploration of the stimulus, flexibility with figure-ground reversals, transcendence over the content of parts in perception of the whole, mental transportation of stimuli from one context to another, etc.). These decentration abilities and reading achievement share a common factor (Elkind, Horn, and Schneider, 1965) and average readers perform better on these decentration tasks than slow readers of the same IQ (Elkind, Larson, and VanDorminck, 1965). Moreover, training on the tasks seems to lead to an improvement in word recognition (Elkind and Deblinger, 1969).

At the heart of initial reading and word recognition is the ability to process more than one letter at a time and later to process more than one word at a time. This ability may be related to what Elkind has called schematization or the ability to transcend the parts of one sort to see a whole of another; an example would be to recognize that a configuration of various fruits had the shape of an animal. More specifically the ability has been investigated directly by Farnham-Diggory and Bermon (1968). They taught a group of conservers and nonconservers the meanings of various logographs for the concepts, *jump, block, over, teacher, walk* and *around*, and found that each group learned the logographs equally well. However, when the logographs were put together in a series, such as *walk-around-teacher* or *jump-over-block*, and the children were directed to act out what the logographs said, the conservers performed at a significantly higher level (7.54 out of 8.00) than the nonconservers (2.31). The conservers seemed able to "read" the logographs or to synthesize the elements into a meaningful whole which directed their action while the nonconservers were not. Denner (1970) found that normal readers were superior to problem readers of the same age in this type of logograph synthesis.

The link between operativity and reading comprehension has been investigated by Rawson (1969) and Stack and Murray (1976). In each study, stories were constructed that illustrated or reflected one or more of the operativity structures. In the Stack and Murray study, these were class inclusion, complementary classes, multiplication of classes, seriation, and multiplication of relations at the concrete operational level, and mechanical equilibrium, probability, proportionality, combinatorial reasoning, and correlation at the formal operational level. Like the earlier example of the fat man and his pie, the chapters in the comprehension story each had one of these concrete or formal operativity structures embedded in it. Comprehension was measured (Rystrom, 1970) by measures of vocabulary, statement recall, statement sequence, inference, role taking, and so forth. The overall correlation between operativity, as measured independently in the traditional way, and comprehension was .69. The correlation was reduced to .51 when IQ and vocabulary (as measured by vocabulary subtest of the Gates-MacGinitie) were partialled out. There were, as well, significant low-positive correlations between each operativity measure and its comprehension counterpart. Performance on the concrete operativity tasks exceeded comprehension of the passages in which these operativity structures were embedded, while surprisingly, comprehension of the formal operational passages exceeded performance on the formal operational tasks themselves. Since the factor structures of the operativity performance and the comprehension task performance were quite different and theoretically sensible, it does not seem that the achievement of this study was simply a measure of operativity in two modes, the traditional assessment paradigm and comprehension of a story passage.

This research indicates that there is a clear link between specific operativity features and specific aspects of reading comprehension. Moreover, at the concrete operational level, operativity may be a sufficient, if not necessary, condition for reading. What the exact contribution of operativity is to the reading process is not clear, but it is possible, and even likely, that it does not influence the process itself as much as it influences the child's understanding of the process. Operativity may only allow the child to be more reflective about what he is doing when he reads, and to appreciate the inherent logic and structure in the activity of reading. Children who read without operativity to support the activity may be like children who count accurately but do not have number conservation. Decoding certainly may occur in an automatic nonreflective manner and operativity presumably contributes very little to it; however, decoding with understanding and intelligence, so to speak, probably depends upon the Piagetian operational structures. Certainly, the language of reading instruction itself, emphasizing as it does the concept of rules, and classroom reading exercises of sorting, ordering graphemes and phonemes may be expected to depend upon operativity. Indeed, in studies of the correlation between operativity and reading, the measure of reading is often such classroom or standardized exercises. The concepts of rule, arbitrariness, and exceptions to rules which underlie orthographic structure and the teaching of it are concrete operational constructions. Piaget's work on moral development, justice, and the child's concept of the rules of a game indicate that these notions have a developmental history like that of operational intelligence.

In sum, the theory should hold that, in principle, written material is a part of the world to be interpreted and understood by the same operations that Piaget has claimed support the child's understanding of the many things in the child's world that Piaget and his colleagues have already researched. Letter, word, sentence, etc., are as valid concepts and appropriate objects for operational processing as are the concepts of number, weight, causality, time, amount, velocity, etc. These and other linguistic conceptual distinctions are amenable to the operations of addition and multiplication of classes and relations that constitute the concrete operational structures as well as the operations of the INRC group of the formal operational period.

As the Stack and Murray study implied, the relationship between reading and operativity may be somewhat different at the formal operational level from what it was at the concrete level. Formal operations are hypothesized by Piaget to describe and explain some additional qualitative changes in the child's reasoning that occur around the ages of 11 and 12 years. At this time, children seem for the first time to reason hypothetically, that is to imagine a situation different from the one that actually exists and to reason from it; they also show initial competence in concepts of probability and proportion, and give evidence of combinatorial reasoning in which they seem able to hold all things constant but one, in their problem solving. The notion here is that language, and by implication, reading, may be a necessary, but insufficient, condition for the development of formal operations (e.g., Elkind, Barocas, and Rosenthal, 1968). There is, of course, evidence that the written compositions and reading comprehension of formal operational children, or at least of children of that age, show clear and scoreable signs of formal operational thought (Lovell, 1971; Hallam, 1967; Goldman, 1968; Stack and Murray, 1976). This may indicate that the mental manipulation provided in language and reading is critical to the development of formal operational thought since it provides the medium for hypothetical and combinatorial reasoning. In a similar manner, Olson (1976) has argued that "the invention of an artifact, the phonetic alphabet, has altered both human culture and human cognition" not so much because of what was read as because of the fact of reading itself. The reading mind differs qualitatively from the nonreading one in this respect. Of course, Piaget insists that formal operations, although not quite as general or universal as was once thought, have their developmental roots not in language but in the fusion of reversibility by negation and reversibility by reciprocity into one system (the INRC group).

Specific recommendations from Piaget's theory for reading instruction should wait for more explicit determinations of the relationships between operativity, decoding, and comprehension. Still, the evidence suggests that the recommendations that might eventually come from the theory would include a general recommendation to delay reading instruction until the advent of concrete operational thought, because these operations probably contribute to a more reflective appreciation of the reading task and because instruction in reading otherwise, while possible, is difficult and takes time from instruction that might contribute to the development of operativity itself. However, rather than wait for the match between cognitive structure and the structure of the decoding task to occur, schools presumably could do some things to facilitate the match and bring about cognitive readiness for reading.

It would be reasonable to attempt to train children on the cognitive and perceptual operations that are related to reading. Rather than fit the child's mind to the task, however, it is also reasonable to attempt to fit the task to the child. Modifications in the reading task consistent with the theory already exist. The initial teaching alphabet (ita), for example, eliminates the need for double classification competence of concrete operations since each phoneme has a unique grapheme. The language experience approach to reading instruction constitutes a significant modification of the reading task since the child reads his own language and spellings and since the task itself is based upon the content and structure of the child's experiences. The match between cognitive structure and the task exists by definition in this instructional innovation.

In sum, the principal recommendation from Piaget's theory for reading instruction hinges upon a conceptualization of reading readiness in terms of operativity. Modification of the child's cognitive structure by instruction and the modification of the reading task itself through a curriculum reform are recommendations that are both consistent with the theory.

4. On the Pedagogical Similarity of the Operant and Cognitive Models

With respect to the differences between the cognitive-constructivist models and the other models of human behavior, the question for the educator is likely to be: "What difference do these separate theoretical accounts make in educational practice?" What does the Piagetian model recommend that the others do not? Are there instructional recommendations from the operant model, for example, that are really inherently different or incompatible with those from the cognitive model? One would think so, but the differences operationally between these models may be minimal and in most cases the pedagogical recommendations could be very nearly the same. In the 1942 *NSSE Yearbook* the leading learning theorists of the era were invited to discuss the implications of various theories of learning for educational practice. Guthrie, a major figure of the time, had the lead article, which he called "Conditioning." In it he described eloquently his theory of learning as the contiguity of stimulus and response and cited a great many clever educational implications of his position. His paper was followed by Clark Hull's, whose theory of learning was antithetical in many important respects with Guthrie's. After some 30 pages, Hull concluded:

> Because of the severe limitations on the space available for the present chapter no attempt will be made to draw detailed educational maxims from the preceding theoretical outline. Despite certain sharp differences between the primary assumptions of Professor Guthrie's chapter and this one, the two systems have a strong kingship. If practical morals or recommendations were to be drawn from the present system, they would agree almost in detail with those put forward by Professor Guthrie. (Hull, 1942, p. 93)

A similar state of affairs exists between the models described earlier, and one needs to think very clearly about the ways in which these models differ with respect to their educational implications because, while they may appear antithetical and while descriptions of the educational practices each engenders may seem incompatible, they may not be. Dewey argued that with any two positions that are in opposition, it is always possible, often with great effort, to find some dimension that links them, because things are only opposite with respect to some dimension, and with respect to that dimension the opposites are also similar. Dewey made that point with respect to the classic debate in education which still goes on. "Is teaching an art, or is teaching a science?" The difference between arts and sciences is not that there are not teachable rules for doing one and not the other, but that the rules for doing the arts have not been discovered. In the case of science, the rules for doing it are established. In this case, arts and sciences reside on a common dimension of "rules for doing x" on which at one end the rules are clear and at the other they are undiscovered.

The same kind of case can be made for the differences between the pedagogical recommendations from the operant model or cognitive-constructivist model. When one comes to talk about practical recommendations for education, the differences really are minimal and where they differ, they differ in a position on some dimension between them. The clearest educational recommendations that come from the operant theory for education are things like programmed instruction, computer assisted instruction (which is the technological extension of the first), contingency managed classrooms, token economies (i.e., bribing children to learn things, telling children what to do and rewarding them when they do it). The unique educational recommendation from the cognitive group (other than certain curriculum innovations like Project Physics or Minnemast in which the curriculum is the structure of the discipline) is discovery learning. Discovery learning is pedagogically what the cognitive position stands for. The notion is that the information the child discovers for himself will be remembered better, learned easier and will be a more permanent acquisition than information acquired in some other way. However, when one teaches by the discovery method, one does very much the same kind of thing one could be doing when one teaches by the operant method. For example, what one does in both cases is to arrange the environment in some way so that some responses are more likely than others to occur and some are made incompatible with the environment. Schools are arranged so that some behaviors students are capable of making are more likely to occur than others. A classroom is arranged so that certain kinds of behavior that pupils are capable of making are more likely to occur than others. In a discovery learning exercise or a programmed learning lesson, the teacher sequences the events so that the pupil begins with some response or skill that he already has. This response is made either to a deliberate statement or some clear direction or in response to an artful manipulation of the materials. Programming and discovery both start where the child is, with his ability level wherever that is or with some presumption about his cognitive structure and what it contains. In both cases, one starts where the child is and one begins to move from there in some systematic way. Now the dimension on which instruction is varied is really the dimension of how much guidance one wishes to give along the way—whether one wishes to prompt at every intersection or whether the materials themselves are to lead the child on. By careful arrangement of the materials and directtions, one tries in either model to move the child from the position that he has now to some position that is the goal of instruction. Finally, when the pupil gets there, or as he gets nearly there, some means for telling him that he's there is provided in both models. He can either be told or verbally encouraged, which is an extrinsic or external device, or he can be provided with some kind of intrinsic feedback or reinforcement by the materials when he arrives at a position which hopefully fits in some coherent way with what he already knows. That feeling of coherence is presumably gratifying—a satisfying feeling that the problem is solved because the solution is coherent with cognitive structure and its content. This intrinsic satisfaction occurs in both pedagogical procedures and is not a peculiar feature of only one of them.

In this argument, the differences between these models, which may be very interesting theoretically, are not great for educational practice. In a very real sense the rat in the Skinner box discovers the solution to its thirst.

However, what of the case where the goal of instruction is really unanticipated, where not enough is known to predict what the child is going to do, and where one may not even know *what* the child is to do? Such a case could be a creativity lesson where the goal is for some creative or novel behavior to occur. All this means for this issue is that the teacher probably should be a human being, because it will take a human being to recognize a particular response, unanticipated as it was at the beginning, and evaluate it, or praise it, or shape it in some way. That means that there is a fair amount of important instruction that can not really be left to machines because in fact we do not know enough about what someone will do in a situation to anticipate and program for all the possible outcomes. However, this fact is a limitation in both the pedagogy of discovery and programming and does not provide grounds for choosing one over the other. If a thing can be taught, it can be programmed, and it can be programmed in such a way as to be indistinguishable from a discovery learning exercise.

The differences between the models do not lead to different pedagogies but only to different explanations of teaching. Both Piaget and Skinner, for example, have different but adequate explanations for such educational strategies as Montessori teaching. Neither explanation influences Montessori practice and Montessori practice is compatible with both models. This should not be a particularly surprising state of affairs for there are many instances in science and elsewhere where different theoretical positions yield the same practical recommendations, but of course for different reasons. Both Ptolemaic and Copernican astronomies yield the same navigational strategies, for example. All learning theories recommend that teachers make provisions for presentation of the item to be learned, the pupil's response to it, and reinforcement of that response. As William James wryly observed, "If the difference doesn't make a difference, it doesn't make any difference."

There is, moreover, nothing inherent in the operant model that prohibits the teacher from taking as his goal the child constructing his world. The teacher would arrange a set of conditions that will make "constructivist behavior" a likely or probable event. When the child gets close to it the teacher will reward him, and when he gets too far away from it the teacher will ignore him or even punish him. There is nothing in the operant model which requires that the teacher be the source of knowledge, nor is there a requirement that the child could not construct knowledge from his own actions. There is nothing in an operant situation which requires telling. Transitivity, for example, could be programmed for construction in an operant situation in which students manipulated little rods or something until they found that if $A = B$ and $B = C$ then $A = C$. Gifted teachers, especially in the arts or athletics, may be able to "teach" their pupils behaviors they themselves do not have, nor may never have had, and pupils may be guided by the teacher to ideas or insights that the teacher has never had.

There is, of course, an area in which the various models may result in differing educational practices and it is based partly on the fact that the connections between theory and practice are vague and imprecise. However, it is clearly possible that the teacher's belief in a model may influence the style of teaching and in this regard the different models may lead to different pedagogical results. Unfortunately, the data on the influence of teacher philosophy and belief on teaching practice and student achievement do not indicate that differences in teaching philosophy lead to significant differences in practice (Stephens, 1967).

Nevertheless, if one is a believer that man is a conditionable organism, then one may treat people as though they were conditionable, and that may not have a neutral influence on the situation. A self-fulfilling prophecy may be created. Similarly, if a teacher were to adopt constructivist viewpoints, he could become sensitized to different things in the classroom than the operant teacher. That there may be important differences in the behavior of operant and Piagetian teachers as their behavior is directed by their beliefs in the two models may be as much a testimony of the restrictive interpretations each makes of the possibilities inherent in and compatible with the models as it is of true differences in the models.

5. General Piagetian Educational Recommendations

The recommendations from the constructivist model, in addition to the ones just mentioned, occur in three categories—assessment, curriculum design, and instruction.

Piaget devised in the face of the behavioristic strain in American psychology a clinical method for evaluating what a child knew. This, he insisted, had to be done in a single subject session in which the experimenter created a situation in which the child made a prediction, or validated his expectations. If the prediction or expectation failed, the experimenter was there to recognize that and to suggest some alternative which again led to another expectation on the part of the child. It is in this series of expectations and predictions that one discovers the general cognitive structural level of the child. Piaget very clearly made his own laboratory work quite difficult and time consuming by insisting that the only valid way to assess intellectual competence and intellectual structure was with this kind of clinical procedure. Presumably, it has equal validity for an educational setting and there is a strong recommendation from this theory for that kind of assessment of academic achievement.

When Piaget worked in Binet's laboratory, he was much more fascinated by the mistakes a child made than by the things he got right. He would look at these errors, these mistakes that schools attempt to extinguish, as really the most interesting things that may be going on, because in that error the child is revealing what he thinks. These creative errors, as Bruner has called them, reveal cognitive structure and thinking and represent pupil behavior that may be more significant than the correct response or answer.

Piaget's primary psychological accomplishments may be viewed, in fact, as the discovery of children's mistakes that virtually no one would ever think they would make. The conservation phenomena is an example of that. Who would have thought that anybody would think that by spreading objects out you might actually increase the number of things that are there. Incidentally, since all the Piaget items have deceptively clear relationships with chronological age, they make, by virtue of that fact alone, excellent candidates for IQ tests. However, Piaget based IQ tests have no greater utility in predicting school achievement than conventional standardized IQ tests (Goldschmid and Bentler, 1968).

The recommendations for curriculum design are clearly that the hierarchical level of stages should dictate the curricular sequence. The principal issue in curriculum design is sequencing and this theory does give some clue about which concepts should come before and after others. Neither model can make any recommendations about the content of the curriculum, but as Piaget does treat various concepts that are normally part of the curriculum, his theory lends considerable empirical support to certain curricular sequences and to consideration of certain topics that the child finds difficult to understand.

There are three primary instructional recommendations. There is a high premium in the theory on self-initiated activities, like discovery learning, and other classical educational innovations, like Montessori or Sylvia Ashton-Warner, Dewey's progressive strategies, and the British Infant Schools. All these innovations have existed quite nicely for some time and have theoretical support in Piaget's account of intellectual functioning. Any educational innovation that places a high premium on self-initiated activity is consonant with this theory.

There is also a high premium placed upon social interaction and social collaboration, since it is the principal device for the breakdown of egocentric thought. Intellectual development is enhanced enormously, and perhaps made possible, by the fact that one's cognitive structure inevitably conflicts with other people's. This conflict motivates resolution and eventual confirmation which promotes ability in cognitive structure.

The third basic pedagogical recommendation is simply that the pedagogy which simulates the processes of human development is most likely to succeed. In the Genevan context those teaching procedures which simulate equilibration are recommended.

In summary, this chapter has set out theoretical differences between various psychological models and has advanced the argument that the differences between two of them for educational practice are not as great as is often assumed. In addition the recommendations of one of the models, Piaget's constructivist account of intellectual development, for educational assessment, curriculum design, and instruction were considered. Particular emphasis was placed upon an analysis of the implications of the theory for reading instruction.

References

Beilin, H., 1971. The training and acquisition of logical operations. In M. F. Rosskopf, L. P. Steffe, and S. Tabock (Eds.), *Piagetian cognitive-development research and mathematical education*. Washington, D. C.: National Council of Teachers of Mathematics.

Beilin, H., 1977. Inducing conservation through training. In G. Steiner (Ed.), *Psychology of the 20th century* (Vol. 7), *Piaget and beyond*. Bern: Kinder.

Brainerd, C. J., and Allen, T. W., 1971. Experimental inductions of the conservation of "first-order" quantitative invariants. *Psychological Bulletin, 75*, 128–144.

Brekke, B. W., Williams, J. D., and Harlow, S. D., 1973. Conservation and reading readiness. *Journal of Genetic Psychology, 123*, 133–138.

Briggs, C., and Elkind, D., 1973. Cognitive development in early readers, *Developmental Psychology. 9(2)*, 279–280.

Carroll, J. B., 1970. The nature of the reading process. In H. Singer and R. B. Ruddell (Eds.), *Theoretical models and processes of reading*. Newark, Dela.: International Reading Association.

Denner, B., 1970. Representational and syntactic competence of problem readers. *Child Development, 41*, 881–887.

DeVries, R., 1974. Relationships among Piagetian I.Q. achievement assessments. *Child Development, 45*, 746–756.

Elkind, D., and Deblinger, J. A., 1969. Perceptual training and reading achievement in disadvantaged children. *Child Development, 40*, 11–19.

Elkind, D., Barocas, R., and Rosenthal, B., 1968. Combinatorial thinking in adolescents from graded and ungraded classrooms. *Perceptual and Motor Skills, 27*, 1015–1018.

Elkind, D., Horn, J., and Schneider, G., 1965. Modified word recognition, reading achievement, and perceptual decentration. *Journal of Genetic Psychology, 107*, 235–251.

Elkind, D., Larson, M., and VanDorminck, W., 1965. Perceptual decentration learning and performance in slow and average readers. *Journal of Educational Psychology, 56(1)*, 50–56.

Farnham-Diggory, S., and Bermon, M., 1968. Verbal compensation, cognitive synthesis, and conservation. *Merrill-Palmer Quarterly, 14*, 215–228.

Furth, H., 1970. *Piaget for teachers*. Englewood Cliffs, N.J.: Prentice-Hall.

Gibson, E. J., 1968. Perceptual learning in educational situations. In R. M. Gagne and W. J. Gephardt (Eds.), *Learning research and school subjects*. Itasca, Ill.: F. E. Peacock.

Goldman, R., 1968. *Religious thinking from childhood to adolescence*. New York: Seabury Press.

Goldschmid, M., and Bentler, P., 1968. *Concept assessment kit-conservation manual*. San Diego, Calif.: Educational and Industrial Testing Service.

Goodnow, J. J., and Bethon, G., 1966. Piaget's tasks: The effects of schooling and intelligence. *Child Development, 37*, 573–582.

Grant, Janet, 1972. *Piagetian development and learning to read*. Unpublished master's thesis, University of London.

Hallam, R. N., 1967. Logical thinking in history. *Educational Review, 19*, 183–202.

Heatherly, A. L., 1972. *Attainment of Piagetian conservation tasks in relation to the ability to form hypotheses as to the probable content of story material among first and second grade children.* Unpublished doctoral dissertation, University of Virginia.

Hull, C., 1942. Conditioning: Outline of a systematic theory of learning in "The Psychology of Learning." In R. B. Henry (Ed.), *The forty-first yearbook*, NSSE (Part II). Chicago, Ill.: University of Chicago Press.

Kaufman, A. S., and Kaufman, N. L., 1972. Tests built from Piaget's and Gesell's tasks as predictors of first grade achievement. *Child Development, 43*, 521–535.

Lovell, K., 1961. A follow-up study of Inhelder and Piaget's "the growth of logical thinking." *British Journal of Psychology, 52,* 143–154.

Lovell, K., 1971. Some problems associated with formal thought and its assessment. In D. R. Green, M. P. Ford, and G. B. Flamer (Eds.), *Measurement and Piaget.* New York: McGraw-Hill, pp. 81–93.

Lovell, K., Shapton, D., and Warren, N. S., 1964. A study of some cognitive and other disabilities in backward readers of average intelligence as assessed by a non-verbal test. *British Journal of Educational Psychology, 34,* 58–64.

Mermelstein, E., and Shulman, L. S., 1967. Lack of formal schooling and the acquisition of conservation. *Child Development, 38,* 39–52.

Olson, D., 1976. Theory of instructional means. *Educational Psychologist, 12,* 14–35.

Plato, 1975. Phaedrus and the seventh and eight letters. Translated by Walter Hamilton. Harmondsworth, England: Penguin Books Ltd., 95–96.

Price, K., 1962. Education and philosophical thought. Boston: Allyn and Bacon, 153–154.

Rausher, S. R., 1970. *The relationship between achievement on Piagetian conservation and spatial measures and reading readiness.* Unpublished doctoral dissertation, New York University.

Rawson, H. I., 1969. *A study of the relationships and development of reading and cognition.* Unpublished doctoral dissertation, University of Alberta.

Rystrom, R., 1970. Toward defining comprehension: A first report. *Journal of Reading Behavior, 2,* 56–73.

Scott, R., 1969. Social class, race, seriation and reading readiness: A study of the relationship at kindergarten level. *Journal of Genetic Psychology, 115,* 87–96.

Smith, F., 1971. *Understanding reading: A psycholinguistic analysis of reading and learning to read.* New York: Holt, Rinehart and Winston.

Stack, W., and Murray, F. B., 1976. *Operativity and reading comprehension.* Paper presented at the Sixth Annual Symposium of the Jean Piaget Society (June).

Stephens, J. M., 1967. *The process of schooling.* New York: Holt, Rinehart and Winston.

Waller, T. G., 1977. Think first, read later. In F. B. Murray (Ed.), *Development of the reading process.* Newark, Dela.: International Reading Association. (Monograph)

7

Genevan Theory and the Education of Exceptional Children

D. KIM REID

1. Introduction

Interest of special educators in Genevan theory is growing, but few serious attempts have been made to approach the education of exceptional children from a Genevan perspective. Piaget's concerns have been with the epistemic subject whose structures are relatively homogeneous. In addition, Genevan theory has focused on development, rather than the acquisition of information and skills. It is not surprising, therefore, that special educators have all but overlooked the potential value of Genevan theory to their work. In the hope of encouraging a narrowing of that gap, this chapter will examine Genevan theory as a suitable framework for the education of exceptional children, its relation to the predominant orientations in special education, research trends relating Genevan theory to special populations, and finally the implications of Genevan research and theory for the education of exceptional children.

D. KIM REID • Department of Educational Psychology, New York University, New York, New York.

2. Individual Differences

Perhaps the initial question one might ask in considering the use of Genevan theory as the framework for the education of exceptional children is whether a structural model (i.e., one concerned with discovering universal regularities in human behavior) is appropriate to the study of individual differences. Although the theory of Piaget and his colleagues provides no systematic position on individual differences (Webb, 1974; Piaget, 1971b), it does enable us to explain and understand them. Individual differences can mean many things: (1) Variations in the rate at which a given child develops: for example, relatively rapid movement from the sensorimotor to the preoperational period leading to the attainment of concrete operations at a much later time. (2) Variations in rate of growth among children: some children attain the level of concrete operations at age 6, whereas others do not attain that level until 8 or 9. (3) Differences in the particular route children take to achieve a given operational structure: e.g., variation in sequence, number, or nature of stages. Some children, for example, learn conservation of weight before conservation of number which is expected to develop earlier (Bovet, 1976; Piaget, 1977c). Frequently, individual differences which vary sufficiently from the norm to earn children the label "exceptional" result from some limitation related to one or more of the four factors of development (Piaget, 1970a).

Piaget accepts the three classical factors of learning and development—maturation, physical experience, social experience—but argues that a fourth factor, equilibration, is also needed to explain development. He does not, however, always define the three classic factors in the usual way, so it is important to examine all of them closely.

Although Piaget (1971a, 1977b) has consistently emphasized a biological model, he is not to be regarded as a maturational theorist. Unlike Gesell (Ilg and Ames, 1955) and Chomsky (1965) (also see Piaget, 1977c), the Genevans do not view development as a reflection of the internal maturation of the nervous system (Piaget, 1959; Inhelder, Sinclair, and Bovet, 1974). Instead, maturation is regarded as providing a *condition of possibilities* not simply for the content of knowledge, but also for the development of its form. This potential must be provoked into existence by interaction with the environment (Piaget and Garcia, 1971).

Experience with the physical environment, the second factor, is indispensable to cognitive development and constitutes a basic condition for learning both in the broad and strict senses.* Piaget (1970a) distinguishes three types of experience: exercise, physical experience *per se*, and logico-mathematical experience. The first of these refers to the repeated application of actions or operations to objects in the environment which does not necessarily lead to new knowledge. Children, for example, may group and regroup the same objects according to some previously acquired classification scheme. The term physical experience is generally used to describe how children gain new knowledge by manipulating objects. In this case, actions on objects allow them to discover the objects' properties, for example, that blocks are heavy, that blankets are soft, or that long, thin metal rods will bend. This process of observing properties of objects is called *empirical abstraction* and refers to the observation of affirmations, i.e., the present, positive characteristics of objects (Piaget, 1975a). The third kind of experience, which is almost never mentioned by other theorists (Piaget, 1970a), is logico-mathematical experience. In this kind of experience, knowledge is gained indirectly from children's actions with objects through a process of *reflexive abstraction* (Piaget, in press). There are two distinct, but interrelated aspects of the reflexive property of this type of abstraction. First, the child reflects or projects (in the sense that a mirror reflects light) what is taken from a lower plane (a motor activity, for example) onto a higher plane or conceptual level. Second, there is a reflection in the sense of a conceptual reorganization. The child constructs a conceptual frame of reference by making inferences which enable him or her to understand why and how the original activity exists (Piaget, 1976, p. 45). Through this process of reflexive abstraction both negations (the nonobservable properties of objects, e.g., the set of objects which are *not* red) and logical rules (e.g., that sum is independent of the order of counting) are constructed. Experience with environmental objects and events provides both the foundation on which logico-mathematical knowledge is built and is itself assimilated into logico-mathematical structures (Piaget and Garcia, 1971).

By social experience (the third factor), the Genevans refer primarily to social relationships, education, and language. That the rate of development varies among children of different cultures indicates that cultural impact can accelerate or retard children's development. The fact that the sequence of stages remains unchanged, however, gives evi-

*Learning in the strict sense refers to acquisitons from the environment. Learning in its broad sense includes learning in its strict sense plus equilibration. It, therefore, encompasses all of development.

dence that, as in the case of maturation, cultural experience cannot explain everything. Social relationships help the child to decentrate by becoming aware of aspects of a problem previously ignored (Doise and Perret-Clermont, 1976). Education both influences the rate at which children progress through stages and determines the particular content to be learned. Language, frequently cited as the essential factor in logical thought, is considered by the Genevans to be effective only when children can assimilate the ideas presented to structures they have already developed (Piaget and Inhelder, 1969; Sinclair, 1973b; Voyat, 1970). Language is certainly important in helping children interiorize action into representation and thought, but it is only one aspect of the ability to function symbolically. Language, like all social experience, is a necessary but not a sufficient condition for learning.

Physical and social experience cannot account for the sequential character of development. Maturation cannot account for the variations among rates of development. There must, then, be a fourth factor which coordinates all the others. This factor Piaget calls *equilibration*. It is through the process of equilibration that the child organizes the other three factors into a coherent whole (Piaget, 1977c). The process of equilibration (Piaget, 1975a), or self-regulation, entails successive states which may be stable or unstable. These states are dependent on the interaction of two factors: observable cues and coordinations. By cues, Piaget means the understanding of the facts, i.e., the data children readily assimilate, including observation of the results of their own actions. By coordinations, he refers to inferences which may be derived from the child's actions or from objects acting on each other. There is, therefore, collaboration on all levels between empirical and reflexive abstractions. At initial levels, forms of equilibrium may be unstable because of gaps, perturbations, and/or contradictions—real or, at least, experienced by the child. Stable forms of equilibration require exact compensations of affirmations and negations.

Exceptionalities, therefore, may be conceptualized (as they are in maturational and learning theories) as resulting from an abnormality of the biological organism (e.g., physical handicap, maturational lag), unusual or inadequate physical or social experience (e.g., cultural familial retardation), or some combination of the two (e.g., blindness). The important contribution of Genevan theory to our understanding of exceptionality, however, is related to the process of equilibration. Only when we consider the child as a coordinated, self-regulated whole can we understand the dynamic quality of the interaction of the four factors of development and how a limitation related to one may affect the functioning of the others. In addition, there is some evidence that the mentally retarded (Stephens, 1972) and the severely emotionally disturbed (Schmid-Kitsikis, 1969) have difficulty with precisely this function.

The individual differences which result are both quantitative and qualitative. A 17-year-old mentally retarded youth, for example, is certainly quite different from a 10-year-old child of similar mental age, both in his rate of development and in the quality of his performance. The same *sequence of stages* in development, however, is observed in nearly all children whether they are intellectually deficient or gifted. Even within normal development, the Genevans discuss the presence of time lags, that is, uneven development within and across stages. A *horizontal* time lag (sometimes called *décalage*) refers to the use of an acquired structure in one or some areas (e.g., conservation of number and weight), but not in all (e.g., conservation of volume). A *vertical* time lag (or décalage) refers to the child's approaching some tasks at one level of functioning while approaching others at a higher or lower level. Children who generally function at the level of preoperations may, for example, solve a very complex problem on a sensorimotor level.

The final consideration one must make in discussing individual differences is motivation. Because cognitive and affective systems are interdependent (Piaget and Inhelder, 1969), motivation, according to Genevan theory, is inextricably linked to the child's level of competence. A young child, for example, asked to group objects may create an assemblage in which relations are determined by juxtaposition (i.e., a triangle and a square may be grouped together because they are both red; a third object may be chosen because it is like the last one selected—it is square). In this case, the child looks for similarities and simply ignores any differences. He puts each new element into a positive relation with the one before it and succeeds in creating a spatial totality (Piaget, 1975a). Encouragement, incentives, or punishment are powerless in eliciting a logical, classificatory grouping. Unless he is in transition to a higher level of functioning, even direct instruction may be inadequate or, at best, may result in a rote mechanical performance (Inhelder *et al.*, 1974).

Thus, Genevan theory provides workers in exceptionality with a framework which focuses on the mechanisms of self-regulation, i.e., the control of the individual over his own development. Even though genetic epistemology seeks to explain an epistemic homogeneous development, the Genevans are consistently concerned with individual differences in affect, interest, motivation, and experience. The theory provides us with a developmental sequence, not tied to age *per se*, which emphasizes the child's mode of functioning. Attention to how children function promises to enrich our understanding and to enable us to develop more appropriate educational strategies.

Special education has in many respects been a Procrustean bed for its consumers. Attempts at individualization have frequently amounted to trying to fit children into neatly packaged programmed materials in reading, writing, and arithmetic. These, of necessity, bind their users to a prescribed style and sequence of thinking. Many children can adapt to these rigid sequences, others cannot (see, for example, the story of Einstein by Patten, 1973). Because of differences in maturation, past experience, or levels of equilibration, different children respond differently and learn different things from the same experience (Schwebel and Raph, 1973). Certainly, there are many avenues to learning.

3. Predominant Orientations

Influenced by the Anglo-American empiricist tradition (Blatt and Garfunkel, 1973), special educators have tended to explain higher-level, cognitive functions in terms of basic elements such as perception, association, habit, and simple learning. They have also viewed language as the major vehicle of learning and development. The result of the adoption of such a mechanistic theoretical position has been to explain cognitive deficit and to conceptualize remedial strategies through recourse to these elements. The major thrust of special educators, therefore, has been to focus almost exclusively on problems of perception, learning, memory, and language.

3.1. Perception

Many writers (cf. Frostig and Maslow, 1969; Kephart, 1971; Getman, 1965) have viewed perception as the basis for cognition and have suggested, therefore, that improved perception would lead to improved cognitive functioning. This perspective fostered the development of "perceptual training programs" which treated perception as an ability prerequisite to thought and as divorced from it. Emphasis was directed solely to empirical abstraction without any recognition of the role of its interaction with simultaneous, reflexive abstraction. Numerous studies carried out to determine whether successful training in perception lead to increased abilities in reading (cf. Coleman, 1968; Erickson, 1969; Hammill, 1972; Hammill and Larsen, 1974; Lyle, 1968) and in other academic skills (cf. Singer and Brunk, 1967) failed to substantiate improved functioning (Hammill and Bartel, 1978). The view of perception (and, therefore, of remediation) was too simplistic (Piaget, 1969). Academic, as well as other types of cognitive tasks, are too complex to be improved by the kinds of exercises and experiences which emphasize only the discovery of affirmations.

Four problems appear to have contributed to this emphasis on perception. First, citing Piaget's work as support for the argument that the child until ages 6 or 7 is predominantly a perceptual being (cf. Hallahan and Cruickshank, 1973) is to ignore his emphasis on activity (Piaget, 1977a). To understand the role of action in learning, one must first understand the distinction between figurative and operative aspects of knowing (Piaget, 1970a; Furth, 1969). Not only perception, but also imitation and the mental image constitute the mechanisms of figurative understanding, i.e., the means to describe the static characteristics of states or transformations. Understanding of the dynamic quality of transformations, however, is dependent on activity, at first actual, then internalized and finally reversible. Although one must be able to describe reality in order to comprehend it, description does not ensure comprehension. Understanding of objects is always attained by successive approximations. The child must act on objects and transform them in order to comprehend their nature.

Secondly, but related to the first issue, is the lack of understanding that the child's level of development affects his perception (Inhelder et al., 1974; Piaget, 1969). The information the child selects as the basis for his mental activity may be due to a physiologically based perceptual distortion or may be influenced by his developmental stage. In either case, even if it is inadequate to the solution of a given problem, it should not be refuted or corrected, but should be used as the foundation for further advancements (Inhelder et al., 1974).

Third, in the Genevan model (Piaget and Inhelder, 1967) perception is regarded as an activity, not as a passive sensory experience or the simple organization of such experience. Perceptual activity (Piaget, 1969) involves the formation of mental images from abstractions of space. The child's understanding of any object, therefore, is dependent on his level of spatial conceptualization rather than on instructional procedures that make properties-to-be-noticed more accessible or dominant.

Finally, the understanding of topological space precedes mastery of Euclidean forms (Piaget and Inhelder, 1967). Freidland and Meisels (1975) suggest three applications of this finding: (1) assessing young children on their ability to reproduce geometric forms may be inappropriate; (2) children with visual discrimination problems in alphabet learning may be topologically dominant (also see Popp, 1964; Voyat, 1970); and (3) it may be more profitable to provide children who have perceptual problems with experiences that foster consolidation of topological understanding rather than to stress Euclidean shapes.

3.2. Learning

Since the predominant theory which serves as the framework for both research efforts and educational programming with special populations is behaviorism (Blatt and Garfunkel, 1973), it is not surprising that we have approached the study of deviancy from a learning paradigm. This approach has been most evident in our efforts to explain mental retardation as a learning deficiency. Iano (1971) points out, however, that even research conducted within a learning orientation has failed to support a learning-deficiency hypothesis. When comparisons between normal and educable retarded groups on a variety of learning tasks were based on chronological age, the performances of retarded children were inferior. When comparisons were made on the basis of level of development, however, often the performance of retardates was equivalent to that of normal children.* In cases where the retarded as a group performed in an inferior manner, there was considerable overlap between groups and considerable variability within the retarded group, which suggests that at least some of the subjects performed as well as normals.

Several studies indicate that a learning-deficiency approach is equally unsatisfactory in regard to the trainable retardate. Zeaman and House (1963) showed that once trainable retardates developed the ability to attend to the relevant stimuli on a discrimination task, they learned as well and as rapidly as their normal mental-age peers. Zeaman and House, therefore, adopted the theoretical position that learning inability *per se* was not characteristic of mental retardation. Clarke (cited in Garrison, 1966) reviewed research related to the learning of trainable retardates. With training, these children were able to develop good space perception, manual dexterity, and a normal response to incentives. In regard to sorting tasks of various kinds, learning and retention both

---

*Level of development is most often operationally defined as mental age (MA). Zigler (1967) argued that mentally retarded persons (excluding those who are organically impaired) differ from the norm in their rate of development (IQ), but not in the cognitive processes they employ in reasoning and problem solving. Kohlberg (1968), on the other hand, suggested that older retardates might be superior to their brighter but younger peers of equivalent MA, because they have had more extensive general experience.

were good. Although the retarded take much longer to learn industrial tasks in a sheltered workshop setting, their performance eventually equals that of normals (Lovell, 1966).

Behaviorists, who fail to distinguish between development and learning (described by Piaget as learning in its broad sense and learning in its strict sense, respectively), view retarded development as the result of slow or inadequate learning. The learning-deficiency approach is based on the assumption that intellectual development is primarily accounted for by learning. The developmentalists (Johnson, 1959; Inhelder, 1966, 1968; Zigler, 1967, 1969), on the other hand, who do make the distinction, assert that the retarded are slow in development rather than in learning *per se* (Iano, 1971). They suggest that learning is accounted for by intellectual development. While learning in its strict sense is the acquisition of content which results from specific environmental experience, development is a more gradual acquisition of structures which result from the interplay of maturation, physical and social experience, and the child's own active construction. Advances in development permit the child to organize, utilize, and to understand his knowledge and to respond to his environment in new ways. Learning simply amounts to acquiring more information or more adequate responses.

Lovell (1966) explains how learning occurs without concomitant understanding. Two schemata may be combined into a single, larger schema (incorporating both of the original schemata), because they are frequently called for one after the other in the same order. Reaching and touching, for example, in the infant become combined into a single activity. As the child's repertoire expands, however, he may form even larger schema comprised of several single schemata (for example, reaching, touching, grasping, holding, pushing, and pulling). Various combinations of these single schemata are often called for in his daily interaction with the environment. Sometimes the child reaches and grasps, sometimes he touches and pushes, and sometimes he simply grasps and pulls. It is the combination of these single schemata into larger schema that allows trial-and-error learning. The child now has several behavioral alternatives at his disposal.

If this larger, trial-and-error schema has within it a subschema or combination of subschemata, which is appropriate in a given situation (for example, when the child is presented with a cup of milk), that particular subschema or combination of subschemata (in this case, reaching, grasping and holding) will become strengthened and the other subschemata (pushing, pulling, etc.) will be inhibited and finally eliminated. Although this combination or recombination of subschemata can account for learning involving a series of actions at the same level of

abstraction, it cannot account for understanding. Reasoning and understanding require higher-order representational schemata which allow
the child to survey, so to speak, all of his available schemata simultaneously, to see which are appropriate and equivalent and to select among
his alternatives. The young child when presented with his cup does not
have this ability. Lovell reports that there is considerable evidence that
trainable retardates rarely form these higher level schemata and that the
educable mentally retarded do so only in adolescence. (Normal children
develop them at approximately 7 to 8.) These higher-order schemata
signal the onset of concrete operations.

In sum, the mentally retarded, like all of us, are quite capable of
learning information and developing more adequate, situation-specific
responses. Learning is not the problem, reasoning is (Stephens and
McLaughlin, 1974). Because of their slower rate of development, the
retarded are limited in terms of what they are able to understand. This
lack of understanding, in turn, contributes to the slower acquisition of
general structures which define learning in its broad sense and embrace
all of development. Where learning in its broad sense is spontaneous in
normal children, retardates appear to need more time and possibly more
help from adults to advance (Droz, 1970).

3.3. Memory and Language

Two more recent developments in the field of special education have
been emphases on the memory and language aspects of disabilities.
These concerns grow out of a tradition which assumes that knowledge is
acquired from the environment, that a copy of environmental reality is
stored in memory, and that language is the essential base for both learning and thinking. The Genevans argue, however, that language and
memory are not the keystones of thought, but rather are parts of a much
more general capacity, that is, representation or symbolic function
(Piaget, 1967).

Representation confers mobility on operations, but is not the source
of such coordinations. Sinclair (1973a) suggests that when children are
unable to relate to verbal or pictoral presentations, the reasons may not
be inattention or faulty memory, but children's deformation of the
stimulus. Children do not simply copy what they have seen or heard,
but instead assimilate it to their own structures. It is the assimilated
knowledge that is maintained in memory. More importantly the nature
of the memory itself varies as the child's level of cognitive understanding changes (Cromer, 1977; Liben, 1977; Piaget and Inhelder, 1973).

Children's memories for seriated sticks, for example, correspond to their developmental stages and change accordingly as new understanding is acquired. The problem in focusing on representational aspects of functioning is the danger (currently apparent in special education curricula) of short-changing the more fundamental, operative aspects of knowing.

4. Research on Exceptionalities from a Genevan Perspective*

A considerable amount of research has been generated both here and in Europe which examined aspects of exceptionality within a Genevan framework. No attempt has been made to compile an exhaustive review of the literature.† Rather, studies have been selected as illustrative of important contributions and/or major trends. These studies have been divided into three groups: (1) those seeking clarification of the performance characteristics of various disability groups, (2) those analyzing regulatory mechanisms, and (3) those related to differential diagnosis, although there is often considerable overlap.

4.1. Clarification of Performance Characteristics

Most of the early research effort with exceptional children was directed toward discovering gaps in performance and toward determining whether the developmental stage hierarchy is preserved (Schmid-Kitsikis, 1973). Studies conducted by the Genevans (for example, studies by Inhelder, Sinclair, and Schmid-Kitsikis) used Piaget's clinical method of exploration and observation. Their results have generally been confirmed later by other Europeans and Americans who adhered rigorously to a psychometric research paradigm. The Genevans at-

---

*In this discussion, *Genevan perspective* refers to a framework used by researchers of many nationalities who base their work, more or less faithfully, on the theory devised by Piaget and his colleagues. The terms *Genevans* and *Genevan School* are reserved for those investigators who are actually connected with the Center of Genetic Epistemology and/or the University of Geneva.

†Those interested in a more comprehensive bibliography of research with special children are referred to Warner and Williams (1975, 1976) and to a collection of papers presented at the Sixth Interdisciplinary Seminar: Piagetian Theory and Its Implications for the Helping Professions (Magary, Poulsen, Levinson, and Taylor, 1977).

tempted to uncover structural mechanisms, while the others assessed more static aspects of performance using a variety of tests and tasks. All groups made frequent comparisons to the development of normal children.

4.1.1. Mental Retardation

The early research with exceptional children was aimed at verifying the hierarchy of stages and in studying the impact of various deficits on mental development. Leading the Genevan School, Inhelder (English edition, 1968) published a study in which she used the method of critical exploration to show that the mentally retarded progressed through the same stages as normal subjects in the same order. She reported, however, that the rate at which they progressed was delayed and that the final level of development attained was determined by the severity of the retardation and was, at best, intermediary in normals. The mentally retarded appeared to exhibit characteristics of thought essentially analogous to those of younger children. Their thought processes revealed rigidity, oscillation between higher and lower levels of functioning, dependence on the concrete aspects of the problems, and a susceptibility to irrelevant influences such as examiner approval. Inhelder (1966) suggests that these children reach a "pseudo-equilibrium."

In England, Woodward conducted a series of studies (1959, 1961, 1962) in which she demonstrated that what often appeared as random behaviors in the severely retarded followed the sequence of sensorimotor substages outlined by Piaget. Her later work is important, because it suggested that development in the retarded might not be so homogeneous as Inhelder's original work (concerned primarily with physical conservations) had indicated (Schmid-Kitsikis and de Ajuriaguerra, 1973). Woodward found homogeneity within a single domain of knowledge, but considerable variation between domains, e.g., number and space.

An American team led by Stephens (Stephens, McLaughlin, Miller and Glass, 1972; Stephens, 1974; Stephens and McLaughlin, 1974; Mahaney and Stephens, 1974; Moore and Stephens, 1974; McLaughlin and Stephens, 1974) conducted a longitudinal study comparing the development of educable retardates with that of normals on Piagetian tasks related to reasoning, moral judgment, and moral conduct.* Results of

*These authors indicate that they followed Inhelder's earlier approach to the study of mental retardation. It should be noted, however, that these studies consisted of a standardized presentation of tasks and the use of statistical analyses. For a critical evaluation of the methodology, see Weisz (1976).

the initial phase of the study supported Inhelder's finding that cognitive development becomes arrested in the retarded. The data collected in the second phase of the study, however, indicated that youths 16 to 20 years old did continue to make progress, although at a decelerating pace (Stephens and McLaughlin). In addition, significant differences between the performance of retardates and normals (not attributable to differences in chronological or mental ages) on conservation and classification tasks appeared to be related to difficulties in categorization, flexibility, and reversibility among the retarded. Findings related to moral judgment (Mahaney and Stephens) indicated that retardates at all ages (even as they approached late adolescence) demonstrated improvement over a two-year period when asked to give opinions regarding which form of punishment might discourage further misdeeds and when asked to make decisions related to holding an entire group accountable for the misdeeds of a single member. Slow and sporadic growth interspersed with regressions characterized their responses to a problem designed to determine whether the seriousness of a deed was dependent on the doer's intent or the consequences of the act. Moral conduct (Moore and Stephens) proved to be developmental both in retardates and normals, with retardates' conduct equivalent to that of normals of similar mental age. Although retardates showed a decline in gains through middle adolescence, in later adolescence they continued to advance. Finally, factor analyses (McLaughlin and Stephens) were conducted to study the interrelations among Piagetian measures of reasoning, intelligence tests, and scores on the Wide Range Achievement Test as well as among cognitive tasks, moral judgment, and moral conduct. Findings indicated that for both normal and retarded groups, standard measures of intelligence and Piagetian measures of reasoning defined separate factors, and that reasoning, moral judgment, and moral conduct became more closely related over the two-year period of the study. In retardates the association between reasoning and moral conduct strengthened. In contrast, although abilities involving reasoning and moral judgment were evolving in normals, they appeared not to be influencing moral conduct.

The preponderance of American research with special groups based on Genevan theory has been done with mentally retarded children. Like the Stephens study, many have investigated the development of retardates vis à vis their normal peers. Other studies, however, were cross-sectional and more limited in scope. Several of them focused on the relation of cognitive tasks (especially conservation) to chronological age, mental age, and IQ (cf. Adler, 1964; Brogle, 1971; Carpenter, 1955; Hood, 1962; Marchi, 1971; McManis, 1969; Wilton and Boersma, 1974). There have also been attempts to train the retarded to perform cognitive tasks (cf. Kahn, 1974) and to study the effects of a number of task variables on children's responses to tasks (cf. Carlson and Michelson, 1973; Dodwell, 1960; Hood, 1962; Rothenberg, 1969; Vitello, 1973).

Schmid-Kitsikis and de Ajurriaguerra (1973) reported two European studies that followed a related line of investigation. Ranson (1950) in France and a team of Genevan researchers headed by Garonne *et al.* (1969) established a correspondence between the level of functioning retarded children attained and their progress in school. This type of research has also been conducted here. Swize (1972), for example, studied the relations among conservation, IQ, and achievement in mathematics and reading recognition skills. Conservation was not correlated with either IQ or reading recognition skills, but was related to mathematics achievement.

The relation between cognition and language in retarded children has also been studied. Sinclair (1967) found that severely retarded children better understood instructions given in the language of preoperational rather than operational children and that the descriptions given by the retardates were analogous to those of normal, younger children. She concluded that language, like other manifestations of the symbolic function, is subject to the laws of operational development. An American study with a similar purpose but using statistical methodology was conducted by Kahn (1975). He examined the relation between Stage 6 functioning at the sensorimotor level and language performance in severely retarded children 47 to 98 months old. His findings supported Piaget's contention that cognitive structures exist which are prerequisite to language development.

4.1.2. Emotional Disturbance

Much of the research aimed at discovering the performance characteristics of emotionally disturbed children has been conducted by Americans and has centered on conservation. Goldschmid (1967) found that emotionally disturbed children evidenced the same sequence of acquisition of conservation as normals, but their progress was delayed. The performance of emotionally disturbed children 2 years older was no better than that of young normals. Goldschmid pointed out, however, that IQ and verbal facility favored the normal group. He suggested that verbal facility might have influenced comprehension of the questions asked and the adequacy of responses.

Filer (1972) in a factor analytic study of cognitive and social-cognitive Piagetian tasks, found that the performance of emotionally disturbed children equaled that of normals on cognitive but not on social-cognitive tasks. Findings were related to the child's developmental level and to social understanding in normals.

In a study of delinquent adolescent girls of borderline IQ, Miller, Zumoff, and Stephens (1974) found them below grade level in school achievement and well below expectations in conservation. These girls tended to respond perceptually to conservation tasks. Evidence of the attainment of formal operations was lacking except in two cases. Moral reasoning was adequate, but not related to moral conduct.

Howell (1972) compared the performance of normal and emotionally disturbed children on classification tasks. Normals tended to receive higher scores on both IQ and classification tasks. Increased performance with age was apparent in normals, but not in the emotionally disturbed, independent of IQ. Howell concluded that his study emphasized the need for increased attention to cognitive education for emotionally disturbed children.

4.1.3. Learning Disabilities

The field of learning disabilities is a relatively new one and very few studies have appeared which have investigated the performances of learning-disabled children from a Piagetian perspective. Genevan researchers have studied children who would be included in this category, but since they have generally analyzed regulatory mechanisms, their results will be reported in the next section of this chapter.

Two Belgian investigators, Klees and Lebrun (1972), compared the operative and figurative performances of dyslexic children. They found that 80% of the dyslexic children studied exhibited disturbances in figurative functioning, which tended to be more pronounced at higher ages (i.e., ages 9 and 10). In addition, these children tended to persist in their use of perceptual strategies even when more operative modes of performance were more appropriate. Finally, comparisons between children who were severely figuratively delayed and those whose figurative functioning was undisturbed revealed that a delay in operativity accompanies figurative problems.

In Canada, Kershner (1975) divided second-grade children into high and low perceptual/operational groups on the basis of two visual-spatial tests (the Frostig Developmental Test of Visual Perception and an operational test of his own devising). He then measured their reading performances. Regardless of perceptual ability, the groups high in operative visual-spatial skills were superior in reading. Kershner described the poorer readers as "characterized by an inability to coordinate multiple

cues, an over-concern for perceptual features, irreversibility of perceptual imagery, and the inability to decentrate" (p. 35). He concluded that
cognitive-spatial competence could allow children to compensate for
poor perceptual skills (which were perhaps more crucial to children at
the preoperational level of functioning). It is important to note, however, that Kershner's subjects were children who were maintained in the
regular classroom and did not demonstrate severe reading difficulties.

4.1.4. Cerebral Palsy

Few studies have been reported which examine cerebral palsied
children from a Genevan perspective. Since most tests of mental development which are appropriate for use with infants are based on physical and motor tasks, Tessier (1970) devised an instrument based on
Piagetian measures to assess sensorimotor development in nursery
school children with motor handicaps. She compared the performances
of normal and both retarded and nonretarded children with cerebral
palsy. She found that children with cerebral palsy who were retarded
were slower in sensorimotor development (although the sequence was
parallel) and object-concept development than were normal and nonretarded cerebral palsied children. Although normal and nonretarded
cerebral palsied children progressed at a comparable rate, responses of
nonretarded cerebral palsied children were qualitatively different (due
to motor disability) from those given by normals: slower rate of response, more trials, more limited range of interaction between objects
and toys, low tolerance for frustration and need for more encouragement. An important finding is that even with a motor disability, nonretarded cerebral palsied children performed as well as normals in sensorimotor tasks. This finding lends support to the Genevan contention
that the more important aspect of activity is reflexive abstraction and not
motor activity *per se* (Inhelder *et al.*, 1974; Piaget, 1977a).

4.1.5. Deafness

Few studies have also been reported concerning deafness. The
studies which do exist, however, have contributed significantly to our
understanding of the importance of language in operational competence
as well as to the performance of the deaf population *per se*. In France,
Oléron (1957; Oléron and Herren, 1961) compared intellectual development in deaf and hearing children. He postulated that the deaf would be
developmentally delayed, because he believed that language played a
much more crucial role in development than Piaget recognized. He

found that the deaf were delayed 5 to 10 years in the acquisition of conservation concepts.

Furth (1966, 1971, 1973), an American, has demonstrated the presence of concrete operations and even formal operational abilities in deaf-mute children and adolescents. His methodology is nonverbal and generally includes training over an extended period of time. Furth argues that when one is assured that the deaf subject understands the requirements of the task (which he infers was clearly not the case in Oléron's experiments), one finds only a slight developmental lag of one to two years. This lag he attributes to lack of adequate cultural stimulation, because "deaf children without linguistic skills performed similarly to intellectually impoverished children who had linguistic mastery" (1973, p. 67). Furth concludes, therefore, that although language constitutes an effective medium for the transmission of information, it does not play a dominant role in the development of operations.

4.1.6. Blindness

It was again a European who carried out the first study of cognitive development in blind children. Hatwell (1966), a French investigator, found, as Piaget had predicted, that the development of operational schemes was impoverished in the congenitally blind, presumably a result of disturbances at the sensorimotor and preoperational levels. Spatial development was particularly sensitive to delay, but predominantly verbal tasks were performed nearly as well as by children with sight.

American studies have been carried out which essentially support Hatwell's findings (Miller, 1969; Friedman and Pasnak, 1973). Gottesman (1971), however, found the level of development of blind children to be similar to that of children with sight (half of whom were blindfolded) on a task of haptic perception of objects and forms. He also discovered that the performances of blind children raised in an urban environment were superior to those of the rural blind.

Stephens (1977) compared children with sight and blind children of equivalent verbal IQ at three age levels (6 to 10, 10 to 14, and 14 to 18). The major findings of the study suggest that the blind appear to have the potential for achieving the level of concrete operations, but that its actualization is painstaking and laborious and requires twice the time needed by sighted subjects. Although older blind children progressed in cognitive areas other than spatial orientation and mental imagery, they were not capable of formal operational tasks. Of particular interest was the finding that Piagetian reasoning scores for blind children were more highly related to verbal IQ scores than those of sighted children.

Stephens suggests that the close association represents a compensation resulting from the blinds' greater need to rely on verbal stimulation. Although interesting, the results of this study must be interpreted with caution. The blind and sighted subjects were drawn from different geographical areas, differed in socioeconomic status, and performed the tasks under different conditions (i.e., the blind were tested on adapted tasks while the sighted performed the traditional tasks while viewing them).

In England Cromer (1973) criticized Hatwell's study on similar grounds:

> (1) She used no control groups of sighted children beyond the age of eight, and the younger sighted children she did test (38 seven- and eight-year olds) made their judgments while being able to view the material. (2) About 50 per cent of her sample of 107 blind children, ranging up to 13 years of age, were from rural areas, but the younger sighted children against whom they were compared were all brought up in an urban environment. (3) Blind children in Paris begin school two years later than sighted children. (pp. 242–243)

Cromer then replicated, as well as extended, Hatwell's study while rectifying her methodological errors. His results indicated that blind and sighted children attained conservation at approximately the same age and that they gave similar explanations for their choices. His results also supported Sinclair's finding (Sinclair-de-Zwart, 1967) that conservers used language which compared materials by coordinating two dimensions (e.g., one is longer, but thinner than the other), while nonconservers tended to refer to only a single dimension (e.g., it's thin). Language used by blind children did not differ from that of sighted children.

4.1.7. Giftedness

Contrary to the decidedly empirical approach which directs research and practice in other areas of exceptionality, the study of the gifted has been guided primarily by the use of Guilford's model (Getzels and Dillon, 1973). Although Piagetian studies (cf. Lunzer, 1965; Hughes, 1965; Peluffo, 1966) have included gifted children, few have concentrated on the performance of the gifted *per se*. The primary question Piagetian researchers have asked in regard to gifted children is whether very bright children move quite rapidly through developmental stages or whether their progress, as Genevan theory would predict, is constrained by needs related to maturation and experience. In separate studies both Lovell (1968) and Webb (1974) found that gifted children at the elementary school level generally failed to reach the level of formal operational thought, but succeeded in a quite superior way in solving concrete operational tasks found difficult by children of average IQ. Lovell suggests that a minimum mental age between 16 and 16½ is required for formal thought. In similar studies investigating much younger gifted children who were potentially precocious in their development of concrete operational abilities, Brown (1973) found that 4-year-olds with a mental age of 6 were less competent on concrete operational tasks than average 6-year-olds. DeVries (1973) also found that 5-year-olds with mental ages of approximately 7 performed less well than older, retarded children with comparable mental ages. It seems, therefore, that gifted children are superior in their performance of within-stage tasks, but the quality of thought is limited by maturational and experiential parameters.

4.1.8. Summary

It is clear from the literature reviewed above that initial studies examining the presence of the hierarchy of stages and the impact of deficits on intellectual development in various disability groups were performed by Europeans, most often by the Genevans. Later studies, both replicating Genevan findings and extending the study of exceptionalities to include additional variables (e.g., task variables, socioeconomic status, nonverbal methodologies) were carried out by other Europeans and by North Americans. It is important to note, however, that although the non-Genevan studies test aspects of Genevan theory, they do not follow a Genevan research paradigm. They represent what Voyat (1977) refers to as "an American attempt to integrate Piaget's thinking into a behaviorist approach" (p. 343). Voyat suggests that implementation of a psychometric approach fosters a "subtle but real reversal of Piaget's intentions, which were never to treat intelligence as a progressive accretion of specific reactions, but rather to analyze it as an overall structure" (p. 345). Piaget and Inhelder (1962) as well as Schmid-Kitsikis (1973) point out that tests reveal only the static results of mental activity. They do not probe the dynamic psychological operations. Many different structures can give rise to a single response. In addition, various responses can derive from the same structure, since a single structure never acts alone (Kamara and Easley, 1977). The result of having substituted tests for structural analyses has produced a rather extensive body of research which generally fails to add anything of substance to Genevan theory or to clarify the cognitive operations of exceptional children. It does, however, serve to confirm Genevan hypotheses with large numbers of children, to provide norms to guide expectations for levels of functioning, and to lend a sense of legitimacy to Genevan theory for those who are steeped in an empiricist tradition.

The substance of these studies and others reporting similar investigations (cf. Gottesman, 1975; Volpe, 1975) has confirmed the presence of an invariant sequence of stages in all children. What varies appears to be the rate of acquisition, the final stage attained, and the quality of performance within a stage.

4.2. Research Analyzing Regulatory Mechanisms*

In their recent studies of special populations the Genevan School used a method of research which is quite different from that used by Anglo-American researchers (Schmid-Kitsikis, 1973; Inhelder, 1966). Each child is studied individually using the method of critical exploration in which each succeeding question is determined by the child's response to the preceding one. The child is given tasks to perform, but emphasis is on the method used to solve the problem rather than on results. The aim of the research is the analysis of dynamic thought processes and underlying structures. There is no attempt to study a wide range of behaviors, nor is there emphasis on a comparison with normal children. The Genevans study the thinking of many children within a disability group so that they might discern common patterns of response among, for example, mentally retarded children, which might differ from the approaches to the same problem used by children of another disability group, for example, the emotionally disturbed.

Because Piaget's model of equilibration emphasizes the interaction between the child and the characteristics of the objects on which he operates, Genevan research attempts to distinguish between two mutually influencing factors (Schmid-Kitsikis, 1973): observable cues (Which cues does the child notice? What are the results of the child's manipulation of the object?) and the child's subjective and logical coordinations (How does the child coordinate his actions? How does he coordinate the action of objects acting on each other?). Research with special groups, like all Genevan research, is designed so that external disturbances prevent the child's activation of his assimilatory schemes. This situation provokes compensations on the part of the child which can lead to a new construction. Researchers study the conditions under which compensatory regulations occur and the types of compensatory regulations used among children of various disability groups.

*An example of this type of research is given on pp. 223–225.

The research applying structural analysis to psychopathology has been dominated by the work of de Ajuriaguerra, Inhelder, and Schmid-Kitsikis.* It has centered around three groups of exceptional children: (1) learning disabled children who manifest either language and/or motor and spatial problems; (2) prepsychotic children, and (3) mentally retarded children.†

4.2.1. Learning Disabled

In an early study (de Ajuriaguerra, Jaeggi, Guignard, Kocher, Maquard, Paunier, Quinodoz, and Siotis, 1963), several researchers studied a group of children who were of normal intelligence and who could communicate verbally, but who exhibited a disorder in the integration of language. They discovered that five key tests differentiated children who had language difficulties, the dysphasics, from those who did not: a test of auditory-verbal perception, a test in which children were asked to maintain the conceptual structure of a narrative, a speech test, a synonyns test, and a vocabulary test. All the dysphasics failed the first four tests. The fifth, if failed, indicated that the child's entire verbal system was poor. In 80% of the cases, interdependence existed among deficits in language comprehension, production, phonetics, and semantics. In addition, these children evidenced a level of operativity which was normal in its progress, but not in its processes (e.g., dysphasic children compensated for their problems by accompanying language with action and gesture). These children also displayed spatiotemporal disturbances. Both level of intelligence and affective stability seemed to influence the severity of the children's problems and the degree to which they were able to compensate.

Inhelder and Siotis (1963) studied the relations between the figurative and operative aspects of thought in dysphasics. Although these subjects exhibited verbal deficiencies, they achieved operativity as well as their linguistically competent peers. It appears that they achieved this through recourse to real or imagined action. On the figurative level, however, difficulties were evident in the potential for recalling and anticipating transformations of spatial configurations. The children coped with their deficient figurative representations by progressively subordinating them to the cognitive operations. Impairment in figurative rep-

---

*Schmid-Kitsikis is also known as E. Siotis.

†Although Inhelder's study (1968) was the forerunner of the research investigations analyzing regulations, it also provided the basis for the stage studies and so has been included in the earlier section.

resentation, therefore, might be expected to slow down the formation of certain operations, but to become enriched and dominated by them once they are constituted.

Schmid-Kitsikis (1969, 1972) studied operativity in dyspraxic children, i.e., those with normal intelligence but with motor and spatial problems. She found that their problems were not related to thinking, but rather to the actualization of their thinking. When required to seriate a collection of sticks, for example, the children often announced that they would put the smallest first and then each of the bigger ones in order until all the sticks were aligned. Although they were quite capable of understanding and describing a correct procedure, they were not able to carry it out. When logical problems could be solved without manipulation, e.g., class inclusion, these children exhibited no difficulties.

4.2.2. Emotionally Disturbed

The Genevans (Inhelder, 1966) also have been conducting research with both prepsychotic and neurotic children. Their results lend credence to Piaget's notion that the emotional and intellectual aspects of development cannot be dissociated. In prepsychotic children the reasoning processes which seem to be most affected are those related to conservation. Operational behavior is characterized by a primitive level of reasoning unlike that used by retardates: their reasoning is characterized by incoherence and a distorted assimilation of reality. Since these children tend to alter reality according to the needs and fears which dominate them, striking discordances in operational activity occur. In gifted psychotics, however, coherent structures do exist (de Ajuriaguerra, Inhelder, Jaeggi, Roth, and Stirlin, 1969). Prepsychotics, gifted as well as others, tended to be uncomfortable with problems related to random factors, probabilities, representations of transformations, and relations between signifiers and signified (Schmid-Kitsikis, 1973). In contrast, neurotic children evidence normal reasoning processes, but those are often characterized by exaggerated oscillations between two successive levels of thought. Operativity, therefore, seems to depend at least in part on an internal motivational force directed toward adaptation to reality.

Schmid-Kitsikis (1969, 1973) reported that the affective disorders of the prepsychotic child interfere with his cognitive development, because affect and cognition are frequently in conflict. There is considerable evidence in her later study, for example, that psychotics do not try to substitute functional for deficient mechanisms, that they transform reality to suit their subjective needs, and that they rather consistently attempt to avoid conflict. During the experiments they created identical situations (e.g., rolling both clay balls into a sausage before giving a response to a conservation question), changed the experimental problems to make them more consistent with their personal views of reality and to reduce task complexity, and wanted to see the results of transformations before giving answers (e.g., they wanted to weigh the sausage before declaring its weight unchanged).

More recently Voyat (in press) obtained similar findings when he and his colleagues used both Freudian and Piagetian paradigms to investigate the relation between affect and cognition in 30 psychotic youngsters. Voyat studied the performances of these children on tasks of one-to-one correspondence, conservation of matter, seriation, and class inclusion. The psychotic children displayed (1) an absence of reasoning by operatory reversibility, (2) discrepancies between modes of operations (e.g., manipulations versus verbal descriptions), (3) a reliance on explanations related to the child's or the experimenter's actions, rather than on observation of the transformations among objects, (4) a general lack of operational reasoning, with no apparent order or relations among performances on the various tasks, (5) no effect of preference for content on task performance, (6) a lack of learning during the experiments, (7) an absence of vacillation in thinking, and finally (8) a fundamental role of egocentrism in justifications. Voyat concluded that psychotic thought processes cannot be described as preoperational regressions. Rather, the consequence of abnormal internalization (i.e., organization without regard for adaptation to an external world) is an equilibrium structurally different from that of the normal child. These results led Voyat to question whether affect has only a functional rather than structural relation to cognition.

4.2.3. Mentally Retarded

Schmid-Kitsikis (1976) compared the mechanisms underlying problem solving in low-functioning psychotic and mentally retarded children by focusing on the coherence of thought processes during their equilibration. (She believes that comparisons with normal-child behavior are dangerous since they foster a negative view of exceptionality.) Her findings include: (1) The retarded develop through a normal, hierarchical sequence of stages, but at a slower rate. Psychotics do not appear to follow normal developmental patterns. They exhibit difficulties in acquiring stable operations even at developmentally lower levels. (2) Retardates' activity leads to stable constructions even though deductive processes are limited. Psychotics, on the other hand, form constructions, but their performances fluctuate to such an extent that they have difficulty attaining a definite level of functioning. "The reasoning processes are linked to spatial and temporal considerations and are formed by simultaneous construction. Each action seems to contain its own causality which prevents the coordinations of the actions necessary for the logical structuring of thought" (p. 254).

4.2.4. Summary

In summary, studies investigating regulatory mechanisms have focused not on what children within various disability groups can do, but rather on how they progress. Learning disabled children with language disorders tend to compensate for their inadequate language by recourse to real or imagined action. Disturbed figurative representations become increasingly subordinated to cognitive operations. A distinction between competence and performance in learning disabled children with motor and spatial problems was highlighted: these children are capable of adequate operational reasoning when concrete manipulations are not required. Emotionally disturbed children's reasoning is characterized by fluctuation between higher and lower levels. Although neurotic children follow normal developmental patterns, psychotic children do not. They do not attempt to improve their mode of functioning, but rather attempt to avoid conflict by transforming reality to correspond to their own subjective views. Mentally retarded children progress slowly, but normally and do attain stable levels of construction. Their behavior, however, is characterized by rigidity, oscillations, and difficulty in generalizing beyond the concrete data of a task (Inhelder, 1968).

4.3. Differential Diagnosis

The major work exploring the use of structural analysis as a clinical, diagnostic tool has been done by Schmid-Kitsikis (1969). She argues that the only other method of inquiry which even approaches the in-depth nature of the analysis of regulations is factor analysis. Factor analytic techniques, however, observe only the results of functioning, where analyses of regulations observe the functioning itself. Factor analysis appears to be most useful, therefore, as a technique to verify operational findings. Factor analysis may have difficulty in the explanation of behavior so necessary to diagnosis. The analysis of regulations seems more appropriate to explanation since its data are the dynamic, rather than the static, properties of thought.

To observe the greater sensitivity of structural analysis for diagnosis, consider the case of TIN, aged 11 years and 5 months (Schmid-Kitsikis, 1969). TIN is described as a child babied by his mother who shows marked tendencies toward hypochrondria. He reads haltingly, but with good comprehension. In mathematics, he solves some problems at grade level correctly, but gives absurd responses to others, even though he remembers the details of the questions. His global score on the WISC is 75. He is a thwarted left-hander whose academically successful older sister is often held up to him as a model. Understanding about TIN's level of acquisition of operatory structures and their functioning can be gained from the protocols in Figures 1, 2, and 3.

Because the adult questioned TIN in such a way as to help him overcome his nervousness and reticence, TIN was able to demonstrate operatory structures corresponding to expectations for children his age, that is, conservation of volume (Figure 3) as well as weight (Figure 1).

TIN demonstrated adequate mobility in his reasoning by the way he modified his arguments. In the conservation of weight problem, for example, he began by explaining that the quantity of matter remained unchanged by an assertion of identity (It's the same amount). Later in response to the adult's objections that the clay is so long, TIN responds by using a system of coordinations: "Yes, but it's long and thin."

TWO CLAY BALLS OF THE SAME WEIGHT	
E	— If one weighs them, what do you think, will they be the same weight or will one be heavier?
TIN	— Yes, the same thing.
E	— How do you know?
TIN	— It's difficult to explain.
E	— Try. I know you can.
TIN	— Because it was in a ball before and you pressed it so that it would become more round, but there is still the same quantity.
E	— Yes, but look, it is completely flat.
TIN	— Yes, but it is rounder, larger, and there is still the same quantity.
VERY THIN SAUSAGE	
TIN	— The same thing.
E	— Explain it to me.
TIN	— Because there is still the same quantity of dough to shape.
E	— Yes, but look how long it is.
TIN	— Yes, but it's long and thin.
	(The words in general are expressed with great reticence, the child perspiring, reddening, and paling in turn.)

Figure 1. Conservation of weight. (From Schmid-Kitsikis, 1969, pp. 58–59. Reprinted with the permission of the author.)

E	—	What is going to happen if you put them in water?
TIN	—	They sink.
E	—	And with the water, what happens?
TIN	—	It rises.
E	—	Tell me, on both hands the same thing?
TIN	—	Yes, because they are both the same thing.
E	—	The what?
TIN	—	The bullets.
E	—	What makes the water rise?
TIN	—	The heaviness.

ONE ALUMINUM AND ONE COPPER SQUARE OF EQUAL SIZE

E	—	What will happen if one submerges them?

(He hesitates a long time.)

E	—	Try to imagine.
TIN	—	I don't know.
E	—	Make an effort, I'm sure you know.
TIN	—	It will not be the same thing because one is heavier than the other.

(One submerges them.)

(He laughs, bothered.)

TIN	—	It's the same thing again.
E	—	Think, what makes the water rise?

(He hesitates and wiggles in his chair.)

E	—	Is it the heaviness?
TIN	—	No.
E	—	What then?
TIN	—	I don't know.
E	—	Try to explain it to me.
TIN	—	It is perhaps the size, they are of the same size.

TWO SMALL ALUMINUM SQUARES, BUT BIGGER THAN A THIRD, SINGLE ALUMINUM SQUARE

TIN	—	Ah! it will not be the same thing. I understand now, it's according to the size.
E	—	Why the size and not the weight?
TIN	—	Because here when one puts it in the water, it leans on the edge and makes the water rise.
E	—	But on the other side it also leans. Why does it rise more on one side?

(He seems completely blocked.)

ONE COPPER AND TWO ALUMINUM SQUARES

E	—	One is going to try another thing. Now?
TIN	—	Not the same thing.
E	—	How do you know?

(Silence)

TIN	—	I don't know.
E	—	Make an effort to explain it to me. It's been going well till now.
TIN	—	Because it is not the same size.
E	—	Why is it the size and not the weight that counts?
TIN	—	It is difficult to explain, when it is bigger, it rises more than when it is smaller.

Figure 2. Dissociation of weight and volume. (From Schmid-Kitsikis, 1969, pp. 58–59. Reprinted with the permission of the author.)

```
┌────────────────────────────────────────────────────────────────────┐
│                  TWO BALLS OF THE SAME VOLUME                        │
│ E    — If one submerges them in the water, what happens?             │
│ TIN  — The water rises the same thing, both are the same thing.      │
│                       FLATTENED BALL                                 │
│ E    — And now?                                                      │
│ TIN  — The same thing because it is the same ball that one has pressed.│
│ E    — Yes, but it is thin?                                          │
│ TIN  — That doesn't matter, it takes up the same space in the water. Ah! I under-│
│         stood a second ago, I explained the size badly. (He suddenly seems more at│
│         ease.)                                                       │
│ E    — What do you mean?                                             │
│ TIN  — It is the space that the bullet occupies that counts and not the heaviness.│
│ E    — How can you explain to me that when it is thin, it occupies the same thing│
│         than when it is a ball?                                      │
│                  (He seems bothered again.)                          │
│ TIN  — That is to say, one pressed it, the ball.                     │
│ E    — And?                                                          │
│ TIN  — Uh, it has become thinner, but it is also longer, so it comes back to the same│
│         thing.                                                       │
│ E    — As what?                                                      │
│ TIN  — As the ball.                                                  │
│ E    — It comes back to the same thing for what?                     │
│ TIN  — For the space it occupies in the water.                       │
│                        METAL BALL                                    │
│ TIN  — It will be the same because it is the same size as that ball of dough.│
│ E    — It doesn't matter that it is so heavy?                        │
│ TIN  — No, it's the same size.                                       │
└────────────────────────────────────────────────────────────────────┘
```

Figure 3. Conservation of volume. (From Schmid-Kitsikis, 1969, pp. 58–59. Reprinted with the permission of the author.)

TIN showed that he had sufficient resources to advance during the course of a test (see Figure 3) and to use what he learned in one test (Figure 3) to correct his incorrect response in another (Figure 2).

Finally, throughout the testing, TIN needed the stimulation and encouragement of the adult in order to pursue his reasoning. Since he is beginning to function at the level of formal operations, where he will not have the security of concrete proofs to aid his progress, the prognosis for TIN is not favorable, unless he succeeds in acquiring a more assertive attitude.

The nature of this investigation and the type of information gathered differs considerably from that obtainable from standardized tests. Schmid-Kitsikis was able to determine that a 75 IQ was not indicative of the child's intellectual functioning, i.e., that the child was not retarded. He needed only encouragement and support to demonstrate his potential. As de Ajuriaguerra and Tissot (1966, cited in Schmid-Kitsikis, 1969, p. 181) point out:

> To determine that a subject does or does not achieve a given performance is different from knowing how he gets there, or why he does not. Definitely, in the clinic it is almost always more important to grasp the structure of reasoning or of a behavior than to measure its results.*

4.4. Summary

The research reported in this chapter is indicative of the development of several trends in research applying Genevan theory to exceptional children. The early research carried out by Genevans focused on an analysis of the gaps in cognitive development and of the hierarchy of stages. Anglo-American researchers are, for the most part, still pursuing these lines of investigation, using empiricist techniques. Genevans, however, have adopted a new strategy: they have begun analyzing the regulatory mechanisms of special children. This newer approach promises to lead to a much richer understanding of the dynamic aspects of behavior in exceptional children. Briefly, the Genevan studies have examined the acquisition of dynamic systems. Anglo-American research, on the other hand, has been primarily correlational. It has examined the static relations between cognitive development and a host of other variables. It has been especially well-focused on a comparison of the performances of normal and exceptional children. It has, in addition, emphasized task variables and training possibilities to a greater extent than Genevan studies. A new thrust, in structural analysis has been its clinical, diagnostic use. This approach has recently been attempted by a few American workers (cf. Delany and Fitzpatrick, 1976; Poulsen, 1976).

5. Implications of Genevan Research and Theory for Special Education

Little research from any theoretical model has been applied directly to educational procedures (Blatt and Garfunkel, 1973; Getzels and Dillon, 1973; Hewett and Blake, 1973). What exists, therefore, in terms of

---

*"Déterminer qu'un sujet atteint ou n'atteint pas telle performance est autre chose que de savoir comment il y parvient, ou pourquoi il n'y parvient pas. En définitive, en clinique il est presque toujours plus important de saisir la structure d'un raisonnement ou d'une conduite que d'en mesurer les résultats."

recommendations for educational practice is based on extrapolation and implication. Genevan theory has been used to challenge current educational practice in regular education (cf. Kamii and DeVries, in press; Schwebel and Raph, 1973) and has some serious implications for education of exceptional children as well.

Piaget (1970b) reminds us that education has a dual purpose: (1) to acculturate the individual and (2) to develop the individual to his fullest potential. The many diagnostic-prescriptive approaches used by special educators are based on empiricist models and generally ignore one or the other of these goals. The areas and methods of diagnosis are both standardized and preestablished, even when a variety of activities and instruments are used. Specific behavioral objectives are delineated either early in or even prior to the beginning of the teaching-learning sequence. These practices assume a passive learner, a fixed body of knowledge and skills to be diagnosed and remediated, and fixed approaches to learning problems. In contrast, an approach consistent with Genevan theory would demand a greater openness for both diagnosis and remediation. The new constructions that result from the child's internal regulations would have to be understood and taken into consideration at each step of the way. The child's own activity, therefore, would, to a great extent, dictate both a conception of the nature of his problem and the corrective or remedial steps to be taken. It is unlikely that any approach which requires the establishment of extensive, fixed programs could be considered adequate in fostering a child's development to his or her fullest potential.

Little mention of teaching through exploration is ever made in texts on teaching special children. These children are more likely to perform exercises and drills rather than to explore their environments and to pursue their own interests. Drill, programmed learning, and M and Ms do not encourage reasoning. Exploration does. Genevan research has shown that exceptional children (with the possible exception of the psychotic) follow essentially the same paths through cognitive development as normals. In those instances where children with particular disabilities vary from the norm in the process of their development, it is because they must compensate for their deficits. Only rates of acquisition and the quality of particular constructions, however, vary. Development, therefore, is dependent on much the same factors in exceptional as it is in normal children.

Miller and Dyer (1975) have shown that preschool programs using behavioral approaches were initially very effective. Their successes decreased over time, however, when compared to the more lasting effects of child-centered programs such as the Montessori. Similar results were obtained by Stallings (1976) in her study of follow-through classrooms. As Miller and Dyer suggest, immediate academic success is not an adequate criterion for the value of educational programs. Certainly children can be taught responses, but that does not ensure that they have the logic to construct the responses.

Special educators have traditionally assumed that exceptional children need specialized and rigorous teaching plans. Christopholos and Renz (1969) and Dunn (1968) among others, however, indicated that mentally retarded children often achieved as well or better in regular classes as they did when given special instruction in a segregated class. Such findings have led to the enactment of Public Law 94-142, The Education for All Handicapped Children Act of 1975 which ensures that all special children will be educated within the least restrictive environment. The mandate of the law is clearly to return the mildly impaired to the mainstream, that is, to the least restrictive, appropriate setting. The law requires that specific instructional objectives be identified for each special child. Plans for teaching must also include the child's present level of functioning and a statement of annual goals (Deshler, 1976). It is important to note that in passing this legislation the United States Congress has actually legislated an empirical approach to the education of exceptional children. This writer does not take issue with the tenor of the law which is, of course, to protect the civil rights of exceptional children. Aspects of the plan, however, are open to criticism.

First, Kamii and DeVries (in press) have shown that the specification of particular objectives is based on the notion that knowledge comes from the environment and is acquired by children through social transmission. The Genevans have demonstrated quite clearly, however, that social transmission is not a sufficient condition for learning. Acquisition of knowledge depends also on maturation, physical and logico-mathematical experience, and, most importantly, equilibration. Those who advocate the use of instructional objectives and similar task-analytic procedures fail to make the distinction between learning in its strict sense and in its broad sense (Piaget, 1959). Specific bits of knowledge are learned only if they can be assimilated into existing structures. In addition, because children's reasoning is qualitatively different from that of adults, who is to determine what sequence of objectives, if any, is most effective? Since children learn through successive approximations, and since disturbances and contradictions lead to the compensations which, in turn, foster reequilibration of structures, it appears that step-by-step acquisitions which attempt to eliminate cognitive disturbances could lead, at best, to the acquisition of information but not to higher levels of development. Kamii and Derman (1971) showed quite clearly

that Engelmann's attempt to accelerate children's acquisition of operational knowledge (He systematically trained kindergarten children on
the "logical structures" of conservation, including specific gravity) lead
to nothing more than the rote application of what was apparently, for
the children, a meaningless rule.

Basing annual goals on current levels of functioning is also a ques-
tionable procedure. Kohlberg and Mayer (1972) describe the practice of
predicting future performance on the basis of measured, earlier performance as completely unjustifiable. They say that educators make two
errors when they define educational goals on the basis of tests: first, they
confuse correlation and causation (e.g., teaching children conservation
tasks in the hope of making them better readers) and second, they
assume that success in school implies success in life. Kohlberg and
Mayer argue that development, not the acquisition of specific skills or
objectives, should be the aim of education.

Another question relating to the law is what achievement is to be
measured. In addition to academic objectives, special educators frequently advocate the assessment of correlated (sometimes called processing) disabilities such as perception, language, and memory. Recent
reviews of research (cf. Hammill and Weiderholt, 1973; Hammill and
Larsen, 1974; Newcomer and Hammill, 1976), however, indicate that
what Mann and Phillips (1971) refer to as fractionalized practices (i.e.,
the division of psychological functions into measurable, teachable parts)
have not proved successful. Is perception understood well enough to be
divided into segments to be measured? Are there indeed psychologically
separate functions or are there arbitrary segments of psychometric imag-
inations? What is needed is the understanding of how correlated functions interrelate and how they facilitate or hinder academic and/or developmental progress. Genevan research has begun to examine the impact of
deficits on development and to examine the ways in which children
compensate for their deficiencies. One important finding of this research
was that the distinction between competence and performance is often
unclear (see the Schmid-Kitsikis, 1969, study on dispraxia). Two separate experiments by Birch and Bortner (1966, 1967) with normal and
learning disabled children also illustrate this point. Children were given
an array of items—a red lipstick case, a blue poker chip, and a spool of
thread—and asked to designate which item was most like a red button.
Younger children responded by choosing perceptually similar items,
i.e., the red lipstick case or the round poker chip. Older children chose
the thread because of its functional relation to the button. The investigators then asked the question as to whether younger children were
capable of responding to the functional relation. A replication of the

study using less compelling perceptual cues, demonstrated that they were. The research literature on mental retardation is replete with similar examples, i.e., the retarded are able to overcome their initial tendency to respond perceptually to cognitive problems when a perceptual solution is clearly ineffectual (cf. Reid, 1974; Schmelkin and Reid, 1976). Kershner's work (1975) with retarded readers suggest, furthermore, that retarded readers may have perfectly adequate perceptual abilities and that those delayed in reading persist in applying them! These findings raise the issue of what an acceptable measure of correlated disabilities might be.

What alternatives would a Genevan approach to the education of exceptional children provide?

For the Genevans, knowledge is not derived from the registration and memory of environmental objects and events. It is, instead, "an internal growth activity of coordinating and structuring, or better, restructuring available schemes which the child applies to situations confronting him" (Furth, 1976). The child learns through resolving discrepancies in simultaneous wholes between the givens in a situation as he observes them and his own mental coordinations. It is not possible to understand, for example, that when dominoes on end are closely aligned, a push on the first will tumble the last, unless one grasps the relations among all the dominoes from the outset (Piaget, 1975b). Understanding that the first is close to and would tumble the second, does not help children to predict what will happen to a fourth when the first is pushed. Tasks, therefore, in teaching would not be presented segment by segment. Emphasis would be on the dynamic aspects of the transformation rather than on the states. Four examples of Genevan-based teaching strategies will illustrate this approach.*

The primary strategy used by Genevans in their studies of learning (Inhelder *et al.*, 1974) is described by Pascual-Leone (in press) as the method of *graded learning loops*. If tasks A_1, A_2, A_3, and A_4, for example, become progressively more difficult, they might be presented to a child in the following manner: A_4, A_3, A_2, A_1, A_2, A_3, etc. Task A_1 is designed to be so simple that the child will solve that task spontaneously. For example, Inhelder *et al.* (1974) report an experiment in which they facilitated the acquisition of class inclusion. First, the experimenter gave a doll a collection of pieces of fruit made up of two subclasses (e.g., peaches and apples). The experimenter then asked the child to give a

*The author does not advocate the adoption of Genevan research tasks as curriculum content. These examples were selected as illustrative of a holistic, dynamic approach to education.

second doll, for example, fewer peaches, but just as many pieces of fruit (A_3). The second part of the training consisted of asking questions (e.g., Does someone have more apples? Does someone have more pieces of fruit?) designed to help children compare the number of items in the superordinate class with the number in one of its subclasses (A_2). Children usually lose track of the superordinate class and compare the items in the subclasses with one another. In the third part of the training, the child was asked to determine whether more peaches or pieces of fruit were in a single collection (A_1). This intrinsic feedback plus the experimenter's encouragement to contrast strategies needed in the solution of various items in the loop generally helps children use the schemes they've applied to solve easier problems in the solution of more difficult ones.

The second example is derived from an attempt by Inhelder (Piaget, 1975c) to help children realize that in the conservation task a displacement is simply a moving of parts and that what is added on one place corresponds to what was taken away in another. Instead of rolling the ball of plasticene into a sausage, the investigators took a piece off and put it back on a different side of the ball. Children acquired stable conservation responses nearly two years earlier than in the classic experiment and performed successfully on that task, too.

A third example is taken from the work of Schmid-Kitsikis (1976). In her experiments with prepsychotic and mentally retarded children, Schmid-Kitsikis used control tasks to observe how children compensated during equilibration. Various modifications of classic cognitive tasks were designated to test invariance. The procedures were slowed down and emphasis was put on the physical dimensions of the objects. The transformations were graduated. For example, in conservation of discontinuous quantity, elements were added and subtracted until the children became aware of equivalences by counting and achieved a correct solution.

A fourth procedure has been developed by Lefebvre and Pinard (cited in Pascual-Leone, in press). The child's attention is focused on relevant aspects of the situation and is monitored throughout the task. Systematic and lengthy repetition of the same sequence of graded items is given. The equilibration process in such induced learning becomes simplified. One must recognize, however, that the model developed by Lefebvre and Pinard is a learning model and, therefore, differs from the Genevan model which studies and explains spontaneous learning within the context of development. When one deals with children whose learning and/or developmental processes have been disrupted, however, one might profit from the use of more structured tasks which foster learning. The point, of course, is to emphasize the dynamic aspects of the transformation, rather than segment the task into isolated, sequential bits.

Each of these strategies is based on an equilibration model which places stress on the child's spontaneous activities (Piaget, 1973). Instruction in the solution of the problem is never didactic. Children are aided in mustering their own resources to solve problems. Emphasis is on reflexive rather than empirical abstraction and on the similarities rather than the differences among objects and events. These strategies also recognize that there is a delay between action and conceptualization (Piaget, 1976) and that conceptualization derives from the periphery to the center, i.e., from accommodation to objects to internal coordinations. Anticipation and choice, because they foster reconstruction of the task on a conscious level, foster conceptualization and lead to plans for behavior. An important teaching strategy to be derived from these models, therefore, is to ask children to predict the results of their manipulations prior to carrying them out. It is equally important to note, however, that either actual or imagined manipulation of objects is (until formal operations) crucial to learning, so that children may experience the disturbances and contradictions which can lead to compensations and the posing of new questions.

Learning of verbal rules is not sufficient for at least three reasons. First, verbal rules do not foster contradiction. Second, success without understanding may ensue. Third, motivation is impoverished and learning becomes narrow in scope. Only the initial goal is given when children are asked to perform tasks, intermediate goals are derived by the children themselves as they tackle problems and struggle with conflicts and contradictions (Piaget, 1975b).

Finally, in a Genevan model, the particular methodology to be used in teaching would be dependent on the child's mode of functioning and on the nature of the task. Piaget (1970b) indicates that lectures are appropriate for children at the level of formal operations. Programmed learning is also efficient and appropriate in fostering learning in which a single formal structure is to be associated with a given content or two contents are to be associated with each other (for example, the sorting of red and blue triangles or the matching of states with their capitals).

Genevans, however, have never been concerned with the learning of such specific information.* They have instead focused on the de-

*The acquisition of information is unquestionably important. It is an overemphasis on facts or the assumption that the accumulation of facts will lead to understanding that is to be avoided.

velopment of the systems of knowing in which the interaction between the effects of objects and the inferences of the child change in the course of cognitive growth (Furth, 1974). Under such a system, the content of knowledge plays an important role in fostering developmental progress. The more challenging the problem, the greater the gains. A perusal of the research findings indicates that problems posed to exceptional children should be as exciting as those posed to other children.

Furth (1973) originally conceived of his thinking laboratory to stimulate cognitive development in deaf subjects, but later argued that all children could benefit from those activities and from others originally designed for special populations (Furth and Wachs, 1974). As he suggested, these types of activities used with normal children might help to prevent faulty learning habits and to eliminate the need for later remediation. When remediation is needed, however, it would appear that surface first-aid such as practice drawing triangles or bs and ds is not sufficient. An analogy might be drawn between Waddington's concept of homeorheses (see Piaget, 1977c) and the goal of remediation, which is to assist children in returning to the place where they would have been if a disruption had not occurred. We see in their efforts at compensation a tendency of exceptional children to begin to do that for themselves.

Most importantly, Genevan theory helps us through its emphasis on the interaction of the four factors of development, and especially equilibration, to view the child as a whole and not in terms of his or her disability. With emphasis on what children can do rather than on what they cannot do, teachers might be more successful in recognizing and fostering children's strengths.

6. Conclusions

Genevan theory provides those teaching special children with a theory which describes a developmental sequence not tied to age and which focuses on the mechanisms of change. Its emphasis on equilibration leads to a view of exceptional children which centers on their capabilities and provides the basis for understanding the compensations these children make between their accommodations to objects and their assimilatory schemes. More traditional approaches to special education have focused on representational rather than operative functions. Exceptional children, however, progress through the same stages of development as normals and in the same order. Variations in rate, final

stage achieved, and quality of within-stage performances may vary, but
with the exception of psychotic children, the process of compensations
is similar and effective in producing higher levels of functioning. Emphasis on the operational aspects of thought would question current
procedures which lead children comfortably, step by step through the
learning of verbal rules. Instead, activities should be designed to foster
anticipation and choice. Manipulation of objects can then lead to disturbances and contradictions and, thereby, encourage the spontaneous
generation of new goals and new questions. One cannot deny that exceptional children need special attention and probably more extensive
guidance and externally imposed structure. But if, as Piaget suggests,
the process of life itself is the acquisition of knowledge, we can no longer
afford to ignore developmental concerns in the education of our exceptional children.

ACKNOWLEDGMENTS

The author wishes to thank Nancy Houghton for translating Figures
1, 2, and 3 and Richard Iano for his helpful comments on an earlier draft
of this chapter.

References

Adler, M. J., 1964. Some implications of the theories of Jean Piaget and J. S. Bruner for
    education. *Canadian Education and Research Digest, 4,* 291–305.
Ajuriaguerra, J. de, and Tissot, R., 1966. Application clinique de la psychologie génétique.
    In F. Bresson and M. de Montmollin (Eds.), *Psychologie et épistémologie génétique: Thèmes
    Piagetiens.* Paris: Dunod.
Ajuriaguerra, J. de, Guignard, F., Jaeggi, A., Kocher, F., Maquard, M., Paunier, A.,
    Quinodoz, D., and Siotis, E., 1963. Organisation psychologique et troubles du dé-
    velopment du language. (Etude d'un groupe d'enfants dysphasiques). In *Problems de
    psycholinquistique,* Symposium de l'APSLF, Neuschâtel, 1962. Paris: Presses Univer-
    sitaires de France.
Ajuriaguerra, J. de, Inhelder, B., Jaeggi, A., Roth, S., and Stirlin, M., 1969. Troubles de
    l'organisation de désorganisation intellectuelle chez les enfants psychotiques.
    Psychiatrie de l'Enfant, 12, 37–69.
Birch, H. G., and Bortner, M., 1966. Stimulus competition and category usage in normal
    children. *Journal of Genetic Psychology, 109,* 195–204.
Birch, H. G., and Bortner, M., 1967. Stimulus competition and category utilization in brain
    damaged children. *Developmental Medicine and Child Neurology, 9,* 402–410.
Blatt, B., and Garfunkel, F., 1973. Teaching the mentally retarded. In R. M. W. Travers
    (Ed.), *Second handbook of research on teaching: A project of AERA.* Chicago: Rand Mc-
    Nally.
Bovet, M., 1976. Piaget's theory of cognitive development and individual differences. In B.
    Inhelder and H. H. Chipman (Eds.), *Piaget and his school: A reader in developmental
    psychology.* New York: Springer-Verlag.

Brogle, J. F., 1971. Performance of normals and retardates on Piaget's conservation tasks. *Dissertation Abstracts, 31*, 6870 6871 B.

Brown, A. L., 1973. Conservation of number and continuous quantity in normal, bright, and retarded children. *Child Development, 44*, 376–379.

Carlson, J. S., and Michelson, L. H., 1973. Methodological study of conservation in retarded adolescents. *American Journal of Mental Deficiency, 78*, 348–353.

Carpenter, T. E., 1955. A pilot study for a quantitative investigation of Jean Piaget's original work on concept formation. *Educational Review, 7*, 142–149.

Chomsky, N., 1965. *Aspects of the theory of syntax.* Cambridge, Mass.: M.I.T. Press.

Christopholos, F., and Renz, P., 1969. A critical examination of special education programs. *Journal of Special Education, 3*, 371–380.

Coleman, H. M., 1968. Visual perception and reading dysfunction. *Journal of Learning Disabilities, 1*, 116–123.

Cromer, R. F., 1973. Conservation by the congenitally blind. *British Journal of Psychology, 64*, 241–250.

Cromer, R. F., 1977. Children's perceptual organization of seriated displays: Evidence against a memory reorganization hypothesis. *British Journal of Psychology, 68*, 165–175.

Delany, F. I., and Fitzpatrick, M., 1976. *The use of structured Piaget-type tasks to investigate cognitive development in seriously disturbed children, aged 3–17.* Paper presented at the Sixth International Interdisciplinary Seminar on Piagetian Theory and Its Implications for the Helping Professions, Los Angeles, Calif.

Deshler, D. D., 1976. Introducing public law 94–142: The education for all handicapped children act of 1975. *DCLD Newsletter, 2*, 10–24.

DeVries, R., 1973. *The two intelligences of bright, average, and retarded children.* Paper presented at the meeting of the Society of Research in Child Development, Philadelphia.

Dodwell, P. C., 1960. Children's understanding of number and related concepts. *Canadian Journal of Psychology, 14*, 191–205.

Doise, W., and Perret-Clermont, N., 1976. *Coordinations sociales et cognitives.* Paper presented at the 21st International Congress of Psychology, Paris.

Droz, R., 1970. *Educational implications deriving from operational attainment of retardates.* Paper presented at the 2nd Congress of IASSMD, Warsaw.

Dunn, L. M., 1968. Special education for the mildly retarded: Is much of it justifiable? *Exceptional Children, 35*, 5–22.

Erickson, R. C., 1969. Visual-haptic attitude: Effect on student achievement in reading. *Journal of Learning Disabilities, 2*, 256–260.

Filer, A. A., 1972. Piagetian cognitive development in normal and in emotionally disturbed children. *Dissertation Abstracts International, 33*, 2342.

Friedland, S. J., and Meisels, S. J., 1975. An application of the Piagetian model to perceptual handicaps. *Journal of Learning Disabilities, 8*, 20–24.

Friedman, J., and Pasnak, R., 1973. Attainment of classification and seriation concepts by blind and sighted children. *Education of the Handicapped, 5*, 55–62.

Frostig, M., and Maslow, P., 1969. Reading, developmental abilities, and the problem of the match. *Journal of Learning Disabilities, 2*, 571–74.

Furth, H. G., 1966. *Thinking without language: Psychological implications of deafness.* New York: Free Press.

Furth, H. G., 1969. *Piaget and knowledge.* Englewood Cliffs, N.J.: Prentice-Hall, pp. 55–67.

Furth, H. G., 1971. Linguistic deficiency and thinking, research with deaf subjects 1964–1969. *Psychological Bulletin, 76*, 58–72.

Furth, H. G., 1973. *Deafness and learning: A psychosocial approach.* Belmont, Calif.: Brooks/Cole.

Furth, H. G. *Psychology in Geneva, 1974.* Unpublished paper, Catholic University.

Furth, H. G., 1976. Review of Inhelder, B., Sinclair, H., and Bovet, M. *Learning and Cognitive Structures.*

Furth, H. G., and Wachs, H., 1974. *Thinking goes to school.* New York: Oxford University Press.

Garonne, G., Guignard, F., Rodriguez, R., Lenoir, J., Kobr, F., and Degailler, L., 1969. La débilité mental chez l'enfant. *Psychiatrie de l'Enfant, 12,* 201–219.

Garrison, M. (Ed.), 1966. Cognitive models and development in mental retardation. *American Journal of Mental Deficiency, 70(4),* Monograph Supplement.

Getman, G. N., 1965. The visuomotor complex in the acquisition of learning skills. In J. Hellmuth (Ed.), *Learning disorders* (Vol. 1). Seattle: Special Child Publications.

Getzels, J. W., and Dillon, J. T., 1973. The nature of giftedness and the education of the gifted. In R. M. W. Travers (Ed.), *Second handbook of research on teaching: A project of AERA.* Chicago: Rand McNally.

Goldschmid, M. L., 1967. Different types of conservation and nonconservation and their relation to age, sex, IQ, MA, and vocabulary. *Child Development, 38,* 1229–1246.

Gottesman, M., 1971. A comparative study of Piaget's developmental schema of sighted children with that of a group of blind children. *Child Development, 42,* 573–580.

Gottesman, M., 1975. *Stage development of blind children: A Piagetian view.* Paper presented at the Fifth Special Invitational Interdisciplinary Seminar: Piagetian Theory and Its Implications for the Helping Professions, Los Angeles, Calif.

Hallahan, D. P., and Cruickshank, W. M., 1973. *Psychoeducational foundations of learning disabilities.* Englewood Cliffs, N. J.: Prentice-Hall.

Hammill, D., 1972. Training visual perceptual processes. *Journal of Learning Disabilities, 5,* 552–562.

Hammill, D. D., and Bartel, N. R., 1978. *Teaching children with learning and behavior problems* (2nd ed.). Boston: Allyn & Bacon.

Hammill, D. D., and Larsen, S., 1974. The relationship of selected auditory perceptual skills and reading. *Journal of Learning Disabilities, 7,* 429–435.

Hammill, D. D., and Weiderholt, J. L., 1973. Review of the Frostig Visual Perception Test and the related training program. In L. Mann and D. Sabatino (Eds.), *The first review of special education (Vol. 1).* Philadelphia: The Journal of Special Education Press, 33–48.

Hatwell, Y., 1966. *Privation sensorielle et intelligence.* Paris: Presses Universitaires de France.

Hewett, F. M., and Blake, P. R., 1973. Teaching the emotionally disturbed. In R. M. W. Travers (Ed.), *Second handbook of research on teaching: A project of AERA.* Chicago: Rand McNally.

Hood, H., 1962. An experimental study of Piaget's theory of development of numbers in children. *British Journal of Psychology, 32,* 300–303.

Howell, R. W., 1972. Evaluation of cognitive abilities of emotionally disturbed children: An application of Piaget's theories. *Dissertation Abstracts International, 32 (9-A),* 5037–5038.

Hughes, M. M., 1965. *A four-year longitudinal study of logical thinking in a group of secondary modern school boys.* Unpublished master's thesis, University of Leeds.

Iano, R., 1971. Learning deficiency versus developmental conceptions of mental retardation. *Exceptional Children, 38,* 301–311.

Ilg, F. L., and Ames, L. B., 1955. *The Gesell Institute's child behavior.* New York: Dell Publishing Company.

Inhelder, B., 1966. Cognitive development and its contribution to the diagnosis of some phenomena of mental deficiency. *Merrill-Palmer Quarterly, 12,* 299–321.

Inhelder, B., 1968. *The diagnosis of reasoning in the mentally retarded.* New York: John Day.

Inhelder, B., and Siotis, E., 1963. Observations sur les aspects operatifs et figuratifs des enfants dysphasiques. In *Problèmes de psycholinguistique*. Paris: Presses Universitaires de France.

Inhelder, B., Sinclair, H., and Bovet, M., 1974. *Learning and the development of cognition*. Cambridge, Mass.: Harvard University Press.

Johnson, G. O., 1959. Relationship of learning rate and developmental rate. *Exceptional Children, 26,* 68–69.

Kahn, J. V., 1974. Training EMR and intellectually average adolescents of low and middle SES for formal thought. *American Journal of Mental Deficiency, 79,* 397–403.

Kahn, J. V., 1975. Relationship of Piaget's sensorimotor period to language acquisition of profoundly retarded children. *American Journal of Mental Deficiency, 79,* 640–643.

Kamara, A., and Easley, J. A., Sr., 1977. Is the rate of cognitive development uniform across culture?—A methodological critique with new evidence from Theme Children. In P. R. Dasen (Ed.), *Piagetian Psychology: Cross Cultural Contributions.* New York: Gardner.

Kamii, C., and Derman, L., 1971. Comments on Engelmann's paper: The Engelmann approach to teaching logical thinking: Findings from the administration of some Piagetian tasks. In D. R. Green, M. P. Ford, and G. B. Flamer (Eds.), *Measurement and Piaget.* New York: McGraw-Hill.

Kamii, C., and DeVries, R. Piaget for early education. In M. C. Day and R. K. Parker (Eds.), *The preschool in action* (2nd ed.). Boston: Allyn & Bacon, 1977.

Kephart, N. C., 1971. *The slow learner in the classroom* (2nd ed.). Columbus, Ohio: Charles E. Merrill.

Kershner, J. R., 1975. Visual-spatial organization and reading: Support for a cognitive developmental interpretation. *Journal of Learning Disabilities, 8,* 30–36.

Klees, M., and Lebrun, A., 1972. Analysis of the figurative and operate processes of thought of 40 dyslexic children. *Journal of Learning Disabilities, 5,* 14–21.

Kohlberg, L., 1968. Early education: A cognitive developmental view. *Child Development, 39,* 1013–1062.

Kohlberg, L., and Mayer, R., 1972. Development as the aim of education. *Harvard Educational Review, 42,* 449–498.

Liben, L. S., 1977. Memory from a cognitive-developmental perspective: A theoretical and empirical review. In W. Overton and J. M. Gallagher (Eds.), *Knowledge and development* (Vol. I): *Advances in research and theory.* New York: Plenum.

Lister, C. M., 1970. The development of a concept of volume conservation in ESN children. *British Journal of Educational Psychology, 40,* 55–64.

Longeot, F., 1969. *Psychologie differentielle et théorie opératoire de l'intelligence.* Paris: Dunod.

Lovell, K., 1966. The developmental approach of Jean Piaget: Open discussion. In M. Garrison, Jr. (Ed.), *Cognitive models in mental retardation.* Monograph supplement to the *American Journal of Mental Deficiency, 70,* 84–105.

Lovell, K., 1968. Some recent studies in cognitive and language development. *Merrill-Palmer Quarterly, 14,* 123–138.

Lunzer, E. A., 1965. Problems of formal reasoning in test situations. In P. Mussen (Ed.), *European research in cognitive development. Monographs of the Society for Research in Child Development, 30,* 19–46.

Lyle, J. G., 1968. Reading retardation and reversal tendency: A factorial study. *Child Development, 40,* 833–843.

Magary, J. F., Poulsen, M. K., Levinson, P. J., and Taylor, P. A. (Eds.), 1977. *Piagetian theory and its implications for the helping professions. Emphasis: The handicapped child.* Los Angeles, Calif.: University of Southern California.

Mahaney, E. J., and Stephens, B., 1974. Two year gains in moral judgment by retarded and nonretarded persons. *American Journal of Mental Deficiency, 79,* 134–141.

Mann, L., and Phillips, W., 1971. Fractional practices in special education: A critique. In D. Hammill and N. Bartel (Eds.), *Educational perspectives in learning disabilities.* New York: Wiley, 314–325.

Marchi, J. Y., 1971. Comparison of selected Piagetian tasks with the WISC as measures of mental retardation. *Dissertation Abstracts, 31,* 6442-A.

McLaughlin, J. A., and Stephens, B., 1974. Interrelationships among reasoning, moral judgment, and moral conduct. *American Journal of Mental Deficiency, 79,* 150–161.

McManis, D. L., 1969. Conservation of mass, weight, and volume by normal and retarded children. *American Journal of Mental Deficiency, 73,* 762–767.

Miller, C. K., 1969. Conservation in blind children. *Education of the Visually Handicapped, 1,* 101–105.

Miller, C. K., Zumoff, L., and Stephens, B., 1974. A comparison of reasoning skills and moral judgments in delinquent, retarded, and normal adolescent girls. *Journal of Psychology, 86,* 261–268.

Miller, L. B., and Dyer, J. L., 1975. Four preschool programs: Their dimensions and effects. *SRCD Monographs,* Serial No. 162.

Moore, G., and Stephens, B., 1974. Two-year gains in moral conduct by retarded and nonretarded persons. *American Journal of Mental Deficiency, 79,* 147–153.

Newcomer, P., and Hammill, D. C., 1976. *Psycholingustics in the schools.* Columbus, Ohio: Charles E. Merrill.

Oléron, P., 1957. *Recherches sur le développement mental des sourals-muets.* Paris: Centre National de la Recherche Scientifique.

Oléron, P., and Herren, H., 1961. L'Acquisition des conservations. *Enfance,* 201–219.

Pascual-Leone, J. On learning and development, Piagetian style: A reply to Lefebvre-Pinard. *Canadian Journal of Psychology,* in press.

Patten, B. M., 1973. Visually mediated thinking: A report of the case of Albert Einstein. *Journal of Learning Disabilities, 6,* 415–420.

Peluffo, M., 1964. La nozioni de conservazione del volume e le operazione di sviluppo del pensuro operatorio in soggetti appartenenti ad ambienti fisci e socioculturali diversi. *Rivista de Psicolozia Sociale, 2,* 19–32.

Piaget, J., 1959. Apprentissage et connaissance (première partie). In P. Greco and J. Piaget (Eds.), *Etudes d'épistémologie génétique* (Vol. 7): *Apprentissage et connaissance.* Paris: Presses Universitaires de France, 21–67.

Piaget, J., 1967. Language and thought from the genetic point of view. In D. Elkind (Ed.), *Six Psychological Studies.* New York: Random House.

Piaget, J., 1969. *The mechanisms of perception.* London: Routledge & Kegan.

Piaget, J., 1970a. Piaget's theory. In P. H. Mussen (Ed.), *Carmichael's manual of child psychology* (Vol. 1). New York: Wiley, 703–732.

Piaget, J., 1970b. *Science of education and the psychology of the child.* New York: Orion Press.

Piaget, J., 1971a. *Biology and knowledge.* Chicago: University of Chicago Press.

Piaget, J., 1971b. *Psychology and epistemology.* New York: Grossman.

Piaget, J., 1973. *To understand is to invent.* New York: Grossman.

Piaget. J., 1975a. *L'équilibration des structures cognitives.* Paris: Presses Universitaires de France. (English edition, New York: Viking, 1977.)

Piaget, J., 1975b. *Réussir et comprendre.* Paris: Presses Universitaires de France.

Piaget, J., 1975c. *On correspondences and morphisms.* Paper presented at the Annual Symposium of the Jean Piaget Society, Philadelphia.

Piaget, J., 1976. *The grasp of consciousness.* Cambridge: Harvard University Press.
Piaget, J., 1977a. The role of action in the development of thinking. In W. F. Overton and J. M. Gallagher (Eds.), *Knowledge and development* (Vol. I): *Advances in research and theory.* New York: Plenum.
Piaget, J., 1977b. From noise to order: The psychological development of knowledge and phenocopy in biology. In H. E. Gruber and J. Voneche (Eds.), *The essential Piaget.* New York: Basic Books.
Piaget, J., 1977c. Problems of equilibration. In M. H. Appel and L. S. Goldberg (Eds.), *Topics in cognitive development* (Vol. 1). New York, Plenum.
Piaget, J., 1977d. *L'Abstraction réfléchissante.* Paris: Presses Universitaires de France.
Piaget, J., and Garcia, R., 1971. *Les explications causales.* Paris: Presses Universitaires de France. (English edition, New York: Norton, 1974).
Piaget, J., and Inhelder, B., 1962. *Le développement des quantités physique chez l'enfant.* Neuchâtel: Delachaux et Niestlé. (English edition: London: Routledge & Kegan Paul, 1974.)
Piaget, J., and Inhelder, B., 1967. *The child's conception of space.* New York: Basic Books.
Piaget, J., and Inhelder, B., 1969. *The psychology of the child.* New York: Basic Books.
Piaget, J., and Inhelder, B., 1973. *Memory and intelligence.* New York: Basic Books.
Popp, H., 1964. Visual discrimination of alphabet letters. *Reading Teacher, 17,* 221–226.
Poulsen, M. K., 1976. *Clinical assessment of semiotic function for the differential diagnosis of young exceptional children.* Paper presented at the Annual Meeting of the Piaget Society, Philadelphia.
Ranson, J., 1950. *Application des épreuves Piaget–Inhelder à un groupe de débiles mentaux.* Lyon: Bosc.
Reid, D. K., 1974. *The effects of cognitive tempo and the presence of a memory aid on conjunctive concept attainment in educable mentally retarded boys.* Unpublished doctoral dissertation, Temple University.
Rothenberg, B., 1969. Conservation of number among four- and five-year-old children: Some methodological considerations. *Child Development, 40,* 382–406.
Schmelkin, L., and Reid, D. K., 1976. *The effects of verbalization and the presence of a memory aid on conjunctive concept attainment in normal and mentally retarded children.* Final report: Bureau of Education of the Handicapped (Grant G00–75–00359).
Schmid-Kitsikis, E., 1969. *L'Examen des opérations de l'intelligence: Psychopathologie de l'enfant.* Neuchâtel: Delachaux et Niestlé.
Schmid-Kitsikis, E., 1972. Exploratory studies in cognitive development. In H. Monks (Ed.), *Determinants of behavioral development.* New York: Academic Press, 51–63.
Schmid-Kitsikis, E., 1973. Piagetian theory and its approach to psychopathology. *American Journal of Mental Deficiency, 77,* 694–705.
Schmid-Kitsikis, E., 1976. The cognitive mechanisms underlying problem-solving in psychotic and mentally retarded children. In B. Inhelder and H. H. Chipman (Eds.), *Piaget and his school.* New York: Springer-Verlag, 234–255.
Schmid-Kitsikis, E., and Ajuriaguerra, J. de, 1973. Aspects opératoires en psychopathologie infantile. *Revue de Neuropsychiatrie Infantile, 21,* 7–21.
Schwebel, M., and Raph, J., 1973. *Piaget in the classroom.* New York: Basic Books.
Sinclair, H., 1967. Conduites verbales et déficits opératoires. *Acta Neurologica Psychiatrica Belgica, 67,* 852–860.
Sinclair, H., 1973a. From preoperational to concrete thinking and parallel development of symbolization. In M. Schwebel and J. Raph (Eds.), *Piaget in the classroom.* New York: Basic Books.

Sinclair, H., 1973b. Some remarks on the Genevan point of view on learning with special reference to language learning. In R. A. Hinde and J. Stevenson-Hinde (Eds.), *Constraints on learning: Limitations and predispositions*. New York: Academic Press, 397–415.

Sinclair-de-Zwart, H., 1967. *Acquisition du langage et développement de la pensée*. Paris: Dunod.

Singer, R. N., and Brunk, J. W., 1967. Relation of perceptual-motor ability and intellectual ability in elementary school children. *Perceptual and Motor Skills, 24,* 967–70.

Stallings, J., 1976. Implementation and child effects of teaching practices in follow through classrooms. *Monographs of the Society for Research in Child Development,* Serial no. 163.

Stephens, B., 1972. *The development of reasoning, moral judgement, and moral conduct in retardates and normals: Phase II*. (Research grant no. 15-p-55121/3-02) Philadelphia, Penn.: Temple University.

Stephens, B., 1974. Symposium: Developmental gains in the reasoning, moral judgment, and moral conduct of retarded and nonretarded persons. *American Journal of Mental Deficiency, 79,* 113–115.

Stephens, B., 1977. Piagetian theory: Applications for the mentally retarded and the visually handicapped. In J. F. Magary, M. K. Poulsen, P. J. Levinson, P. A. Taylor (Eds.), *Piagetian theory and the helping professions*. Los Angeles, Calif.: University of Southern California.

Stephens, B., and McLaughlin, J. A., 1974. Two-year gains in reasoning by retarded and nonretarded persons. *American Journal of Mental Deficiency, 79,* 116–126.

Stephens, B., McLaughlin, J. A., Miller, C. K., and Glass, G., 1972. Factorial structure of selected psycho-educational measures and Piagetian reasoning assessment. *Developmental Psychology, 6,* 343–348.

Swize, L. M., 1972. The relationship between performance on Piagetian conservation tasks and intelligence and achievement in educable mentally retarded children. *Dissertation Abstracts International, 32,* 3806.

Tessier, F. A., 1970. The development of young cerebral palsied children according to Piaget's sensorimotor theory. *Dissertation Abstracts International, 30(11-A),* 4841.

Vitello, S., 1973. Facilitation of class inclusion among mentally retarded children. *American Journal of Mental Deficiency, 78,* 158–162.

Volpe, R., 1975. *Social experiences and the development of social cognition in disabled and nondisabled children*. Paper presented at the Fifth Special Invitational Interdisciplinary Seminar of Piagetian Theory and Its Implications for the Helping Professions. Los Angeles, Calif.

Voyat, G., 1970. Minimizing the problems of functional illiteracy. *Teachers College Record, 72,* 171–186.

Voyat, G., 1977. In tribute to Piaget: A look at his scientific impact in the United States. In R. W. Rieber and K. Salzinger, *The roots of American psychology: Historical influences and implications for the future*. New York: Annals of the New York Academy of Sciences (Vol. 291).

Voyat, G. *Psychosis: A cognitive and psychodynamic perspective*. Proceedings of the 8th Annual Interdisciplinary Conference on Piagetian Theory and the Helping Professions. Los Angeles: University of Southern California, in press.

Warner, B. J., and Williams, R., 1975. Piaget's theory and exceptional children: A bibliography, 1963–1973. *Perceptual and Motor Skills, 41,* 255–261.

Warner, B. J., and Williams, R., 1976. Bibliography: Supplement to Piaget's theory and exceptional children, 1963–1973. *Perceptual and Motor Skills, 43,* 212–214.

Webb, R. A., 1974. Concrete and formal operations in very bright 6- to 11-year-olds. *Human Development, 17,* 292–300.

Weisz, J. R., 1976. Studying cognitive development in retarded and nonretarded groups: The role of theory. *American Journal of Mental Deficiency, 81,* 235–239.

Wilton, K. M., and Boersma, F. J., 1974. Eye movements and conservation development in mildly retarded and nonretarded children. *American Journal of Mental Deficiency, 79,* 285–291.

Woodward, M., 1959. The behavior of idiots interpreted by Piaget's theory of sensorimotor development. *British Journal of Educational Psychology, 29,* 60–71.

Woodward, M., 1961. Concepts of number of the mentally subnormal studied by Piaget's method. *Journal of Child Psychology, 2,* 249–259.

Woodward, M., 1962. Concepts of space in the mentally subnormal studied by Piaget's method. *British Journal of Social and Clinical Psychology, 1,* 25–37.

Zeaman, D., and House, B. J., 1963. The role of attention in retardate discrimination learning. In N. R. Ellis (Ed.), *Handbook of mental deficiency.* New York: McGraw-Hill.

Zigler, E., 1967. Familial mental retardation: A continuing dilemma. *Science, 155,* 292–298.

Zigler, E., 1969. Developmental versus difference theories of mental retardation and the problem of motivation. *American Journal of Mental Deficiency, 73,* 536–556.

8

Piagetian Theory and Neo-Piagetian Analysis as Psychological Guides in Education

JUAN PASCUAL-LEONE, DOBA GOODMAN, PAUL AMMON, and IRENE SUBELMAN

1. Reflections on Piaget and Education

Chapters in this volume reflect the strong conviction that Piaget's work has important implications for education. We share that conviction and wish to explore it further by emphasizing problems and suggesting solutions. The need for further exploration is shown in the other chapters by the way they display, and even acknowledge, a fundamental dilemma found in the vast literature on Piaget and education. The dilemma is that psychologists or educators, who presumably started from the same Piagetian theory, often arrive at very different conclusions regarding practice, and sometimes these conclusions seem less in keeping with Piaget than with other theoretical approaches. There is no question that

JUAN PASCUAL-LEONE and DOBA GOODMAN • Department of Psychology, York University, Downsview, Ontario, Canada. PAUL AMMON and IRENE SUBELMAN, School of Education, University of California, Berkeley, California. Preparation of this chapter was facilitated by Grant S76–0694R1 of The Canada Council to the senior author.

some of these problems have resulted from incomplete or erroneous interpretations of Piagetian theory, as is often suggested in this volume by DeVries, Gallagher, or Reid. However, our own view is that even relatively sophisticated attempts to apply Piaget's theory to education will continue to be plagued by ambiguities and contradictions until some basic theoretical problems have been solved.

When we maintain that major obstacles to the productive use of Piagetian theory lie within the theory itself, we are referring to Piaget's *explicit psychological theory*, particularly the ways he has characterized the stages of development and the process of equilibration. The fundamental *genetic-epistemological theory* of Piaget already has enormous heuristic value for education—a value that other contributors to this volume have clearly emphasized (e.g., Easley, Gallagher, Lickona, or Reid). From a strict psychological viewpoint, however, genetic epistemology is an *empirically based* constructive rationalist *meta*theory, i.e., a set of guidelines along which different psychological theories of cognitive and personality development could be built. In this regard Piaget is to developmental psychology and to "active" education what Pavlov has been to Russian psychology and to physiological and learning theories everywhere, i.e., the scientist against whose monumental empirically based metatheory new useful insights and more explicit theories must be contrasted. Piaget's models of stages and equilibration might in fact be most appropriately viewed as a part of this metatheory—as (approximately) valid *descriptive structural* models of the psychological system's competence. We will claim that psychological theories, by contrast, must be *process-structural*; a causal account of the processes of equilibration and the manifestation of general stages must include an explicit representation of the step-by-step temporal *functioning* of the developing system.

Recent work from Geneva (e.g., Inhelder, Sinclair, and Bovet, 1974; Piaget, 1975) acknowledges the need for psychological theorizing and process modelling. Our attempt in this chapter can be best understood as another and largely complementary manifestation of the same concern. We hope to demonstrate that educators should and can ask for more, diversified and better, psychological Piagetian theorizing than is currently provided; they should ask for psychological theories that have the power to explain (and predict) the development of individuals and their performance in specific types of situations—whether learning situations or problem-solving situations, or social/personality or psycholinguistic or perceptual/cognitive situations. We believe that such explicit psychological theorizing can be built on foundations laid down by Piaget.

To illustrate the desirability and the possibility of stronger versions of Piagetian psychological theories, we will review some of the problems that have been brought to light in connection with Piaget's current theory (when interpreted psychologically and not just genetic-epistemologically). We will then summarize a neo-Piagetian theory that may "correct" these problems and briefly sketch the kinds of approaches to educational application suggested by this psychological theory.

1.1. Stages and Equilibration as a Basis for Instructional Planning

The relevance of developmental stages for the timing of instruction has been a focal theme in Piagetian educational research. If the child's intellect develops through a sequence of stages involving increasingly powerful ways of thinking; if developmental stages have the kind of breadth and generality that Piaget has suggested with his notion of *"structure d'ensemble"*; then, given a "relatively simple" diagnosis of the learner's current stage, along with an assessment of the cognitive demands entailed in learning various contents, one should have a sound basis for selecting the immediate objectives of instruction across the entire curriculum.

However, it is now widely known that one cannot make a single diagnosis of a child's Piagetian stage and then apply it effectively to theoretically related instructional contents. The failure of such a general approach is already indicated in Piaget's own work; tasks that presumably entail the same logical structure have often been observed to vary in developmental difficulty—they present "horizontal décalages." Piaget has attributed these variations among tasks to differences in task "resistance" to assimilation by the necessary operative structure (a "resistance" caused somewhat by the task's "content"); but this notion of resistance has not been adequately defined (e.g., Pascual-Leone, 1969, 1972, 1976c; Scardamalia, 1977). Without an adequate theoretical explanation of resistance, the actual specification of horizontal décalages is only possible *post-facto*. Thus, given the empirical abundance of horizontal décalages, considerable ambiguity exists as to just how useful Piaget's stage notion, as a psychological theory, might be to the practitioner, and in what ways.

In the face of this ambiguity, different writers on educational practice have suggested different ways to use the Piagetian stages while avoiding the complications that could arise from horizontal décalages. One approach has been the planning of curricula on the basis of indices of cognitive development that come from tasks that are highly similar in terms of their specific content and the behaviors they elicit, to those involved in actual instruction. This strategy is illustrated in the chapter by Lovell and Shayer. They describe a project involving large numbers of British students, aged 9 to 14. Normative data for a battery of Piagetian tasks was collected; the "conceptual demand" of content items in the British Nuffield science courses was carefully analyzed, either by means of direct analogies between the science lesson material and the science-type tasks employed by Inhelder and Piaget (1958) in their research on formal operations, or by application of a set of descriptive behavioral criteria abstracted from the work of Inhelder and Piaget. The goal of the project was to identify areas in which the existing curriculum made excessive demands on its intended population of students. On the face of it, their approach appears to minimize the problem of décalages between predictor and criterion tasks—the cognitive assessment tasks are similar in many respects to the lesson material in the science courses, and both cognitive level and conceptual demand are characterized in terms of specific behaviors associated with Piaget's descriptive substages, such as Stage IIB, "late concrete operations, " or Stage IIIA, "early formal operations. "However, the ultimate test of this approach lies in its ability to predict the performance of individual pupils on specific parts of the curriculum. Lovell and Shayer, recognizing the importance of this test, present some relevant data. Items testing achievement in science were classified by their levels of conceptual demand (IIB, IIIA, or IIIB) and performance on them was examined as a function of the pupils' Piagetian levels (IIB or IIIA). Pupils diagnosed as Stage IIIA did pass more items overall than those diagnosed as IIB, and both groups passed fewer items as the assessed level of demand increased. But in neither group did children pass even *half* of the items that were judged to be appropriate for their own level of development. It is unlikely that this last result was due entirely to inadequate opportunities for specific learning, because the Stage IIIA pupils were able to pass 77% of the IIB items—over twice as many as the IIB pupils themselves. It appears, rather, that in many instances, the theoretical analysis of the test material underestimated its cognitive demand relative to pupil capabilities, as assessed by the predictor tasks. Of course, once this state of affairs has been detected, appropriate adjustments can be made in the curriculum; but the more the planning of instruction depends on such *post hoc* adjustments, the more it resembles the "empirical" approach that Lovell and Shayer criticize in traditional science education.

Murray suggests another method for establishing a fit between instruction and pupil development in his chapter on Piagetian implications for instruction in reading. After noting a number of logical correspondences between aspects of reading and the kinds of tasks Piaget has characterized in terms of concrete operations, along with some empirical correlations between reading achievement and performance on Piagetian tasks, Murray concludes that operativity at the concrete level is "sufficient" for initial reading acquisition. He seems to mean that beginning reading instruction will at least be more likely to succeed with children who have concrete operations (unless the reading tasks are modified to make them more accessible to preoperational children, or unless the child has acquired "some competence system other than the one Piaget has identified"—a loophole or ill-defined possibility that he invokes to account for the common phenomenon of preoperational readers). One implication of Murray's analysis is "to delay reading until the advent of concrete operational thought"—an approach that would be analogous in principle to the one illustrated by Lovell and Shayer, and would probably pose the same problems in practice. In addition, Murray suggests that "it would (also) be reasonable to train children on the cognitive and perceptual operations that are related to reading." Several investigators have reported success in training children to perform specific "operational" tasks. From a Piagetian perspective, we must assume that successful training has either (a) promoted consolidation of, or assimilation to, an operative structure that was already present in some form, or (b) provided a special figurative structure for performing more easily the training task. In either case, it is conceivable that the newly acquired capability could in fact be used to advantage in a criterion learning task such as reading. But this outcome is far from certain, for it would depend on the extent to which the criterion task (i.e. reading) contained those conditions necessary for the new capability to be realized in performance. Piagetian theory does not provide a clear way of specifying those conditions, and thus we are often left without a basis for predicting when positive transfer of training will occur and when it will not (i.e., when a horizontal décalage will occur).

The training of operations that may transfer to reading seems especially problematic if the training is to be accomplished through the sorts of tasks that have typically been used in experimental training studies. Murray suggests, for example, that children could be trained on transitivity if they "manipulated little rods or something." Enhanced reading achievement would appear more likely (though not a foregone conclusion) if the training of relevant operations were conducted in the context of reading itself. But then one would have to ask what, if anything, is uniquely "Piagetian" about the approach, as the same sort of procedure would be implied, for instance, by the "learning hierarchies" of Gagné (1968). Perhaps that is why Murray concludes that the educational implications of Piaget's theory are not noticeably different from those of an *S–R* operant approach. It may also explain, in part, why DeVries contends that past attempts to "apply" Piaget have often turned out to be more empiricist than constructivist in their epistemological character—a result that DeVries attributes more to misguided interpretations of Piaget than to limitations of his theory *per se.*

DeVries proposes another solution to the problem of fitting instruction to student developmental level. She suggests that misapplications of Piaget's theory have generally resulted from an overemphasis on the structural aspects of the theory, rather than its constructive aspects as represented by the process of equilibration. That is, development is reduced to a sequence of stages and the stages are reduced to logical structures, which are further reduced to particular Piagetian tasks. It follows from this series of reductions that training on these same tasks will suffice to promote intellectual development in some general way. It is clear to DeVries—and to us—that this derivation does *not* follow from the basic tenets of Piaget's genetic epistemology. In our view, however, Piaget's explicit theory of structural stages, when psychologically interpreted does invite exactly the kind of reductionism described above, and the rest of the psychological theory is not sufficiently explicit to provide a clear alternative to the reductionist interpretation.

This last point can be supported by a critique of the principal Piagetian "implication" emphasized by DeVries. Instead of training on prescribed operational tasks, DeVries argues that the educational activities "with the highest priority are those which engage the child's active interest in such a way that intelligence is more exercised." The exercising of intelligence can be facilitated by "maximizing the child's opportunities to create and coordinate many relationships of which he is presently capable." In other words, it is a kind of general *operative* enrichment approach. However, in order to implement this approach effectively, one must first be able to determine exactly what the child's present capabilities are and which ones could be more productively developed. We have already seen that stage assessment does not provide a satisfactory basis for predicting what a given child (as opposed to the idealized age-group child—the epistemic subject) can and cannot do—a point with which DeVries apparently agrees, judging from her comments about the overemphasis on Piagetian structures. DeVries recommends an alternative approach: "When children are interested in an activity, one must observe and try to figure out what is the focus of their interest and what possibilities the activity offers for the exercise of reasoning." In other words, one might try to deal with the problem of determining what the child *can* do by observing what the child *does* do, spontaneously, among cognitive-developmental activities or tasks, and then create additional opportunities for the child to do more of the same.

While the idea of capitalizing on the child's spontaneous activity certainly has merit, it also poses some problems. For one thing, there is again the problem of psychological equivalence across activities or tasks: it would be useful to know, in advance, what constitutes *another* opportunity to exercise *the same* structural sort of reasoning already observed in spontaneous behavior. Secondly, it seems unlikely that children's spontaneous activity will always reflect their thinking at its best. As an illustration, consider the comments of Lovell and Shayer on "incorrect assumptions" in problem solving; many task situations—the conservations are a good example—create a misleading context that evokes irrelevant or inappropriate performance, regardless of the child's true competence. This is particularly likely to be the case for those children who are more in need of professional educational help—such as children with certain cognitive styles (e.g., field-dependent, impulsive, cognitively low-adaptive), children with emotional disturbances, or children with deficient repertoire of school-oriented executive/motivational structures. Consequently, a teacher who is guided primarily by the pupil's demonstrated interests and abilities might be misled into promoting activities that are not at the growing edge of the child's developing intelligence, and which, therefore, do not exercise it effectively. Thus, there is still a need for some way to determine the child's current maximum capability or at least suitable remedial activities.

Even if that problem were solved, there would then be a further question as to whether all activities reflecting the child's thinking at its best were equally productive in terms of further growth. If one assumes that growth is toward a new general structure of the sort described by Piaget, then the answer to this question may appear to be yes; any content could do, as long as it was consistent with the developing structure. But since general structures are unsatisfactory models as representations of a child's present developmental status (because of the horizontal décalages and the local formation of specific concrete-operational structures) the question should be raised about whether the educational goals must not, after all, be oriented toward developing properly chosen specific cognitive skills. General structures will, if Piaget is right, develop as a by-product of this specific structural learning. Even those educators who would prefer not to focus their early curriculum on specific cognitive skills development may find it necessary to decide which are (for each age level or child) the important targets for instruction.

DeVries's attempt to shift the focus away from Piaget's structural stages and toward equilibration, i.e., toward Piaget's constructivist view of intellectual development, exemplifies the growing emphasis in educational research on the process of equilibration. The basic educational implication of Piaget's theory of equilibration is taken to be, not surprisingly, that instruction should attempt to promote or simulate the process of equilibration. The question of crucial importance, then, is how to realize this goal in actual practice.

At the core of the equilibration process, as Piaget describes it, is the child's own, self-regulatory activity. Consequently, it is often suggested that the instructional activities of pupils should be *self-initiated*. The literature on Piaget and education contains several variations on this same theme—including references to "discovery" learning (e.g., Murray) or learning through exploration (e.g., Reid). The essential idea throughout is that those instructional activities that grow out of the pupil's natural curiosity and interests will lead to greater developmental progress than those that are imposed on the pupil at the behest of a teacher. We noted with respect to DeVries's approach of using self-initiated activity as a clue to the pupil's present level of development, that such activity is not necessarily a reliable indicator of developmental stage. By the same token, it does not appear to be a sufficient basis for designing an educational program in keeping with Piaget's notion of equilibration. Piaget says as much himself when he remarks that good instruction is not a matter of letting pupils do whatever they want but of seeing to it that they want to do whatever they do (1970).

Another consideration that has often been mentioned in the past is the overt manipulation of objects and events; self-regulatory activity has sometimes been defined, at least tacitly, as overt behavior—especially activity on the physical world. Proponents of an emphasis on physical activity compare it favorably to approaches that rely heavily on verbal instruction by the teacher and/or the training of language skills in pupils (see Chapters 3 and 4). We agree that the latter approaches could be quite inconsistent with Piagetian theory (and may also be ineffectual), in particular if language is used without a figurative (concrete or abstract) context of reference about which it can emphasize aspects and assign meaning and by means of which the language itself is disambiguated. Without some sort of a figurative context the child's construction of the *meanings* that underlie the language of instruction remains unchecked. But the same may be said as well of an emphasis on physical activity. Much physical activity is self-regulatory in character, but not all self-regulation entails physical activity. Indeed, those regulations essential for cognitive growth during the school years—the reflexive abstractions discussed by Gallagher and others—are mental activities. Physical activities may be useful in bringing such mental activities about, but they do not automatically guarantee that productive mental activity will occur, and, in fact, may not even be necessary.

A third type of activity frequently recommended by Piagetians is *social interaction*, particularly with peers (see Chapters 3 and 6). The value of social interaction is suggested to be that it confronts the child with points of view different (but not too different) from his own, producing both "disequilibrium" and guidance toward a more adequate form of equilibrium. The problem, here too, remains that it is not possible, with the Genevan models of equilibration, to specify with precision the conditions under which, and the mechanisms by which, peer interaction will lead to general structural change.

To sum up: The Piagetian structuralist models of stages and equilibration have proven to be elusive as practical guides for instructional planning. We suggested earlier, and will amplify this claim below, that the problems of application stem from the lack of explicit representation of the functional processes by which the stage competences are generated, and manifested, in performance. In this sense, the basic theoretical problem cannot be escaped through the sort of practical strategies we have discussed here.

One further important comment should be made in this review of problems: The work thus far reviewed refers largely to purely cognitive performances in anxiety-free situations (mainly the work summarized in the chapters by DeVries, Lovell and Shayer, Murray, and some aspects of the chapters by Easley, Gallagher, and Reid). In this area Geneva's unique genetic-epistemological tradition and its descriptive-structural psychological theorizing has immense heuristic value. We can best propose new psychological theories by using critically, correcting and pursuing further, possibilities that Piaget and Inhelder have initiated. However, a different situation exists in the areas of affective and personality development, so excellently covered in the chapters by Lickona and Reid. These areas exhibit well the heuristic power of Piaget's genetic epistemology; but they also show the fact that Piaget has not contributed much toward a psychological theory of affective/personality development, beyond some valuable presuppositions hidden in the general notions of scheme, structure, and constructive abstraction.

As Lickona and Reid's reviews intimate, affective and emotional factors and personality structures (ego structures, "will power," values, emotional-defense structures, etc.) are very important and often interact with purely cognitive factors in social/moral development and excep-

tional development. A Piagetian psychological theory capable of representing these affective and personality structures, and their interactions
with cognition, is not available from Geneva at the present time, not
even in rough sketch. Until such a psychological theory becomes available, a Piagetian approach to social/moral development and to exceptional development can only be genetic-epistemological. In fact, these
affective and personality factors are also found in the cognitive domain,
as good Piagetian users of the critical-exploration method know. In this
regard as well, educators should be made aware that the Piagetian
psychological theory is incomplete.

2. The Metasubject inside Piaget's "Epistemic Subject"

Educational research has clearly exposed the problems within the
psychological models of Geneva: the theory of structuralist stages (and
its corresponding probabilistic equilibration model) has no clear explanation of the process of change from one stage to the next and no clear way
of predicting the appearance of horizontal décalages; the new dialectical
equilibration theory (e.g., see Chapters 3, 5, and 1), although describing
well the stage transitions in performance, does not causally account for
these performatory transitions.

In this section, we will suggest a new approach to the psychological
modelling of Piaget's genetic-epistemological theory, which may in the
long run be more productive, in terms of application, than the Genevan
models. This approach—formalized in Pascual-Leone's Theory of Constructive Operators (TCO)—seeks to represent explicitly the underlying
mechanism of dialectical equilibration and structural growth. The TCO
integrates three sorts of organismic constructs (*schemes, basic factors, and
basic principles*) within a process model of the psychological organism
(which is called *metasubject* to emphasize that it is a highly active hidden
organization, causally responsible for the subject's performances). Our
plan in this section is to describe very briefly the three sorts of organismic constructs, focussing in particular on the *schemes*.* The TCO is an
abstract and technical theory that does not lend itself easily to brief
summarization; our summary is intended only to highlight aspects in
which this neoPiagetian theory differs from Piaget's formulations and
which have direct relevance for educational practice, as we shall discuss
in the third section.

---

*For a more comprehensive formal presentation of the theory, see the Pascual-Leone
references in the bibliography and Pascual-Leone and Goodman (1976).

2.1. Schemes and Their Affective/Personal/Cognitive Classification

Schemes are the *subjective operators* of the metasubject, because they determine (and operate upon) both the content of the subject's experience and his performance. A scheme is "an organized set of reactions that can be transferred from one situation to another by the assimilation of the second to the first" (Piaget and Morf, 1958, p. 86). Structurally, all schemes have the same form: if a set of *conditions* is minimally satisfied by the input and/or the internal state, the scheme will tend to assimilate, i.e., *to apply* (and will do so unless some other dominant scheme prevents its application); when a scheme applies, the set of *effects* (physiological reactions, patterns, meaning, action possibilities, mental blueprints, expectancies, etc.) which it carries are used by the metasubject to further or to modify its ongoing activities.

We distinguish two basic sorts of schemes, purely affective and cognitive. *Affective* (i.e., purely affective) schemes are subjective operators which are activated by the subject's mental state (cognitive and/or affective) and which when they apply generate two kinds of effects, *physiological* reactions (e.g., blushing with embarrassment, paling with fear, perspiring with anxiety, etc.) and *conative* or *motivational* effects (the conative effect of fear is an incrementing of the activation weight of cognitive schemes involved, e.g., in escaping; the conative effect of embarrassment is an incrementing of the activation weight of cognitive schemes involved, e.g., in a personal withdrawal). The conative effects of affective schemes serve to generate *affective goals* that boost (A boosting) the activation of corresponding schemes. Cognitive schemes can be of two basic sorts, figurative and operative, which we will discuss below. Schemes develop by content differentiation (C learning, see below) and by coordination among themselves (L learning, see below). The pool of habitual (i.e., enduring, habit-like) cognitive schemes of the subject is described as constituted by the C and the L repertoire. The pool of affective schemes is the A repertoire.

Habitual structures coordinating both cognitive and affective schemes are called *personal schemes* or *personal structures* (values, cognitive styles, personality, belief structures, etc.). Subjects develop (and are also born with) special sorts of cognitive schemes closely connected with personal schemes. These are the control executives or controls that function as organismic biasing mechanisms (cf. Pribram, 1971), *biases* for short, in charge of monitoring the various organismic resources (i.e., basic factors and basic principles) in accordance with the current performance requirements. The pool of both personal structures (including

beliefs) and biases, of the subject are described in our theory as constitut-
ing the B repertoire.

We now will present a fairly detailed summary of the TCO. Readers
who are not interested in such a summary but who want to see the
educational applications can on first reading proceed directly to page 271.

All schemes follow the same functional general rules. We will summarize them in five points with reference to cognitive schemes.

(SC 1). Functionally, a scheme is an indivisible *unit*. This implies
that whenever two objects or two aspects of the environment are somewhat different or play different functions (even if they look alike), they
will have to be represented by the metasubject *separately*, in two different
schemes, if the organism is to perceive, treat, or use them differently.

(SC 2). A scheme is a sort of recursive function—the conditions
and/or effects of any scheme could in turn be constituted by schemes.

(SC 3). From a functional viewpoint there are two types of schemes,
figurative and *operative* (operative schemes can in turn be classified as
either *subordinate operative* or *executive* schemes; we discuss here operative schemes in general, while executive schemes are discussed in the
next section). *Figurative schemes* are *predicates* (simple or complex
compound-predicates) which, by applying separately or conjointly with
others, generate a *mental state* description or phenomenal
representation—some figurative configuration, meaning, or expectancy.
Operative schemes are either *transformations* or *operative expectancies* (i.e.,
means-end-readinesses of type $s_1 r_1 \rightarrow s_2$ in Tolman's technical sense,
Tolman, 1959). Subjective transformations effectively change (in the
sense of *actually* subtracting or adding properties or relations) the mental
(and/or physical) state on which they apply. An operative expectancy
reflects the consequences of a transformation, without actually effecting
a transformation. Referring to current Piagetian terms, a "sensorimotor
transformation" is, of course, a transformation—the blueprint for an
action; a "mental transformation" is either an interiorized transformation (i.e., the silent activation and application of an action blueprint) or
an operative expectancy.

The concepts may become clearer with the following example.
When a 9-month-old baby reaches for a rattle in order to shake it because he likes its sound, his behavior results, cognitively speaking and
disregarding affective factors, from a performatory synthesis: the coordination and application of several operative expectancies, predicates,
and transformations.

Let us list the schemes involved (in this list the content of the pa-
rentheses within quotation marks which follow each scheme serve, together with the arbitrary numbering, for their identification). The sym-

bols are a pictographic shorthand for compactly representing schemes. Readers may observe that ψ stands for transformations, ϕ for predicates, $\dot\psi$ for operative expectancies and $\dot\phi$, used later in this chapter, for figurative expectancies. In the case of expectancies the three subscripted numbers, e.g., 2, 1, and 3 in $\dot\psi_{213}$, designate the practical meaning "If transformation ψ_2 applies on mental state ϕ_1, then mental state ϕ_3 will be brought about":

ϕ_1 : "(1: visual rattle)"

$\dot\psi_{213}$: "(2: reaching and grasping; 1: visual rattle; 3: touched-and-handheld rattle)"

ψ_2 : "(2: reaching and grasping)"

ϕ_3 : "(3: touched-and-handheld rattle)"

$\dot\psi_{435}$: "(4: shaking; 3: touched-and-handheld rattle; 5: sound-producing rattle)"

ψ_4 : "(4: shaking)"

ϕ_5 : "(5: sound-producing rattle)"

$\dot\psi_{678}$: "(6: apply 7 in order to apply 8; 7: $\dot\psi_{213}$; 8: $\dot\psi_{435}$)"

Using this notation the temporally structured performatory synthesis exhibited by the 9-month baby could be as follows (where a dot "$\cdot$" indicates the *simultaneous* activation and/or application of the interconnected schemes, an arrow "$\rightarrow$" indicates the *successive* activation with brackets separating the processing steps):

$$\phi_1 \rightarrow (\phi_1 \cdot \dot\psi_{435}) \rightarrow (\phi_1 \cdot \dot\psi_{435} \cdot \dot\psi_{678} \cdot \dot\psi_{213} \cdot \psi_2) \rightarrow (\phi_3 \cdot \dot\psi_{435} \cdot \psi_4) \rightarrow (\phi_5 \dots)$$

This example of a Secondary Circular Reaction illustrates, in the context of a very simple performance, the notions of simple figurative schemes (i.e., *ordinary predicates* ϕ_j), simple operative schemes (i.e., *transformations* ψ_i) and more-or-less complex operative schemes (i.e., operative expectancies $\dot\psi_{ijk}$, which for reasons stated below, we prefer to call *operative fluents*). In addition, this example shows that performatory syntheses often result from the activation of operative schemes by *applied figurative* schemes (which constitute the subject's *mental state*) and the application of the operative schemes to the latter which in turn brings about the activation and application of new figurative schemes (which constitute a new mental state).

This example is simplified and incomplete in several regards. One oversimplification occurs with regard to the figurative schemes. A child in Piaget's fourth (or third) sensorimotor stage does not just have simple predicates such as ϕ_1: "(1: visual rattle)" or ϕ_3: "(3: touched-and-handheld-rattle)" or ϕ_5: "(5: sound-producing rattle)" but already has a complex figurative scheme, which integrates such predicates and many other aspects of the *ob*ject. Such an *ob* structure represents (reflects the constraints of) the distal object in terms of mental states (i.e., applied figurative schemes) which the distal object has satisfied in the past when the subject's operative schemes were applied onto it (Piaget's generalizing assimilation and constructive abstraction). An *ob* is thus (Pascual-Leone, 1969; 1976a; Pascual-Leone and Smith, 1969) a compound predicative structure that stands for the whole manifold of discriminative, manipulative, and functional aspects or facets of the distal object.

In the case of the sensorimotor child of our example, the ob structure in question could be symbolized as OB "(rattle: 1, 3, 5, ... j ... k)", where 1, 3, and 5 stand for *re*presented versions of the figurative schemes ϕ_1, ϕ_3, and ϕ_5 mentioned above, and where .. j..k are many other different figurative schemes representing other facets of the ob in question.

Usually, interconnecting the various facets of an ob are also the descriptions of operative expectancies that reflect the possible movements from one facet to another, including, as Tolman (1959) pointed out, the operative option of attentive waiting. The baby's ob for the rattle contains not only predicates ϕ_1, ϕ_3, ϕ_5, ... ϕ_j ... ϕ_k but also generic transformation-representing predicates such as ψ "(scan in order to visually see)," $\dot{\psi}$ "(move fingers in order to feel/touch)," etc. These operative aspects we have not symbolized above. As this example illustrates, all obs are in fact *figurative expectancies,* embodied in habitual structures of the sort illustrated above for simple *operative* expectancies. The difference is that in figurative expectancies the semantic-pragmatically important constituents are figurative (Tolman and learning theoreticians often called these expectancies $s_1 - s_2$ associations). Note that figurative expectancy structures, as much as operative expectancies, are a product of the subject's operative functioning—constancies and conservational invariants of all sorts (those are figurative expectancies) could only emerge, Piaget and others have often emphasized, as the subject experiences through his Action the constraints of his environment or of his own body.

Functional structures embodying operative expectancies or figurative expectancies result from the constructive-abstraction processes (which we call below logical/structural learning or *L* learning) described by Piaget (e.g., 1975). Since constructive-abstraction processes are recursive—can apply on their own results—very complex functional structures can result. Figurative examples of these structures are the concrete-operational generic or specific obs of children standing for their parents and friends, for tools (furniture, TV, toys, etc.), for playgrounds, schools, churches, etc. When activated, these obs are, as Tolman first emphasized, "cognitive maps"* of specific or generic entities of the child's environment (people, objects, places, etc.) that require particular operative handling and present a variety of aspects or *facets* lawfully interrelated by means of operative acts (operants!). Examples of complex operative expectancy structures are the subject's motor and logical/structural modular representations of complex strategies for doing "jobs"—i.e., enduring mental blueprints of *procedures* which, for short, we call *pros* (Pascual-Leone, 1976a). Examples of pros are numerous: from the preoperational child's routines related to "school readiness," "good manners," and "getting dressed," to the many concrete-operational "basic skills" (counting, classifying, etc.), to the concrete or formal-operational "scripts" (cf. Schank and Abelson, 1977) of generic procedures for specific types of situations ["eating in the OB '(restaurant)'," "visiting with the OB '(friends)'," etc.] as well as the "proper conduct" and "how to . . ." tacit procedures for hundreds of social, interpersonal, or cognitive situations.

(SC 4). Expectancy-carrying structures, whether figurative or operative, are *temporally organized;* they are transformation-representing predicates, which, as illustrated above, embody temporal relations of inter-activation or coactivation, i.e., habitual coordinations, between or among schemes. To emphasize that the *flow* of time-ordered events and possibly time itself are metasubjectively created by (operative and figurative) expectancy-carrying structures, Pascual-Leone has proposed to call this type of scheme a *fluent*—a term coined by the computer scientist McCarthy for a concept not unlike this one (cf. Pascual-Leone, 1972, 1973, 1976a). The need for a name to denote expectancy-carrying schemes exists; not only because Piaget does not have a name for this important type of scheme, but because Tolman's own names (means-end-readinesses or "sign-gestalten") are cumbersome and the terms often used in the current literature, i.e., expectancies or beliefs (e.g., Hintzman, 1978) are misleading. They are misleading for a reason which Tolman (1959) emphasized: psychologically speaking expectancies do not exist unless the corresponding operative or figurative fluents are activated and apply to determine a suitable mental state. Properly speaking expectancies are not habitual schemes but dynamic mental states. Notice the importance of this distinction for education: properly speaking expectancies cannot be taught but the corresponding fluents can. Whether and when, once the fluents have been learned, the expectancies appear in the subject as mental states depends on equilibration processes; and these processes involve the learned fluents as well as any

---

*Cognitive maps are spatio-temporal and semantic-pragmatic modular "frames"—detailed frame-of-reference representations.

other, perhaps incompatible, schemes activated in the metasubject by the situation. In other words, acquired fluents (and operational structures are fluents, see below) may not necessarily be manifested in all of the subject's performances. As Tolman already emphasized in 1932, much learning may remain latent until appropriate circumstances allow it to appear in performance.

In addition, beliefs are not, contrary to what Tolman and other psychologists think (e.g., Tolman, 1932, 1959; Hintzman, 1978), ordinary expectancies; they are rather conscious, habitual expectancies of expectancies (cf. Pascual-Leone, 1976a; Rozeboom, 1970). The distinction is important to educators because mental states that we can call beliefs are constructively more complex than the expectancy they contain (i.e., if the expectancy results from the application of one or more fluents, the corresponding belief results from the application of a constructively abstracted fluent of fluents—a developmentally more advanced and complex habitual structure). For instance, the expectancy "(the teacher does not like me)" could be an *ephemeral* mental state reached by a child via an equilibration process, as a result of the clash between the teacher's style (or conduct) and the child's own personally based expectations. It may thus not require from the teacher explicit attention. However, the belief "(I believe that the teacher does not like me)" is likely to be a mental state reflecting a *habitual* structure, and may thus necessitate that teacher and child "talk it over." It may be useful to point out that this distinction between ordinary expectancies and beliefs is likely to be important in moral development; the role of consciousness/ awareness-raising discussions on moral development, which Lickona mentions, may be useful in changing or structuring moral beliefs.

The explicit concept of fluent is necessary to Piagetians (and in particular to Piagetian educators) because, as the analyses of Piaget and Inhelder clearly show, operational structures are but particularly complex and reversible fluents of fluents, sometimes related to belief structures in that they have a conscious representation. Yet, not all fluents are operational; the earliest acquired fluents are the Secondary-Circular-Reaction schemes clearly exhibited by infants during the fourth Piagetian sensorimotor stage.

(SC 5). Possibly both operative and figurative fluents (both of which emerge from sensorimotor activity) are the psychogenetic roots of operational structures. This is implicit not only in the (metasubjective) analysis of mental processing suggested above, but also in Geneva's insistence on the importance of the symbolic function for operational thinking and its definition of operations as reversible, interiorized transformations incorporated into a structured whole.

Still, as Piaget and Inhelder would insist, operative fluents are the leading structures in operational thinking. This is shown, quite clearly, when the problem of purpose in temporally structured directed thinking is examined. This problem, which after Koffka (1935) has come to be known as the problem of the executive (e.g., Anderson, 1975; Miller, Galanter, and Pribram, 1960; Neisser, 1967), has been brought to new light by computer simulation.

2.2. Executive Schemes

Executive schemes constitute the "plans" and the "control structures" of the psychological organism. As Koffka already saw (and modern neuropsychology has corroborated, using different terminology, e.g., Pribram, 1971; Luria, 1973), executive schemes mediate between the subject's motives (i.e., his affect-defined goals) and his other cognitive schemes that are needed for pursuing the affective goal.

Executive schemes are a special sort of operative fluents that usually (i.e., in plans) stipulate types of procedural segments, strategic moves, or generic operative modules. These modules monitor, in every mental processing step, the coordination of relevant figurative and operative schemes (those are the *step* plan-executives); they also may organize the sequence of steps that the subject's directed thinking or behavior follows (those are the *temporal* plan-executives). Executives are, directly or indirectly, responsible for the creativity or productivity (i.e., Piaget's *operativity level*) of the subject's performance, i.e., his ability to produce truly novel solutions to problems or tasks never encountered before. These *performatory syntheses*, as we called them above, are the mark of the subject's *operativity* in Geneva's sense of the word.

Note in passing that, as Geneva's recent emphasis on dialectical equilibration tacitly shows (Inhelder, Sinclair, and Bovet, 1974; Piaget, 1975; and in this volume see Chapters 3, 5, and 1), the subject's *operativity level* and the level of his *acquired operational/logical structures* are not the same. In developmentally normal subjects, the level of operativity is always more advanced than the level of the operational/logical structures currently available in the subject's repertoire. (This neglected but educationally important idea, the consistent ordering of *operativity level* over *logical-structural level*, is implied by Geneva's division of Stages in two phases, attainment and consolidation.) The operativity level of subjects, i.e., the complexity of performatory syntheses they can generate (beyond and above the power of their habitual operational/logical schemes) results not only from the repertoire of executive schemes they possess, but from the ability of the organism to mobilize the equilibration mechanisms (i.e., the organismic resources, basic factors, and principles). These equilibration mechanisms help the executive schemes to synthesize a truly novel, temporally structured performance out of the bits and pieces (executive modules, figurative, or operative schemes) that are provided by the subject's repertoire.

An illustration of the point just made is given by the example offered above of a Secondary Circular Reaction. In our earlier analysis of this example, however, we left implicit the affective goal, "to hear the rattle's sound." (This affective goal—call it αg—will be created by virtue of the baby's OB "rattle" which contains the expectancy of sound.) We did, however, explicitly represent an executive plan; the operative expectancy we labeled ψ_{678} stipulates a plan of action—"to obtain sound, first reach-and-grasp, then shake."

Note also that, prior to the psychogenetic acquisition of this executive scheme, the baby must have attempted to "shake the rattle in order to obtain its sound" in situations when the rattle is not hand-held but is visible (i.e., when "visual rattle" applies). This is Piaget's generalizing assimilation. The baby's repeated failure to produce the rattle's sound under these circumstances and his lack of a suitable executive scheme such as ψ_{678} must necessarily have produced (Piaget's accommodation) two habitual negative expectancies to the effect that (1) the rattle's sound *is not* obtained and (2) it *cannot* be obtained. These negative expectancies will be embodied in what Piaget (1959, pg. 43) has called a *negative scheme*, i.e., a scheme which forewarns of failure to obtain satisfaction for the affective goal under these circumstances (i.e., when the rattle is seen). Even when the (now older) baby has available an executive plan of action ψ_{678}, the "visual rattle" will activate this negative scheme (the "rushing-to-apply" assimilatory disposition of schemes!) and its application will recreate the negative expectancy that the sound-producing rattle *cannot* be obtained in this situation. Since this negative expectancy negates (cancels, contradicts) the affective goal αg, it will prevent ψ_{678} from being activated by αg. (Notice that this paralyzing effect of negative expectancies, clearly implied by Tolman's and Piaget's theories, has been studied and made popular recently by Seligman (1975) and Maier and Seligman (1976) under the name of *learned helplessness*. When a subject such as the baby develops the negative expectancy that some affective goal cannot be attained in a given situation, the actual attainment of the goal when it becomes possible is made much harder. The educational relevance of this negative-expectancy mechanism is considerable.)

Thus, the executive scheme ψ_{678} will not be boosted by αg because of the interference from a previously constructed negative scheme. Under these conditions, an executive scheme that is not directly cued by the situation can only acquire the assimilatory strength needed for monitoring performance from the mental arousal (i.e., mental effort or M energy—Piaget's mental centration) which it mobilizes in connection with the "frustrated" affective goal αg. This M energy, a situation-free organismic factor jointly monitored by the current "frustrated" *affective* goal αg and its dominant *executive* scheme, can "shift the balance of power," so that the executive scheme which it boosts together with other schemes relevant for the implementation of the executive plan come to control performance.

To clarify further the notion of executive schemes and their relation to the Piagetian operational/logical structures, we will now present five remarks on Executive schemes (whether sensorimotor or formal operational).

(*EX 1*). There are two sorts of executive schemes, *plans* and *controls*. Plan-executive schemes were illustrated above: they are directly involved in monitoring the metasubject's dealings with his environment by way of performances. Control-executive schemes, in contrast, monitor not the dealings with the environment, but rather the use and regulation of organismic resources. For example, *arousal* executives will mobilize M energy (they are M controls); *memory retrieval* executives will create mentally produced activation of relevant habitual schemes—L or C controls; *affective control* executives (A controls) will regulate affective reactions, such as the psychoanalysts' "defense mechanisms," etc.

These controls (cf. Gardner, Jackson and Messick, 1960; Witkin and Goodenough, 1977a,b), which are at the root of the so-called cognitive styles, are often but special-purpose plan-executive modules which have been developed in special circumstances and are normally operating silently to regulate the use and strength of the organismic resources M, L, C, A, I, F, etc. They will be discussed again below when we describe these basic organismic factors.

(*EX 2*). Executive schemes have five main functional characteristics: (1) They are first activated by the currently dominant affective goal (αg) as potential plans for its satisfaction. (2) The dominant *executive (one or more compatible executive schemes*) embodies a module(s) or segment(s) of a plan, more or less long or detailed. For as long as this executive is dominant the direction of performance results from its plan. In this sense, *any instructions* received by a subject (or self-administered) are metasubjectively represented by a dominant executive. Instructions, as understood by the subject, are carried by the executive schemes. (3) A part of the dominant executive, call it the arousal executive (an M control) mobilizes M energy (mental arousal). M energy is mobilized whenever there are figurative and/or operative schemes relevant for the executive's implementation (and thus the satisfaction of the dominant αg) that have a low assimilatory strength. This low strength occurs because of lack of situational cues (weak relevant C factor), lack of sufficient logical/structural learning (weak relevant L factor), or presence of strongly activated misleading incompatible schemes (error factors—misleading L or C factors). (4) Another part of the dominant executive, the *task plan executive*, allocates the mobilized M energy (M power) to the various goal-relevant figurative and/or operative schemes related to the executive in question. As we emphasize below, the subject's M power is limited; if the number of relevant schemes with low assimilatory strength is excessive relative to the subject's M power, the executive implementation, and thus the executive, will fail. A new choice of executives will then occur. (5) Dominant executives, in addition to mobilizing and allocating M energy to their relevant schemes, can *interrupt* (this is an "interrupt" control)—they can monitor the inhibition of activated schemes that are irrelevant to them. This "interrupt" function of executives ensures that schemes mobilized by M under the monitoring of a dominant executive come to dominate irrelevant schemes and thus determine performance. Important educational and individual-difference issues may be related to this interrupt function. Some sorts of impulsivity, distractibility or forgetfulness may well be related to underfunction of this interrupt. In the same vein we remark that Witkin's field-dependent subjects seem, on the basis of their cognitive performance, to exhibit a weak "interrupt" function (Pascual-Leone, 1969, 1974; Witkin and Goodenough, 1977a,b).

(*EX 3*). Unlike Piaget's operational/logical structures, which can only be found after the preschool years, executive schemes are found from the fourth sensorimotor Piagetian stage on. Yet, *executives* (each a dominant cluster of compatible executive schemes, one or several) are very different in content and qualitative structure, depending on whether they belong to *sensorimotor* subjects (and tasks) or to *mental-processing* subjects (and tasks). This difference is clearly implied by Piaget's stage theory. A sensorimotor task is, generally speaking, one which does not necessitate imparted or self-administered verbal or symbolic instructions; a mental-processing task is one which needs them.

The intuitively most obvious distinction between sensorimotor executives and mental-processing executives is the greater informational complexity (greater number of schemes involved) in the latter. The educationally-crucial characteristic distinguishing these two types of tasks is, however, to be found elsewhere: in connection with the affective goal αg motivating the task. In sensorimotor tasks (whether the ones of babies or of adults) the affective goal αg is *motivationally immediate* in the sense that it is directly cued by the immediate input and that it boosts (activates) most or all the schemes involved. Except for one step, the sensorimotor example given above illustrates this case. In contrast, mental-processing tasks present affective goals that are *motivationally mediated* in the sense that soon after the actual task's work begins the immediate operative process ceases to be directly relevant to αg, so that the operative process itself must be kept alive in a mediated manner by M power and strong executives endowed with a powerful Interrupt function.

Any Piagetian concrete-operational task is usually a good example of motivationally mediated processing. The question of the Piagetian psychologist or educator (e.g., Equivalence Conservation: If you would eat the whole of this ball and I would eat the whole of this sausage, should we have eaten the same amount of food or different amounts?) provides the task instructions which the subject's executive must encode and implement. The immediate affective goal αg, however, is not to implement these instructions but rather to please the friendly, warm, engaging Piagetian and/or to meet the challenge to the subject's personality structures (self-esteem, etc.) which the task's problem represents. Thus αg ceases to boost directly the immediate plan as soon as the task's work, monitored by the executive, begins. As a result of this mediated motivational character of the affective goal, αg cannot easily activate the schemes of the executive. Thus, in mental-processing tasks the executive must usually keep itself alive by allocating M energy to boost its own schemes and by developing a strong interrupt function.* To emphasize these processing characteristics, Pascual-Leone (1970, 1976b) has suggested that in mental-processing tasks the subjects' M power is functionally divided into two parts: M^e which is spent in boosting the executive and M^k which is used to boost relevant operative and figurative schemes, i.e., $M = M^e + M^k$.

We stress here these distinctions because the important Piagetian principle of *assimilatory praxis* (the tendency of all and any scheme or structure to apply whenever it can) and its derived notion of *intrinsic* cognitive motivation (e.g., Hunt, 1965) could and has often been misunder-

---

*Note that to emphasize the strong interrupt (I) function of this mental-processing executive cluster, Pascual-Leone denotes it by the generic symbol ϵ_I. Note further that M^e (i.e., the e fraction of M power) represents the power of mental centration that the child develops throughout his sensorimotor period (first two years of life)—an M power later used to boost the executive cluster ϵ_I in mental-processing tasks.

stood by educators as implying that motivation is not needed in educational practice, and a laissez-faire attitude is always sufficient. In fact, given the cognitive complexity of mental-processing tasks and subjects (given that any one of these tasks often activates, in any one of these subjects, a multiplicity of often incompatible schemes belonging to different stage levels), the intrinsic motivation of assimilatory praxis turns out to be motivationally ambiguous (too many activated schemes and too many executive alternatives). This motivational ambiguity of assimilatory praxis must be resolved, in the manner intimated above, by suitable mediated affective goals "planted" in the child by the educator. This necessary educational practice (see for example, Piaget, 1977a, and in this volume Chapters 3, 2, and 7), together with our preceding analysis, points to the need to help the child in developing varied and strong executive schemes (via executive skill training) and strong Interrupt functions.

(*EX 4*). Implicit in what we said above is an important idea (cf. Pascual-Leone and Bovet, 1966; Pascual-Leone, 1969, 1970, 1976b, 1976c, 1977b). Namely, the *executive demand* and *M-power demand* of a task (i.e., the sophistication of the executive it requires and the M power it necessitates) increase with: (1) the mediated motivation of its affective goal; (2) the number and salience of misleading cues, i.e., of elicited and applied schemes that are incompatible with the correct performatory synthesis; (3) the need to go beyond the information given, i.e., need to activate internally, through executive memory retrieval and M boosting, relevant schemes that are not activated by the current situation.

Since Piagetian operativity (developmental intelligence) is precisely measured as the capacity to cope with tasks with progressively stronger parameters (1), (2), and (3), the need to develop selectively (practice, train, educate) each and all the mechanisms discussed above should be apparent.

(*EX 5*). If, as Geneva has so often emphasized, Piaget's operational/logical structures are interpreted as representing sophisticated and abstract metasubjective schemes, the connection between executive schemes and operational structures becomes important, for the former could well be constructive precursors of the latter.

The analyses presented above and the work of the group using our neoPiagetian theory point in this direction. While operational structures represent the executive/operative organization of a task as a whole, executive schemes cover only *modular segments* of one of the task's performatory strategies. Thus, executives are more narrowly defined and simpler than operational structures. Implementation of the whole strategy often necessitates a sequence of different executives (together with their relevant figurative and operative schemes, and their activation-boosting organismic factors). This sequence of executives is often assembled serendipitously by equilibration processes—interaction effects produced by organismic factors and principles. If and when, by the virtue of thoughtful (M boosted) practice, the whole strategy as implemented and all its variations come to be learned rationally (i.e., LM learned— mentally automatized, constructively abstracted), the resulting general structure would be (provided that all the variations and aspects of the strategy have been explored) an operational/logical structure.

The educational implication of this analysis is that Piaget's operational structures can be decomposed, by means of task analysis, into sequences of executive modules as implemented (i.e., with their figurative and operative schemes, and requisite organismic factors). If these executive modules can be taught to children, and the organismic resources needed for the implementation of executive sequences are available to the children, Piaget's operational structures can be taught. The unknown key to this prescription is the amount and quality of organismic resources needed. We turn now to discuss this issue.

2.3. Organismic Resources and the Equilibration Process: I. Basic Factors

In addition to schemes, a metasubjective theory must include, as we suggested above, organismic resources (basic factors and principles) capable of generating temporally structured performatory syntheses out of the bits and pieces provided by executive, figurative, and operative schemes in the repertoire. From a formalist's viewpoint, organismic resources are *metaconstructs*, not only because they operate on the schemes to modify their state, but because they are inferred across *types of types* of situations and/or types of subjects (cf. Pascual-Leone, 1976d, 1977b, 1978). They are inferred to account for the data's "lawful anomalies" which theories recognizing only schemes and structures cannot explain. In this regard the metaconstructs of the TCO can be said to be an explicit theory for the "regulatory mechanisms" responsible for equilibration. From a dynamic viewpoint there are two types of metaconstructs: *silent operators* (i.e., basic organismic factors) and *basic principles*.

Silent operators function as scheme boosters (or antiboosters) i.e., they increase (or decrease) the activation weight (assimilatory strength) of the schemes on which they apply. Silent operators, like schemes, have conditions that stipulate when they will be activated and where (on which schemes) they will apply: unlike schemes, however, their application does not have direct effects on the metasubject's current mental state (this is why they are called "silent"); silent operators only have *side effects:* either they construct schemes out of the current mental state (learning), or they increment or decrement by some amount the activation weight of the schemes they apply on.

A detailed presentation of silent operators and basic principles is beyond the scope of the present chapter. Instead, we will list the main silent operators included in the theory, suggesting their relation to Piaget's constructs and indicating their related executive controls:

1. C: *Content* learning, related to Piaget's *empirical experience* and to the Pavlovian and learning-theoretical notions of simple conditioning and simple perceptual learning. C also stands for the schemes formed via C learning. Through repeated cumulative practice (overlearning), C schemes can become "chunked" into coordination structures which we call LC structures. LC learning is typically a very slow cumulative process (Pascual-Leone, Parkinson, and Pulos, 1974). Executive controls for C take the form of automatized scanning patterns which, adjusted to appropriate expectancies raised in a given situation, can generate C cues beyond those immediately activated by the situation and thus minimize the effect of misleading or distracting perceptual field factors.

2. L: *Logical* (in the formal sense of purely structural) learning, related to Piaget's *logico-mathematical experience* (constructive abstraction) and to the learning-theoretical notions of configural, structural, or "mediated" learning (cf. Razran, 1971). L also stands for the schemes formed via L learning. Examples of L controls are memory-retrieval strategies that create mentally produced activation of relevant L schemes; or decentration strategies that monitor decentrations in Piaget's sense—shifts in level of analysis, e.g., from perceptual to conceptual.

3. M: *Mental* attentional energy, or mental arousal, related to Piaget's *centration mechanism* and to the modern information-processing notions of mental effort (e.g., Kahneman, 1973), working memory or central processor and STM. The M operator represents a reserve of mental energy that can be allocated to raise the activation weight of task-relevant schemes. This reserve of M energy (maximum M power) may be measured by the maximum number of different schemes that M can weight in a single mental act of centration, i.e., in the same M operation. M is monitored by the current dominant executive ϵ_I which contains an arousal control (M control) for its mobilization. M is the or-

ganismic developmental construct of the theory. It has previously been described (Pascual-Leone, 1969, 1970) as the transition rule for Piaget's developmental stages; its power increases regularly approximately every two years, from a value of $e + 1$ (see above, EX#2) at three years to $e + 7$ at 15 years of age. This developmental growth of M power is represented in Table I. Notice that normal children who are not field-independent (e.g., Witkin and Goodenough, 1977b) may not exhibit in their performance as much effective M power as they potentially have. The M controls (arousal executives) can be adjusted through learning so that they mobilize an amount of M energy proportional to the evaluated difficulty of the task. These M arousal controls may be connected with general affective arousal which possibly regulates their driving power.

4. F: *Field* factor, related to the Piagetian *field effects*, figural factor, and "pregnance figurale"; even more closely related to the gestaltist autochthonous field factor or *Pragnanz*, and the neogestaltist minimum principle (Hochberg, 1957; Attneave, 1972) and S–R compatibility factor (e.g., Fitts and Seeger, 1953, Fitts and Posner, 1967). F controls are likely to be indirect: either C controls (scanning patterns for avoiding those situational features that induce the misleading F effects) or $I/\bar{I}$ controls (see below).

5. A: *Affective* factors. These are *general affective arousal* as well as *specific* instinctual affects, needs and emotions (i.e., affective schemes) which Piaget has little studied. Affective goals (αg) and the Pavlovian Orienting Reaction (αOR) are cognitive expressions of this organismic resource. A also stands for all affec-

Table I. Predicted M Capacity Corresponding to the Average Chronological Age of Normal, Field-Independent Subjects: Piaget's Developmental Substages

Predicted maximum power of M $m(M) = e + k$	Piaget's substage	Average chronological age (in year pairs)
$e + 1$	Low substage of preoperational period	3–4
$e + 2$	High substage of preoperational period	5–6
$e + 3$	Low concrete operations	7–8
$e + 4$	High concrete operations	9–10
$e + 5$	Substage introductory to formal operations	11–12
$e + 6$	Low formal operations	13–14
$e + 7$	High formal operations	15–adults

tive schemes, which can develop via C learning or combine with C or L schemes via L learning. Specific controls regulate the amount of affect applied in a given situation. A good example is given by psychoanalysts' "defense mechanisms."

6. B: Personality *biases* and *beliefs*—ego structures, values (axiological schemes), cognitive and personal styles (stylistic schemes), social, cultural, and humanistic characteristics of the subject. B stands for all these sorts of schemes—complex structures often formed via L learning, by constructively combining A, C, and L schemes alone or with other B schemes. B structures are thus essentially superordinate structures that reflect interactions, in particular types of situations, among all the silent operators. It follows that *all* control executives are to some extent B controls.

7. I: *Interrupt* function, which Piaget has neglected. Under the monitoring of the current dominant executive ϵ_I and its interrupt control, the interrupt applies on the schemes that are irrelevant for the implementation of this ϵ_I and actively cuts down (i.e., interrupts) their assimilatory strength. It is therefore an "antibooster." It is related to the Pavlovian notion of "external inhibition," to the neuropsychological notions of lateral or collateral inhibition (e.g., Pribram, 1973) and, more remotely, to the common theoretical notion of an attentional "filter" (e.g., Kahneman, 1973). A related inhibitory (antiboosting) function—the Pavlovian "internal inhibition" or "habituation"—is mentioned below as a part of the *SID* principle. There are *interruption* (strengthening, I controls) and *de-interruption* (weakening, $\bar{I}$ controls) executives that regulate the strength of the Interrupt and whose functioning can be developed through learning. The interruption controls cause phenomenally a "narrow beam" of attention and/or a state of strong attentional "filter." The de-interruption controls cause a "wide beam" of attention and/or a state of "openness to the input." Clearly the $I/\bar{I}$ functions are, together with M power and ϵ_I, the mechanisms of Piaget's centration/decentration.

All these silent operators have, we believe, innate roots. Their strength (or weight) develops via maturation and perhaps also with practice, within innately prescribed limits (whether practice can directly affect M, F, or I needs to be investigated). The mutual relative strengths of silent operators are a major set of parameters explaining individual (and developmental) differences. The other major set of parameters in individual differences is contained in the subject's total *repertoire H* of *habitual* schemes; i.e., it is contained in the qualitative structure of schemes of any sort (C schemes, L schemes, A schemes, and B schemes). The silent operators *directly* responsible for cognitive development, and thus for the emergence of Piaget's stages, are M, C, L, and I.

2.4. Organismic Resources and the Equilibration Process: II. Basic Principles

We conclude our presentation of the TCO with a consideration of the basic principles of this theory. Principles serve two functions: to outline (make explicit) the theoretical and epistemological presuppositions of the theory and to formulate the basic rules governing functional relations among the constructs of the theory. For this reason, presentation of principles serves as an overview of the theory. The theory's presuppositions (all but the last one found in Piaget's genetic epistemology) are:

(PR 1): Principle of Psycho-Logical Modular Organization. The metasubject is some sort of organismic logical machine, which can be decomposed into a set of relatively autonomous components or *modules.* In Piaget's theory, these modules are the schemes and structures; however Piaget's theory also contains nonmodular constructs, the unexplained "regulatory mechanisms." In the TCO, the modules are, of course, the habitual schemes (i.e., the subjective operators) and the silent operators.

(PR 2): Principle of Assimilatory Praxis. The modules of the theory, in particular subjective operators, are generally highly active and, unless prevented by some other incompatible and stronger module, will tend to apply (in accordance with their rules but under *minimal* conditions of satisfaction or stimulation) to determine performance. This is Piaget's assimilation function.

(PR 3): Principle of Equilibration. The modular organization (i.e., the metasubject) tends, as a result of its activity, to undergo enduring changes (modular restructurations) that pursue three goals: (a) they maximize the internal consistency within and among modules; (b) they maximize adaptation (functional payoff) in its dealing with the environment, i.e., maximize the number of different types of situations with which the organism can successfully interact; and (c) they minimize internal complexity within and among its modules, i.e., organize its psychogenetic and generative constructive processes in such a manner that (a) and (b) are satisfied with a minimum of learned and innate

resources. This is a reformulation of Piaget's equilibration principle (cf. Pascual-Leone, 1972, 1976c).

(PR 4): Principle of Bilevel Psychological Organization. An assimilatory modular system with equilibratory mechanisms necessitates two interdependent systems of modules: the subjective system (or level) of *schemes* and the silent system (or level) of *metaconstructs.* The modules in the subjective system are situation specific and are predominantly activated by (environmental or organismic) local/relational events. The modules in the silent system are situation free (to the extent that they do not reflect collective aspects of subjective modules, such as the denominations of *C, L, A,* or *B*): they are predominantly activated by organismic holistic/relational events.

(PR 5): The Principle of Schematic Overdetermination of Performance or SOP Principle. This is a basic functional rule describing the metasubject's government. According to the SOP principle, clusters of schemes that are compatible (i.e., which can apply together) sum their activation weights in order to increase their degree of dominance. Clusters of schemes that are incompatible compete for their application (for their control of the performance output). The SOP principle stipulates that at any moment of the generative process the dominant cluster of schemes will apply (i.e., will bring to bear its effects on the current mental state or on the input). The *criterion of dominance* is determined by the terminal activation weight W (i.e., *assimilatory strength*) of each cluster of schemes relative to the W of the other clusters. The *terminal activation weight W of a scheme* is the weight it has after the various scheme boosters and antiboosters (i.e., *C, A, L, B, M, F, I*) have applied on it.

(PR 6): The Principle of Scheme Inhibition and Decay (SID Principle). A modular dynamic organization that follows the principle of Assimilatory Praxis must contain active mechanisms for the deactivation of modules. The alternative is a breakdown due to universal modular excitation. Scheme inhibition can occur by either one of two mechanisms, which according to the model of Pribram (1971, 1973) and to cognitive-style psychological data, may be interrelated. One of these inhibitory mechanisms is the silent operator Interrupt which we mentioned above. The other inhibitory mechanism is psychological habituation. *Habituation* is an active interruption of dominant schemes (figurative, operative, and executive) which, because of lack of environmental and/or organismic change, have lost their (affective/orienting reflex) novelty value. Notice that habituation could be regarded as an *internal interrupt,* "internal" because it interrupts the very schemes that are internal to the dominant executive process. With this terminology the Interrupt would be an *external interrupt* because it interrupts schemes external (irrelevant) to

the dominant executive process. This terminology seems particularly apt because the degree of strength (antiboosting weight) of the Interrupt and Habituation operators seems to be correlated: whenever the Interrupt (i.e., external interrupt) is strong (weak) the habituation operator (i.e., internal interrupt) is strong (weak). Their strength is correlated. There may also exist a *decay mechanism:* an active scheme that is not boosted by any silent operator (or by the input) could be exposed to the decay of its assimilatory strength as a function of time.

3. Toward a Piagetian Metasubjective Technology for Education

In the first part of this chapter, commenting on other chapters of this book, we suggested the need for an explicit and detailed psychological theory that conforms to the main tenets of Piagetian genetic epistemology. Unless such a psychology is fully developed, the problem encountered in applying the Piagetian views to education may not be solved.

In the second part of this chapter, we sketched our proposal for such a theory. We tried to present a condensed and yet useful description of a rather abstract and technical neoPiagetian dynamic theory. We regard this theory to be a model of the psychological organism (*the metasubject*) which is at work inside Piaget's "epistemic subject" for each age group, as much as inside the particular children which educators encounter. We have reasons to believe that our theory can handle the Piagetian stage data and the process of stage transitions (i.e., dialectical equilibration), as well as learning, cognitive style and individual differences in cognition and learning. No less is needed from a theory geared to cognitive-educational applications.

In this last section, we will attempt to suggest the potential usefulness of our approach for education, by selectively discussing some key issues. We begin with the old philosophical problems of whether, when, and what to teach.

If the metasubject is a modular organization endowed with assimilatory praxis, anything should be teachable that can be broken down into a sequence of modules simple enough for the subject to learn. This progressive practical orientation, successively made popular by Bruner, Gagné, by "direct" or "compensatory" approaches to education (e.g., Bereiter, 1970; Bereiter and Engelmann, 1966) and by behavior modification approaches, is indeed technologically explained by our theory in terms of the trade-off between the subject's M power (power of his mental centration mechanism) and the M demand of the task. This trade-off is mediated by the quality of the repertoire of schemes (executive, figurative, and operative) that the subject possesses; the more powerful the habitual structures (the chunks of information) of the subject, the less M power he will necessitate to cope with the constructive complexity of the task.

But to say that something can be taught early (and not everything can), does not imply that it should be. We will discuss this matter by considering the following sets of questions: (1) What does "simple enough to be taught early" mean?, which are the limits of this "enough"? That is: What is it that *cannot* be simplified enough for a child of a given age to learn? (2) Assuming that anything, subject to restriction (1), can be taught in some manner to young children, what is the possible cost for the child in learning, via a special technology, skills he may learn later in an easier way? (3) Assuming that no cost or harm to children is involved in the early teaching of many specific skills (whether particular behavioral routines or control executives for silent-operator monitoring), how should educators select those that should be taught?

We discuss the three sets of questions successively, relating them to the theory of constructive operators (TCO). Other issues and methods based in the TCO that are relevant to education have been discussed elsewhere.*

3.1. The Limits of Educational Simplification

Piaget's constructivism has persistently emphasized that all knowledge, whether figurative, operative, or executive, consists in the internalization (interiorization) of invariants, i.e., recurrent mental states and/or their semantic-pragmatic interconnections (fluents) generated within or across types of situations. The diversity of mental states, interconnections, and types of situations involved in abstracting an invariant determines its *constructive complexity*. The limits of educational simplification appear in terms of four sorts of factors: (1) the nature of the situations and performances involved; (2) the kind of organismic resources (including the total repertoire H of habitual schemes) available to the learner; (3) the desired degree of generality (applicability across situ-

---

*E.g., Ammon (1977); Bachor (1976); Burtis (1976); Case (1974, 1975, 1978); DeAvila, Havassy, with Pascual-Leone (1976); DeRibaupierre (1975); Miller (1975); Parkinson (1975); Pascual-Leone, (1976b); Pascual-Leone and Bovet (1966); Pascual-Leone and Goodman (1976); Pascual-Leone and Smith (1969); Scardamalia (1977); Toussaint (1974).

ations) of the to-be-learned task structures; and (4) the amount of time available for the learning to take place.

In terms of the situations and performances involved, simplification can be achieved (via task analysis) by breaking down the constructive complexity involved into sequences of wisely chosen learning steps. The advantage of this method of *sequential cumulative learning* is the lowering of the M demand of the task, since this demand is a function of the M demand of the step that is constructively most complex (as measured by the number of schemes which must be simultaneously coordinated in it). In addition to (2), (3), and (4), an important condition restricting this common method of sequential cumulative learning is the *minimal dimensionality of the task* (i.e., the constructive complexity that must be preserved in some steps of the sequence in order to preserve the lawfulness of the to-be-learned invariant).

Since the method of sequential cumulative learning which Gagné and Skinner made popular is widely used by educators, it may be appropriate to examine these four restrictions of the method starting with the concept of minimal dimensionality of a task.

We use the term dimensionality or rank of a problem-solving strategy (or an invariant) to mean the minimal number of organismically-distinct semantic dimensions (conditions) that must be considered for the problem to be solved (or the invariant detected). A classic example, well analyzed by Piaget although he did not explicitly examine the issue of dimensionality, is that of "conservations" (Inhelder, Sinclair, and Bovet, 1974; Piaget, 1941, 1956, 1977; Piaget and Inhelder, 1962). It may be convenient to use this example here since Easley in his chapter uses the same example to illustrate the recent Genevan work. We will sketch the analysis of conservation of substance and weight with plasticine, in order to illustrate this notion.

The dimensionality of the substance problem, for the usual identity-reversibility or historical strategy, involves three conditions plus the formulation of the executive problem, which we designate by the letter e (cf. Pascual-Leone, 1969, 1976b, 1977a, 1977b). A representation of this conservation of substance–equivalence task appears in Figure 1 and a brief description of the $(3 + e)$ dimensions of this problem follows.

1. The first semantic dimension of this problem is the relation existing between the two original balls of plasticine a and b (value: equal amount versus unequal).

2. The second semantic dimension is the actual transformation T (e.g., rolling a ball on the table) which produces the "sausage-like" piece b' out of b.

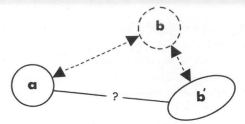

Figure 1.   The conservation of substance-equivalence task.

3. The third semantic dimension is the relevant type (or class) of transformation to which *T* belongs (value: quantity-preserving transformations as opposed to quantity-changing ones). Note that this semantic dimension, the discrimination of the type of transformation performed on the ball *b*, can only exist for subjects whose repertoire of figurative and operative fluent *L* structures contains obs (i.e., distal object representations) that can represent the distal object "ball of clay" as a (sensorimotor-based) spatial arrangement of particles ("molecules") that originally are thought to change in amount with different rearrangements. The quantity-preserving transformation is recognized by the metasubject as a spatial rearrangement of the "molecules" of an object that changes its surface appearance (its *perceptual facet*) but does not remove or add "molecules" to the object.* This discrimination of a quantity-preserving transformation psychogenetically leads to the emergence of the metasubject's representation of substance (i.e., metasubjective quantitative identity) as a generic ob. That is, as a (naive) "molecular" aggregate of particles, each particle defined by an invariant quantum of surface-mass (mass for which weight and volume are not yet invariant); and such that the whole object is the sum of all the surface-mass quanta. Constructively, the substance of an object emerges in the organism as the invariant generated under quantity-preserving transformations.

Finally, the executive problem is to estimate whether or not the amounts of substance found in *a* and *b'* are equal. The quantity of substance of an object is first defined by the organism as the object's value under the concrete action "perceptual exploration of the object's surface, and estimation (in length of scanpaths, exploration time cost, or some

---

*This explanation of spatial rearrangement of the molecules is similar to Piaget's (1975, 1977) concept of generalized commutativity in the revised explanation of conservation. Pascual-Leone (personal communication) used a spatial rearrangement explanation in his early writings. [Eds.]

other cumulative recording mechanism) of this amount." Later, after the problems (contradictions) created by this formulation in the context of conservation tasks are solved (see below), quantity of substance comes to be defined in terms of a transperceptual cognitive invariant acquired via logical/structural (L) learning. This transperceptual invariant, a differentiation of the generic ob mentioned above, is a *habitual* (i.e., habit-like) fluent representation of the distal object in question in terms of its various facets, and of the identity-preserving transformation (e.g., displacements of matter in the case of substance conservation) that transform one facet (aspect) of the object into another. Substance conservation problems are generally solved at about 7 years of age.

Consider now the weight conservation task, which uses the same situation to compare the weights of a and b'. There are several possible strategies and all seem to have the same dimensionality, although they make use of different actual dimensions. The *identity-reversibility weight strategy*, often discussed by Piaget (1941; Piaget and Inhelder, 1962), requires a fourth dimension in addition to dimensions (1), (2), and (3) of substance equivalence, as well as different executive structures.

(4) A (naive) "molecular" representation of matter as constituted by an aggregate of surface-mass particles endowed with their own weight, so that the weight of the object is the sum of these particle weights.

The executive problem is to estimate whether a and b' weigh the same and thus to anticipate the outcome of placing a and b' on the two plates of the balance. The weight of an object is first defined by the organism as its value under the concrete actions "its pressure on the hand" (kinesthetic weight) or "its pressure on the balance plate." Note that the procedure by which the balance scale translates the relative weight of two objects into a position of the scale marker (values: equal weight, more weight, less weight) has been taught by the tester in advance and thus is chunked with the weight scheme, i.e., (4).

Conservation of weight problems are often spontaneously solved at about 9 to 10 years of age (unless subjects are field-dependent, see below), but not sooner.

Conservation of volume with plasticine, which Piaget and Inhelder (1962) have called "displacement volume" is spontaneously solved at about 11 or 12 years of age. Solution strategies for this task reveal a dimensionality of at least $5 + e$ (Pascual-Leone, 1969, 1972; Parkinson, 1975).

The same functional relation between the psychogenetic difficulty of these tasks and the dimensionality of their problem-solving strategies can be found in many Piagetian tasks: problems with dimensionality of $3 + e$ are usually spontaneously solved at 7 or 8 years (if the subject's background and cognitive style are adequate); problems of rank 4 + *e* are similarly solved at 9 or 10 years; problems of rank 5 + *e* at 11 or 12 years. This intriguing linear relation extends from age 3 or 4 to 15 or 16 years.

The analyses presented above illustrate, we hope, the notions of dimensionality of a task and dimensionality analysis. Note that recent work has confirmed the dimensionality predictions for conservation tasks (e.g., Case, 1977; Parkinson, 1975; Pascual-Leone, 1976b) as well as for other Piagetian tasks (e.g., Case, 1974; DeRibaupierre, 1975; Parkinson, 1975; Pascual-Leone, 1969; Pascual-Leone and Smith, 1969; Scardamalia, 1977; Toussaint, 1976).

The minimal dimensionality of a task is the dimensionality that results when (1) misleading *F* factors, *L* factors, *A* factors, etc., elicited by the task's situational context are removed by changing features of the situation and/or by training the subject (extinction of error factors); and (2) the subjects are trained so as to "chunk" the relevant pieces of information stored in memory (internal activation of relevant *L* or *C* structures through *L* or *C* retrieval controls); and/or (3) subjects are trained to explore or scan appropriately the situation so as to notice the relevant cues (task executive training and *C* control training).

The fact that the dimensionality of a task can be reduced, up to a minimum, by training methods, is related to the intriguing question of why dimensionality analysis often predicts the stage-level (developmental difficulty) of Piagetian tasks. These issues, very pertinent to our present concern, can be made clearer by examining the error patterns and misleading factors exhibited by subjects of different ages in the tasks. These methods show, as is already known, that Piagetian tasks usually present *misleading situations* (e.g., Pascual-Leone, 1969, 1976b, 1976c, 1977a, 1977b; Pascual-Leone and Bovet, 1966; Pascual-Leone and Smith, 1969) that can be contrasted with the "facilitating" type of situation represented by typical learning tasks. The situations are misleading because they elicit powerful *error factors* in Harlow's sense (1959) that produce erroneous strategies or responses. Two of the most common kinds of error factors are: (1) over-learned (i.e., *LC*) schemes or structures, developed in other situations where they were relevant, which are irrelevantly elicited in the new situation by salient yet misleading cues; and (2) the organismic disposition to produce performances or responses (i.e., percepts, behaviors, cognitive judgments) which are congruent with the dominant features of the field-activated figurative, perceptual, and/or cognitive schemes. This *F* factor is misleading in many Piagetian tasks, as the typical errors of young children attest.

In the conservation tasks these two error factors are quite strong. In substance conservation, for instance, they appear as: (1) A habitual

scheme that equates amount of perceptual surface with amount of substance. This habitual scheme results from the LC learning of the organism that internalizes the empirical probabilistically-invariant relation
usually found between the visible surface and the expectable substance
of objects. This empirical L structure is in fact an instance of the preoperational structures Piaget calls "unidirectional functions." It constitutes
an empirical rule, unwittingly developed and generally true in everyday
life, which is as misleading in conservation tasks as it is in the packaging
of supermarket products. (2) An F factor that induces subjects to assimilate the conceptual structure of the problem (i.e., the real quantity) to its
perceptual structure (i.e., the perceptual quantity). This tendency to
organize conceptualizations (e.g., the conservation judgment) in con-
gruence with the perceptual organization of their data is a cognitive
manifestation of the well-known S–R compatibility disposition.

These error factors turn conservation tasks (and many other Piagetian and gestaltist problem-solving situations) into mental teasers or
(unconscious) cognitive conflicts, where the correct solution (strategy X)
to the problem must assert itself, if it can, against the strong interference
provided by error-factor facilitated wrong solutions (strategies Y).

The existence of these conflict situations and their powerful error
factors raises the issue of the mechanism that allows strategy X to assert
itself against strategy Y, when subjects spontaneously and for the first
time solve the problem. This mechanism cannot be "simple" discrimination learning (e.g., Gibson, 1969) or even logical/structural cognitive
learning, as Piaget's traditional conception of operational/logical learning, or Klahr and Wallace's (1976) production-system model of conservation acquisition, would suggest. That is, the orthodox interpretations,
according to which cognitive competences, such as conservations, are
spontaneously acquired when and if the appropriate logical structures,
such as the grouping of "correspondences" (Piaget, 1977) or the specific
production systems (Klahr and Wallace, 1976), are acquired, actually beg
the question. They beg the question because, as we indicated above, in
order to acquire operational/logical structures the metasubject must go
through the experience of solving the tasks. To say otherwise implies a
learning paradox (Pascual-Leone, 1973, 1976a, 1977b).

Pascual-Leone has proposed (Pascual-Leone, 1969, 1972, 1973,
1976b, 1977a) the following account of acquisition. As the conservation
of plasticine task proceeds, children's executive, figurative, and operative schemes encode the events that take place. They are led by the
experimenter to verify that a has the same amount as b and retain the
scheme ϕ "$(a = b)$" which in Figure 1 is represented by a double arrow
—this is dimension (1). This scheme ϕ "$(a = b)$" must be kept activated,

perhaps through M boosting, while b is transformed into b' generating the scheme $\phi\,''(Tbb')''$—this is dimension (2). Finally, while schemes $\phi\,''(a = b)''$ and $\phi\,''(Tbb')''$ are being boosted by M, a quantity-preserving transformation type classifier, an operative fluent $\psi\,''(Class\ T)''$ (dimension 3 of the task) is applied onto $\phi\,''(Tbb')$.'' The application of $\psi\,''(Class\ T)''$ onto $\phi\,''(Tbb')''$ yields the scheme $\phi\,''(b = b')$,'' an expectancy implied by the successful assimilation of $\psi\,''(Class\ T)$.'' This scheme is represented in Figure 1 by a double arrow.

Note that Figure 1 should be interpreted as the cognitive map or problem representation of the child at this point. This cognitive map will be needed to solve the conservation task because the F and L error factors discussed above prevent the subject from directly concluding via "simple associations" (i.e., C learning) that a is equal to b'. Note further that this cognitive map can only be reached by the child if he can boost with M simultaneously the three schemes $\phi\,''(a = b),''$ $\phi\,''(Tbb')''$ *and* $\psi\,''(Class\ T).''$ The reason why the three schemes must be simultaneously M boosted is because they are not boosted by the input when the conservation question is asked: they must be recalled.

They are not cued by the input, in spite of the physical presence of ball a and sausage b', because a and b' are actually assimilated by perceptual schemes OB''(ball a)'' and OB''(sausage b')'' and this assimilation will make the features of a and b' unavailable for cueing the conceptual schemes $\phi\,''(a = b),''$ $\phi\,''(Tbb')''$ and $\psi\,''(Class\ T)''$. This occurs because the perceptual schemes are different from the conceptual schemes (see p. 254, SC 1), and the former become misleading vis-à-vis the latter. Thus M has to boost the latter to activate them after a "historical-strategy" executive (i.e., an identity–reversibility strategy) has taken over the direction of mental processing.

We may notice in passing that this situation is strictly similar to the one of quanitification of class inclusion (i.e., Do I have in my hand more daisies or more flowers?—when there are 8 daisies and 2 roses). To succeed in this inclusion of classes, children must simultaneously think of the daisies they see as being a "collection of daisies" and as being "members of the class of flowers". In all these cases the subject must be able to apply to the same object two different schemes such that the first is perceptual and the second, which includes the first as a part, is a logical or infralogical fluent. Since the first is directly cued by the input while the second involves remembering, the second necessitates M boosting and/or a strong *decentration executive* to monitor the shift from the first to the second.*

---

*Inhelder, Sinclair, and Bovet (1974) did in fact find that training on inclusion of classes emphasizing this decentration scheme produces considerable facilitation to subsequent performance in substance conservation. Our task analysis explains their results.

Thus, the emergence in the child's mind of the cognitive map symbolized in Figure 1 necessitates the spontaneous activation of a historical-strategy executive and a strong decentration executive as well as an M power of measure $m(M) = e + 3$. This M power, made necessary by misleading error factors F and L and by the failure of a and b' to cue directly the relevant schemes, is the cause of the task's dimensionality (i.e., its M demand).

Note that, as this example illustrates well, the dimensionality of a task can be reduced if the misleading error factors are removed by training or by situational manipulation and if the necessary executives, such as the historical-strategy (identity–reversibility) executive and decentration executive, are taught to the child. The immense literature on conservation training with preoperational children or preschoolers fully confirm this theoretical conclusion (cf. Pascual-Leone, 1972, 1976b): Under these training conditions the dimensionality of the task usually becomes $2 + e$, since the schemes ϕ "(Tbb')" and ψ "(Class T)" are chunked (L structured) by the training, and the misleading F, L factors are reduced or the decentration executive directly trained. A dimensionality of $2 + e$ can be handled by the M power of 5 year olds easily ($m(M) = e + 2$). Which explains why, after suitable training, 5 year olds solve conservation tasks and often exhibit good generalization and durability of the results. Undoubtedly, the dimensionality (M demand) could be brought down further by training to $1 + e$, making the task accessible to suitably-trained 3 and 4 year olds ($m(M) = e + 1$), but then the learning should not generalize easily across tasks.

This lengthy example illustrates a very important point: the minimal dimensionality of a task is relative to the power of the subject's repertoire of structures—up to an absolute minimum below which the relevant invariant cannot emerge (e.g., no training can bring the dimensionality of volume conservation below the one of substance conservation).

Consider again the four main factors that set limits to educational simplification: (1) the minimal dimensionality of the task; (2) the kind of organismic resources available to the learner; such as his M power, the strength of his (task facilitating and/or misleading) F and L factors, the strength of his task-related affective goals, etc.; (3) the desired degree of generality (applicability across situations) of the to-be-learned structures—as we minimize the dimensionality of the invariant being taught, thus minimizing the number and the abstractness of its semantic conditions (e.g., bringing the dimensionality of substance conservation down to $2 + e$ or even $1 + e$) the invariant being taught necessarily becomes more concrete and situation specific, which in turn reduces the generality (generalizability across situations) of the structure; and (4) the amount of time available for the learning to take place.

It should be clear from the example and comments presented above, that there is a trade-off system or dialectical equilibration among these four factors: the gain (i.e., educational improvement) in one usually carries a cost in the others. For instance, (a) if we could determine and fix the desired generality of the structure to-be-learned, then its minimum dimensionality would come to be fixed, which in turn would impose limits to the minimum M power of the learner and the minimum time required for training; (b) if we choose to minimize the required learner's M power (i.e., teach children as early as possible, a "progressive" educational goal) then the dimensionality of the structures (i.e., the task-as-solved) will have to be equally minimized; which in turn will minimize the generality of the learned skill and maximize the requisite time of acquisition (since the number of relevant schemes coordinated in any given step will have to be minimized to accommodate the subject's low M power).

3.2. The Educational Cost of Wholesale Early Efficient Education

The discussion above may have already intimated that the method of sequential cumulative learning draws its efficiency from the educator's (or trainer's) clever, whether conscious or tacit, minimization in the task of misleading factors (F, L, C, A, and B). When all contingencies are arranged so as to make salient the relevant cues (i.e., features of the situation matching releasing conditions of relevant schemes) and exclude or extinguish misleading or even irrelevant ones (so that no misleading or even irrelevant scheme is activated) the situation is a *facilitating situation* (cf. Pascual-Leone, 1969; 1974; 1976b; Pascual-Leone and Smith, 1969; Pascual-Leone and Bovet, 1966). Facilitating situations make sequential cumulative learning efficient and so they are customarily used by behaviour-modification and learning-oriented educators. They are good for learning easily certain skills (specific, concrete figurative-operative-executive performatory packages or scripts). But they present the problem when overused, of diminishing the subjects' opportunities to experience misleading situations and distracting situations. A *misleading situation* (or conflict) is one that elicits misleading schemes that interfere with the activation and application of relevant schemes.* A *distracting situation* is one eliciting irrelevant schemes that

---

*Pascual-Leone (1969, 1974) has called misleading a situation that elicits both (task) relevant and non-relevant schemes, where these schemes are such that at least some relevant

may distract from the activation and application of relevant ones. Experiencing and learning to cope with misleading and distracting situations is important for children not only because these types of situations are quite common in curricular (e.g., mathematics, physics, abstract languages and reasoning, problem solving, human interactions, and social or linguistic communication, etc.) as well as extra-curricular activities (deals in the marketplace, jobs and career choice and achievement, sportive and risk-taking activities, love relations, etc.) but also because humans are able to develop organismic controls (i.e., control executives) for cognitively coping with misleading and distracting situations. Since excessive and exclusive early concentration on skill learning from facilitating situations (which we for short call a "facilitating" education), could later hinder the learning of these controls, the cost of efficient "facilitating" education appears to be quite considerable.* We wonder whether excessively polarized human typologies such as the ones of being a "learner" versus a "problem-solver," or of having "intelligent" versus "creative" versus "clever" minds, are not fostered by lopsided educational (and interpersonal) practices at school and at home. Namely, an excessively "facilitating" directed education versus exclusively or excessively "misleading" and "distracting,"nondirective educations. Warnings against these two extreme types of education have also been raised by Piaget (e.g., 1977), and, in this volume, by DeVries and Lickona.

To illustrate the important new concepts of "organismic controls" (control executives) and "education of controls" it may be useful to refer

---

schemes share input releasing features with nonrelevant schemes and these nonrelevant schemes have a very high initial assimilatory strength because they are directly cued by obvious features in the input. Nonrelevant schemes of this sort are called misleading vis-à-vis the relevant schemes cue-related to them. Note that all learning theories, Piaget's included, would predict that, under these circumstances, the misleading schemes apply first, thus subtracting some potential cues from their cue-related relevant schemes. As a result, the probability of subsequent activation of these relevant schemes will be lower, unless the executive uses M power to boost these relevant schemes which are not misleading. Note that in the conservation example discussed above the schemes OB "(ball a)" and OB "(sausage b')" were misleading, respectively, vis-à-vis schemes ϕ "$(a = b)$" and ϕ "(Tbb')."

*Piaget's notion of assimilation (i.e., our principles of Assimilatory Praxis and Schematic Overdetermination of Performance) already implies this possibility. Once skills developed in facilitating situations are varied and strong enough (including the "facilitating" skills of asking for help, seeking a "facilitating" teacher or giving up and avoiding the problem situation) an adequate learning of controls for misleading and distracting situations may not be possible under ordinary circumstances—thus the well-known life-long stability of cognitive styles such as Field-dependence-independence (Witkin, Goodenough, and Karp, 1967).

again to the conservation of substance analysis. As we suggested above, silent operators (i.e., basic organismic factors, M, L, F, etc.) intervene both in producing the incorrect performances and in bringing about the correct results. Incorrect performances are induced by the misleading error factors F and L as well as by the misleading character of perceptual schemes OB "(ball a)" and OB "(sausage b')," "i.e., a misleading C factor, vis-à-vis conceptual schemes ϕ "($a = b$), " ϕ "(Tbb')" and ψ "($Class\ T$)." These misleading factors are overcome by the active interaction of four kinds of operators:

1. An appropriate repertoire of relevant figurative and operative schemes
2. Several sorts of executives (e.g., a plan or task executive; an M control or arousal executive; an L control or decentration executive*; an I control or interruption executive)
3. The silent operator M (mental attentional energy)
4. The silent operator I (The Interrupt function)

Relevant now are the executive controls: arousal executive, decentration executive, and interruption executive. The first one mobilizes M energy; the second makes possible the cueing and activation of the conceptual schemes by cancelling the interference of perceptual schemes OB"(ball a)" and OB"(sausage b')"; the third monitors the "interrupt" so as to reduce the assimilatory strength of the various misleading and irrelevant schemes. By the good service of these controls the cognitive map of Figure 1 gets formed. But once the relevant cognitive map for the task solution has been attained, the task is by no means solved. The subject must still *provoke* the serendipitous emergence of the correct response by using again executive controls and silent operators.

Pascual-Leone has proposed (1969, 1973, 1976b) that the factor provoking this serendipitous emergence of the correct response is the silent operator F. Indeed, if the cognitive map of Figure 1 is maintained (M centrated) by the child and if he feels compelled to give an answer to the question "Is there as much amount in a and b'?" (perhaps because he likes to please the experimenter—a mediated affective goal) he may experience the terms of the cognitive map $a = b$ and $b = b'$ as a mental stimulus–situation (an S array) that induces, via the F factor, a strong

*Note that we use the term "decentration" in Piaget's sense. As Pascual-Leone (1969, 1974) pointed out there are two sorts of decentration, simple de-centration or "scanning" (whether visual, auditory, etc.) and hierarchical de-centration (e.g., de-centrating from the "eye" or the "nose" to the corresponding "face"; de-centrating from the "roses-as-objects" to the "roses-as-flowers"). Hierarchical de-centration is what Piaget means by decentration.

tendency to respond (R pattern) with a relation of equality $a = b'$ which is compatible with the equality relation found in the other terms of the cognitive map.

This $S–R$ compatibility tendency induced by F serendipitously leads, in this situation, to the solution.* Note that after the appropriate cognitive map has been formed by overcoming misleading factors, a strong F factor actually facilitates the correct performance. Good problem solvers should actually have a way of making the F factor weak when the task's context is F-misleading (i.e., before the formation of the appropriate cognitive map) *and* making F strong when the task becomes F-facilitated. Neuropsychological research (e.g., Pribram, 1971, 1973) as well as scattered work in perception and cognition suggest that these controls exist and are in fact related to the interruption executive (I control) and *de-interruption* executive ($\bar{I}$ control)—the controls regulating the interrupt function. With interruption (which neuropsychologically corresponds to active inhibition of lateral inhibition) the F factor becomes weaker; with de-interruption (which neuropsychologically corresponds to active lateral inhibition) the F factor becomes stronger.

We have engaged in these detailed analyses of conservation to emphasize a general idea which is new and quite important in education: people must learn to control their organismic resources (their centration/decentration, their mental energy, their attentional "filters," their field factor) and the training grounds for these controls are properly chosen misleading or distracting situations. Furthermore, schools are doing very little to train children in these controls and they should be doing more.

3.3. Offers of Directed Training That Children Cannot Refuse

In an epoch when technology and skills become obsolete as rapidly as in ours, children should be brought up to be problem solvers and not "facilitating task" learners. Furthermore, they should be brought up to be problem solvers via much directed training of their silent-operator controls and some directed training of relevant plan executives on the appropriate basic content areas. Methods should be developed to train all the major control systems, but this could necessitate major ideological

---

*Because of its possible relevance to the domain of education in moral development, we may point out that in this conservation situation as well as in other cognitive and social/personality situations, the F factor behaves much as the Heider-inspired theory of Balance and other Congruency theories would predict (Zajonc, 1960).

changes in the school boards (in particular for the A controls—affective controls and defense mechanisms; and for the stylistic B controls— cognitive style retraining methods). More immediately possible is the training of C controls (e.g., sensorial/perceptual automatic scanning that is guided by the expectancies in the current mental state—essential for reading skills); the training of L controls (e.g., mental decentration executives, memory-retrieval executives, and the so-called metamemory); the training of M controls (e.g., arousal executives which regulate the amount of M energy mobilized according to the sort of task encountered, task executives which allocate M energy optimally for the task— only to *relevant* schemes with *low* assimilatory strength and in the right order); and the training of I controls (e.g., interruption and de-interruption in accordance with the type of situation and rapid shifting from the one to the other). Methods for training some of these control-executive skills already exist, often developed by researchers with a philosophy of education which we Piagetians criticize (but technology does not know where it comes from). Other methods will have to be invented. To contribute some ideas to this effort we conclude the chapter by summarizing two general methods that could prove useful for a start: the method of Graded Learning Loops (Pascual-Leone, 1976b) and the Executive Time Sharing.

3.4. Two Methods in Lieu of an Epilogue

The method of *Graded Learning Loops* is a formalization of a frequent Genevan practice (e.g., Pascual-Leone, 1969; Inhelder, Sinclair, and Bovet, 1974). Its purpose, from our present viewpoint, is to provide a cognitive-conflict context (misleading and distracting situation) in which the difficulty is controlled and such that a modicum of near-spaced "successes" would be ensured to any child. It is understood that the chosen items would be task-analyzed so as to choose (and properly regulate the strength of) the different control executives and plan executives involved. In this method children are exposed to a sequence of minitasks (i.e., items), all belonging to the same *process-structural family* (i.e., all presenting at least in part the same or a related problem-solving process structure), and varying in difficulty.*

---

*The change in item difficulty is obtained in the manner that Pascual-Leone and Bovet (1966, 1967) and Pascual-Leone (1969) first explicitly suggested and used: by minimizing in some of the minitasks the executive processing demand, by minimizing the amount of requisite information, and by maximizing the task-facilitating field characteristics of the situation.

The order in which items from the process-structural family are organized is crucial. Items are ordered so as to form a graded series of learning loops. That is, if the basic sequence of items is A_1, A_2, A_3, B_1, C_1, C_2, C_3, D_1, E_1, etc., *and* items A_1, A_2, and A_3 (or C_1, C_2, and C_3) constitute a *learning loop segment*, these items are such that (a) A_1 is more difficult than A_2, which in turn is more difficult than A_3, and (b) A_1, A_2, A_3 belong to the same process-structural family of tasks. In fact, the last item of the learning loop segment is usually as easy as possible, being maximally facilitated by field factors and learning factors (e.g., sets of habitual schemes). This last item is often spontaneously solved, resulting in *intrinsic* (self-produced or reafferential) *feedback* which facilitates the learning of schemes useful to the solution of harder items. If the subject fails all of the early items in the learning-loop segment but succeeds on the last one, say A_3, the learning loop is implemented by successively retesting items A_2 and A_1, one or several times, returning to A_3 as needed. The executive and operative schemes developed in solving the easy items can help in solving the harder ones; to facilitate further this solution, the experimenter leads the subject (by asking for justifications and comparisons) to contrast the items in the loop with respect to the strategies he used in them. Successive learning-loop segments and ordinary items are ordered in graded difficulty, the easier ones first. In this manner, earlier segments may assist the subject to develop spontaneously (i.e., without being directly taught) the plans and control executives needed to solve the latter segments.

Pascual-Leone (1976b) has discussed in detail a concrete instance of this method utilized by Inhelder, Sinclair, and Bovet (1974).

Consider now briefly the *Executive Time Sharing* method. The purpose here is to develop decentration executives, M controls and, in particular, $I/\bar{I}$ (interruption/de-interruption) controls: the paradigm is analogous to those sometimes found in experimental studies of attention and of working memory, but used with a different (educational) purpose.

The child is required (within a game format with short-term affective goals, e.g., with "token" rewards) to shift rapidly back and forth between (or to carry concurrently) two performances which present opposing demands with regard to a given silent operator. For instance, one task may require strong interruption (or F minimization) while the other demands strong de-interruption (or F maximization). If the contingencies were suitably arranged, the child would in this manner exercise and thus develop his control of $I/\bar{I}$ alternation.

We hope that the educational issues we have raised with the help of our neoPiagetian theory will entice some readers to read more on the work of our group.

We also hope to have shown with the example of our own approach that metasubjective theories are needed to explicate psychologically the important problems raised by Piaget's genetic-epistemological theory of dialectical equilibration.

ACKNOWLEDGMENTS

We wish to acknowledge the comments of Carl Bereiter and Marlene Scardamalia on an earlier draft of the chapter.

References

Ammon, P. R., 1977. Cognitive development and early childhood education. In H. L. Horn and P. A. Robinson (Eds.), *Psychological processes in early education.* Academic Press, New York, p. 157.

Anderson, B., 1975. *Cognitive psychology: The study of knowing, learning, and thinking.* New York: Academic Press.

Attneave, F., 1972. Representation of physical space. In W. W. Melton and E. Martin (Eds.), *Coding processes in human memory.* Washington, D.C.: Winston and Sons.

Bachor, D., 1976. *Information processing capacity and teachability of low achieving students.* Unpublished doctoral dissertation, University of Toronto, (O.I.S.E.).

Bereiter, C., 1970. Genetics and educability, educational implications of the Jensen debate. In J. Hellmuth (Ed.), *Disadvantaged child* (Vol. 3). New York: Brunner-Mazel, p. 279.

Bereiter, C., and Engelmann, S., 1966. *Teaching disadvantaged children in the preschool.* Englewood Cliffs, N.J.: Prentice-Hall.

Burtis, P. J., 1976. *A study of the development of short term memory in children.* Unpublished doctoral dissertation, York University, Ontario, Canada.

Case, R., 1974. Structures and strictures: Some functional limitations on the course of cognitive growth. *Cognitive Psychology, 6,* 544.

Case, R., 1975. Gearing the demands of instruction to the developmental capacities of the learner. *Review of Educational Research, 45,* 59.

Case, R., 1977. Responsiveness to conservation training as a function of induced subjective uncertainty, M-Space, and cognitive style, *Canadian Journal of Behavioral Science, 9,* 12.

Case, R., 1978. Piaget and beyond: Towards a developmentally based theory and technology of instruction. In R. Glaser (Ed.), *Advances in instructional psychology* (Vol. 1). Hillsdale, N.J.: Lawrence Erlbaum.

DeAvila, E. A., Havassy, B., with Pascual-Leone, J., 1976. Mexican-American School Children: A neo-Piagetian Analysis. Washington, D.C.: Georgetown University Press.

DeRibaupierre, A., 1976. *Cognitive space and formal operations.* Unpublished doctoral dissertation, University of Toronto.

Fitts, P. M., and Posner, M. I., 1967. *Human performance.* Belmont, California: Brooks/Cole.

Fitts, P. M., and Seeger, C. M., 1953. SR compatibility: Spatial characteristics of stimulus and response codes. *Journal of Experimental Psychology, 46,* 199.

Gagné, R., 1968. Contributions of learning to human development. *Psychological Review, 75,* 177.

Gardner, R. W., Jackson, D. N., and Messick, S. J., 1960. Personality organization in cognitive controls and intellectual abilities. *Psychological Issues, 2(4)*, Monograph 8.

Gibson, E. J., 1969. *Principles of perceptual learning and development.* New York: Appleton-Century-Crofts.

Harlow, H. F., 1959. Learning set and error factor theory. In S. Koch (Ed.), *Psychology: A study of a science* (Vol. 2). New York: McGraw-Hill, p. 492.

Hintzman, D. L., 1978. *The psychology of learning and memory.* San Francisco: W. Freeman and Company.

Hochberg, J. E., 1957. Effects of gestalt revolution: The Cornell symposium on perception. *Psychological Review, 64*, 73.

Hunt, J. McV., 1965. Intrinsic motivation and its role in psychological development. *In Nebraska Symposium on Motivation.* Lincoln: University of Nebraska Press, p. 189.

Inhelder, B., and Piaget, J., 1958. *The growth of logical thinking from childhood to adolescence.* New York: Basic Books. (Originally "De la logique de l'enfant à la logique de l'adolescent," 1955, Paris: Presses Universitaires de France.)

Inhelder, B., Sinclair, H., and Bovet, M., 1974. *Apprentissage et structures de la connaissance.* Paris: Presses Universitaires de France.

Kahneman, D., 1973. *Attention and effort.* Englewood Cliffs, N.J.: Prentice-Hall.

Klahr, D., and Wallace, J. F., 1976. *Cognitive development: An information processing view.* Hillsdale, N.J.: Erlbaum.

Koffka, K., 1963. *Principles of gestalt psychology.* New York: Harcourt, Brace & World, Inc. (originally published 1935).

Luria, A. R., 1973. *The working brain.* New York: Penguin Books.

Maier, S. F., and Seligman, M. E. P., 1976. Learned helplessness: Theory and evidence. *Journal of Experimental Psychology, General, 105*, 3.

Miller, G. A., Galanter, E., and Pribram, K. H., 1960. *Plans and the structure of behavior.* New York: Holt, Rinehart and Winston.

Miller, M. S., 1975. *Associative and conceptual learning: Towards a neo-Piagetian evaluation of Jensen's intelligence thoery.* Unpublished M.A. thesis, York University, Ontario, Canada.

Neisser, U., 1967. *Cognitive psychology.* New York: Appleton-Century-Crofts.

Parkinson, G. M., 1975. *The limits of learning: A quantitative developmental investigation of intelligence.* Unpublished doctoral dissertation, York University, Ontario, Canada.

Pascual-Leone, J., 1969. *Cognitive development and cognitive style: A general psychological integration.* Unpublished doctoral dissertation, University of Geneva.

Pascual-Leone, J., 1970. A mathematical model for the transition rule in Piaget's developmental stages. *Acta Psychologica, 32*, 301.

Pascual-Leone, J., 1972. A theory of constructive operators, a neoPiagetian model of conservation, and the problem of horizontal decalages. Paper presented at the annual meeting of the Canadian Psychological Association, Montréal, Québec, Canada.

Pascual-Leone, J., 1973. Constructive cognition and substance conservation: Toward adequate structural models of the human subject. Unpublished manuscript.

Pascual-Leone, J., 1974. A neo-Piagetian process-structural model of Witkin's psychological differentiation. Extended version of a paper presented at the Symposium on Cross-Cultural Studies of Psychological Differentiation at the annual meeting of the International Association for Cross-Cultural Psychology, Kingston, Ontario.

Pascual-Leone, J., 1976a. Metasubjective problems of constructive cognition: Forms of knowing and their psychological mechanisms. *Canadian Psychological Review, 17(2)*, 110. (Errata for this paper appeared in volume *17(4)*, 307.)

Pascual-Leone, J., 1976b. On learning and development, Piagetian style: I. A reply to Lefebvre-Pinard. *Canadian Psychological Review, 17(4)*, 270.

Pascual-Leone, J., 1976c. On learning and development, Piagetian style: II. A critical historical analysis of Geneva's research programme. *Canadian Psychological Review*, *17(4)*, 289.

Pascual-Leone, J., 1976d. A view of cognition from a formalist's perspective. In K. F. Riegel and J. A. Meacham (Eds.), *The Developing Individual in a Changing World* (Vol. I). The Hague, Netherlands: Mouton.

Pascual-Leone, J. 1977a. Stages and décalages: A neo-Piagetian view. Paper presented at the meeting of the International Society for the Study of Behavioral Development, Pavia, Italy.

Pascual-Leone, J., 1977b. Constructive problems for constructive theories: The current relevance of Piaget's work and a critique of information-processing simulation psychology. Paper presented at the conference of the Institut für die Pädagogik Kiel, Germany, September, 1977, to appear in R. Kluwe and H. Spada (Eds.), *Developmental models of thinking*. New York: Academic Press, in press.

Pascual-Leone, J., 1978. Compounds, confounds, and models in developmental information processing: A reply to Trabasso and Foellinger. *Journal of Experimental Child Psychology*, in press.

Pascual-Leone, J., and Bovet, M. C., 1966. L'apprentissage de la quantification de l'inclusion et la théorie opératoire. *Acta Psychologica*, *25*, 334.

Pascual-Leone, J., and Bovet, M. C., 1967. L'apprentissage de la quantification de l'inclusion et la théorie opératoire, Partie II: Quelques résultats expérimentaux nouveaux. *Acta Psychologica*, *26*, 64.

Pascual-Leone, J., and Goodman, D., 1976. Intelligence and experience: A neoPiagetian approach. Unpublished manuscript, York University, Ontario, Canada.

Pascual-Leone, J., and Smith, J., 1969. The encoding and decoding of symbols by children: A new experimental paradigm and a neo-Piagetian model. *Journal of Experimental Child Psychology*, *8*, 328.

Pascual-Leone, J., Parkinson, G., and S. Pulos, 1974. Constructive abstractions (structural learning) and concept development. Paper given at the meeting of the Canadian Psychological Association, Windsor, 1974. Unpublished manuscript.

Piaget, J., 1941. Le méchanisme du développement mental et les lois du groupement des opérations. *Archives de Psychologie*, *28*, 215.

Piaget, J., 1956. Logique et équilibre dans les comportements du sujet. In L. Apostel, B. Mandelbrot, and J. Piaget (Eds.), *Logique et équilibre*. Paris: Presses Universitaires de France.

Piaget, J., 1959. Apprentissage et connaissance. In P. Greco and J. Piaget (Eds.), *Etudes d'épistémologie génétique* (Vol. 7): *Apprentissage et connaissance*. Paris: Presses Universitaires de France.

Piaget, J., 1970. *Science of Education and the Psychology of the Child*. New York: Orion Press (originally published 1969, Denoel, Paris.)

Piaget, J., 1975. L'équilibration des structures cognitives (Problème central du développement). Paris: Presses Universitaires de France.

Piaget, J., 1977. Some recent research and its links with a new theory of groupings and conservation based on commutativity. *Annals of the New York Academy of Sciences, 291*, 350–371.

Piaget, J., and Inhelder, B., 1962. *Le développement des quantités physiques chez l'enfant*. Neuchâtel: Delachaux et Niestlé.

Piaget, J., and Morf, A., 1958. Les isomorphismes partiels entre les structures logiques et les structures perceptives. *In* J. S. Bruner, F. Bresson, A. Morf, and J. Piaget, *Logique et perception*. Paris: Presses Universitaires de France.

Pribram, K. H., 1971. *Languages of the brain.* New York: Prentice-Hall.

Pribram, K. H., 1973. The primate frontal cortex—executive of the brain. In K. H. Pribram and A. R. Luria (Eds.), *Psychophysiology of the frontal lobes.* New York: Academic Press, p. 293.

Razran, G. H. S., 1971. *Mind in evolution: An east-west synthesis of learned behavior and cognition.* Boston: Houghton Mifflin.

Rozeboom, W. W., 1970. The art of metascience, or, what should a psychological theory be? *In* J. R. Royce (Ed.), *Toward Unification in Psychology.* University of Toronto Press, Toronto, Canada.

Scardamalia, M., 1977. Information processing capacity and the problem of horizontal decalage: A demonstration using combinatorial reasoning tasks. *Child Development, 48,* 28.

Schank, R., and Abelson, R., 1977. *Scripts, plans, goals, and understanding: An inquiry into human knowledge structures.* Hillsdale, N.J.: Lawrence Erlbaum.

Seligman, M. E. P., 1975. *Helplessness.* San Francisco: W. H. Freeman & Company.

Tolman, E. C., 1932. *Purposive behavior in animals and men.* New York: Century.

Tolman, E. C., 1959. Principles of purposive behavior. In S. Koch (Ed.), *Psychology: A study of a science* (Vol. 1). New York: McGraw-Hill.

Toussaint, N. A., 1974. An analysis of synchrony between concrete-operational tasks in terms of structural and performance demands. *Child Development, 45,* 992.

Toussaint, N. A., 1976. Mental processing capacity, anticipatory and retroactive abilities, and development of concrete-operational structures. *Canadian Journal of Behavioural Science, 8,* 363.

Witkin, H. A., Goodenough, D. R., and Karp, S. A., 1967. Stability of cognitive style from childhood to young adulthood. *Journal of Personality and Social Psychology, 7,* 291.

Witkin, H. A., and Goodenough, D. R., 1977a. Field dependence and interpersonal behavior. *Psychological Bulletin, 84(4),* 661.

Witkin, H. A., and Goodenough, D. R., 1977b. Field dependence-independence revisited. Princeton, N.J.: Educational Testing Service Research Bulletin.

Zajonc, R. B., 1960. Balance, congruity, and dissonance. *Public Opinion Quarterly, 24,* 280.

Index

Abstraction, 84, 95, 100, 124
Abstractions
  in formal-analytic thought, 105
  in hypothetical-deductive thought, 101
  in transitional stages, 120
Action schemes, 95, 222
Activity
  in early education, 79, 83–84
  and internal regulations, 227
  in Piagetian theory, 15, 18
  self-initiated, 250
Activity School, 45–46
Adaptation, 10, 221
Affect, 221, 251–253
Altruism, 26
Assessment
  of competence in science, 116–117
  of continuous quantities, 148
  of geometry skills, 205
  of horizontal décalage, 110
  of intellectual ability, 141, 194–195
  levels of formal thought, 125–126
  Loevinger Sentence Completion Test, 41
  Piaget's stages of, 119–120, 223–225
  of reading ability, 187
  of visual spatial skills, 213
Assimilation, 8, 15, 169
Assimilatory praxis, 263–264, 269
Autonomy
  in early education, 88
  in moral development, 24

Behaviorism, 177, 194–195

Causality, 105
Classification, 96
Compensations
  of affirmation and negation, 101
  and exceptional children, 216, 218–219
  and explanation, 7
  and reflexive abstraction, 16–17
Competence, 203
Commutativity, 156
Compromise, 25
Conservation
  plasticine experiment, 163–164
  spontaneous discovery, 171
  tasks, 223–225
Constructions
  in analogy problems, 11–12
  explanatory, 158
  of imperceptibles, 6
  internal reconstructions, 10
  inventing concepts, 145
  mental, 179
  of negatives, 201
  and special education, 221
Constructive process, 48–49, 85–87, 145
Context
  independence, 85
  and reading, 247
  and retarded children, 208
  in scientific investigation, 112, 120
  solving problems, 283
  and teaching content, 79
Continuous quantities, 26, 33–34, 142
Coordination
  of abstractions, 6, 207
  of classes and relations, 142–143